THE ANTHONY BOURDAIN READER

THE ANTHONY BOURDAIN READER

FOREWORD BY
PATRICK RADDEN KEEFE

EDITED BY
KIMBERLY WITHERSPOON

BLOOMSBURY PUBLISHING
LONDON · OXFORD · NEW YORK · NEW DELHI · SYDNEY

BLOOMSBURY PUBLISHING

Bloomsbury Publishing Plc

50 Bedford Square, London, WC1B 3DP, UK

Bloomsbury Publishing Ireland Limited,

29 Earlsfort Terrace, Dublin 2, D02 AY28, Ireland

BLOOMSBURY, BLOOMSBURY PUBLISHING and the Diana logo
are trademarks of Bloomsbury Publishing Plc

First published in the United States by Ecco in 2025
First published in Great Britain in 2025

A catalogue record for this book is available from the British Library

ISBN: HB: 978-1-5266-9656-4; TPB: 978-1-5266-9654-0; eBook: 978-1-5266-9658-8;
ePDF: 978-1-5266-9655-7

2 4 6 8 10 9 7 5 3 1

Typeset by Six Red Marbles India
Printed and bound in Great Britain by Clays Ltd, Elcograf S.p.A

To find out more about our authors and books visit www.bloomsbury.com
and sign up for our newsletters
For product-safety-related questions contact productsafety@bloomsbury.com

Contents

Foreword

When Anthony Bourdain spoke about his life, he tended to describe it as a series of happy accidents, as if it all just fell in his lap. Tony was always a high priest of his own mythology, and he leaned into this image of the lucky guy from New Jersey with nothing going for him but his curiosity and his megawatt charisma, the humble chef who became a druggie, then a novelist, then a memoirist, then a famous globe-trotting TV adventurer. In rough outline it's all true, of course. But Tony was also very cool, and attuned to coolness in its many forms, and it is not cool to talk about how much you had to work to will the life you wanted into being. The TV career really *was* a fluke: After Tony became (overnight, in his midforties) a famous author, he was approached by a pair of visionary producers who had the idea of building a travel show around him. But in a sense, he'd already made it, at that point. He was a successful writer, and while it's true that the idea of hosting a TV show might never have occurred to him until somebody else brought it up, Tony had wanted to be a writer all his life.

In high school, he drew comics. He'd grown up in a family that put a lot of stock in the written word: His father loved to spend long hours lying on the sofa reading novels; his mother worked as a copy editor at the *New York Times*. He kept a journal (which is excerpted in this collection) and even as he plunged headlong into the world of professional New York kitchens and developed an increasingly demanding drug problem, he was always writing. When I was working on a profile of Bourdain for *The New Yorker* in 2017, I got a tip that there might be some interesting material in the archives of a now-defunct downtown literary zine called *Between C and D.* In the library at New York University, I discovered early short stories that Tony had submitted, featuring characters who often bore a resemblance to the shady creatures he was mixing with during that period, in restaurants and on the streets. Often, these submissions had little cartoon embellishments in the margins, and in his cover letters, he was unusually forthright about his overriding passion to be a writer. Tony even took a writing workshop at Columbia with the legendary fiction editor Gordon Lish. He had ambition—and specifically *literary* ambition—right from the start, and what the prevailing myth of Anthony Bourdain often misses is that he wasn't a chef who was suddenly reborn, as if by immaculate conception, as a writer. He was a frustrated writer who spent the two decades before he finally hit it big working as a chef.

You can feel Bourdain's yearning—and a tinge of his lifelong self-loathing—as he confesses, in "The Typewriter or the Television," that he wants "success as a writer." He has been laboring under the misapprehension that his life would be "a work of art," he writes, but now there is nothing for it but to sit down and do the work. And he *did* work at his writing, with the same furious discipline he applied to prepping his station or turning out three hundred orders on a brunch shift. After a long night at the restaurant, followed by several further hours of boozy decompression, he would rise before dawn, light the first of many cigarettes, drag himself to the keyboard, and start typing. He describes this process, with characteristic insouciance, as a "hurried disgorging of sentences," and it's true that for many years he lacked the luxury of time and had to write quickly, between shifts. But again, the slightly flip, self-denigrating register in which Tony often spoke about himself tends to obscure the real, arduous, careful work that he put into writing, and to getting better at writing, which you can behold for yourself in the handwritten revisions he left on some of the manuscript pages reproduced in this compendium.

Over time, he honed his voice. In his memoir and novels and essays, even in his recipes, Bourdain wrote like he spoke: wry, conversational, with flashes of occasional hyperbole, as if he were sitting on the bar stool next to you, relating a great story. And when he spoke, at least in the voice-over for his TV show, all that casually philosophical musing was in fact a carefully written script. He had a knack for dialogue, even his own. It is ironic to think that it was this voice, which he initially found on the page, that would become the secret ingredient of his success in TV. From its earliest iteration, Bourdain's television show was a written thing.

In whatever medium in which he was writing, Bourdain always had a salty vernacular, a jaded sense of humor, and an eye for the telling detail. Apart from childhood trips to France and a few vacations in adulthood to the Caribbean, he had never seen much of the world until he reached his midforties. In that respect he was not so different from most Americans; more than half of all Americans do not own a passport. When he first started going abroad, he turned out to have an uncanny ability to capture a place and its people in a few deft strokes. He was always an enthusiast, which helped: Whether rhapsodizing about some obscure tripe preparation or recounting a beer-buzzed conversation with a new friend he'd only just met or describing what it feels like to watch the sun set over the Sahara, he wanted to convey, in as fresh and undiluted a manner as possible, the sheer wonder he was experiencing—to bottle it up and serve it to us. But he also had an uncanny ability, developed in his fiction writing, to select the vivid, indelible detail: his evocation of riding home at night in a yellow New York City taxi, a slight breeze coming through the open window; his observation that one ubiquitous sight in virtually any poor country is raggedy plastic bags, strewn everywhere, because there is no municipal trash collection; his description of lobsters as "cross-eyed."

For all the swagger of his persona, Bourdain's writing was also imbued with great humility. One of the paradoxes of his life was that he was so closely associated in the public mind with chefs and restaurants and cooking, but as he would be the first to admit, he was never a great chef himself. He was *friends* with great chefs—his best friend was one of the greatest, Eric Ripert—and he was certainly a champion and a chronicler of great chefs. He was also a very capable chef himself, and he took great pride in his skill and experience in the kitchen. But he knew that there was some gene of inspiration that a chef like Ripert possessed and he lacked. I sometimes think that living with this constant reminder of his own limitations is part of what made Tony so humble and so open to the world.

One night in October 2017, about nine months before his suicide, we had a public conversation in Manhattan as part of the New Yorker Festival. We talked about his concern that in some ways the prevailing mood in the United States seemed to have turned against his way of seeing the world. In America and in many places abroad, tribalism and xenophobia were on the ascendant. This was a function of politics—but not exclusively. It also had something to do with social media, and the ways in which societies become atomized when everybody spends so much time on their phones. Tony spoke about how his decades in restaurant kitchens had given him an appreciation and respect for immigrants of every stripe. To him, difference was not something to fear or resent, but something to celebrate and be inspired by. On virtually every page of this wonderful collection you can feel that curiosity about other people and that abiding generosity of spirit.

Since Tony died, the most extraordinary thing has happened. His books are still being read, old episodes of his show are still being watched, and on Instagram and TikTok, he's become the source of a thousand memes. He's developed this resonant afterlife on the Internet, with people sharing little videos or photos of him accompanied by memorable quotes. Part of this may just be the cool thing; like no writer since Joan Didion, the man photographed well. But I think there's more to it than that. Bourdain was very taken with *How to Live*, Sarah Bakewell's 2010 book on Michel de Montaigne. He got a tattoo on his forearm, in Greek, of Montaigne's motto: "I Suspend Judgment." In the breaking of bread, he found a way to close the distance between himself and strangers the world over, often people whose lives might have seemed unbridgeably different from his own. In these days of heightened division, suspicion, and hostility, we can learn much more from Anthony Bourdain than the backroom secrets of restaurant life or the best place for street food in Singapore. Part of the reason he still feels so alive to his many friends and fans and devoted readers is that there was an important lesson, in the way he lived his life, for how to live our own, and how to treat one another as we move through this world. May we heed it.

—PATRICK RADDEN KEEFE

Preface

I was Anthony Bourdain's literary agent and friend for over twenty years and I am still discovering his writing. I mean that in a literal sense—there are pieces in here I had never read or even knew existed before I began to assemble this collection—and in the sense that every time I reread his work, I find something new. I have no idea how many times I have read the essay "Don't Eat Before Reading This" ever since it was first published in *The New Yorker* nearly thirty years ago, but I was thrilled to sit down and read it again, for the purpose of assembling this book. It is surprisingly prescient. What seemed back in 1999 to be a brash (ornery?) cri de coeur by a young maverick chef now reads to me more like a mature, visionary essay, especially when published here alongside so much of his writing that preceded it. He saw the future of restaurants, chefs, fame, and so much more. He also married writing and eating in a way that few other chefs (or writers) ever have. Eating and reading went hand in hand in Tony's life, from the beginning to the end.

Of course that's not all he wrote about. While many readers will always think of Tony, first, as a chef and author, it is surely the case that he reached his largest audience through television, and by taking viewers along with him on his travels around the world. Television, though, did not mark the end of his writing. Not by a long shot. He read widely for his travel shows, met people from all walks of life, and the scripts that he wrote for his shows reflect that boundless curiosity. He also continued to write essays, novels, comic books, cookbooks, and more. He never stopped. Those of us who worked with him can also attest to the sheer entertainment value of his e-mails and texts. Whatever he was writing, and to whomever, he was always unequivocally himself. His voice was not a literary conceit. It was who he was.

It is his voice that emerges from this collection. I feel a deep responsibility to honor that voice, because it really is who he was. It always was. From childhood, he wrote. Diaries, letters, stories, plays. And it is all, for lack of a better word, authentic. His voice is witty, angry, musical, passionate, and empathetic. Always empathetic. He always had empathy for the down-and-out and dispossessed, and you'll see here how that manifested throughout his life in his fiction, with his lovingly depicted addicts, gangsters, and lowlifes of all kinds.

As he traveled widely, that empathy spread and took new forms. Always an instinctual fan of the underdog, he came to despise injustice more broadly, especially when it was imposed by powerful forces on people who simply wanted to live their lives, raise their children, take pride in their homes, and cook their meals. People all around the world welcomed him into those homes, and cooked and ate with him. He was trusted. He had an innate ability to generate trust, and to trust others in return. We all benefited from this exchange.

From the moment I began assembling this collection, I was confronted with some tough choices. There was a mountain of material, of course, including much that has never been published anywhere, and it is always hard to distill a life's work into a single volume. Then there was the issue of "polish." In some of this material, there are errors and indiscretions, and there's always a tendency in a situation like this to want to go back and "clean things up"—tighten sentences, smooth transitions, sand down some of the language. But with Tony that was the last thing I wanted to do. Once I rejected that tendency, I realized it would have been absurd to even try: This is who Tony was. And he was who he was: imperfect, (mostly) unapologetic, often brilliantly messy. Instead of representing him as something he wasn't, I have left Tony alone in these pages. I hope that when you read it you feel that he's almost sitting opposite you, sharing a meal, a beer, and you're listening to a great storyteller go to work. Sometimes he might get distracted (or interrupt himself to crack a joke). That's just part of the fun.

I also hope that you are surprised by what you find. Over the last few years, I have heard from a wide range of Tony's fans who miss him, as I do, and who express a basic appetite for more. More shows, more books, more speeches. More Tony. One thing I have noticed is that many of these fans know him primarily through one or another channel: perhaps they are longtime viewers of his travel shows, or perhaps they know him almost exclusively from his big bestselling collections of essays, *Kitchen Confidential* and *Medium Raw*. There are others who have all his cookbooks. With this collection, my hope is that these different audiences will find opportunities to spread their appreciation to other parts of his work. It was in his writing more than anything else that Tony expressed the whole gamut of his talents, ideas, and personality. Fans of any part of his career will find much they recognize and enjoy in these pages, but I hope and believe they will find new and surprising pieces as well.

To that end, I've organized this collection in a way that I hope maximizes serendipity and discovery. I did not separate his writing by format or medium, and I did not want to lay it all out chronologically. Perhaps because Tony has always "sounded like Tony," the chronological approach seemed almost irrelevant: Yes, he matured and developed as a writer, but his voice is remarkably consistent throughout this writing, which begins when he was a teenager. Instead, I have created the categories you'll see in the table of contents, categories that I think emphasize some of his most resilient moods, subjects, and beliefs.

This approach also frankly mirrors Tony's life, which never developed in a straight line, but followed his curiosity as it bounced from kitchen to kitchen, and then all around the world, and back again.

This has not been easy work. His loss in 2018 was unimaginable. The process of assembling this collection has involved mourning him again. Every word I read, I hear his voice in my head. It is simultaneously comforting and heartbreaking. But more than that, it has been profoundly motivating: I want to make sure this collection honors him and his voice, and also honors the emotions of his millions of readers and fans, each of whom feels they have a connection with the man. I hope as you read this you will feel that that connection is warranted.

Tony never shied away from talking about his demons. He was open about his addiction, his struggles with depression, his woundedness on behalf of people he loved and wished to protect. That was all a part of him. But I hope it is clear that his openness, humanity, and artfulness extended well past all of that. It was the only mode he knew, and he engaged with everything and everyone with the same humanity. As much as he wrote to understand the world and all of its many diverse parts, he wrote also to understand himself, both his pain and his joy. I shared a lot of that pain and joy with him for many years as his friend, and I was able to once again reading these pages. Like I said, it was not easy work. It helps that, among so many other things, Tony was very funny. There are so many laughs in this book to go along with the tears. And now I am very happy the work is done, and this book will last forever. I will read it again and again.

This book will not establish Tony's legacy and it is not intended to. It cannot. His legacy is secure in the minds and memories of millions of his fans.

However, it will play a part. It is my honor to play a part in it. It is my honor especially to help make sure that his legacy will include at its core the fact that Tony was a writer. Almost above everything else, he was a writer. He loved writing, he loved writers, and he loved reading. He loved the world and tried to fit it all into his writing. Even when he struggled, even when the world vexed him, he wrote.

I hope you will be inspired, provoked, and entertained. He never failed to do the same to me. I hope I have done him justice.

—**KIMBERLY WITHERSPOON**

THE
ANTHONY
BOURDAIN
READER

I

Eating and Drinking

Where else to begin? Whether something as humble as bread and butter, or as exotic as ortolan, it was always food that inspired Tony's greatest bursts of literary extravagance. Even before he went to culinary school, food featured in his stories and diaries, but it was later on in his career, when he experienced the sensory onslaught of restaurant kitchens, that he refined his ability to write about food in a way that made it glisten, bleed, ooze, drip, and jump off the page, like in old Dutch still lifes with grapes and rabbit viscera. He really, really loved viscera.

Lust

An excerpt from *Medium Raw: A Bloody Valentine to the World of Food and the People Who Cook*, published in the UK by Bloomsbury in 2010.

It's nighttime in Puebla and there is a taco lady and her husband standing behind a cart, one naked lightbulb dangling overhead, serving *tacos de lengua*, strips of beef tongue, seared with onions on a griddle. When the edges of the tongue are browned and the air fills with deliciousness, she scrapes them off the hot metal with a spatula, drops them into soft, still-warm corn tortillas, double layered—and quickly drags a spoon of salsa verde across them. She sprinkles them with fresh cilantro and a little raw, chopped onion and hands them over on a paper plate so thin it barely supports their weight without buckling. You quickly shove one of the tacos into your mouth, wash it down with a big pull from a can of cold Tecate—which you've previously rubbed with lime and jammed into a plate of salt, encrusting the top—and you can feel your eyes roll up into your head.

Standing there in the dark, stray dogs cowering expectantly just outside the corona of light from the one bulb, you've got all sorts of scary, blissed-out expressions flashing across your face. A father, mother, and two kids sit on kitchen chairs that the couple has dragged out into the street for their customers—and you hope that the kids, catching a look at you in the weird light, aren't frightened by what they see.

It's a fucking Everest of shellfish, an intimidating, multilevel tower of crushed ice and seaweed, piled, heaped—festooned with oysters from nearby Belon, and slightly farther away Cancale. There are periwinkles, whelks, palourdes, two types of gargantuan crabs—their claws reaching angrily for the sky over the carcasses of many lobsters, a tangle of meaty claws—their large bodies surrounded by the smaller ones, beady-eyed prawns and langoustines scattered about like the victims of a bus crash. What's striking is that everyone in this small café has an identical mountain range of seafood in front of them: the older couple at the table next to you, tiny figures at the next table, silently cracking and slurping their way through an ungodly amount of seafood—they look too feeble for the kind of damage they're doing, but *mais non*, the waiters scurry to keep up with the ever-filling discard bowls of empty shells. The elegant-looking woman eating by herself, the large table of Parisians—down for the weekend—they've ordered *more*. Everyone is drinking wine—whites and rosés—and, with incongruous delicacy, smearing local butter on little slices of the thin but dense brown bread before returning to the carnage that ensues when they grab ahold of a lobster tail and yank, with one jerking movement, tail meat from the shell—one brutal movement—or gnash and suck their way through the broken carapace of a spider crab, dripping eggs and back fat onto their hands without care. This, too, is a good place to be. You will be in need of a nap after this. A small hotel by the port, perhaps. Pillows a little too hard, a redundant bolster, and sheets that smell slightly of bleach. The people around you, however, will be going out for dinner.

The morning in Kuching, Borneo: a hangover so bad you don't and can't even look anyone in the eye so certain are you that you said or did something truly awful after a night of *langkau*—the local rice whiskey—and (to the best of your recollection) fucking *tequila*. (And whose great idea was *that*, anyway?) You're oblivious to the view of the river, and the sights and smells of morning, focusing only on the chipped white bowl of steaming *laksa* coming your way—the promise of relief. The smell hits you first as the waiter deposits it in front of you with a clunk you feel in your pineal gland: a rich, fiery, hearty, spicy steam of fish and coconut gravy. You dig in with chopsticks and spoon, slurp your first mouthful of noodles—a powerful hit of *sambal* grabbing hold of you, exorcising the Evil. Ensuing mouthfuls bring shrimp, cockles, and fish cake . . . more spicy-sweet gravy . . . more noodles. It burns. It burns so good. You're sweating now, the poison leaving your pores, brain kick-starting . . . something that might just be hope secreting from somewhere in your shriveled, sun-dried, terribly abused cortex.

It's another one of those agriturismos. *They're all over Italy, little mom-and-pop joints, for the most part thrown up quickly in farmhouses, private homes, on picnic tables under the trees—serving out of hearths, field kitchens.* This one's in Sardinia, and what's on your plate is the simplest thing in the world: *spaghetti alla bottarga*—pasta, tossed quickly with local olive oil (through which a clove of garlic and a hot pepper have briefly been dragged) and the local salt-cured mullet eggs, which are the specialty of the region. There's no explaining why this is so good. It just . . . is. The salty and frankly fishy flavor of the eggs cuddles up to the more subtle taste of the durum pasta—the tiniest notes of heat from the pepper—and the sharp yet lush tang of freshly pressed extra-virgin olive oil. You wash this down with a sneakily compelling Cannonau—the local red whose rough charms have lately got a serious hold on you. You don't care about the big Bordeauxs anymore. The high-maintenance Burgundies with their complex personalities. The Baron Rothschild could back his car up to the door, trunk full of monster vintages, he's drunk and offering them for free—and you would decline. Here? Now? Mopping olive oil and a few errant fish eggs from the bottom of your plate, swilling this young and proudly no-name wine, there is *nothing* you would rather be drinking.

When you ask the proprietor where the wine comes from, he points to an old man sitting in the corner reading a soccer magazine, a cigarette dangling from his lips.

"It came from him," he says.

The salarymen are getting boisterous in Shinjuku district, their worka-day personalities filed away till tomorrow, rapidly being replaced—with every beer, every reciprocally poured sake—with their real *personalities.* Drunk—they're loud, friendly, angry, maudlin, horny. Over yakitori—lovingly grilled bits of artisanal chicken bits—you are particularly well placed to observe Japan's uniquely kooky national schizophrenia. A man with a headband carefully turns skewers of sizzling poultry over glowing charcoal in a metal trough. Someone gives you another beer—an oversized bottle of Sapporo in an undersized glass. The room is filled with smoke from the dripping chicken fat flaring up on the coals, from many cigarettes. You can barely see the men at the tables, sitting or leaning cross-legged in their stocking feet, some of them slumped over, falling to the side, red-faced and sweating. The thick smoke hanging in the air obscures their upper halves. Now and again, one group or another, sitting by a window, will open it for a few minutes and try to air the place out.

You're sitting at the counter, the wooden cup in front of you bristling with naked, recently gnawed skewers—a hedgehog display of dead soldiers. You've had the soft bone (breast cartilage), knee bone, thigh, chicken meatballs dipped in raw quail egg. There have been many orders of chicken hearts; chicken livers; Kobe beef tongue—little, uniformly sized bits impaled neatly on bamboo and slowly turned until perfectly cooked, salty and slightly redolent of the handmade charcoal, garnished with sea salt—or red pepper. You've had many skewers of chicken skin—threaded and wrapped tightly around the slivers of bamboo, then slowly grilled until crispy, chewy, and yet still soft in the center. But now it's all about ass. You got the last six of them and you're pretty pleased with yourself about that. That fatty protuberance of rich skin, each one containing fatty nubbins of flavorful, buttery meat divided by a thin layer of cartilage—it's the single best piece of meat and flesh on the chicken. And, of course, there's only one of them per animal, so supply is limited. The man fighting a losing battle with verticality across from you, his head teetering on one elbow, then sliding down his forearm from time to time, recovering just before his head bounces off the counter—he's looking at your chicken asses and he's angry. You don't know what he's griping about to the chef—who's heard it all before—but you suspect that he's complaining that the lone gaijin in the room got the last pieces of ass. You buy him a sake.

At the deli on Houston Street, they haul the pastrami steaming out of a giant warmer and slice it thickly by hand. It's moist and so tender you wonder how the guy gets his knife through without mashing it. He piles the dark pink meat between too-fresh rye bread smeared with the bright yellow mustard indigenous to these parts. Later, at the table, the bread gives way, crumbling beneath the weight and wetness of the pastrami. You push the salty, savory flesh around your plate with a wedge of dill pickle, wash it down with a Dr. Brown's. The salty, peppery, savory, spicy, and sour are cut just right by the sweetness of the soda.

Fifty miles out of Prague, the halved carcass of a freshly killed hog hangs, still steaming in the cold, from what looks like a child's swing set. It's a wet, drizzling morning and your feet are sopping, and you've been warming yourself against the chill by huddling around the small fire over which a pot of pig parts boils. The butcher's family and friends are drinking slivovitz and beer, and though noon is still a few hours off, you've had quite a few of both. Someone calls you inside to the tiled workspace, where the butcher has mixed the pig's blood with cooked onions and spices and crumbs of country bread, and he's ready to fill the casings. Usually, they slip the casing over a metal tube, turn on the grinding machine, cram in the forcemeat or filling, and the sausages fill like magic. This guy does it differently. He chops everything by hand. A wet mesa of black filling covers his cutting board, barely retaining its shape—yet he grabs the casing in one hand, puts two fingers in one open end, makes the "V" sign, stretching it disturbingly, and reaches with the other—then buries both his hands in the mix. A whirlwind of movement as he squeezes with his right hand, using his palm like a funnel, somehow squirting the bloody, barely containable stuff straight into the opening. He does this again and again with breathtaking speed, mowing his way across the wooden table, like a thresher cutting a row through a cornfield, a long, plump, rapidly growing, glistening, fully filled length of sausage engorging to his left as he moves. It's a dark, purplish color through the translucent membrane. An assistant pinches off links, pins them with broken bits of wooden skewer. In moments, they are done.

Back in the cold backyard, you're on your fifth slivovitz when the sausages arrive in a cloud of vapor, straight from the pot. Everybody's damp and a little drunk; hard country people with rough hands and features for whom a mist of cold rain is apparently no obstacle to a meal. There is goulash, mopped with crusts of bread, and there is blood soup and many sausages. The whole of the pig is very well represented. But it's the blood sausage that sings—or, more accurately, spurts. You cut into it with your knife and it explodes across the plate like a Hollywood bullet hitting a skull—and again you think of Zola, the greatest of food pornographers, that wonderful scene in the charcuterie, our tragically absurd hero starving in the midst of ridiculous bounty. His in-laws stirring blood and spices for *boudin noir*, filling their glass display case with enticingly described delights he is unwelcome to try. It smells here like that room must have: blood and onions, paprika and a touch of nutmeg, notes of sweetness, longing . . . and death. The woman at the end of the table with a face like a concrete pylon sees you close your eyes for a second, appreciating, and she smiles.

Six o'clock in the morning is when the pains aux raisins *come out, and* already the customers are lining up in the dark outside this tiny Parisian *boulangerie* waiting for the first batch. The baguettes are ready—piping-hot from the brick oven, fabulously, deliberately ugly and uneven in shape, slashed crudely across the top. They're too hot to eat but you grab one anyway, tearing it open gingerly, then dropping two fingers full of butter inside. It instantly melts into liquid—running into the grooves and inner spaces of white interior. You grab it like a sandwich and bite, teeth making a cracking sound as you crunch through the crust. You haven't eaten since yesterday's lunch; your palate is asleep and just not ready for so much sensation. The reaction is violent. It hurts. Butter floods your head, and you think for a second you're going to black out.

*On Fifty-ninth Street, at a fancy Italian joint and fortified with Negro-*nis, you're ready for a good meal—but you're not ready for the little *cicchetti* that arrive unexpectedly at the table: little pillows of sea urchin roe sitting atop tiny slices of toasted bread. Wonderful enough, one would think, but the chef has done something that goes beyond mischievous, possibly into the realm of the unholy: Melting onto each plump orange egg sac is a gossamer-thin shaving of *lardo*, the lightly cured and herbed pork fat made in marble caverns in the mountains of Tuscany, slowly curling around its prey, soon to dissolve. You hurry to put it in your mouth, knowing it's surely a sin against God—and are all the happier for it. It's too much. Way too much. Beyond rich . . . beyond briny-sweet. Beyond decency. You call the waiter over and ask for more.

The prawn comes from particularly deep waters, you are told by the man tending the coals. Special waters. He makes the charcoal himself—two different mixes. The grills are of his own design as well—gleaming, spotlessly clean metal squares, each raised and lowered to specifically selected heights by the turn of a wheel. He puts almost nothing on what he cooks. Sea salt. A spritz of Spanish olive oil from a pump bottle. He's smiling as he places the prawn in front of you and you eat the tail first, stripping away the shell and taking it in two bites. But then comes the head, twisted free and waiting for you. You raise it to your mouth and suck out the soup of hot brains, squeezing it like a toothpaste tube. Silence for a moment, then, from outside, you hear the sheep bleating faintly in the hills. The man smiles, pleased you've properly appreciated his prawn. He has something else. He removes another small pile of burning coals from one of the wood-burning ovens and places it beneath one of his jury-rigged grills, lowers the grid all the way, fans the embers. He produces another device of his own making—a sauté pan that looks more like a strainer than any known cooking vessel—sprays it lightly with oil. He heats it for a few seconds over the glowing coal, then quickly—quickly, but delicately—drops in a handful of tiny, translucent baby eels, sprinkles them with a few granules of salt while he makes them leap once, twice in the pan. In seconds, they are off the fire and into a bowl. They are, you fully appreciate (at this time of year, anyway), the rarest of the rare of God's edible creatures. Each linguine-thin eel has swum here all the way from the Sargasso Sea, upriver into northern Spain—to be caught live. The man has killed them only minutes ago, poisoning them with tobacco. During the two or three weeks you can get them (in the unlikely event you can get them at all), they sell for upwards of a thousand dollars a kilo. They are barely cooked. They don't need to be—they shouldn't be cooked more. Twirled on a fork and lifted to the mouth, they whisper secrets. This, you tell yourself, is a flavor one shouldn't speak of.

*Sichuan hot pot is where you find out some very dark things about your-*self. You look around at the others in the crowded, painfully bright dining room in Chengdu, wiping the backs of their necks with cold napkins, their faces red and contorted with pain. Some of them hold their stomachs. But they plow on, as you do, dipping chopsticks loaded with organ meats, fish balls, and vegetables into the giant woks of dark, sinister-looking oil. It's like that Victorian brothel in London you've read about, the one that had a spanking machine—could paddle forty customers at a time. There's that kind of consensual perversion going on here. As if we are, all of us—though strangers to one another—bound by an awful compulsion we share. The liquid boils and bubbles like witch's brew, opaque, reddish-brown distillate of the mind-blowingly excessive amounts of dried Sichuan chilies bobbing and roiling up throughout. The oil is cooking down, reducing by the minute and growing yet more powerful. You drag a hunk of tripe through the oil; it disappears below the surface, where it shrinks, then hardens like an aroused nipple; and then you remove it from the hellbroth and into your mouth. The heat from the dried peppers nearly lifts your head off—but there is something else. Tiny black flower peppers, floating discreetly alongside their more aggressive cousins, have an eerie numb-ing effect, first on your tongue—and then your entire head. There's the by now familiar floral dimension: You smell it everywhere in this part of China—it's in the air . . . But now it comes on strong, comes to the res-cue; like an ice cube applied to abused flesh, it counteracts the pain and burn of way more hot pepper than any man can or should reasonably bear. Sweating through your shirt, resisting the urge to double over in pain, you begin to understand.

Pain—followed by relief.

Burn, followed by a pleasing, anesthetizing numbness. It's like being spanked and licked at the same time. You were, after many years on this planet and what you thought had been a full and rich life, pretty sure you didn't go for such things. The film *9½ Weeks* left you unmoved. At no point in your youthful misadventures would the offer of even playful discomfort have appealed—even if the person offering was a German supermodel in assless latex chaps.

Pain, you were pretty sure, was always bad.

Pleasure was good.

Until now, that is. When everything started to get confused.

Invasion of the Walking Glands

An unpublished short story that Tony wrote for his English class in 1971.

THE INVASION OF THE WALKING GLANDS, STARRING HOWARD N. ROSENTHAL AND A CAST OF AT LEAST A THOUSAND

The gravity on asteroid A-127 was such that human intestines could not function properly.Space Commander Howard Rosenthal gave himself an enema in the bathroom of his space ship and headed toward the food dispensary.A quarter in one of the wall of vending machines brought him a small plastic pouch containing his meal for the day.Opening it,he removed the small vial of brown liquid and set it aside.Then, removing the crisp, sanitary paper, he fitted the shiny, new needle onto his model B-12 Space-Issue hypodermic, sucked the contents of the vial into it,and injected it into the permanent metal valve, which had been installed into his arm. Then, his hunger quenched for the next 24 hours, he walked heavily to his bunk,where he quickly fell asleep.

The Glands had been planning for a long time.From their orbitting space ships, they parachuted to the fecal-smelling surface of asteroid A-127.Stalking through the space barracks,filled with sleeping astronauts, they finally came upon the food dispensary where they were dissappointed to find no food or supplies aside from the little vials of brown fluid and countless enema tubes, The glands were starving. Seeking advise from their mother ships, they were advised of the proper form of action. A supply ship of Naugahyde chairs crashed in Bayonne New Jersey,while on aseroid A-127, there was no noise save the sound of a thousand glands feeding on the disemboweled vitals of the sleeping(now dead) astronauts.

Wow, great story, well written. interesting

See Ray Bradbury

H.P. Lovecraft

Space Asimov

Robert Heinlein

Salty Horse

An excerpt from Tony's *Hungry Ghosts*, issue number 2, written with Joel Rose and illustrated by Leonardo Manco, published by Dark Horse in 2018.

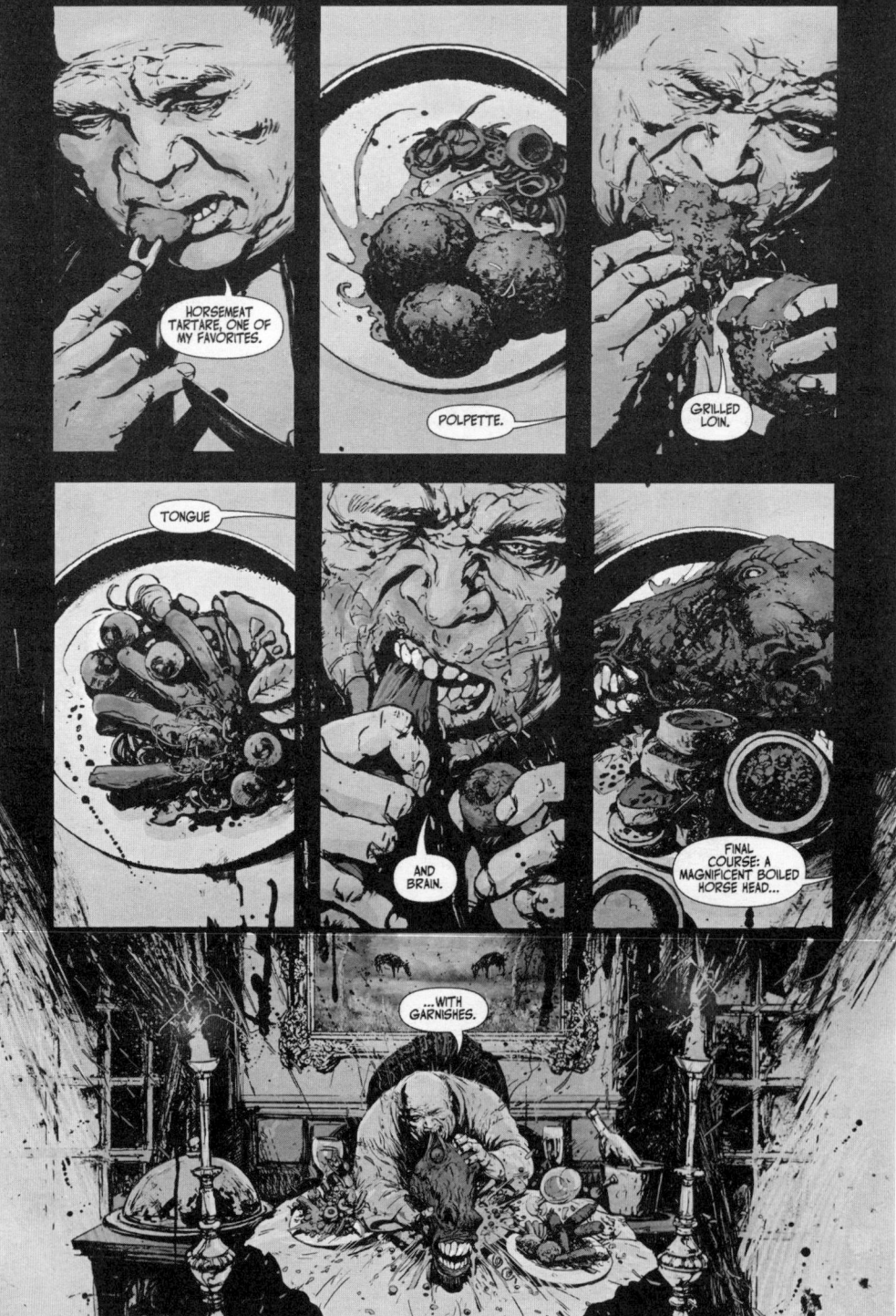

How to Drink Vodka

An excerpt from *A Cook's Tour: In Search of the Perfect Meal*, originally published by Bloomsbury in 2001.

I ate my way around Saint Petersburg for a week, with Zamir, Alexej, and Igor coming along. Alexej had loosened up considerably around me. One night, he invited me back to his flat, where his wife had made blintzes. It was in an uninviting-looking workers' block, with thick graffitied concrete walls, and dark hallways. But behind the multiple door locks, Alexej lived like a New York City nightclub owner: raised carpeted floors, recessed lighting, an enormous bathroom with hot tub, Jacuzzi, and full sauna, a wet bar, home recording studio, wide-screen TV, and entertainment center. My Russian driver lived far better than I do! I was introduced to his lovely wife, and his young son, who, along with his father, treated me to some Stevie Ray Vaughn covers on a brand-new drum kit and Stratocaster guitar.

On another night, we ate braised reindeer in juniper at the Podvorye restaurant, a steeply gabled log structure on the outskirts of Pushkin Park, where Catherine the Great's gaudy summer palace still stands. Gaping at the gigantic gold and pastel-colored behemoth set in a wooded estate and surrounded by the stately former homes of nobles and retainers, one could easily understand the rage of the peasantry in pre-Revolution days. The palace must have been a grotesque affront to a largely starving, uneducated, downtrodden peasantry, people who were struggling even for bread. Looking at this gorgeous Italian-designed abomination, where maybe ten people and their servants lived, one could understand the blind exultation they must have felt when the Romanovs were brought down.

At Podvorye, while a Georgian folk band played, Zamir showed me, step by step, how to drink vodka while we waited for our reindeer to be served. First, if at all possible, make sure you have food present. Even a simple crust of bread will do. We had an enticing selection of traditional appetizers in front of us: pickled garlic, cucumbers, mushrooms, some smoked eel, a little sturgeon, some salted salmon roe, and a loaf of heavy country bread.

Step one, demonstrated Zamir, is the toast. To others present, to your parents, to your country—anything will do. Hold a full shot of vodka in one hand and food—bread is easiest—in the other hand. Exhale. Inhale slowly. Knock back your entire shot in one gulp, immediately inverting your glass over the table to allow the microscopic last drop to fall out, proving you're not a wuss or a reactionary revanchist Trotskyite provocateur.

Then take a bite of food. If you don't have any food, a long, lingering sniff of your wrist or cuff will do. (I know it sounds strange but trust me.) Repeat the procedure up to three times every twenty minutes throughout the drinking period. This is about as fast as your system can absorb all that alcohol. If you follow this regimen carefully, you can and will retain a state of verticality throughout the entire meal and into the post-meal drinking.

In all likelihood, you will make it away from the table without disgracing yourself. You will probably make it home without help. After that, however, you're on your own. Remember: They're professionals at this in Russia, so no matter how many Jell-O shots or Jäger shooters you might have downed at college mixers, no matter how good a drinker you might think you are, don't forget that the Russians—any Russian—can drink you under the table.

Be prepared, by the way, no matter how bad you might feel when you wake up, to do it again—with breakfast.

Zamir and I finished our reindeer (which tasted like slightly gamier venison) and strolled outside in the knee-deep snow. Near the restaurant, an area had been cleared and iced for skating. Kids played around a straw figure representing winter; it would be burned in effigy that night at the Farewell to Winter festivities. Families with children and toboggans and sleds slogged in heavy overcoats and fur hats from nearby homes, looking cheerful and excited, red-faced in the cold.

"I should put reindeer on our Christmas menu," I mused out loud. "Can you picture it? All those crying kids, wondering if that's a chunk of Rudolph or Blitzen lying on their plate?"

"I take it you don't have children," observed Zamir.

We ate piroshki in town, at a Russian fast-food joint. Adorable-looking women in white-peaked caps and spotless red-and-white uniforms with low décolletage dished up pastries filled with meat, fish, cabbage, and sausages. Put out of your mind, by the way, any idea that Russian women are all wide-bodied babushkas with faces like potatoes. They're not. I'd never seen so many tall, beautiful, well-dressed women in one place in my life. That they seem about as soft and cuddly as a fistful of quarters is beside the point—they're gorgeous. At a blintz place, My Mother-in-Law's Blintzes, more creamy-white-breasted girls behind a spotless counter efficiently prepared and served made-to-order crepes wrapped around various sweet and savory fillings.

We ate *ukha*, a clear fish soup, and wood-roasted trout on Krestovsky Island, a two-story structure by a frozen pond. The cooks were out back, dressed in paratrooper camos in the snow, feeding fish into wood-burning ovens in a windblown lean-to. We drank tequila in a cellar bar filled with Russian kids, a band playing phonetic English versions of ska, country-western, and blues standards. I bought the obligatory fur hat, then went ice fishing on the frozen Neva River with my two companions, factory workers, who came a few times a week to get away from their families. When I saw their catch—tiny whitebait-sized fish, which they said they gave to their cats—I got the idea that these guys weren't there to catch the big one. When one of them cracked open a lunch box at eight o'clock in the morning and offered me a slug of vodka, I got the full picture.

"Zamir," I said, "you've been dunking me in frozen lakes, involving me in reindeer killing, poisoning me with vodka. Let's go someplace nice and eat some high-end stuff. Some fish eggs. Let's dress up and go out for one last blowout."

That night, we trudged through the snow and a vicious wind on Vasilevsky Island (Saint Petersburg is made up of about 120 islands). It was dark and extremely cold.

Zamir and I stepped into the Russkaya restaurant, a cavernous but cozy, rustically elegant space with wide wood floorboards, a plain plaster interior, dramatic ceilings, and a big brick-and-mortar oven in the dining room. A relaxed flathead in a tight jacket sat by the coat check, providing security, a suspicious-looking bulge under his left shoulder. We were greeted right away by a friendly host, who helped us peel off our layers and then showed us to two large glass jars of homemade vodka and another jar of cloudy greenish liquid.

"Homemade mustard seed and horseradish vodka," I was informed. The greenish liquid was "cucumber juice," essentially pickle brine. The idea was to down a shot of the spicy, throat-burning vodka, then chase it immediately with a glass of brine. Sounds pretty loathsome, right? And either element alone would indeed have been troublesome. But in correct order, the searing neutral spirits followed by cooling and oddly mellowing brine was delicious, sort of like my earlier experience at the *banya*: sweating and burning, followed by dunking and freezing. Together, somehow, it works.

We sat down and had a few more of these "one-two punch" concoctions and some bread. Our waitress, a cute but unusually assertive young woman, seemed to materialize regularly with more of the stuff. "Don't vorry," she said, "I am strong. If you get drunk, I can carry you home." She was fairly petite, but I believed her.

Now, I famously hate salad bars. I don't like buffets (unless I'm standing on the serving side: Buffets are like free money for cost-conscious chefs). When I see food sitting out, exposed to the elements, I see food dying. I see a big open petri dish that every passing serial sneezer can feel free to drool on and fondle with spittle-flecked fingers. I see food not held at ideal temperature, food rotated (or not) by person or persons unknown, left to fester in the open air unprotected from the passing fancies of the general public. Those New York delis with the giant salad bars where all the health-conscious office workers go for their light, sensible lunches? You're eating more bacteria than the guy standing outside eating mystery meat on a stick. I remember my own words when designing buffets at a large club: "Fill 'em up on free salads and bread, so they go light on the shrimp."

Russkaya's first-course salad bar, however, was not bad. It helped that the restaurant was empty, and the food looked fresh. A long white table was covered with goodies: *pashket* (a liver pâté), *grechnevaya kasha* (buckwheat groats with mushrooms and onions), pickled beets, smoked fish, pickled herring, potato salad, potato latkes, and shaved paper-thin slices of chilled, uncooked pork fat. It was the perfect accompaniment to the early stages of what I was beginning to understand would be a marathon vodka-drinking session. A full bottle of Russian Standard had already hit our table when Zamir and I returned from the buffet, and our waitress, watching us like a severe schoolmarm, seemed hell-bent on seeing us both carried out on stretchers.

Two huge plates loaded with osetra caviar and the traditional garnishes arrived at our table. We eyed the big mound of gray-black fish eggs, lemon wedges, separated hard-cooked egg yolks and whites, finely chopped onion, sour cream and chives, and a warm stack of fluffy, perfectly cooked buckwheat blinis. Then I dug in, not messing about with garnishes, shoveling about half an ounce into my mouth in one bite. The blinis were perfect, the little eggs bursting between my teeth.

"She says there is a problem with our table," said Zamir, our waitress standing at his shoulder with a grave expression on her face. "Our waitress says we are not drinking enough vodka. She is concerned."

I searched my waitress's face, trying to find a hint of a smile. Was she kidding? I didn't know.

Try to imagine this happening in an American restaurant or bar. Your waiter comes to your table and says he doesn't think you are consuming enough booze, that you need more alcohol, and you need to consume it quickly. Our highways would be demolition derbies of colliding muscle cars overloaded with drunken frat boys, senseless Yuppies, and out-of-control secretaries stoked on spritzers and woo-woos. In Russia, though, this is apparently normal. At the time of their deaths, three out of five Russian men, I am told, are found to have a blood-alcohol level exceeding what one needs to qualify for a DWI. That doesn't mean the booze killed them, just that the majority of Russian men happen to be drunk when they die. Hundreds, if not thousands, do die every year directly from the effects of drinking cheap rotgut—bathtub brews sold as vodka but more like lighter fluid or paint remover. I shudder to think what the threshold for "intoxicated" is if pulled over by a cop in Russia. I'm guessing about fifty rubles.

After we'd knocked off maybe four ounces of caviar and a half bottle of vodka, our entrée arrived, a whole roasted sterlet. Already smashed, Zamir and I were not off the hook. Even though we were well past the "I love you, man" stage, exchanging slurred toasts every few minutes, our waitress returned to our table to admonish us.

"You will both be considered traitors to your countries and your people if you do not drink more!"

When we finally staggered out into the street, it was snowing hard, the wind howling off the river, a half bottle of Russian Standard sloshing around in our stuffed bellies. Zamir and I exchanged loud expressions of friendship and devotion, our coats flapping open in the frigid wind.

The Purpose of the Hamburger Bun

An excerpt from Tony's last cookbook, *Appetites*, published in the UK by Bloomsbury in 2016.

Brioches are very nice.

For breakfast.

Do *not* think for a second that a brioche roll is a good idea for a hamburger. The brioche is a French innovation. The French, however vital to all things culinary, have no cultural understanding of—or historic sympathies for—the American hamburger.

The purpose of the hamburger bun is to support and enhance the meat. Hamburger meat is, by definition, supposed to be fatty. A certain amount of grease is desirable. The bun is supposed to counteract the runoff and absorb it. It is supposed to last, in direct proportion to the amount of meat left, until the last bite.

Brioches are greasy. They *add* grease. They also crumble and break apart in the hand as the burger reaches its butt end. It is not a reliable partner or friend. The potato bun, however, is the perfect delivery system for a fatty patty (or patties). It should be soft, pillowy, reliable, and decidedly proletarian.

Like sushi—another perfect food—a hamburger should be austere, seemingly uncomplicated, yet prepared with pride and precision.

One must continue to ask oneself, as if arranging flowers in the Japanese manner, "Is this necessary?," stripping away that which does not serve the meat. The meat is the star.

Does one need a tomato slice? Does it really add anything? Here, a cost-benefit analysis is required. The tomato may be in season, and at its height of deliciousness, but will including it in the delicately constructed hamburger be worth the possible damage to its structure and "eatability"?

Cheddar or processed American food? One must ask oneself constantly what one is willing to sacrifice for presumed "quality." American cheese, clearly, is texturally and structurally superior as a binding agent—and has the added force of tradition on its side.

Lettuce? I'm not a fan. I'll have my salad on the side. But I understand the desire for crunch. If you're putting mesclun or baby arugula on your burger, though, Guantánamo Bay would not be an unreasonable punishment. Use finely shredded iceberg. Or *maybe* romaine. Period.

Onions add something to the party, but they must be thinly sliced. Paper thin. And fresh, *please*. Caramelized? No. Not a fan. Burgers should not be sweet. Any sweetness in a burger should come from the ketchup alone.

Speaking of which: Do not put "house-made chutney" on my hamburger. Please. Let ketchup do its job. And don't make "house-made ketchup" either. Why would you do that? If it's not broken, as they say, why the fuck would you fix it? Is your ketchup *really* better than the stuff that's been our trusty condiment companion for decades? A waiter asks me if I'd like some "house-made" ketchup and I tense up, anticipating further blows: Will Mumford and Sons suddenly emerge from the kitchen and begin playing tableside?

Mayonnaise? Maybe, if applied judiciously. You don't want that burger shooting out from between the buns and landing on your genitals. It's a tough call. How much do you really like mayonnaise? A cost/benefit analysis is called for here.

Bacon? By all means. But as with anything you put on a burger, serious attention must be paid to thickness, doneness, and cut, which is to say, use a standard-issue thin slice of bacon, and cook it to well-done. And don't overload your burger with it. You can, as it turns out, have too much bacon.

Fugu Fish in Tokyo

An excerpt from *A Cook's Tour: In Search of the Perfect Meal*,
originally published by Bloomsbury in 2001.

F ugu. The deadly puffer fish of legend. It's a delicacy. It's expensive. You must be licensed by the state—after a long and comprehensive course of training and examination—to prepare and serve it. It can kill you. And every year in Japan, it does kill a score or so of its devotees, who are poisoned by the potentially deadly nerve toxins in its liver. First comes a feeling of numbness around the lips, a numbness that rapidly spreads through the central nervous system, paralyzing the extremities. Quickly followed by death.

Sounds cool, right? If I'd had a top ten list of things I absolutely had to try while in Tokyo, fugu would have been right near the top. I had high hopes. I was ready. I wanted the exhilaration of a near-death experience. I'd scheduled my whole trip around fugu season. As I understood it—from careful study of barroom speculation and an episode of *The Simpsons*—a fugu meal was a game of chicken with all those delicious, if potentially fatal, toxins. There had to be a psychoactive, or at least a physical dimension, to the fugu experience, maybe just enough of the liver in each portion to give you a momentary peek into the void, maybe a sharp but pleasant sensation in the belly after eating, an artificial sense of well-being, a slight MDA-like high as traces of nerve toxin flirted with heart muscles and synapses.

I chose the Nibiki restaurant, run by chef/owner Kichiro Yoshida. Mr. Yoshida's father was the first licensed fugu chef in Japan. Nibiki has been operated by the Yoshida family for eighty years without incident or fatality. You get one shot at running a fugu restaurant. One strike and you're out. Nibiki is a homey-looking little place with a large plastic puffer fish hanging over the door, an open kitchen with counter, and a raised dining area with tables and cushions.

Mr. Yoshida welcomed me into his kitchen and gave me the short course in fugu. A large example of the fabled fish lay on a spotless white cutting board, looking similar to monkfish with its scaleless, slimy, and knife-resistant skin. The anatomy was similar to monkfish, as well: a center spine, no pin bones, skin that had to be peeled off, and two meaty tenderloin-shaped fillets on each fish. Yoshida-san quickly zipped off the skin and began carving away some dark bits. A small metal waste container with a hinged lid and padlock stood next to the cutting board. The chef removed a key from a chain and gravely unlocked it. The toxic parts—every toxic part—of the fugu, he explained, must, by law, be disposed of like medical waste, segregated and secure at all times. He trimmed away any remaining skin, a few parts around the gills, some tiny, innocuous-looking dark spots on the flesh, then soaked the clean white meat repeatedly in cold water. The liver, I have to say, was lovely: creamy café au lait–colored, engorged-looking, with a foie-gras consistency. It looked appetizing, like monkfish liver. "Do you eat any of the liver?" I asked hopefully. "No," said Mr. Yoshida. Many are tempted, he explained. Most of the fatalities from fugu, he assured me, occurred among fishermen and fishmongers who were unable to resist the tasty-looking livers—and whatever holistic, restorative powers they might believe the deadly but attractive organ to have. According to Mr. Yoshida, the problem is that there's no way to tell how much toxin occurs in any particular fish. A big fugu with a large, plump liver might have relatively little toxin in its liver. Take a nibble or prepare a *nabe* (broth in a pot) with a tiny bit, and you might well be fine. Conversely, a small fish's liver might well be overloaded with toxin; take one lick and you keel over stone-dead. A daredevil fugu fan might become emboldened by the occasional nip of liver, only to take one toxin-heavy bite of another one and check out for good.

As the chef carefully cleaned and washed the fish again and again, I began to get the idea that I would not be risking my life at all. I sat down to a very nice, very fresh meal. There was a tray of fanned-out slices of fugu sashimi, arranged in a chrysanthemum pattern, with a garnish of scallion sticks and a dipping sauce. The flavor was subtle, bordering on bland. It needed the sauce and scallions. A *nabe* of fugu arrived next, served in a hot pot on a tableside burner—also excellent, but hardly the white-knuckle experience I'd hoped for. A batter-fried fugu dish was next, indistinguishable from a deep-fried fish fillet at any of a thousand New England seaside seafood barns. Had I not been expecting a brain-bending, lip-numbing, look-the-devil-in-the-face dining adventure, I would have been thrilled with the meal. That it was only excellent was not enough. I had gotten it wrong. Maybe next time, I'll hook up with those fishermen. They sound like party animals.

Fire over England

An excerpt from *A Cook's Tour: In Search of the Perfect Meal*,
originally published by Bloomsbury in 2001.

You have only to visit an English pub in, say, Bristol or
Birmingham—once-proud strongholds of British culinary
tradition at its simplest and most unvarnished—to see that
the enemy has reached the gates and is pounding on the door. A vegetarian menu! Right there—next to the steak and kidney pie and the
bangers and mash! Worse—far worse—is when you look over at the bar
and see Brits, brewers of some of the finest alcoholic beverages in the
world, gorgeous beers, ales, and bitters, once served in that most noble
of drinking vessels—the pint glass—sucking Budweisers from long-
necked bottles.

It's war. On one side, a growing army of hugely talented young
British, Scottish, Irish, and Australian chefs, rediscovering their own
enviable indigenous resources and marrying them with either new and
brash concepts or old and neglected classics. On the other? A soul-
destroying tsunami of bad, fake reproductions of what was already bad,
fake New York "Mexican" food. Gluey, horrible nachos, microwaved
never-fried "refried" beans, fabric softener margaritas. Limp, soggy,
watery, and thoroughly dickless "enchiladas" and catsupy salsas. Clueless "Pan-Asian" watering holes where every callow youth with a can of
coconut milk and some curry powder thinks he's Ho Chi Minh. (Forget
it. Ho could cook.) Sushi is almost nowhere to be found—in spite of the
fact that the seafood in the UK is magnificent.

You get more heart, soul, and flavor at an East End pie shop than
at any of the rotten, fake, dumbed-down "Italian," "Japanese fusion,"

or theme purgatories. Even the cod—the basic ingredient of fish and chips—is disappearing. (I raised that subject with a Portuguese cod importer. "The damned seals eat them," was his answer. "Kill more seals," he suggested.)

Fortunately, Fergus and other like-minded souls are on the front lines, and they're unlikely to abandon their positions. Sitting at St. John, I ordered what I think is the best thing I have ever put in my mouth: Fergus's roasted bone marrow with parsley and caper salad, croutons, and sea salt.

Oh God, is it good. How something so simple can be so . . . so . . . absolutely luxurious. A few Flintstone-sized lengths of veal shank, a lightly dressed salad . . . Lord . . . to tunnel into those bones, smear that soft gray-pink-and-white marrow onto a slab of toasted bread, sprinkle with some *sel gris* . . . take a bite . . . Angels sing, celestial trumpets . . . six generations of one's ancestors smile down from heaven. It's butter from God.

A few years ago, the neighborhood around St. John was about as fashionable as a fistula. Now, there are faces and bodies one usually associates with tofu snacks and soy milk smoothies, skinny, well-dressed women, mussing their lipstick as they enthusiastically gnaw bones, ooh and aah over the glories of pork belly, pig's trotter, tripe—all that lovingly cooked offal. It's where the people who truly love food, who know what's good about wiping grease off their chins, can congregate without fear, safe from the dark clouds of processed food gathering over Europe. A meal at St. John is only one of the great dining experiences one can have in England. I'm not going to bother to give you an overview—reciting the names of all the sharp, ambitious, well-trained chefs who have, in recent years, completely reversed the widely held perception that English food was crap. Suffice it to say that most of these guys could kick their French counterparts' asses around the block. An Englishman in the kitchen—be it in New York, Melbourne, or anywhere else—is a promise of good things to come. A meal at St. John is not just one of the great eating experiences on the planet—it's a call to the barricades.

Because it will not end with the marrow (which already has to be imported from Holland). The enemy wants your cheese. They want you never again to risk the possibility of pleasure with a reeking, unpasteurized Stilton, an artisanal wine, an oyster on the half shell. They have designs on stock. *Stock!* (Bones, you know—can't have that.) The backbone of *everything* good! They want your sausage. And your balls, too. In short, they want you to feel that same level of discomfort approaching a plate of food that so many used to feel about sex.

Do I overstate the case? Go to Wisconsin. Spend an hour in an airport or a food court in the Midwest; watch the pale, doughy masses of pasty-faced, Pringle-fattened, morbidly obese teenagers. Then tell me I'm worried about nothing. These are the end products of the Masterminds of Safety and Ethics, bulked up on cheese that contains no cheese, chips fried in oil that isn't really oil, overcooked gray disks of what might once upon a time have been meat, a steady diet of Ho Hos and muffins, butterless popcorn, sugarless soda, flavorless light beer. A docile, uncomprehending herd, led slowly to a dumb, lingering, and joyless slaughter.

Bobby Eats Out

An excerpt from the novel *The Bobby Gold Stories*, originally published by Bloomsbury in 2003.

Bobby Gold in black Armani suit (from a load hijacked out of Kennedy), skinny black tie, black silk shirt, and black Oxfords sat on the banquette of 210 Park Grill and looked uncomfortably at Eddie Fish's sourdough dinner roll. Eddie had torn the thing apart but hadn't eaten any; the bits of bread and crust lay scattered on his plate like an autopsied crime victim. When the drinks came, vodka rocks for Bobby, Patrón straight up with a side of fresh lime juice for Eddie, Bobby drained his in two gulps, exhausted already.

At thirty-eight years old, Eddie Fish had not once in his life had to wash his own shirt, clean an ashtray, pick up after himself, or take public transportation. He was a little man; five foot four in heels, and impeccably dressed today: a charcoal-gray pinstriped suit from an English tailor, ultra-thin Swiss timepiece, hand-painted silk tie, shirt from Turnbull and Asser, and Italian shoes made from unborn calfskin. His nails were buffed and polished, and his hair, trimmed twice a week by the same man who'd cut his father's, was neat and curiously untouched by gray. Eddie Fish's skin was golden brown, burnished by the strong Caribbean sun, and his pores were clean and tight after a morning visit to his dermatologist. He looked pretty much like the man he imagined himself to be: a successful businessman, a nice guy, a democrat, and a citizen of the world.

"They love me here," said Eddie Fish, one arm over his chair back, motioning for a waiter.

"Can't you just pick something and order?" pleaded Bobby, knowing it was hopeless.

"I need a minute," said Eddie, his eyes darting around inside his head like trapped hamsters.

The waiter arrived and asked if they were ready to order.

"Would you like a few moments to decide?" inquired the waiter politely after Eddie ignored him, his nose buried in the menu.

"No . . . no. Stay," commanded Eddie.

For Eddie Fish, menus were like the Dead Sea Scrolls, the Rosetta Stone, the Kabbalah, and *Finnegans Wake* all rolled into one impenetrable document. There were hidden messages, secrets that had to be rooted out before it was safe to order. There was, there had to be, Eddie was convinced, some way of getting something better, something extra—the good stuff they weren't telling everybody about. Somebody somewhere was getting something better than what appeared here. Someone richer, taller, with better connections, was getting a little extra and Eddie was not going to be denied.

Brow furrowed, the muscles in his jaws working furiously, he scrutinized each item on the menu, each listed ingredient, his eyes moving up and down the columns, then back again.

Bobby had decided on onglet medium-rare thirty seconds after picking up the menu and he looked around the room, killing time, waiting for Eddie. It was mostly women here; long-legged ones with foreign accents and faces pulled tight, a few weedy-looking men who looked like their moms had dressed them. They were packed in three-deep at the bar, a host hurrying to air-kiss new arrivals. Their waiter, still waiting on Eddie, looked nervously at the rest of his rapidly overflowing station.

"The oysters . . . ," began Eddie. "Where are they from?"

"Prince Edward Island, sir," replied the waiter. "Nova Scotia. They're excellent."

"You have any Wellfleet oysters?" inquired Eddie, looking grave. Bobby nearly groaned out loud. Eddie wouldn't have known a Wellfleet oyster if one had climbed up his leg, fastened itself on his dick, and announced itself in fluent English. He must have seen them on another menu.

"I'm sorry, sir. No. We don't have them," said the waiter. "We only have the Prince Edward Islands."

"And . . . what kind of sauce do they come with?" asked Eddie. "I don't want any cocktail sauce . . . that red stuff. I don't want that."

"They're served with a rice-wine wasabi vinaigrette," said the waiter.

"Like it says on the fucking menu . . ." he could have added.

"Uh-huh . . . ," said Eddie, processing this last bit of information, wondering no doubt if the waiter was trying to trick him somehow. Wasabi . . . Wasabi . . . Was that a good thing or a bad thing?

Bobby saw something being resolved. A decision had been made on the oyster question. "Can you ask the chef to make me some of that sauce with the shallots in it? What do you call that? Mignonette! I want mignonette sauce. It's like . . . red . . . red wine vinegar and shallots. And some black pepper. The shallots—you gotta chop 'em up real small. Can you do that?"

"Mignonette," repeated the waiter, thinking visibly. Which would be worse, thought Bobby: telling Eddie fucking Fish, known gangster associate, that he couldn't have the fucking mignonette with his oysters—or approaching a rampaging prick of a three-star chef in the middle of the lunch rush and telling him to start hunting up some shallots and red wine vinegar?

"I'll have to ask the chef, sir," said the waiter. "But I'm pretty sure we can do that for you."

By the time he started in ordering his entrée, Eddie had kept the waiter at his elbow for five full minutes, the rest of the poor man's station shooting daggers at him from their tables. Eddie, oblivious to Bobby's discomfort, began the tortuous process of grafting together elements from different menu items, designing an entrée for himself, figuring out the way it should be served, instead of the way everyone else was getting it. Only fools, as Eddie liked to say, settled for less.

"The hanger steak. How is that prepared?"

"With saffron cous-cous, sir," said the waiter. "It's pan-seared, then roasted to order and served with a reduction of Côtes du Rhône, demi-glace, and caramelized whole shallots. It's very good." The waiter's offer of an opinion doomed that selection. Eddie wasn't having any.

"And the tuna?"

"That's grilled rare . . . served with roasted fingerling potatoes, braised fennel . . . and a citrus herb reduction," said the waiter, the first hint of frustration creeping into his voice. It made no impression on Eddie. The poor bastard could hop up and down holding his crotch, get down on one knee, and bark like a dog—it wouldn't make any difference to Eddie, who seemed to slip into some kind of a fugue state when ordering from a menu.

"Okay . . . Okay . . . ," pondered Eddie. "How about . . . let me . . . get . . . the . . . the monkfish. The saddle of monkfish."

"One monkfish," repeated the waiter, gratefully, the clouds beginning to part, one foot already pointed toward the kitchen.

"But . . . let me have that with . . . with the sauce from the hanger steak," said Eddie. "And like . . . the roasted finger potatoes. That sounds good . . . And what came with the tuna? What was the vegetable with that?"

"Uh . . . braised fennel," stammered the waiter. Bobby saw the light go out in his eyes. He got it now. He understood, finally, what was happening. Eddie was never letting him go. All hope was gone. This vicious, malevolent little creep wasn't going to be happy until his whole station was up in arms, until his other customers were so pissed off they tipped 10 percent, until the chef was pushed to the point of murder. Chefs blame waiters for the sins of their customers, the waiter was probably thinking, and this chef, when he saw Eddie Fish's order, was going to unscrew his head and relieve himself down his neck.

"Forget the monkfish," said Eddie, changing tack. "Let me have the turbot instead. Yeah. I'll have the turbot. It's fresh?"

"Yes, sir," said the waiter. "It came in this morning."

"Then I'll have the turbot. Grilled . . . with the balsamic reduction and baby bok choy from this pork dish here . . ."

"Yes, sir," said the waiter, picturing his imminent dismemberment in the kitchen.

"Wait!" commanded Eddie, as the waiter began to turn away. "Before you bring the fish . . . could you lemme have a Caesar salad?"

"I'm sorry sir," said the waiter. "We don't have—"

Eddie was not deterred. He'd expected this. "It's simple. You tell the chef, take some egg yolks . . . and some garlic. Fresh garlic . . . and some anchovies . . ."

It went on like this . . . and on. It always did. Bobby had known Eddie since college. Nearly twenty years—and every meal was like this. When the order was, at long last, finally taken, the waiter dispatched to the kitchen to meet his fate, Eddie was still looking at the menu, unsatisfied. He'd study it for a few more minutes, to see, Bobby thought, where he might have gone wrong, doing an after-action report in his head, analyzing where he might have missed something. By now, Bobby had completely lost his appetite. The customers at the tables around them glared, murmuring in French. Bobby, easily the largest man in the room, felt like a circus bear, staked in place, trapped and uncomfortable.

Eddie straightened his tie and put down his menu.

"Isn't this place great? You can't get reservations here. Six-month wait."

"You murder these waiters," said Bobby.

"Are you kidding me? They love me here!" said Eddie, shooting his cuffs, then rubbing his hands together in anticipation of his oysters and his Caesar. "You know how much I tip when I come here?"

Yeah, thought Bobby. *Twelve percent.*

Guts and Glory
An Adventure with Offal

An unpublished piece Tony wrote in 2008 around the tenth anniversary of Les Halles. Tony later went on a speaking tour with the same title, Guts and Glory.

Is there anything more disturbing to the young American mind, more terrifying to the uninformed palate, than the sight of Mom approaching with a thick slice of calf's—or worse, beef—liver? The appearance of entrails in *any* context, we have come to believe, is a violation of the basic order of the universe, a sign, judging from the classic horror films of our youth, that things have gone horribly wrong and will, in all likelihood, only get worse. Guts, movies, books, and television strongly suggest, belong on the *inside* of things—and should stay there. One need only recall the frightening black and white images of zombified cannibals feasting on organs in *Night of the Living Dead* to relive that first twinge of revulsion at Mom's earnest offer. "Try it! It's *good* for you!"

As the chef of the defiantly working-class brasserie Les Halles, I have long been initiated into the French concept of "use everything," so I am no stranger to offal. And as an obnoxious, lifelong show-off, always eager to shock, I take unseemly delight in introducing the timid but curious to the power and glory of French organ-meat classics. Even tripe, which I think smells like wet sheepdog, gives me a slight frisson of pleasure when I cook it. It feels, somehow . . . naughty.

We're coming up on our tenth anniversary at Les Halles, the Big Day falling on October 31, Halloween, an evening where traditionally we dress up our butcher counter with a lurid, Grand Guignol–esque display of contorted and rudely defiled calves', sheep's, and pigs' heads, offal, and stage blood. I take personal charge of the gory tableau, fancying myself a sort of low-rent Damien Hirst (as imagined by Sam Peckinpah). This year, since this is a particularly significant birthday, I thought I'd try a weeklong offal-fest to go along with the theme: Seven days of classic French offerings like *rognons de veau Bercy* (kidneys), *ris de veau financière* (sweetbreads), tripes *à la mode de Caen*, *foie de veau persillé* (liver), and possibly *cervelle au beurre noir* (brains). I know it'll be a tough sell. But I've come to love many of these dishes and hope our diners will too. *How cool!* I thought while assembling recipes. *How scary! How French!*

Well—not entirely. Researching a project recently, I began spending time at the New York Historical Society, perusing old menus from turn-of-the-century America. I was astonished by what I found. In the late nineteenth century and early part of the twentieth, offal was everywhere! Rather than the crude, unsophisticated menus I'd imagined for pre-Julia, pre–Henri Soulé America, I found evidence of a fearless, indulgent, food-crazy, and often Francophilic dining public. Lunchrooms and saloons offered fried brains, roasted ox hearts, sweetbreads, and kidneys. Raw oysters were everywhere. At the high end of the spectrum—in the legendary dining rooms of Rector's, Delmonico's, and Sherry's—often, an entire course was dedicated to offal. Guts were the rule—not the exception! What happened? Where did they all go? What ruined offal for subsequent generations? Was it horror movies? I don't think so, as graphic violence didn't appear in films until the sixties. Was it one overzealous mom too many? I think not. I think we just got lazy. In the prosperity that came with the postwar years, Americans no longer HAD to eat the more challenging parts of the animal. With the appearance of convenience food, supermarkets, and roadside chains, diners could feel free to eat the white, boneless breast of chicken—already prepared or butchered for them—and simply ignore the rest. Why bother with liver, or kidneys, or even shank or shoulder for that matter, when *all* meat could be fatless, boneless sirloin—and all chicken a skinless, processed cutlet of breast? Junior doesn't want the liver? Fine! There's plenty of ground sirloin in the Frigidaire—and if he doesn't like that, we can call out. Offal became pet food—for our expanding population of cats and dogs, hell, there was plenty to eat; why *not* get a cute pooch, a nice kitty?

As decades passed and Hollywood began to break the "splatter barrier," the new "realism" only reinforced our morbid fear and loathing of the unseen palpitating and gurgling things inside us. The Brits, however, continued to do it right. On a book tour a few weeks ago, I had the opportunity to eat around England and Scotland. Though the sinister American influence of fast, convenient food has left its mark, steak and kidney pie is still everywhere on pub menus. Black pudding is still a popular breakfast item—particularly in Scotland. And the new generations of British chefs, many French trained, are exuberantly featuring animal parts that would cause squeals of discomfort if seen on a New York menu. Marco Pierre White, in the early nineties, took particular pleasure, judging from his cookbooks, in such defiantly old-school French-inspired dishes as pig trotters stuffed with sweetbreads and roast woodcock (with brains), a thick tranche of calf's liver—and his many acolytes have continued fusing classic French and British offal recipes in exciting, beautiful, and delicious ways. But for most unapologetically retro, old-school British practitioners of the hoof, snout, ears, tongues, bones, tails, and guts school of cookery, the remarkable Fergus Henderson of London's awesome meat-district bistro St. John appears to be the leader of the pack. His in-your-face menus (which change nightly) proudly showcase the neglected parts of pigs and sheep in straightforward but spectacular fashion. His roasted bone marrow with parsley salad and toast nearly had me weeping with pleasure at my table, and that was before I tucked into the grilled ox heart. Henderson's cookbook, titled *Nose to Tail Eating*, is a compendium of simple, unassuming, and uniquely British fare but sheer exotica to me: rolled pig's spleen, jellied tripe, dried salted pig's liver, duck's heart on toast, four preparations of lamb's brains, blood cake, lamb's tongues, deviled kidneys, lamb kidneys in suet, along with tasty-looking recipes for pigs' ears, tails, and feet. Henderson advises in his introduction: "Don't be afraid of cooking as your ingredients will know and misbehave," boiling down the accumulated wisdom of generations of professionals into one simple and concise sentence.

St. John's austere white undecorated dining room is an incredible experience, especially if you can sit close, facing the open kitchen. Watching Henderson's very serious-looking crew toiling over pork bellies and sifting through organs, making kidneys jump in the pan, is an all-too-rare delight for a coddled American visitor. St. John's sister restaurant in Soho, the revered theatrical hangout the French House, also features some fine offal dishes, like fried lamb sweetbreads and calf's tongue, in its cozy second-floor dining room. A few half-pints of Guinness at the downstairs bar and you might feel daring enough to meet the challenge.

In Scotland, as I was now actively seeking offal in all its forms, I finally scaled the Everest of Entrails, that punch line to a thousand Scottish jokes, the Holy Grail of America's idea of the Thing Never to Be Eaten: haggis. If you didn't know, haggis is a truly petrifying-sounding mixture of sheep's "tuck" (basically the heart, windpipe, lungs, liver, and intestines) minced and folded with oatmeal and allspice and stuffed into the sheep's stomach. Now, haggis is serious business in Scotland. My innocent inquiries in Glasgow on the subject of where to eat good haggis in Edinburgh (where I was headed early the next morning) brought the unvarying reply, "Not in Edinburgh! Not Scottish enough! It's too bloody English!" Scots sneered at some of the newer preparations of their beloved dish at the many upscale "fusion" restaurants, like haggis in phyllo or roast goose with haggis sauce. It was nearly impossible to get a definitive answer as to where and in what circumstances I should eat my first haggis. Every attempt inspired passionate discussion—bordering on argument that threatened to continue into the wee hours. It was not really haggis season, I was informed—especially if I wanted to do the whole haggis with neeps and tatties (turnips and potatoes) route. Two popular brands of haggis available in markets were suggested. "You should really cook it at home," some said, but no two people could agree on a brand. Half-hearted mentions of various tourist-friendly restaurants with "traditional" preparations of haggis on the menu were made, but with the same sad tone and pitying expressions as one might have sending an out-of-town relative off to Planet Hollywood or the Hard Rock Cafe in New York.

When I arrived in Edinburgh, it was festival time, and the streets were clogged with kilt-wearing Japanese and fanny-packing tourists—all looking for a haggis-related thrill. A Glasgow crony agreed to tag along to a place suggested in the guidebooks as being perfect for Real, Authentic Scottish cuisine, but, already dubious of all things Edinburgh, unimpressed by the theme park re-creation of a Real Scottish restaurant, he took one look at the dining room, packed with tittering rubes, and put his foot down. "We're leaving," he said. "Get your bloody haggis in a chip shop, like the rest of us," he said, lurching toward the maître d' to tell him that the "silly American" had changed his mind and "wouldn't be needing a table after all." The good stuff, apparently, had been right under my nose all along. We walked right around the corner, and there, batter-dipped, pre-fried, and kept warm under the heat lamps, were stacks of tube-shaped haggis, right next to the fried cod fillets and the Scotch pies. I ordered some to carry out, with a pile of limp, vinegar-doused chips, and brought it back to my flat. Starving by now, and my stomach roiling after a long night of Tennent's and Guinness and whiskey with my Glaswegian friend, I flipped on the telly to Britain's national obsession, *Big Brother* (the UK inspiration for *Survivor*), and, while watching the tabloid-famous Nasty Nick conspire against his flatmates for the Big Money, wolfed down my haggis. It wasn't "okay," as I'd expected. It was wonderful. Crunchy and crispy on the outside, fluffy and moist on the inside, it tasted like a lighter, more complex version of *boudin noir*—the perfect thing to sop up all that beer—the perfect late-night munchie food. I was hooked, I wanted more. Like all truly great meals, my haggis experience had everything: good-tasting stuff, atmosphere (I was staying in a seventeenth-century stone building down a dark cobblestone lane), the shock of the new and different, and an element of fear. Enjoying my meal felt like a personal triumph, like one's first raw oyster or first taste of foie gras, sushi, or monkfish liver. Fear can be good.

It's Cruel and Unforgiving Terrain

An unpublished piece written by Tony in 2000.

It's cruel and unforgiving terrain, the New York restaurant scene, a fickle, fiercely competitive feudal society where new places open and close, successful ones multiply like cancer cells, and failures leave a residual cloud of doom, infecting even those who follow. It's not a landscape friendly to bold, new ideas—the pressure to survive is too great, and restaurateurs, all too aware of the capricious nature of the dining public, tend to move in packs for protection, embracing the latest "concept" in dining or cuisine en masse, afraid of being separated from the herd, abandoned, devoured. You know the feeling. Suddenly, one wakes up, and it appears that every knucklehead in town who can drag an old couch into his saloon has opened up a "restaurant/lounge."

We've survived a rash of utterly witless theme restaurants—culminating in the Terrordome-like All-Star Cafe; narrowly avoided a magic-themed David Copperfield eatery; seen Comedy Nation shrivel and die. (It always seemed to me that a successful comedy-themed restaurant would be likely to cause a high incidence of choking on food. "All Our Servers Are Trained In the Heimlich Maneuver!") There was a Pacific Rim explosion, Asian fusion, tapas, Nuevo Latino, a flurry of Brazilian all-you-can-eat. Probably the last great wave of cookie-cutter establishments was the spread of brewpubs and "microbrewery" restaurants of a few years back, dooming a generation of beer drinkers to raspberry-wheat ale and honey-mocha lager and ersatz American Regional food.

Now, it's "brasserie." They're sprouting up everywhere, like malevolent weeds, painstaking, even artful re-creations of a century-old concept, with their bright red awnings and antiquey signs reading TRIPES and ASSIETTES FROIDS and BEAUJOLAIS, their enlightened policy of "no reservations" (kinda). The phenomenon has even caused bistros—around for ages—to have identity crises, hanging out new shingles and identifying themselves with their bigger sisters. Why? one might well ask. And what the hell is a brasserie anyway? What exactly is the difference between "brasserie" and "bistro"? How can I tell if I'm in one? What does it all mean?

Let's clear up "bistro" first. Bistros, simply put, were originally smaller, mom-and-pop-type operations that grew up around the mid-nineteenth-century central marketplace in Paris, Les Halles, servicing workmen, market gardeners, and customers of the gargantuan food pavilions. A humble fishmonger or tripe vendor could knock off work, limp over to a neighboring bistro with a pilfered fish head, maybe a spare hoof or snout, and the bistro owner would frequently cook it for them for free. One often paid only for wine. Menus, such as they were, were small, consisting of whatever regional or specialized items Mom and Pop considered themselves good at. The clientele was closely associated with whatever tradesmen drank themselves silly there each night. They were small. They were individual in character. They were not brasseries.

"Brasserie," roughly translated, means "brewery." They came of age in the Alsace region of France, an area where for years, Germans had been constantly marching in and out with their beer and their sausages and their smoked meats, and the early brasseries were unsurprisingly Germanic in their characteristics—efficient mass-feeding operations built around the copious consumption of lager, complete with lederhosen, oompah bands, and public urination. It was only around the turn of the century, when the wily Parisians at the 1900 Exposition Universelle recognized they needed a workable means of feeding millions of tourists and visitors, that they welcomed their suspiciously "non-French" cousins from the east and began opening up brasseries to handle the crowds. The idea was to "get them in and get them out," a concept any veteran of a pre-theater restaurant is familiar with, and they were wildly successful. Unlike the personal imprint menus of the bistro, brasserie menus tended to be nearly identical, offering continuous service, day and night, of steak frites, choucroute, *frisée aux lardons*, boudins, *pieds cochons, soupe a l'oignon gratinée*, and a bacon-heavy repertoire of Alsatian classics, usually listed in compartmentalized menus. No matter what brasserie you went to, the menu was pretty much the same. They were almost always open—no pause between lunch and dinner—and they were decidedly informal. A central irony of the recent brasserie explosion is that America has had its own brasseries for years—even before those silly brewpubs. We called them "diners."

So, why are brasseries so hot right now? New Yorkers are certainly no strangers to the concepts of herding large numbers of people in and out of a feeding facility, standardized menus, French food, or beer. Maybe it's the informality of it all. It's a relief (isn't it?), to eat French food on the fly, in a nonintimidating environment, where one can feel free to be loud, smoke between courses, rest one's elbows on the table, chatter into a cell phone. But are there hard and fast rules? With so many operators busily rubbing tea and wood stain into perfectly new ceilings to give them that "authentic brasserie" nicotine-stained look, carefully damaging new mirrors, and picking out mismatched bar stools and floor tile to get that lived-in "I don't give a fuck" ambiance of their frugal French role models, how does one tell if it's really a brasserie? Some suggested ground rules follow. A brasserie should have: Continuous service. Onion soup—hopefully good onion soup. *Frisée aux lardons* (extra points for poached egg on top). Sausages or tripes (extra points for choucroute). Steak frites. Good fucking french fries. It's the steak frites issue that separates out the real from the pretender. A brasserie should have a decent french fry. Is that so much to ask? It would be nice—certainly more authentic, for sure—if all these budding brasseries served a tasty, slightly chewy, but juicy rump steak, cheap, delicious, and absolutely authentic, but most, sadly, assume the worst of their clientele, figuring that the silly, boobish Americans won't accept a piece of steak that isn't sirloin. So most offer bloodless, fatless, almost entirely flavorless Cryovac-packed sirloin steaks—the sort of ballless meat you get in first-class cabins on airplanes. And the *frites*! You'd think that if Americans could do one fucking thing right, it would be french fries. God knows, we have enough experience. But, shockingly, even after spending millions, scouring the French countryside for just the right antique zinc bar, just the right cane-backed chairs, all those absolutely authentic Tour de France posters and promotional ashtrays for aperitifs no one will ever order—even after putting TRIPE on the menu ('cause it looks so cool on the sign out front)—these would-be La Coupoles and Brasserie Lipps and Au Pied de Cochons don't even bother to turn out a decent french fry! The hottest, busiest, most gorgeous re-creation of the classic Parisian brasserie in town—you know which one I'm talking about—has too-thin, too-crisp *frites* that, though hand-cut, are indistinguishable from the frozen Simplot Classics they serve at the Times Square theme domes.

Another place, also painstakingly crafted to look like the real thing, has gummy, stuck-together, undercooked *frites* that lie limply on the plate like victims of a bus plunge. This second joint compounds its food crimes by offering a particularly gutless onion soup—barely-caramelized onions; dishwatery stock; generic, unbrowned cheese, more reminiscent of Polly-O string cheese than any Gruyère. There's another outpost in my neighborhood, the sort of "French" brasserie you'd expect to see in a Disney resort—in the "French Village" attraction—a bizarre re-creation of something funky and unpretentious by the dispassionately corporate—as if a brasserie had been reconstructed from old photographs and magazine clippings by some alien cargo cult. This place's owner has caused my neighborhood to have two restaurants facing each other from across the street: one a French restaurant that isn't really French, and the other an American "diner" (complete with authentic-looking neon signs and molded stainless steel) that isn't really a diner, forming a canyon of inauthentic mediocrity.

Okay—so some of these new places are bogus French. Does that mean that this brasserie wave is a bad thing? Au contraire. You can eat French food without a tie or a jacket. You can talk loudly—with your mouth full. Even if they're doing it for the wrong reasons at times, restaurants are offering tripe. Chefs are feeling freer than ever to chuck around huge quantities of bacon, duck fat, foie gras, stinky cheese, pork belly, and blood sausages. That's all for the good. People are tucking into red meat again—with abandon, and forsaking postage-stamp-sized portions of herb-infused lawn clippings for Flintstones servings of cassoulet. The vegetarians are again relegated to the fringes—as they should be—sitting silently by while their dinner companions gnaw loudly on bloody boudins, tunnel for bone marrow, nibble on rillettes and swollen goose livers. *Onglet* rules. *Tête de veau, rognons, jarret de boeuf,* beef cheeks, and things *"en crépinette"* are popping up on menus all over town. Smokers are ascendant.

The whole idea of French food as intimidating, unapproachable, undemocratic, and expensive is evaporating. As in Paris, one can decide, on the spur of the moment, at eleven o'clock at night, to drop in to a brasserie and have a platter of oysters, a gamey slab of *onglet*, a pile of *frites* to dip with the hands into a chipped crock of béarnaise. You can smoke again. What's not to like?

II

Family

Tony became a father later in life and he wondered if that was why he immediately took so much satisfaction and happiness from the simple acts of everyday parenthood: changing diapers, holding crying babies, and, of course, making pancakes. His last cookbook, *Appetites* (which is excerpted here), reflects this change: It's a collection of recipes for home, for family, for breakfasts and snacks and all the informal in-between times of family life. Of course, Tony being Tony, he also commissioned a cover painting from Ralph Steadman, whose work you probably know most from his collaboration with Hunter S. Thompson.

Back to the Beach

An excerpt from *A Cook's Tour: In Search of the Perfect Meal*, originally published by Bloomsbury in 2001.

My younger brother, Chris, is about as different from me as anyone can be. While I've spent my whole life living a hand-to-mouth existence, paycheck to paycheck, letting the good times roll, not giving a fuck, a rapidly aging, now-aged hipster, Chris has always been the responsible one, the good son. He never smoked weed. He certainly never did drugs. His hair was never, ever too long or too short for the times. He graduated from an Ivy League school—probably (if I know him) with distinction. I've never seen him roaring or staggering drunk. He saved, and continues to save, his money, never having wasted it on a fast car or a loose woman or (as in my case) some cool-looking high-tech surveillance equipment, which looked good in the catalog when under the influence. He owns a house in Westchester, has a beautiful wife and two adorable, bright, and well-behaved children. If he doesn't drive a Volvo, he probably should. His job, as best as I can understand it, is as a currency specialist for a bank; I think what he does is fly around and advise various South American, European, and Asian investors when to drop dollars and buy yen, when to trade deutsche marks for baht or dong or drachmas. If there's an evil streak in there, I have yet to find it. And I've been looking my entire life.

Chris has no particular reason to love me. I bullied him without mercy as a child, tried, in a fit of jealous rage, to bludgeon him to death as an infant (fortunately for us both, my chosen instrument was a balloon), blamed him constantly for crimes of which I was invariably the true perpetrator, then stood by and listened gleefully as he was spanked and interrogated. He was forced to watch the endlessly unfolding psychodrama at the dinner table when I'd show up late, stoned, belligerent, a miserable, sullen, angry older brother with shoulder-length hair and a bad attitude, who thought Abbie Hoffman and Eldridge Cleaver had it about right—that my parents were fascist tools, instruments of the imperialist jackboot, that their love was what was holding me back from all the psychedelic drugs, free love, and hippie-chick pussy I would have been getting had I not been twelve years old and living at home. The fights, the screaming matches, the loud torments of my painful and pain-inducing early adolescence—he saw it all. And it probably screwed him up good. On the plus side, however, I had taught the little bastard to read by the time he was in kindergarten. And I did keep my mouth shut when he finally decided he'd had enough and coshed me over the head with a pig-iron window counterweight.

There were, I guess, at least some good memories of growing up with Tony, and I think our summers in France as kids might have provided some of them. Each of us had been, for most of those times, the only English-speaking company the other had had. We hung out together, explored the little town of La Teste, spent hours playing army with little green plastic men in the back garden of my aunt's house there. We traded *bandes dessinées*, Tintins, Lucky Lukes, and Asterixes, played with firecrackers, and, when really bored, ganged up on my poor mother. Surprisingly or not, over the years we've become very close. When I suggested a trip together down memory lane, Chris didn't hesitate.

"Let's do it," he said. It was probably the most madcap thing he's ever done.

The idea was to leave our loved ones behind and, just the two of us, reexperience the France of our youth. We'd visit the house in La Teste. We'd eat in all the same places in town, and in neighboring Arcachon. We'd go out at the crack of dawn to the oyster parks in the *bassin* where I'd enjoyed my first all-important oyster and had my first real food-related epiphany. (Chris actually ate and liked the tasty bivalves now.) We'd climb the dune of Pyla again, gorge on sugary pastries (without having to ask permission), drink as much Bordeaux as we pleased, buy lots and lots of firecrackers and throw them into the German blockhouses we'd played in as kids at the beach. Who could hinder our good time now? Who could stop us?

We'd gorge on *saucisson à l'ail*, *soupe de poisson*, big bowls of hot chocolate with buttery baguettes—and we'd drink as many Kronenbourgs and La Belles and Stellas as we damned well pleased. I was forty-four; Chris was forty-one. We were grown-ups now: a respected currency analyst and a bestselling author. Our mother was in New York and had decades ago given up trying to correct our behavior. Our father, though never really a disciplinarian, had died back in the eighties. We could do whatever we wanted. We were free to act like children again. It was the perfect way and the perfect place, I thought, to look for the perfect meal, in our old stomping grounds near the beaches of southwest France.

We met in Saint-Jean-de-Luz, Chris coming from Switzerland, I from Portugal. Together, we drove in a rented car to Arcachon, stopping only for *gaufres*, the hot waffles covered with powdered sugar, which we'd gotten as a post-beach treat as kids. We could eat as many as we wanted now. It's mostly flatland in the southwest—mile after mile of pine trees, planted over a century ago to dry up the mosquito-infested marshes and to keep the long strip of seaside dunes from burying the interior in sand. There's not a lot to look at, but we were happy enough recognizing the familiar names on the signs, smelling French diesel fuel again, getting closer and closer to a place we hadn't been to together in over twenty-eight years.

It was night when we arrived in Arcachon, the summer resort town next door to the tiny oyster village of La Teste-de-Buch. It was January, about as off-season as off-season can be: cold, windy, with a constant drizzle of penetrating, bone-chilling rain. When considering the heady, sentimental, exciting implications of recapturing the past, I'd overlooked such earthly matters as temperature and precipitation—and the fact that we'd very likely be freezing our asses off in a boarded-up ghost town. We checked into a dark, drafty clapboard and chintz House of Horrors hotel on the water, an insane tchotchke-filled barn, decorated with Art Deco stained glass, fake Tiffany lamps, Austro-Hungarian figurines, moldy carpets, rococo furniture, and absolutely no other guests. Picture Norman Bates operating a "romantic getaway" in the Catskills, off an old, no-longer-used highway, and you'll get the idea.

Depressing is not sufficient to describe it. Outside my window, beyond a concrete patio and a pool filled with floating clumps of dead leaves, the Bay of Biscay lay flat and gray, a few fishing boats scudding along its surface, the beach empty except for a few gulls, the lights of Cap Ferret winking in the black distance across the water.

The first night, I slept badly, dreaming of my aunt, Tante Jeanne, yelling at me for throwing firecrackers into the outhouse: *"Défunte! Prison!"* she shrieked. Even my dreams seemed penetrated by the smell of dank, musty upholstered chairs and the peeling pink wallpaper.

Chris woke up looking cheerful and excited. Not me. I declined breakfast in the hotel, wondering when they'd seen their last guest—and if he'd survived the experience. My brother and I hurried to the station and took the short ride to La Teste. It may not have been summer, and we may well have been two silly old farts bundled up to our chins, but for a few moments of anticipation, after stepping off the train, we might have been kids again. Neither of us had said a word the whole way, only smiled, a giddy inability to put into words what we both were feeling. Just standing there on the platform, I felt for a brief moment as if it really were 1966 again. The bare telephone pole that I'd shimmied up as a kid to win a chocolate bar during the Fête du Port was still there in the square in front of the station. The port, with its sagging moorings and old-style *pinasses* (flat-bottomed fishing boats), the oyster boats, the two-story cinder block and stucco homes with their red tile roofs—all looked exactly the same.

Shoulder to shoulder, we strolled down empty streets under a cold gray sky, doing our best to ignore a quiet mist of rain. "It's this way," said Chris in a hushed voice. "Past the fire station and the gendarmerie."

"I can't believe I'm here," I said. "I can't believe it."

We found rue Jules Favre just where we'd left it, and after one block, then two: our house. Or what used to be our house. The driveway had changed. It being winter, there were no roses blooming in the front garden beyond the hedges. The wooden shed to the right, where my father had posed for a photograph as a little boy—in beret and short shorts—where my brother and I later posed (in the same much-hated outfits), was still there. But the swinging gate we'd leaned upon, trying desper-

ately to look cool, or at least less ridiculous, was gone. The house where
our neighbor, the oyster fisherman Monsieur Saint-Jour, had lived had
been torn down and a new home erected in its place. The house my uncle Gustave had begun before his death (I remembered clearing bricks
with him) was much the same. Beyond a new white picket fence and
well-trimmed hedges stood our old summer home. There were a few
seconds of stillness as Chris and I peered over the gate.

"That was my room," said Chris, pointing to a window on the second floor.

"Mine was across the hall," I whispered.

"Yeah. You got the better one."

"I'm bigger."

"Tante Jeanne and Oncle Gustave were downstairs there."

"Why are we whispering?" I muttered.

"Should we knock on the door?"

"You go. Your French is better. I want to see the back garden."

My brother hesitantly approached the house and rang the bell. Soon,
the current owner emerged, a short older man, completely unfazed by
the appearance of two tall, goofy-looking Americans and a camera-toting
TV crew in the middle of winter. After a brief chat with Chris, he agreed
to let us look over the old place, leading us around the side, through an
old gate, to the rear patio and garden area, where Chris and I had played
as kids: trapping lizards, exterminating snails, re-creating D-Day with
our little army men. Beyond a low wall was a table where Tante Jeanne
had served us *salade de tomate*, potato omelettes, steamed mussels, sautéed sole, buttery *haricots verts*, those big bowls of hot chocolate and Banania. The hand-cranked water pump was gone, and the old well from
which it drew long plugged. The chipped ceramic pitcher we'd had to
fill before visiting the outhouse was, of course, no longer there, but the
outhouse still stood, and the compost heap behind it. Next to it, the lone
American-style bathroom in southwest France, which my mother had
insisted on building. Next to that, the outdoor fish kitchen and shed,
where I'd stashed my Kronenbourgs and cigarettes as a twelve-year-old.
The stone archway and heavy wooden door were still there, leading to
a back alley. And around front, the garage, where my uncle had kept a

1930s Citroën sedan up on blocks, and his wine cellar—much the same. The garden was all grass now.

"Think there are still little plastic army men buried in there?" I asked.

"Unquestionably," said Chris. "Probably still raise a company at least."

We didn't go inside. It would have been too . . . weird. I often have nightmares about returning to our old house in New Jersey and finding strangers sleeping in my bed. I didn't want to experience that for real.

"I'm kinda excited . . . and kinda bummed out," I confessed to Chris as we walked slowly out.

"Yeah. Me too," said Chris. "Let's get some *pain aux raisins* around the corner at the *boulangerie*. It's gotta still be there."

We had one bit of unfinished business on the property. Assuming the position, we posed for a photograph, roughly where we'd stood as children so many summers ago. We had on no berets this time, thank God. And we were both, without any possibility of argument, finally old enough for long pants.

Le stade municipal (the stadium), where we'd watched the young men from the town chase and be chased by bulls, and *la forêt* (the forest), where the menacing hermit had lived, appeared to be housing developments now. The vacation homes with their summery names like Le Weekend and La Folie were shuttered and forlorn looking in their emptiness.

We walked down the middle of rue Jules Favre, turned a corner, and found the *boulangerie* still open. Entering with the customary "*Bonjour, madame*," we were greeted with a warm, sweet-smelling waft—brioches, and baguettes baking. We bought a bag of *pain aux raisins*—the sticky raisin Danishes we'd had so often as kids—a baguette, a croissant, and a brioche, eager to try it all, to see if it tasted the same.

"The same," said Chris, exuberant.

I was not so thrilled. Something was holding me back. The baked goods, after all this time, were identical in taste and appearance. The shop smelled just as it had twenty-eight years ago. But something was missing.

There was once a little café around the corner called Café Central. It had become our default dinner of choice on those nights when my mother had not felt like cooking or when we'd been unable to agree on where to go or what to eat. It had been a simple neighborhood joint with chipped plaster and whitewashed walls, football posters, a few local fishermen drinking *vin ordinaire* in the small dining room. I had fond, maybe overly fond, memories of their dark brown *soupe de poisson*, their clumsy but delicious *crudités variées*, their *bavette à l'échalote* (flank steak with shallots) with limp but tasty *frites*.

It was called Le Bistro now, and it had been decidedly gussied up. There were candles on the tables, tablecloths, framed paintings of oyster boats on the pastel-colored walls, furniture that didn't wobble. But the fish soup was the same: dark brown, flecked with shreds of fish and milled bone, redolent of saffron, garlic, and anise; it was accompanied, just as I'd remembered, by little fried croutons, grated Gruyère cheese, and a little crock of rouille, the garlic and pepper mayonnaise. It was delicious. My first taste in almost thirty years of a soup that had seriously inspired me in my professional life. As a young chef, I had toiled mightily to re-create it, again and again, chasing the recipe, fooling with ingredients and amounts and procedures, until I'd finally gotten it right. Fact is, however wonderful the soup might have been, mine is better now. I use lobster. I roast the shells. I garnish mine with hunks of claw meat, making, finally, a heartier, more luxurious version. It may have tasted the same, but, like visiting an old girlfriend and wondering, *What the hell did I ever see in her?*, I guess things had moved on.

Desperately seeking epiphany, I ordered oysters—which couldn't have been better—a plate of *rouget*, the tiny, bony but delicious fish from the Med, fried sardines, a pan-roasted *magret de canard* (duck breast) in green pepper sauce, and a *bavette* for good measure.

But it still wasn't happening for me. It's not that I wasn't happy. It was great to sit at a table in France again, to look up from my food and see my brother again, to watch him unrestrainedly enjoying himself, bathing in the normalcy, the niceness of it all. Compared to most of my adventures, this was laudable. Gentle. Sentimental. No one to get hurt.

Waste, disappointment, excess, the usual earmarks of most of my previous enterprises, were, for once, totally missing from the picture. Why was I not having the time of my life? I began to feel damaged. Broken. As if some essential organ—my heart perhaps—had shriveled and died along with all those dead clumps of brain cells and lung, my body and soul like some big white elephant of an Atlantic City hotel, closed down wing by wing until only the lobby and façade remained.

We walked off dinner by the port. "See that dock over there?" I said to Chris, pointing out a sad-looking wooden structure collapsing slowly into the water. "I remember sitting on that dock when I was fifteen. Sam and Jeffrey and Nancy—all my friends—were in Provincetown that summer. And I was stuck here. Jesus! I was miserable here then! I was a lonely, bitter kid. I never got so much as a hand job in this fucking town . . ."

"That was later. That was the last year we were here. When we were kids, it was fun, wasn't it?"

"I guess so. I don't know. I'm still pissed about those shorts. Those berets. Jesus! What a thing to do to a kid."

Chris started to look worried. "Calm down. It's over. No more shorts. Put it behind you. Let it go."

"If you see a phone booth, let me know. I'm thinking about calling Mom. I got a few scores to settle. Those shorts . . . And maybe I should settle the Pucci incident while I'm at it. Did Pucci really have to be put down? I have my suspicions, let me tell you! And what kind of a name is that for a puppy? Puccini? There should be a law against pet names that cute . . . And no Cocoa Puffs! Remember that? All my friends were eatin' Cocoa Puffs, Trix, all the Lucky Charms they wanted! What did I get? 'Too sweet. Bad for your teeth.'"

His big brother appearing to be on the verge of some sort of psychotic break, Chris did his best to pull me out from under whatever dark cloud was gathering. "Relax! You need a drink or something? Jesus, Tony. You can have all the Lucky Charms you want now! I saw a *supermarché* in Arcachon. We can go buy a box right now."

"It's okay," I said, jolted back into the present. "I don't know. I think I miss Dad."

"Me too," said Chris.

We set off for the dune of Pyla, Europe's largest sand dune, a favorite outing long ago. Where once my brother and I scampered up its steep face on young legs, we now slogged, wheezing in boots in the loose sand, pausing every few yards to catch our breath in the wind and cold. Pyla is a gargantuan pile of sand, skyscraper high and miles long, rising over the Bay of Biscay on one side and spilling slowly into pine forest on the other. There used to be blockhouses, pillboxes, and gun emplacements on top, but when we finally reached the summit, they appeared to have long ago been buried in the sand. We stood there, Chris and I, with a thin spindrift of sand hissing along the dune's surface, grit catching in our teeth, looking out at the gray-blue water, the seemingly endless pines and scrub, yearning for . . . something.

Our father had come here as a child, too. Back in the hotel, my brother had shown me an old hand-tinted stereoscopic slide my uncle must have taken back in the thirties. In it, young Pierre Bourdain, age eight or nine, skin browned by sun, stands triumphantly at the dune top, no doubt anticipating the best part of a child's day trip to Pyla: the run down the dune face, leaping faster and faster, momentum and gravity pulling his legs out from under him, until he would topple over onto his face, to finish the trip in a whirl of sand, rolling dizzily, ecstatically, to the bottom. His worried parents would have been waiting for him at the bottom—as ours were years ago—ready to treat him to a *gaufre* at the stand a few yards away. That's how I imagined it anyway.

"C'mon, Chris," I said, running straight at the precipice. "Race you to the bottom."

Doing the best I could to imagine myself ten years old, I hurled myself into space, dropped, then ran as hard as I could, finally falling and rolling, Chris right behind me. There was no waffle stand at the bottom. No *gaufres*. Two confused-looking backpackers in comfortable Scandinavian hiking boots watched bemused as two overaged American knuckleheads rolled to a stop near their feet. The souvenir stands were closed. Not a Pschitt, an Orangina, a Banania, or a *citron pressé* to be had. Cold silence but for a few rustling pines.

What is an oyster if not the perfect food? It requires no preparation or cooking. Cooking would be an affront. It provides its own sauce. It's a living thing until seconds before disappearing down your throat, so you know—or should know—that it's fresh. It appears on your plate as God created it: raw, unadorned. A squeeze of lemon, or maybe a little mignonette sauce (red wine vinegar, cracked black pepper, some finely chopped shallot), about as much of an insult as you might care to tender against this magnificent creature. It is food at its most primeval and glorious, untouched by time or man. A living thing, eaten for sustenance and pleasure, the same way our knuckle-dragging forefathers ate them. And they have, for me anyway, the added mystical attraction of all that sense memory—the significance of being the first food to change my life. I blame my first oyster for everything I did after: my decision to become a chef, my thrill-seeking, all my hideous screwups in pursuit of pleasure. I blame it all on that oyster. In a nice way, of course.

At five thirty A.M., Chris and I set out on an oyster boat with Dominique and Jérôme, two local *pêcheurs d'huîtres*. Their vessel was not the quaint *pinasse* of my childhood. Those days, Dominique explained, were long gone. What *pinasses* remained were used principally as pleasure boats, or to ferry tourists around on day trips and picnics. This craft was a long, flat beast without gunwales—more suitable for loading sacks of oysters—and with a winch and an aft wheelhouse.

It was pitch-black on the bay when we set out, Chris and I clinging to the edges of the wheelhouse, Dominique piloting, Jérôme navigating. We putt-putted cautiously out to the middle of the bay, the sun slowly beginning to announce itself, the sky turning purple and black, shot through with hues of gold.

Things had changed on the bay since we'd last floated out with our neighbor Monsieur Saint-Jour to visit his tiny oyster park in 1966. Back then, we'd waited until the tide ran out and the boat came to rest on the bay floor, surrounded by a crude hand-constructed stockade that delineated his property. Oysters then were strewn directly on the bottom, raked, picked over, and sorted on site.

A few years ago, said Dominique, the oysters died—all of them. The bay was reseeded with "Japanese" seedlings, which took to the water well. This was not the first time this had happened. Originally, oysters had naturally occurred on the region's beds. When they'd gone, "Portuguese" oysters spilled during a wreck had been encouraged, successfully, to proliferate. In 1970, those had mysteriously died off. Things were better now. In fact, young oysters from here were now exported to Brittany and elsewhere, as conditions were particularly favorable for them here. The number of independent oyster fishermen like my old neighbor had shrunk considerably, though, with only a few larger outfits working in much more spread-out areas. The dreaded European Union regulations—which have been wiping out artisans and independents across the Continent—make it much more difficult for small one- or two-boat partnerships to survive.

The oyster parks looked different, too. It is no longer necessary to allow the tide to completely recede. Oysters are kept sorted by size and age in mesh sacks of varying gauge, on raised platforms, just beneath the water's surface. The sacks allow water and nutrients to flow through the oysters, while keeping most predators out. Raised from the seabed and restrained in bags, the oysters are less likely to experience breakage or damage, though an astonishing 25 to 30 percent will be eventually discarded as unsuitable.

Dominique pulled the boat alongside a few hundred feet of racks, and immediately the two men suited up in hip waders and dropped into the frigid water. They worked in shirtsleeves and rubber gloves (which filled with water right away), seemingly impervious to the cold. While they loaded heavy, dripping sacks of jagged shellfish onto the deck, they smoked and chatted casually, in no apparent hurry to finish their work and leave the water. The oysters they were loading were still young. They'd be taken back to their shack on shore, sorted again, rebagged, and returned to the water the next day. Chris and I huddled under thick waterproofs, two layers of sweaters, scarves, and long underwear while the two fishermen prattled on happily about food: lamprey bordelaise (not in season), entrecôte bordelaise (always in season—though the bone marrow for the sauce was increasingly difficult to get and had to be purchased in Holland because of mad cow disease). They talked also of foie gras, and their preferences in oysters.

Jérôme had a relative in San Francisco and had tried West Coast oysters there, but he hadn't thought much of them.

They hauled wet bags on deck for about an hour, stacked them neatly, then showed us where the seedlings were raised nearby. This process had not changed at all. Oyster larvae, before their shells fully develop, are at their most vulnerable. Ages ago, fishermen found that the oyster larvae would cling comfortably to the curved surfaces of terra-cotta roof tiles (after a process of whitewashing and sanding them), adhering themselves to the insides. The tiles could be stacked and restacked easily, and then, at the appropriate time, scraped free.

Oysters, by the way, are bisexual in ways undreamed of by career-minded actors. They actually change sex from year to year. If you were to tell an oyster "Go fuck yourself," it would probably not be offended. The males of a particular year spew their reproductive juices into the water in a generalized, omnidirectional way—a ubiquitously impregnating cloud that fertilizes whatever's female that year. Picture the swimming pool at Plato's Retreat back in the 1970s. That fat guy at the other end of the pool with the gold chains and the back hair? He's getting you pregnant. Or maybe it's the Guccione look-alike by the diving board. No way of knowing.

Loaded up with about two thousand pounds of young oysters, we headed back to port, Dominique and Jérôme smoking rollups and still talking about food. Back at their shack, the two men demonstrated their oyster-scrubbing apparatus, which blasted off the outer silt and dirt, the automated sorting equipment—a multilayered array of large-gauge strainers that bounced back and forth over a conveyor belt, accompanied by unbelievable noise and vibration, as it shook the oysters through. There was a storage and cleaning pool, where the oysters were soaked in clean, strained bay water—nutrients still intact but dirt and silt strained away—useful for leaching out internal impurities. The day's work done, we retired to their shack for a tasting of their wares, a few dozen fresh Arcachon oysters and a bottle of dry white Bordeaux. It was eight o'clock in the morning.

In a previous book, I have described my first oyster on Monsieur Saint-Jour's *pinasse* as a seminal experience. I've never forgotten that moment: that big, scary, ugly shell in my neighbor's knobby hand, the way he popped it open for me, still dripping from the bay, the way its pale blue-gray flesh caught the light, pulsated, the mother-of-pearl-like interior of the shell like a jewel box—promising adventure, freedom, sex, as-yet-unencountered joys.

I'd hoped that all that would come rushing back when I slurped down one of Dominique and Jérôme's finest. I knew I was trying too hard. I knew I was forcing things. It was as ludicrous as buying your girl-friend not only flowers, jewelry, perfume, and candy but also the bathing suit Ursula Andress wore in *Dr. No*, then plainly stating you expect the best sex of your life. Doubtful in the extreme that events will live up to your expectations. I don't know whether I really expected to swoon, fall to the floor, start weeping with joy, or what. No, I do know. I expected the perfect damn meal. I'd thought for sure that this would be it. But did my first oyster fresh from the *bassin* in thirty-four years do it for me? Did it transport me immediately to some culinary version of the Elysian Fields, as I'd hoped? Was it the perfect meal I'd so hoped to find?

Nope. Not really. It's no reflection on the oysters, which tasted much as I remembered them, briny, not too cold (oysters should not, by the way—contrary to conventional wisdom in the States—be buried in ice for hours and served chilled to frigid temperatures; it may make opening them easier for the shucker, but it diminishes the flavor). They were very fine oysters. Maybe even the best. My brother, just as before, was by my side. I'd re-created, as best I could, all the factors present in my youth. But once again, I felt restrained from pure enjoyment. Some-thing was still missing. This was not what I was there for, I realized. This whole enterprise was a sham—the search for "the perfect meal." That's not what I'd been looking for at the water's edge in Arcachon, in La Teste's empty streets, in the overgrown garden at number 5 rue Jules Favre, or atop a windy sand dune in January.

My father was, to me, a man of mystery. He probably would have been pleased to hear that, as he considered himself, I think, a simple, uncomplicated sort of a guy. Though warm, sentimental, and passion-ate about things like literature, art, movies, and especially music, his appreciations ran deep, so deep that what I always suspected was his true nature, that of a secretly disappointed romantic, was nearly out of sight. A shy man with few friends, uncomfortable with confrontation and with large groups, a man who dreaded tie and jacket, unpretentious, amused by hypocrisy, affectation, with a sharp sense of the absurd and ironic, he took a childlike joy in simple things. He was a sucker for films about French schoolkids—the films *The 400 Blows* and *Zéro de conduite* resonate particularly in my memory. The mischievous, borderline-delinquent children in both films were as close as I ever got to imagining my father as a kid. Despite the fact that he was raised by his widowed French mother in the very neighborhood where I now live, I know almost nothing about his life there. I can't picture him playing with friends in Riverside Park, just outside my window, as he surely must have. I can't picture him emerging from the apartment on Claremont with a stack of schoolbooks under one arm. I can't see him at private school in jacket and tie. I do have one of his old schoolbooks from the time: *Emil et les détectives*, in French, with his doodlings of goofy Nazis and Stuka dive-bombers in the margins. He used to read to me from that book—the English version—as he read from *The Wind in the Willows*, *Dr. Dolittle*, and *Winnie the Pooh*. And I remember how he'd do the voices of Toad, Eeyore, and Piglet.

He was in the army as a young man, as a supply sergeant in postwar Germany—about which I also know nothing, only that it seems to have left him with a lifelong appreciation of "funny" German accents and a suspicion that behind every German accent lurks a terrible wartime secret. He found Mel Brooks's take on Germans entirely in keeping with his own, but his laughter masked, I always suspected, some deeper bitterness and cynicism. He saw something ugly yet fascinating there, I'm sure. He loved, in later years, bleak, multilayered espionage thrillers like those of John le Carré and Len Deighton, adored films like *The Man Inside*, *The Third Man*, *Funeral in Berlin*, and thought *Dr. Strangelove* was the funniest movie ever made.

I guess I knew him best from what seemed to make him happiest: lying on the couch on his days off, reading Jean Lartéguy in French, endless John D. MacDonald novels—adventure stories, usually romantic, a little bit sad, set in faraway climes; watching a new Kubrick film;

listening to a new record on his giant JBL studio monitors; fiddling with the dials on his old Marantz radio; or sitting on the beach at Cap Ferret during the two or three weeks he could get away from his job at Columbia Records and join us in France. Eating *saucisson à l'ail* between crusty French bread, sipping *vin ordinaire* in his white terry-cloth shirt and boxer-style swimming trunks, wiggling his toes in the sand, he always looked most completely at ease. He'd charge into the rough surf with me or Chris on his shoulders and try to scare us about the incoming breakers.

Back then, when we'd become bored with the beach blanket and our Tintins and our sandy sandwiches and Vittel, Chris and I would rush off to explore the dunes of Cap Ferret. We'd build forts out of the plentiful driftwood on the wild, usually deserted stretch of beach, play in the massive poured-concrete blockhouses the Germans had left behind, exploring the spider holes, the tunnels that often extended underground from the central gun emplacements. We'd play army—on a real battlefield—hunting the dead Nazis rumored to be still decomposing under the sand, and hurl firecrackers down ventilation pipes and into crumbling, sand-filled stairwells. It was a paradise for kids; scores of ominous gray piles loomed up out of the sand in the vast, barren dunes, set back from the water's edge to provide interlocking fields of fire, overlooking that wild and magnificent surf and a beach that seemed to extend forever.

I had the brilliant idea that Chris and I should rent motor scooters and retrace the long drive from Arcachon, through La Teste and Gujan-Mestras, all the way around the bay to Cap Ferret. We'd made the trek many times as a family, first in the old Rover sedan, later in rented Simcas and Renaults. It would be, I thought, more tactile and immediate on scooters. We would be able to smell the air, get a better view of the towns as we passed through, unobstructed by dashboards or windows. That it was freezing cold and drizzling made no impression on me, caught up as I was in reverie. We dressed for the weather as best we could, packed the traditional Bourdain family lunch of *saucissons*, stinky cheese, baguettes from the La Teste *boulangerie*, Vittel, and a bottle of Bordeaux red, and set out for the beach. Chris crashed his scooter straight out of the hotel parking lot, smacking a street sign and falling over, skinning a significant portion of his shoulder and back. But he clambered gamely back on his bike and soldiered on—good sense having long ago been dispensed with by both of us.

It was cold—extremity-numbingly cold. My bike could speed along at a good clip (I'm bigger—I got the good one), but Chris's bike putted along at twenty-five miles an hour, slowing our progress considerably. Our helmets were too tight. In our zeal to recapture the past, we hadn't really checked them for fit beyond a cursory look. My head soon felt like I had a drill bit lodged behind my right eye. The rain whipped and lashed our faces, even at our reduced speed, and soaked us to an ambient, dispiriting damp.

But we were cruising past the boarded-up villas, shuttered restaurants, and businesses we'd so often passed in our youth. This was a bold and heroic venture, wasn't it? A noble attempt to reconnect with our past, to bond, however foolhardy it was to be trying this in January.

The trip took about two hours, maybe a bit more, given the frequent pit stops to unhelmet and allow our aching brainpans some relief. We finally arrived at a sandy turnoff, drove slowly down a scrub-pine-lined road, parked, dismounted by a dune fence, and began the half-mile walk to the beach. There was nothing but wind, the sound of our heavy hiking boots in the sand, the distant thudding of surf.

"I recognize that one, I think," said Chris, pointing out a graffiti-covered blockhouse in the distance, midway between beach and pine forest, just visible in the rolling dunes.

"Picnic site?" I suggested.

"Plan!"

We trudged over dunes, berms, hillocks, slow going in the sand, then finally clambered up a thick, sloping concrete wall and sat atop the thing, exactly where we'd played as kids. I laid out a blanket and our little picnic lunch and we chewed silently, our fingers stiff in the cold wind coming off the sea. The *saucisson* tasted the same, the cheese was good, and the wine proved serviceable.

I produced a package of firecrackers, and soon two men in their forties were playing army, as they'd done three decades or more ago:

dropping explosives down rusted vents, jamming them into discarded bleach bottles, the dull *bang* of the explosions whipped immediately away by the wind, to disappear into the sand. We chased each other around the blockhouse for a while, and when we got tired of blowing stuff up—or, more accurately, when the firecrackers ran out—we nosed around inside, exploring the stairwells and doorways where we'd played Combat and Rat Patrol those many summers ago.

We ambled awkwardly down to the beach, stepped over driftwood and debris that once, when we were children, had promised untold possibilities for construction projects and play but now appeared sad and dreary. My brother and I stood by the water's edge looking out at a violent surf, neither of us saying anything for a long while.

"Dad would have loved this," I said.

"What?" asked Chris, snapping back from his own thoughts.

"The whole idea of this. That we came back. That we came back here again—just the two of us. He would have liked it. He would have liked hearing about it."

"Yeah," said my little brother, no longer littler, taller than me now. The mature one.

"Fuck . . . I miss the guy."

"Me too," said Chris.

I'd been looking to hook into the main vein on this stretch of my around-the-world adventure. I'd thought everything would be instant magic. That the food would taste better because of all my memories. That I'd be happier. That I would change, or somehow be as I once was. But you can never be ten years old again—or even truly feel like ten years old. Not for an hour, not for a minute. This trip, so far, had been bittersweet at best. I hadn't, I realized, returned to France, to this beach, my old town, for the oysters. It wasn't the fish soup, or the saucisson, or the pain aux raisins. It wasn't to see a house in which strangers now lived, or to climb a dune, or to find a perfect meal. I'd come to find my father. And he wasn't there.

Thanksgiving
A Tactical Primer

An excerpt from *Appetites*, published in the UK by Bloomsbury in 2016.

Thanksgiving
A Tactical Primer

Preparing a holiday meal can be a stressful affair. It's no mystery why murder rates spike between mid-November and late December, what with all those relatives convened awkwardly around a table, many of whom see each other only rarely, some with long-simmering resentments and grudges that festered all year. It takes only one ill-considered remark or unfairly apportioned drumstick to turn what should have been a festive gathering into a slaughterfest of senseless butchery. And when you look at the list of "must-have" dishes expected, the prep work seems daunting, a logistical nightmare.

No need.

The following recipes may *look* long and complicated, but they're really not if you remember that the key to a relatively easy, smooth-running, violence-free Thanksgiving is to adopt the following three-day strategy, which calls for a stunt turkey, a business turkey, and an understanding, at all times, that the real point of Thanksgiving is the leftovers. That at the end of the whole ordeal, when all the guests have gone home and you are alone in the house, you can smoke a little weed, sit there in front of the TV in your underwear, and enjoy a nice roast turkey sandwich with some reheated stuffing and gravy.

Thanksgiving shopping, prep, and cooking should be broken down as follows:

DAY 1

✳ **In the morning (or the weekend before Thanksgiving), buy all the shit you'll need, store it in organized fashion, and cross-check it against your recipes to make sure there isn't anything you've forgotten.** If there is, you've still got plenty of time.

In addition to extra turkey parts (see next page), various aromatic vegetables, herbs, butter, oil, wine, bread, fruit, nuts, and seasonings, there's the matter of the bird—

or actually, birds. You'll need both a small "stunt turkey" and a large "business turkey," which, if frozen, you should start defrosting immediately.

✳ **Make your stock.** This is where the extra turkey parts come in. By all means, reserve the necks and wing tips from your stunt and business turkeys, and make the most of the pan drippings and the "fond," or scrapings, from the bottom of the roasting pan. But you'll need a solid turkey stock before you start fucking around with any actual turkeys. This means buying a separate bag of wings and necks, about 5 to 7 pounds total, to make the stock that will give the stuffing its essential turkey flavor and provide the base for what you might call "gravy" but what is, in fact, a sauce.

✳ **Leave the bread out to get stale for stuffing.**

DAY 2

✳ **Turn your turkey stock into turkey sauce** or, if you must, "gravy." Don't worry, you can still enhance it with pan drippings at the last minute.

✳ **Assemble and bake the stuffing,** *covered,* **so that it doesn't yet brown at all.** Tomorrow you can jack it with turkey grease and brown it a bit on top when you roast the birds.

✳ **Make your cranberry relish and store it in the fridge.** It'll be even better tomorrow.

✳ **Knock out your side-dish prep.** Trim and halve your Brussels sprouts, trim your baby onions if you're doing creamed onions, dice your slab bacon, and scrub your sweet potatoes. Label, group, and refrigerate everything, so that you can quickly finish side dishes tomorrow, while the birds roast.

DAY 3

✳ **Roast the (small) "stunt turkey."** This is the pretty one that you'll display for your guests. Keep it moist and shiny—moist towels and a light brush of oil—as it cools out of the way of the action. Ready your garnishes and feel free to dress it up like a showgirl: such embellishments as chop frills, elaborate fruit garnishes, a bed of old-school curly parsley or kale, and a bit of stuffing to obscure the bony cavity entrance are all totally appropriate visual fireworks to be employed liberally here.

❋ **While the turkeys roast, finish your side dishes.** Brussels sprouts and creamed onions have already been prepped, potatoes just need to be peeled, and the sweet potatoes can go straight into the water unpeeled. You can get everything done on the stovetop while the birds are cooking, and hold it for quick reheating just before dinner.

❋ **Roast (and dismantle) the business turkey.** By the time your guests arrive, the business turkey should be ready, which is to say, just completely cooked, breasts removed from the bone and ready to slice, legs removed, drumsticks and thighs separated, wings good to go, moist towels on top.

❋ **Jack your stuffing with turkey grease and brown it, *uncovered*, in a hot oven.**

❋ **Display the intact, artfully garnished stunt turkey in all its glory, which should elicit much oohing and ahhing from your amazed guests.** Then, whisk it into the kitchen, presumably to be carved.

❋ **In the relative privacy of your kitchen, pull out your business turkey, which is ready to slice, and get busy.** The whole process should take only a couple of minutes. Use a good serrated knife to ensure that each slice of breast comes with a strip of golden skin. To build the platter, I like to put a heap of stuffing in the center, cross the drumsticks decoratively, then slice and shingle first the dark thigh meat, then the breast meat, like a deck of cards around the stuffing. Throw on some parsley or watercress, if you like, and the effect is complete. No embarrassing and inept hacking at a whole turkey while your family looks on with horror: This bird is ready to serve.

Just be *sure* that you've stashed away some choice turkey bits. Later, after you've packed up thoughtful leftover kits for your guests to take home, you want to be certain that after all your hard work, you've got plenty of the good stuff for yourself.

THANKSGIVING GRAVY, STUFFING, AND TURKEY

1 small (8- to 10-pound) turkey (aka "the stunt turkey")

1 large (18-pound) turkey (aka "the business turkey")

5 pounds total turkey wings and necks, cut into 3 to 6 pieces each

Salt and freshly ground black pepper to taste

1 cup dry white wine

2 large yellow onions, peeled and finely diced

4 ribs celery, finely diced

2 large carrots, peeled and finely diced

6 to 8 sprigs fresh thyme, plus 2 teaspoons fresh thyme leaves

1 large loaf of white bread

2 cups dry red wine

2 shallots, peeled and coarsely chopped, plus 4 shallots, peeled and finely chopped

⅔ cup all-purpose flour, or as needed

A few splashes of Thai fish sauce (optional)

Worcestershire sauce (optional)

1½ cups peeled chestnuts

½ pound (2 sticks) unsalted butter, plus more as needed

¼ cup finely chopped fresh sage, plus 2 additional sprigs

1 pound mixed wild mushrooms, finely chopped

⅓ cup finely chopped fresh parsley

2 large eggs, beaten

Worcestershire sauce, soy sauce, or Kitchen Bouquet (a flavor and color enhancer; optional)

DAY 1: DEFROSTING

If they're frozen, start your turkeys defrosting in the fridge as soon as you get them home. If they're fresh, use a heavy chef's knife or poultry shears to remove the wing tips and wishbones from both turkeys, and remove the necks and giblets from the inside of the birds. Refrigerate the giblets, which will go into the gravy, and the turkeys themselves. (If the birds are frozen, you'll deal with all of this later.)

Make the turkey stock. Preheat the oven to 425°F. Assemble the wings and necks, and anything you have harvested from your fresh turkeys, if applicable, on one or more stovetop-ready roasting pans and season them with salt and pepper. Roast in the oven until nicely browned and fragrant, about 45 minutes, rotating the pans (and possibly the wings and parts themselves, if they're looking very browned on one side) about 20 minutes in, for even roasting. Remove from the oven.

Transfer the roasted wings and bones to a large, heavy-bottom stockpot. Pour the excess grease and juices from the pan into a small bowl or jar, and cover and refrigerate it. (You will use it

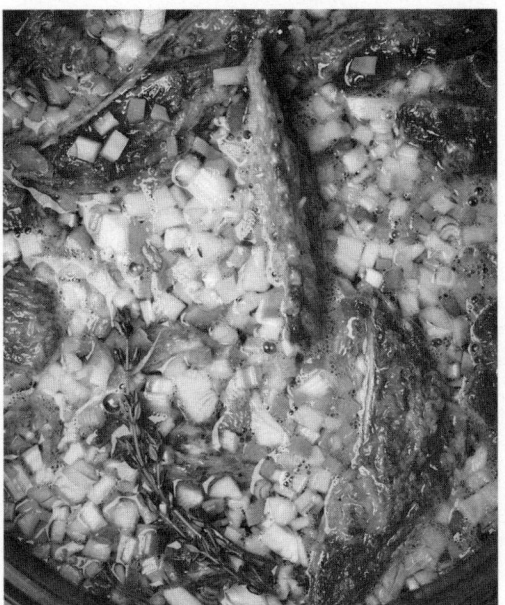

SPECIAL EQUIPMENT

Heavy chef's knife

Poultry shears (optional)

2 (or more) roasting pans, at least
1 of which should be stovetop-
ready, and at least 1 of which
should have a rack

Serrated knife (or better yet, an
offset serrated knife)

Bulb-top turkey baster

Instant-read thermometer

Large carving board, ideally with
trenches to catch juice

later, to build the roux for your gravy.) Place the roasting pan
over medium-high heat and stir in ½ cup of the white wine,
scraping the bottom of the pan with a wooden spoon to dislodge
the fond, or browned bits. Cook until the alcohol smell no longer
remains. Transfer this liquid to the stockpot along with the
bones, and add half of the onions and celery, the carrots, and
4 to 6 thyme sprigs. Cover with cold water and bring to a high
simmer (*not a boil*). Use a ladle to skim off and discard any scum
that floats to the top. Reduce to a medium simmer and cook for
about 5 hours.

Pour the stock into a wide bowl to cool down at room
temperature for about 20 to 30 minutes, stirring occasionally
to release steam and speed cooling. Transfer it into quart-sized
plastic or glass containers or sturdy zip-sealed plastic bags and
refrigerate. If you've done it right, the stock should be dark golden
brown and have a definitively gelatinous quality. With 5 to $\longrightarrow$

7 pounds of bones in a full 4-gallon stockpot, you can expect to get around 4 quarts of good-quality stock.

Prep your bread for stuffing. While the stock simmers, use a serrated knife to dice the bread for stuffing. You're looking to yield about 10 to 12 cups of diced bread. Scatter the bread cubes in a single layer on sheet trays and leave them out to dry.

DAY 2: TURN YOUR STOCK INTO GRAVY

Pull 3 quarts of turkey stock from the fridge and pour it into a medium, heavy-bottom pot. Add the red wine and coarsely chopped shallots, and bring to a high simmer. Cook, stirring occasionally, for about 30 to 45 minutes, until reduced by half. Strain the mixture into a bowl, discard the shallots, and return it to the pot.

Retrieve the container of reserved turkey fat and drippings from yesterday and scrape off enough fat—it will self-separate from the drippings in the refrigerator—to equal ⅔ cup. (You may supplement, if necessary, with butter.) Place the fat in a medium, heavy-bottom pot. Measure out ⅔ cup flour and, with your whisk and wooden spoon handy, heat the fat over medium heat until hot. Sprinkle the flour into the fat, whisking the mixture together to make a roux. Swap your whisk for the wooden spoon and continue to cook over medium heat for 1 to 2 minutes, stirring until the flour is lightly toasted and fragrant. Whisk in the stock and red wine mixture. Switch back to the wooden spoon and continue to stir and scrape to ensure that you pull up all the roux. Once the mixture comes to a boil, reduce to a high simmer, continuing to stir regularly until the gravy is thick enough to coat the back of the wooden spoon.

Taste and season as desired with salt and pepper. Some people use a hit of fish sauce, which I endorse. If the emotional needs of your guests require a darker gravy, you can brown it up with some Worcestershire sauce, soy sauce, or Kitchen Bouquet. Tomorrow, you can further enhance the flavor with drippings from the turkey roasting pans.

Make stuffing. Preheat the oven to 375°F. Remove the remaining quart of stock from the fridge and bring it to a high simmer in a medium saucepot. Turn off the heat and cover the pan to keep the stock warm.

Arrange the chestnuts in a single layer on a sheet pan and roast in the oven until browned and fragrant, about 10 minutes. Remove from the oven, let cool for about 5 minutes, then chop them to a medium-coarse consistency, as you would for chopped walnuts. Place the chestnuts in a large mixing bowl along with the bread cubes.

In a large sauté pan, heat 4 tablespoons butter over medium-high heat until it foams and subsides. Add the finely chopped shallots and the remaining onions and celery and sauté until translucent and fragrant, 3 to 5 minutes. Season with salt and pepper and stir in the thyme leaves and chopped sage. Continue to cook for another minute or two, until the herbs are fragrant, then transfer the mixture to the mixing bowl with the chestnuts and bread cubes.

In the same pan, heat another 4 tablespoons butter until it foams and subsides. Add the mushrooms and sauté, seasoning with salt and pepper and stirring regularly until they release their juice and it sizzles away. Deglaze the pan with the remaining ½ cup white wine, scraping the bottom to gather browned bits of mushroom. Add the mushrooms and reduced wine to the mixing bowl.

Grease another roasting pan with 2 tablespoons butter.

Add the parsley, eggs, and warm stock to the mixing bowl and mix with a light touch to get everything incorporated without compressing it too much. Transfer this mixture to the greased roasting pan, cover with foil, and cook in the oven for about 45 minutes. Remove from the oven and let cool for about 15 minutes without the foil, then re-cover it tightly and refrigerate until tomorrow, when you'll jack it with drippings and brown the top.

Make your cranberry relish (page 195) while the stuffing bakes, and do the prep for Brussels sprouts (page 201) and creamed onions (page 197). $\longrightarrow$

DAY 3

Roast the business turkey. Preheat the oven to 425°F. If you haven't already, trim off the wing tips and remove the neck and the wishbone from the business turkey; these things can be saved in the freezer for your next round of stock-making. Set those giblets, and the ones from the stunt turkey, in a medium saucepot and fill it about halfway with cold water. Bring to a boil.

Rub the turkey all over with 2 to 3 tablespoons butter, and season inside and out with salt and pepper. Place it in a roasting pan with a rack, pour 2 cups of water into the pan, and transfer to the oven to roast. Periodically rotate the pan and use the bulb-top baster to baste the turkey with the grease and juices from the pan. An 18-pound bird should take just under 4 hours to cook through; the thickest part of the thigh should register 165°F on the instant-read thermometer.

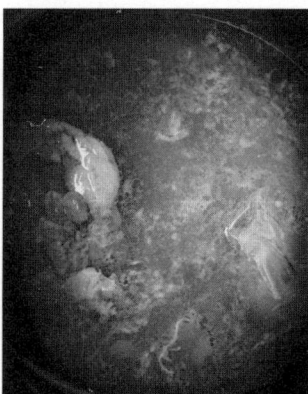

Are your giblets boiling yet? Good. Let them cook for about 5 minutes, then drain and discard the water. Wash out the pot, and return the giblets to it. Add the remaining thyme and sage sprigs, cover with cold water, then let cook at a low simmer as the roasting continues.

About 15 minutes before you take the business turkey from the oven, remove the giblets from the pot, strain them, and discard the cooking liquid. In a medium sauté pan, heat 2 tablespoons of the butter over high heat. Season the giblets with salt and pepper and sear them to golden brown in the butter. Remove from the pan, cut them into fine dice, and set aside.

Once your business turkey is done, take it out of the oven, transfer it to the carving board, and let it rest for at least 15 to 20 minutes. Reserve the juices and turkey grease from the pan in a bowl or jar.

Finish the creamed onions (page 197) and Brussels sprouts (page 201) while the business turkey roasts. Make the sweet potatoes (page 200) and, if you have time, mashed potatoes (page 196).

Roast the (small) "stunt turkey." Rub the outside of the stunt turkey with 2 tablespoons of the butter and season it inside and out with salt and pepper. Place it in a roasting pan with a rack, pour about 2 cups of water into the pan, and roast in the oven. As it roasts, periodically rotate the pan and use the bulb-top baster to baste the turkey with the grease and juices from the pan. A 10-pound bird should take about 2½ hours; the thickest part of the thigh should register 165°F on an instant-read thermometer. Remove from the oven and let it rest for 15 minutes, then carefully transfer the turkey to your serving platter to be garnished at will. Add the turkey grease and juices from the roasting pan to those you collected from the business turkey.

Finish those side dishes that you haven't yet finished. Pull the stuffing out of the fridge and let it come to room temperature. Increase the oven's heat to 425°F.

Dismantle the business turkey. Remove each leg, at the thigh joint, from the carcass. Separate the thigh from the drumstick, and pull or cut the meat from the thigh bones. Run your knife down the center of the breast, just to the left and right of the bone that divides them, and continue to guide your knife to the ribs, gently cutting the intact breast muscle away on either side. Place all the meat on a sheet tray, cover with damp, clean towels, and stash it out of sight of nosy guests.

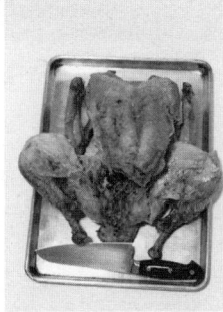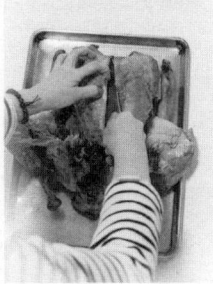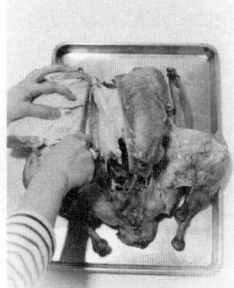

Jack the stuffing with grease, drippings, and giblets. Fold the reserved cooked giblets into the stuffing, and add enough reserved grease and juices so that it glistens. Slide the stuffing, uncovered, into the oven for about 15 to 20 minutes, until it's sizzling at the edges and browned on top. $\longrightarrow$

←

After you have received big praise and glory from your guests for the presented stunt turkey, return to the kitchen to finish the job. You may wish to enlist a trusted accomplice for this. Get all your side dishes and your gravy gently warmed in the oven or on the stovetop. Whisk some reserved turkey grease and drippings into the gravy as it simmers, if desired. Carefully slice the breast meat, making sure to leave a strip of skin intact on each piece. Mound the stuffing in the center of the serving platter. Arrange the thigh meat around the stuffing, then top the thigh meat with shingles of breast meat, attractively arranged. Serve the platter, with gravy and all side dishes.

Serves 10 to 12, with leftovers

You Need Money

An excerpt from the novel *Bone in the Throat*, originally published by Villard Books in 1995.

They sat at one of the better tables, near a gurgling fountain in the garden patio at the rear of the restaurant. Bright green ivy grew on the trellises behind them, and there were yellow tulips everywhere. Wealthy old ladies chatted in small groups at the other tables.

"You need money," his mother said, a statement, not a question. The chef nodded, trying to smile sheepishly.

"Remember how we used to make breakfast?" asked the chef's mother, changing the subject. "In France?"

"With the chocolate?" asked the chef, grateful his mother wasn't chiding him about the money.

"Yes," she said, "with the baguette, the Normandy butter, and the big bowl of hot chocolate. We'd serve it in those big blue bowls."

"I loved that," said the chef. "I miss it. Can't do it here, it's not the same."

"It's the butter," said his mother.

She was tall and thin and elegant in a dark blue dress and a single strand of pearls. Her silver hair was put up in a tight bun, giving her countenance a severe aspect. Her face was pale and white, offset by the single slash of dark red lipstick. She sat ramrod straight in her chair and, with two long, manicured fingertips, removed a piece of tobacco from the tip of her tongue. Without turning her head, she sensed the waiter's approach, and she extinguished the unfiltered Gitane in a cut-glass ashtray.

The waiter placed an oversize china plate in front of her, saying, "Madame." She inspected the *carré d'agneau* without moving her head or changing her expression. Three tiny rib chops, impeccably trimmed, were crisscrossed on a stripe of sauce in the middle of the plate. An arrangement of baby vegetables, tied into little bundles with blanched bits of leek, surrounded the lamb. The waiter came around the table and put the chef's turbot down in front of him.

"Look how many truffles they put," said his mother in her slight French accent.

The chef smiled broadly. "Is that cooked to your liking, Maman?" he asked her.

"*Parfait*," she responded. She liked it when he called her Maman.

The waiter poured her a little more Côtes du Rhône, then lifted a bottle of Pouilly-Fuissé from a silver ice bucket and refilled the chef's glass. He asked the chef's mother, in French, if there was anything else she would care for. She dismissed him, also in French.

The chef picked up a big piece of black truffle from the top of his turbot with his fingers and popped it in his mouth.

"Oh! Michel!" protested his mother. "Not with the hands!"

The chef shook his head and picked up his fork and took a first bite of fish.

"Is it all right? It's moist in the center? It's not cooked too much?" asked his mother, peering across the table.

"It's fine," said the chef. He picked up the oversize white-wine glass and drank half its contents.

"You just got your fish and you've almost finished your wine," she said.

"I can always drink the rest of yours," he said. "You've hardly touched it."

"And stop squirming in your chair like that. Why can't you get comfortable? Something is always eating you," she said.

"Sorry," said the chef.

"And you drink too much," she added.

"I don't drink like this on a regular basis," said the chef. "It's just good wine. I don't drink a lot of wine this good. I'm trying to make the most of it."

She nodded and took a delicate bite from the center of her lamb chop. "I wish you had ordered some meat. You don't look well."

"Maybe it's my liver. *Une crise de foie.* I left the window open last night. The drafts, the night air . . ."

His mother frowned. "Don't make fun of me, Michel. It's not funny. You don't look well. I worry."

"I'm fine, I'm fine," scowled the chef. "I'm just working too damn hard. Not enough sleep."

"You don't even have health insurance. That terrible man you work for can't even give his people, his chef, health insurance. It's disgraceful."

"He can't afford it right now," said the chef. "I can't afford it."

His mother shook her head disapprovingly. "You could have worked here maybe. I could ask my friends. I'm sure he treats his people correctly here. You should let me ask."

"I couldn't be the chef here," said the chef. "I want to be in charge. I need the money, I can't afford to be just a commis."

"All right," she said. "Not here then, somewhere else, where you could be the chef. Like this."

The chef shook his head slowly. "I couldn't work like this. I can't get up at four in the morning and go down Fulton Street and put my nose in a bunch of fish gills. I can't do fifteen, sixteen hours a day, six, seven days a week. And I'm just not that good to do this sort of food. Not as the chef anyway."

"That's a terrible defeatist attitude," said his mother. "You didn't always feel like this."

"Yeah, well, I'm getting older," said the chef.

"Exactly. Yes. You are getting older," said his mother. "And you still live like some sort of gypsy. Never enough money. Changing jobs, every two years another place, another apartment. No family, no insurance, you own nothing."

"I've always got you, right?" he said with a smile.

"Yes. For now. I won't always be here," she said. "I won't be here to help forever. Don't they pay you at your job?"

"They pay me," said the chef. "It's just everything is so expensive, you know. And I owe people money."

"You always owe people money. It's terrible to owe money. I don't owe anybody anything. I don't know how you live like that. And your friends, they look like a . . . like a motorcycle gang, not *cuisiniers*—"

The chef laughed and hurried to change the subject.

They ate quietly. His mother methodically stripped the last bits of fat from the lamb, leaving three thin white rib bones on an otherwise empty plate. The busboy appeared and removed the plates. The waiter pushed a cheese cart alongside the table. The chef's mother reached into her purse for her glasses and, perching them at the end of her nose, leaned over to inspect the cheese. After a moment's reflection she chose a runny-looking Pont-l'Évêque. The chef, without looking, requested a wedge each of Saint André and Camembert.

"I guess we like soft cheeses," said the chef.

"The cheese here is not the same. They ruin it for export," said his mother.

"They pasteurize it," said the chef.

"It's not the same," said his mother.

"Maybe you should live in France."

"Then how could I help you when you get in trouble. Who would give you money for your debts. Besides, I could not go back. It's a communist country now," she said.

"Socialist," corrected the chef.

"The same thing. De Gaulle should have put them all in prison. After the war."

The chef's mother took a last bite of cheese, dotted her mouth with the point of a napkin, and leaned forward. "Do you use a condom?" she asked.

Shocked, the chef tilted his head. "What?"

"When you, when you go out with your friends, maybe to meet a girl, some girl. Do you use a condom? I've been reading articles in the magazine."

"Yes, Maman," said the chef, embarrassed. He glanced at the surrounding tables to see if anyone else had heard. The old ladies at the next table were busy drinking martinis and commenting on the busboy's buttocks.

"Well, that is something. That's good. You should always use one," said his mother, satisfied.

"What have you been watching, Oprah or something?" asked the chef.

"What is Oprah?" inquired his mother.

"Forget it. Joke," said the chef.

"*Qu'est-ce que vous voulez comme dessert, madame?*" inquired the waiter as the busboy whisked the cheese plates off the table. The chef's mother strained to see the dessert cart.

"Tell bucket-head to bring the cart closer," said the chef, slightly tipsy.

"*SSSH! Ça suffit!*"

The waiter had already moved over to the cart and was bringing it alongside the table. The chef's mother carefully scrutinized each item on the three-tiered pastry cart. "Ah!" she exclaimed. "Paris-Brest. Will you look, Michel, Paris-Brest. Remember?" She pointed a finger, and the waiter cut and served a portion. "Gimme one a those, too," said the chef to the waiter. When the waiter disappeared, his mother scolded him. "You shouldn't speak like that. I eat here every week."

"I'm sorry, Ma. Just enjoying myself. Loosen up. I'm having a good time, see?" said the chef.

"You like the dessert? You remember the last time we had it?" she asked.

"In Chagny? It was that place with all the dogs, right?"

"Yes. Chez Denis. Paris-Brest is absolutely my favorite. They made it so well. This is also excellent. Do you like it?"

"It's great," said the chef, shoveling an enormous mouthful into his face, crème Chantilly gathering at the corners of his mouth. "This was a great meal. Outstanding."

"And I suppose I'm paying for it," said his mother.

"Well," said the chef.

"And you said you need money," said his mother, reaching into her purse. She handed him a check for a thousand dollars, written in her spidery, old-lady scrawl. "I'm only giving you this if you promise to get a haircut. You look like a cannibal like that." She held on to one end of the check. "And make sure they trim your sideburns, I don't want people thinking you are, you are some sort of terrorist."

"Sure, Maman," said the chef. She released the check.

The chef put his soiled napkin over his empty dessert plate and sat back in his chair. André, the chef and owner of the restaurant, came over to the table to pay his respects. He wore a spotless white chef's coat with Chinese buttons and the French tricolor adorning the collar. His name was embroidered over the chest pocket in flawless blue script, his starched toque piled high up over his head. He spoke in French for a few moments with the chef's mother, inquiring about the meal and her health. They discussed mutual friends. She turned to the chef and in English said, "André, allow me to present my son, Michel. He is a chef also."

The chef sat up in his chair and extended his hand. He wanted to die.

How Anthony Bourdain Came to Be Anthony Bourdain

An essay that originally appeared in *Bon Appétit* on Father's Day 2012.

I was shucking oysters at a raw bar in the Village when my father died. He was fifty-seven years old, an age I'm rapidly approaching. I think about that a lot—and about my father, whose face I see in my own more and more with the passing of the years. There's a picture of me with my then four-and-a-half-year-old daughter that was taken at a food festival in the Caymans last January. She's sitting on my lap, eyes closed. I'm holding her tight, my face sunburned and blissed out with the joys of fatherhood. I've never looked so much like him.

My father was, as he liked to say, "a man of simple needs." He grew up with a French mother, a French name, speaking French, and spent many summers in France. But this history wasn't really a factor in my childhood. It always came as a shock to me when he'd break into French with a Haitian cabdriver as there was, seemingly, nothing "French" about him, or us, or how we lived. He liked wine (on the rare occasions when some came our way), making pronouncements like "all wine is red," but couldn't have cared less whether it was a Chateau de Something or a *vin de table*—as long as it was from Bordeaux, near where his family came from.

To him, all food was either "marvelous" or not worth mentioning. A decent steak frites at a crummy brasserie was as good as a fine-dining meal. (During my early vacations in France, our family's crummy brasserie of choice was the unpromising-sounding Quick Elysee, where a thin slice of humble rump steak with curiously blond *frites* soon became a treasured taste memory.) In his view, France and New Jersey, where we lived, were the same; he seemed equally attached romantically. France had runny, pungent cheeses and sausages that were "marvelous." But the Jersey Shore, where we were more likely to vacation, had steamer clams, not to mention the occasional lobster with drawn butter.

He taught me early that the value of a dish is the pleasure it brings you; where you are sitting when you eat it—and who you are eating it with—are what really matter. Perhaps the most important life lesson he passed on was: Don't be a snob. It's something I will always at least aspire to—something that has allowed me to travel this world and eat all it has to offer without fear or prejudice. To experience joy, my father taught me, one has to leave oneself open to it.

The world, in his view, was filled with marvels. George C. Scott's manic eyebrows in *Dr. Strangelove* were deemed "marvelous." But then so, potentially, was any food that was new. Wherever you were, he taught me, was an opportunity to eat something interesting.

Growing up in New Jersey, American food was Italian. Chinese. Jewish. Diner. (I still drive out to Hiram's roadhouse in Fort Lee to order my father's favorite birch beer.) It took a trip "across the bridge" to be able to delve into the exotic worlds of "smorgasbord," "sukiyaki," "German," and old-school bistro French. Chinese food was deemed worth investigating as a family—and investigate we did, venturing frequently into Manhattan on weekends for fabulously gluey and bright-colored Cantonese on Upper Broadway and in Chinatown. Visits to my father's office in Manhattan would yield trips to Wienerwald for foreign sausages steamed with sauerkraut; salty pretzels and charred roast chestnuts from street carts; the mysterious joys of the dirty-water hot dog.

He was delighted by different. Thrilled by discovery. In the early seventies, he "discovered" sushi because it was being served in the signless, somewhat sinister back room of a run-down hotel on Fifty-fifth Street that some Japanese colleagues had tipped him off to. When he walked me, fourteen years old, through the shabby hotel lobby for the first time, opened an unmarked door, and ushered me into a smoky room crowded with Japanese people eating raw fish, he was bubbling over with childlike glee.

There's a photo of my father. My favorite. He's sitting on a beach at Cap Ferret in France, near the oyster village of La Teste-de-Buch, where he'd spent many summers as a kid. My younger brother, Christopher, and I are with him—we must have been about ten and twelve, respectively—eating sandwiches: *saucisson à l'ail* or *jambon blanc*. I remember very well the texture of crusty baguette, the smear of French butter, the meat, the inevitable grain of sand between the teeth. Surely, somewhere nearby, there was Orangina or Pschitt for us kids, and a bottle of warm Evian or Vittel—all wildly exotic to my brother and me at the time.

There might well have been a comically runny cheese. My father, upon unwrapping it, would have joked about it, comparing its reek to "old socks," calling my brother and me by our alternate names in Dad language: Oscar and Eggbert. He was generally a pretty serious man, prone to escaping into books and music—a moody one, too, I suspected. But with us, he was almost always goofy and without vanity. I think it was that day—the day of the photograph, or another very much like it, sitting by the edge of the rough Atlantic, perhaps after a swig of rough red table wine—that I first heard him make that statement: "I am a man of simple needs." An expression of genuine satisfaction with the moment.

It left an impression. I remember those words every time I find myself made ridiculously happy by a bowl of noodles eaten while sitting on a low plastic stool, sucking up the smell of burning joss sticks and distant wafts of durian, the sight of Vietnamese families on their motorbikes around me.

I feel myself moving like him. I feel his face in mine when I pick up my daughter. I hear his voice in mine when I say something silly, make myself ridiculous for her entertainment. When we eat together, I can't help but try, like my father, to portray what we eat as potentially awesome or funny—as "marvelous." While I feel strongly that to try and make a small child into one's own image as a pint-size "foodie" would be at best annoying and at worst a form of child abuse, I am secretly proud when she reaches for a hunk of salty Pecorino, a caper, or an anchovy, as she is apt to do on visits with my wife's family in Italy. I admit to shamelessly praising her when she, to our surprise, became enamored with oysters on the half shell.

I was made proudest in Paris last year. My daughter came along for dinner with me, my wife, and Eric Ripert—the grown-ups eating oysters and clams, whelks and periwinkles from an enormous seafood tower at La Coupole. She had been picking at her pasta with butter and moved on to oysters. She looked up at what must have seemed, from her perspective at near eye level with the tabletop, an Everest of crushed ice and sea creatures. Her gaze traveled up and up, past the giant crabs on the second tier, settling on the two steamed lobsters dueling at the top.

"Sebastian!" she cried, misidentifying one of the lobsters as the adorable crustacean sidekick of Ariel, the heroine of the Disney film *The Little Mermaid*. Without blinking, she reached up, grabbed her little friend, and began devouring him without hesitation or remorse.

I thought, That's *my little girl*.

I'm quite sure my father, had he been there, would have been just as proud—of both of us.

That's Our Family and This Is Our Family Cookbook

An excerpt from *Appetites*, published in the UK by Bloomsbury in 2016.

INTRODUCTION

All happy families are alike . . .

—Leo Tolstoy, *Anna Karenina*

Tolstoy clearly never spent any time with my happy family.

My eight-year-old daughter, Ariane, does a terrific imitation of my wife threatening to choke a taxi driver. It's something she's seen often enough to get dead right—my wife's Italian accent, her anger, her exasperation as the driver takes yet another wrong turn on the way to my daughter's school, and finally the kicker: "I'm going to *keel* you with my bare-a hands!"

It has been many months, maybe years, since anyone has seen my wife out of her regular attire of rash guard and spats. She's a martial artist, a purple belt in Brazilian jiujitsu, and she trains full-time, seven days a week. Most of her efforts are spent practicing horrifying new ways to quickly, forcibly manipulate opponents' feet, ankles, and knees in such ways as to permanently damage their tendons and ligaments.

I travel the world for a living. On any given day, I'm as likely to be found in a longhouse in Sarawak, Borneo; in a cafe in Marseille; or in an airport transit lounge in Doha as I am to be found at home. My daughter is used to seeing her father's face on TV and on the sides of city buses, accustomed to seeing him approached by strangers—and is decidedly unimpressed.

Her best friend, Jacques (pronounced "Jax"), from whom she has been inseparable most of her life, is Filipino, part of an extended family who easily spends as much time in our home as anywhere else. English, Italian, and Tagalog are heard interchangeably. My daughter is increasingly fluent in Italian. I am not.

What is it that "normal" people do?

What makes a "normal" happy family?

How do they behave? What do they eat at home? How do they live their lives?

I had little clue how to answer these questions for most of my working life, as I'd been living it on the margins. I didn't know any normal people. From age seventeen on, normal people had been my customers. They were abstractions, literally shadowy silhouettes in the dining rooms of wherever it was I was working at the time. I looked at them through the perspective of the lifelong professional cook and chef—which is to say, as someone who did not have a family life, who knew and associated only with fellow restaurant professionals, who worked while normal people played, and who played while normal people slept.

To the extent that I knew or understood normal people's behaviors, it was to anticipate their immediate desires: Would they be ordering the chicken or the salmon?

I usually saw them only at their worst: hungry, drunk, horny, ill tempered, celebrating good fortune or taking out the bad on their servers.

What they did at home, what it might be like to wake up late on a Sunday morning, make pancakes for a child, watch cartoons, throw a ball around a backyard—these were things I only knew from movies.

The human heart was—and remains—a mystery to me. But I'm learning. I have to.

I became a father at fifty years of age. That's late, I know. But for me, it was just right. At no point previously had I been old enough, settled enough, or mature enough for this, the biggest and most important of jobs: the love and care of another human being.

From the second I saw my daughter's head corkscrewing out of the womb, I began making some major changes in my life. I was no longer the star of my own movie—or any movie. From that point on, it was all about the girl. Like most people who write books or appear on television, who think that anyone would or should care about their story, I am a monster of self-regard. Fatherhood has been an enormous relief, as I am now genetically, instinctually compelled to care more about someone other than myself. I like being a father. No, I love being a father. Everything about it.

I'm sure my wife has a different view on this, but if I could go back to the diaper-changing, wake-up-in-the-middle-of-the-night-to-soothe-crying-baby phase of fatherhood? I'd be overjoyed.

I recognize that I am, in some ways, overenthusiastic about this late-in-life move into responsible parenting. And that I have a tendency to try to make up for lost time. Since so many of my happiest memories of childhood—summer vacations at the Jersey shore, off-season Montauk, trips to France—are associated with the tastes and smells of the things I ate, I feel uncontrollable urges to smother the people I love with food. I've become the sort of passive-aggressive yenta or Italian grandmother stereotype from films who's always urging people, "Eat! Eat!" and sulking inconsolably when they don't.

This pathology is further complicated by my time as a professional. I have developed work habits that, over three decades, imprinted on me the need to be organized, to have a plan, to rotate stock, to label prepared foodstuffs, and to keep a clean work area.

So on top of my desire to make up for lost time, and my psycho–Ina Garten–like need to feed the people around me, I am obsessive-compulsive in my work habits and anally retentive in ways that you'd find ideal in a professional brunch cook, but probably disturbing in a husband or parent.

That's our family. And this is our family cookbook.

These are the dishes I like to eat and that I like to feed my family and friends. They are the recipes that "work," meaning they've been developed over time and have been informed by repetition and long—and often painful—experience.

As happens in the restaurant business, I will, from time to time, make small incremental sacrifices in "quality" for the often more important matter of serviceability. While it is a laudable ambition to prepare the best risotto in the world, that doesn't mean shit if your guests are sitting around with their stomachs growling, getting progressively drunker, while you dick around in the kitchen, interminably stirring rice.

Fish served on the bone is admittedly "better." You, uncertain of your knife skills, struggling to lift a fillet from a cooked Dover sole, tableside, in front of eight guests, might not be.

There is nothing remotely innovative about the recipes in this book. If you are looking for a culinary genius to take you to the Promised Land of next-level creativity, look elsewhere. That ain't me.

Mostly, these recipes are direct lifts from imperfect memories of childhood favorites: things my mom fed me, things I liked or loved to eat during the happier moments of my life—the kind of food memories I like to share with my daughter—along with a few greatest hits from my travels, and some boiled-down wisdom on subjects like breakfasts and Thanksgiving dinner, presented in an organized and tactically efficient, stress-free way.

One of the first things I discovered as I transitioned into my new "Daddy" phase was that I was usually more frantic preparing a dinner party for five friends at home than I was cranking out five hundred à la carte dinners in a restaurant. The remedy for this anxiety, I've found, is to treat my friends or family just like another five-top in a sea of customers—until the food is served. Then I can sit down with them, relax, and enjoy their company. Just like a "normal" dad.

A Note About My Daughter

My daughter, Ariane, is eight years old at the time of this writing. She is mostly obscured in the photos in this book. Being recognized by strangers is as weird and unnatural a thing as I have ever known, but I'm a big boy. I made my bed, and I won't complain when I have to lie in it. If I'm running through an airport, frantically looking for a bathroom, and a fan stops me for a photograph, this is a small price to pay for all the freedoms and the good things that being the sort of person who gets recognized in airports has brought me. It sure as shit beats working a busy brunch shift. I made an informed decision by writing book after book, by choosing to appear on television. At eighteen, my daughter will be old enough to make those kinds of decisions for herself. It would be wrong for me, or anyone else, to make those decisions for her.

The Happy Ending

An excerpt from *Medium Raw: A Bloody Valentine to the World of Food and the People Who Cook*, published in the UK by Bloomsbury in 2010.

I was born at what is now NewYork-Presbyterian Hospital in New York City in 1956, but I grew up in the leafy green bedroom community of Leonia, New Jersey.

I did not want for love or attention. My parents loved me. Neither of them drank to excess. Nobody beat me. God was never mentioned—so I was annoyed by neither religion nor church nor any notions of sin or damnation. Mine was a house filled with books and music—and, frequently, films. Early in my childhood, my father worked days at Willoughby's camera store in Manhattan—and on weekends would come home with a rented sixteen-millimeter projector and classic movies. Later, when he became an executive at Columbia Records, I got free records for most of my adolescence. When I was twelve, he'd take me to the Fillmore East to see the Mothers of Invention or Ten Years After or whoever I was listening to that year.

Summers meant barbeques and Wiffle ball games in the backyard. In school, I was not bullied any more than the next kid—and maybe even a little less. I got the bike I wanted for Christmas. My counselor at camp did not molest me.

I was miserable. And angry.

I bridled bitterly at the smothering chokehold of love and normalcy in my house—compared to the freedom enjoyed by my less-well-looked-after friends. I envied them their dysfunctional and usually empty houses, their near-total lack of supervision. The weird, slightly scary, but enticing stashes of exotica we'd find in their parents' secret places: blurry black-and-white stag films, bags of weed, pills . . . bottles of booze that nobody would notice when missing or slowly drained. My friends' parents always had other, more important things on their minds, leaving their kids to run wild—free to stay out late, to sleep over when and where they saw fit, to smoke weed in their rooms without fear of being noticed.

I was pissed about this. How come *I* couldn't have that? As I saw it, my parents were the only thing standing between me and a life spent taking full advantage of the times.

Much later, standing in some particularly bullshit kitchen, more of a saloon than anything resembling a real restaurant, I wasn't the sort of person to look back in puzzlement and regret, wondering where I might have gone wrong. I never blamed bad choices—like the heroin, for instance—or bad companions for my less than stellar career trajectory. I don't and never did refer to my addiction as my "disease." I'd *wanted* to become a junkie, after all, since I was twelve years old. Call it a character flaw—of which drugs were simply a manifestation, a petulant "fuck you" to my bourgeois parents, who'd committed the unpardonable sin of loving me.

At any given moment, when I'm honest with myself, I can look back and say that, on balance, I'd probably make exactly the same moves all over again. I *know* what brought me to those crummy kitchens, the reeking steam tables, the uncleaned deli slicer, yet another brunch shift—I did.

Life, even in the bad old days, had been perfectly fair to me. I knew this.

Even when it was McAssCrack's Bar and Grill I was working at, I knew I was pretty lucky. Lucky to be alive, given the precarious business of scoring dope every day in the eighties in New York City. Lucky to be in reasonably good health, given what was happening around me—and all the people who came up with me who weren't around anymore. There was even love in my life through it all, however improbable—a criminal partnership of long standing.

As much as I hated standing there in the bad times, pre-poaching eggs for service, letting them slip off the spoon into a bus tub of ice water, I couldn't blame anybody. Like I said, I made my choices. One after the other.

Then again, I could blame my dad, I guess. For all the joy he brought me when he came home with the *Sgt. Pepper* album. Or *Disraeli Gears*. An argument could be made, I guess, that this kind of exposure at an early age could lead one to an appetite for distraction—if not destruction. And maybe nine years old was a little young to see *Dr. Strangelove*—to find out that the world was surely going to end in a nuclear apocalypse (and soon). And that it would be funny when it happened. Perhaps this contributed to the nihilistic worldview I'd adopt later as a world-weary eleven-year-old.

If they ever find me with a crawl space full of dead hookers, I'll be sure to point the finger at Dad—and Stanley Kubrick.

But if we're playing the blame game? Top of the list for "it's all your fault—you made me this way!" goes to two children's classic films: *The Red Balloon* and *Old Yeller*.

What exactly was the message of *The Red Balloon* anyway? Every time our teachers didn't show up, they'd haul out the projector and show us this supposedly heartwarming and inspiring story of a little French boy and his enchanted balloon friend.

But wait a minute. The poor kid is impoverished and clearly unloved. He wears the same clothes every day. Immediately on finding his balloon, he's ostracized by society, banned from public transportation, chastised at school, even ejected from church. His parents are either dead or have abandoned him—as the hideous crone who cruelly throws his balloon out the window at first encounter is clearly too old to be his mom. The boy's schoolmates are a feral, opportunistic bunch who instinctively seek to destroy what they don't understand and can't possess. In fact, nearly every other child in the film is depicted as part of an unthinking mob, fighting viciously among themselves even as they pursue the boy and his balloon through the streets, like a pack of wolves. The boy runs away, is assaulted, separated from his only friend—then reunites with it only to watch it die slowly before his eyes.

The happy ending? Balloons from all over Paris converge. The boy gathers them together and is lifted aloft. He drifts away, dangerously suspended over the city. The end.

Where's the kid going? To an unspecified "better" place—for sure. Or to a fatal drop when the balloons empty of their helium (as we've seen them do just previously).

The message?

Life is cruel, lonely, and filled with pain and random acts of violence. Everybody hates you and seeks to destroy you. Better to opt out altogether, to leap—literally—into the void, escape by any means necessary. However uncertain or suicidal the way out.

Nice, huh? May as well have put a crack pipe in my hand right then. Why wait? Maybe *this* was why I never worked at the French Laundry.

Then there's *Old Yeller*. Even worse. A more cynical and unconscionably bleak message one could hardly imagine.

The story of a boy and his dog. A *Disney* story of a boy and his dog—which, as all children's accumulated experience teaches them, means that *no matter what kind of peril the heroes go through, things will always turn out okay in the end*. This, by the time we sat down in that darkened theater, excited, sticky with Twizzlers, we had come to accept as an article of faith. A contract between kids everywhere, our parents, and the fine people at Walt Disney Studios. This was as powerful a bond as we knew, an assurance that held an otherwise uncertain universe together. Sure, Khrushchev was maybe going to drop the Big One on us, but goddammit, that dog was gonna make it out okay!

So, when Old Yeller gets sick with this rabies thing, little Tony is, naturally, not concerned. Pinocchio, after all, got out of that whale situation no problem. Sure, things looked bad for him, too, for a while, but he figured it out in the end. Bumpy ride with Bambi, what with Mom dying, but that ended okay. Like Mom and Dad never forgetting to pick you up at school, the Happy Ending was a dead cert.

It will be okay. It will turn out fine.

No one will hurt a fucking *dog*.

That's what I'm saying to myself, sitting there between Mom and Dad, staring up at that screen, breath held, waiting for the miracle.

Then they go and blow Old Yeller's fucking brains out.

I sit there stunned. "What do you *mean* there's no cure for rabies? I don't give a *fuck* they hadda put Yeller 'out of his misery'! What about *my* misery, cocksucker! They were supposed to fix things! He was supposed to get *better*!! Don't talk to me about *reality*! I don't care if it's a magical fucking rainbow shining out of a fairy princess's ass that makes him better. He's supposed to get *better*!!!"

From that moment on, I looked at my parents and the whole world with suspicion. What else were they lying about?

Life was clearly a cruel joke. A place with no guarantees, built on a foundation of false assumptions if not outright untruths. You think everything's going okay . . .

Then they shoot your fucking dog.

So, maybe *that's* why until I got my first dishwashing job, I had no respect for myself and no respect for anybody else.

I should probably sue.

I'm Dancing

An excerpt from *Medium Raw: A Bloody Valentine to the World of Food and the People Who Cook*, published in the UK by Bloomsbury in 2010.

I'm dancing.

The twist, actually—or something very much like it. And though I am mortified by the very thought of dancing in front of witnesses, I am not alone in this room. Around me, nine or ten Filipina nannies and their charges are also swiveling their hips and moving to the music in their stocking feet. My dance partner is a two-year-old girl in pink tights and a tutu. The red stuff beneath my fingernails is, I suspect, vestigial Play-Doh.

This, I am fully aware, is not cool. This is as far away from cool as a man can get. But I am in no way troubled by such thoughts. I crossed that line a long time ago. If anything, I'm feeling pretty good about myself—in the smug, Upper East Side, Bugaboo-owning, sidewalk-hogging, self-righteous kind of a way indigenous to my new tribe. I am, after all, the only parent here on this fine Tuesday afternoon, alone among the gyrating nannies, the little Sophias, Vanessas, Julias, Emmas, and Isabellas. My daughter, grinning maniacally as she jumps and twists about three feet below me, is very pleased that I am here. "That's right, I *do* love you *more* than the mothers of all these other children love *them*. That's why Daddy's here—and they're *not*. *They're* getting their fucking nails done, having affairs, going to Pilates class, or whatever *bad* parents do . . . I'm here for you, *boo* . . . twistin' my heart out—something I would never ever have done for any other person in my whole life. Only for you. I'm a good daddy. *Goooood* Daddy!"

Later, if she's good, there will be ice cream. I will seat her prominently next to me, facing the street in her Petit Bateau jumper, secretly hoping that passersby will notice how beautiful she is, how cute we are together, what a *great* dad I am. Holding her little hand, or carrying her on my shoulders, I will float home on a cloud of self-congratulation.

I'm through being cool. Or, more accurately, I'm through entertaining the notion that anybody could even consider the possibility of coolness emanating from or residing anywhere near me. As any conscientious father knows in his bones, any remaining trace elements of coolness go right out the window from the second you lay eyes on your firstborn. The second you lean in for the action, see your baby's head make that first quarter-corkscrew turn toward you, well . . . you know you can and should throw your cherished black leather motorcycle jacket right in the nearest trash bin. Clock's ticking on the earring, too. It's somehow . . . undignified now.

Norman Mailer described the desire to be cool as a "decision to encourage the psychopath in oneself, to explore that domain of experience where security is boredom and therefore sickness and one exists in the present, in that enormous present which is without past or future, memory or planned intention."

I encouraged the psychopath in myself for most of my life. In fact, that's a rather elegant description of whatever it was I was doing. But I figure I put in my time.

The essence of cool, after all, is not giving a fuck.

And let's face it: I most definitely give a fuck now. I give a huge fuck. The hugest. Everything else—*everything*—pales. To pretend otherwise, by word or deed, would be a monstrous lie. There will be no more Dead Boys T-shirts. Whom would I be kidding? Their charmingly nihilistic worldview in no way mirrors my own. If Stiv Bators were still alive and put his filthy hands anywhere near my baby, I'd snap his neck—then thoroughly cleanse the area with baby wipes.

There is no hope of hipness.

As my friend A. A. Gill points out, after your daughter reaches a certain age—like five—the most excruciating and embarrassing thing she could possibly imagine is seeing her dad in any way threatening to rock. Your record collection may indeed be cooler than your daughter's will ever be, but this is a meaningless distinction now. She doesn't care. And nobody else will. If you're lucky, long after you're gone, a grandchild will rediscover your old copy of *Fun House*. But it will be way too late for you to bask in the glory of past coolness.

There is nothing cool about "used to be cool."

All of this, I think, is only right and appropriate. Too much respect for your elders is, historically, almost always a bad thing. I want my daughter to love me. I don't necessarily want her to share my taste for Irish ale or Hawaiian bud.

When you see the children of the perennially cool—on shows like *Behind the Music*—they look sheepish and slightly doomed, talking about their still-working rock-'n'-roller dads, as if they are the reluctant warders of some strange breed of extravagantly wrinkly and badly behaved children. Kids may not be old enough to know what cool *is*, but they are unerring in their ability to sense what *isn't*.

No kid really wants a cool parent. "Cool" parents, when I was a kid, meant parents who let you smoke weed in the house—or allowed boyfriends to sleep over with their daughters. That would make Sarah Palin "cool." But, as I remember, we thought those parents were kind of creepy. They were useful, sure, but what was wrong with them that they found us so entertaining? Didn't they have their own friends? Secretly, we hated them.

Turning thirty came as a cruel surprise for me. I hadn't really planned on making it that far. I'd taken seriously the maxims of my time—"Never trust anyone over thirty" and "Live fast, die young"—and been frankly shocked when I found that I'd lived that long. I'd done everything I could think of to ensure the opposite result, but there I was—and without a Plan B. The restaurant business provided a degree of stability in that there were usually people who expected me to get up in the morning and go somewhere—and heroin, if nothing else, was useful in giving me a sense of *purpose* in my daily movements. I knew what I had to do every day for most of my early thirties: get heroin.

Of my first marriage, I'll say only that watching Gus Van Sant's *Drugstore Cowboy*—particularly the relationship between Matt Dillon's Bob and Kelly Lynch's Dianne—inspires feelings of great softness and sentiment in me. It's a reminder that even the worst times can be happy ones—until they aren't.

By my late thirties, I found that I was still lingering, and I admit to a sense of disappointment, confusion—even defeat. *What do I do* now? I remember thinking. Detoxed from heroin and methadone and having finally—*finally*—ended a lifelong love affair with cocaine. Where was my reward for all this self-denial? Shouldn't I have been feeling good? If anything, all that relative sobriety pointed up a basic emptiness and dissatisfaction in my life, a hole I'd managed to fill with various chemicals for the better part of twenty-five years.

At forty-four, shortly after writing *Kitchen Confidential*, I found myself suddenly with a whole new life. One minute, I was standing next to a deep fryer, pan-searing pepper steaks—and the next, I was sitting on top of a dune, watching the sun set over the Sahara. I was running roadblocks in Battambang; tiny feet were walking on my back in Siem Reap; I was eating at El Bulli.

Shortly before the breakup of my first marriage, I embarked on the equivalent of a massive public works project in my apartment: new shelves, furniture, carpets, appliances—all the trappings, I thought, of a "normal" and "happy" life—the kind of things I'd never really had or lived around since childhood. I wrote a crime novel around that time, in which the characters' yearnings for a white-picket-fence kind of a life reflect my own far more truthfully than any nonfiction I've ever written. Shortly after that, I cruelly burned down my previous life in its entirety.

There was a period of . . . readjustment.

I recall the precise second when I decided that I wanted to—that I was going to be—a father.

Wanting a child is easy enough. I'd always—even in the bad old days—thought fondly of the times my father would carry me aloft on his shoulders into the waves off the Jersey Shore, saying, "Here comes a big one!" I'd remembered my own five-year-old squeals of terror and delight and thought I'd like to do that with a child someday, see that look on my own child's face. But I knew well that I was the sort of person who shouldn't and couldn't be a daddy. Kids liked me fine—my niece and nephew, for instance—but it's easy to make kids like you, especially when you're the indulgent "evil uncle."

I'd never lived in an environment where a child would have been a healthy fit—and I'd never felt like I was a suitably healthy person. I'd think of fatherhood from time to time, look at myself in the mirror, and think, *That guy may* want *a child; he's simply not up to the job.* And, well, for most of my life I'd been way too far up my own ass to be of any use to anyone—something that only got worse after *Kitchen Confidential*.

I don't know exactly when the possibility of that changing presented itself—but sometime, I guess, after having made every mistake, having already fucked up in every way a man can fuck up, having realized that I'd had *enough* cocaine, that no amount in the world was going to make me any happier. That a naked, oiled supermodel was not going to make everything better in my life—nor any sports car known to man. It was sometime after that.

The precise moment of realization came in my tiny fourth-floor walk-up apartment on Ninth Avenue. Above Manganaro's Hero-Boy restaurant—next building over from Esposito Meat Market. I was lying in bed with my then-girlfriend—I guess you could diplomatically call it "spooning"—and I caught myself thinking, *I could make a baby with this woman. I'd like to make a baby with this woman. Fuck, I'd not only be happy to make a baby with this woman, I think . . . I'm pretty sure . . . I'd actually be good at it.*

We discussed this. And Ottavia—that was (is) her name—also thought this was a fine idea, though of my prospects for a quick insemination she was less optimistic.

"Baby," she said (insert a very charming Italian accent—with the tone and delivery of a busy restaurant manager), "you're old. Your sperm. Eez—a dead."

Assuming a long campaign, we planned to get at it as soon as I returned from shooting my next show. In Beirut.

Of that episode I've written elsewhere. Long and short of it: My camera crew and I were caught in a war. For about a week, we holed up in a hotel, watching and listening to the bombs, feeling their impact rolling through the floors. After some drama, we were evacuated from a beach onto landing craft utilities by American navy and marine personnel and taken first to a cargo vessel in the Med and then on to Cyprus.

My network had very generously provided a private jet to take me and the crew back home. None of my crew had ever been on a private jet before, and we slept and played cards and ate omelettes prepared by the flight attendant, finally landing on a rainy, gray morning in Teterboro, New Jersey. We walked across the tarmac to a small private terminal, where Pat Younge—the president of the network—and Ottavia, as well as the crew's wives and family, were there to meet us. It was, to say the least, an emotional homecoming with much hugging and crying.

I took Ottavia back to my crummy apartment and we made a baby. Nothing like eight days of fear and desperation to concentrate the mind, I guess. A few weeks later, we were in a car on the way from LAX into Los Angeles, where I was about to appear as a judge on *Top Chef*, when we got the news from Ottavia's doctor over the phone. There are photos of me, sitting on a bed in the Chateau Marmont, holding five different brands of drugstore pregnancy tests—all of them positive—a giddily idiotic grin on my face. Strangely, perhaps, I had no fear. At no time then—or since—did I have second thoughts. *What am I getting into?* never flashed across my brain.

I was the star pupil at Lamaze class. If your water ever breaks at the supermarket and I'm nearby? I'm your boy. I know just what to do.

I look back on my less well-behaved days with few regrets. True, the responsibilities of marriage and fatherhood demand certain behavioral adjustments. But my timing couldn't have been better. I find myself morphing—however awkwardly—into respectability just as things are getting really hot on the streets for any of my peers who are even semi-recognizable. The iniquitousness of Twitter and food- and chef-related websites and blogs has totally changed the game for anyone with a television show—even me. You don't have to be very famous at all these days to end up with a blurry photograph on DumbAssCelebrities.com. You don't want your daughter's little schoolmates reading about her daddy, stuttering drunk, two o'clock in the morning, at a chef-friendly bar, doing belly shots from a chunky and underdressed cocktail waitress—something that could well have happened a few years ago. In a day when a passing cell phone user can easily get a surreptitious photo of you, slinking out of the porn shop with copies of *Anal Rampage 2* and *MILFBusters* under your arm, and post it in real time, maybe that's a particularly good time to trade in the leather jacket for some cotton Dockers.

I love the saying "Nobody likes a dirty old man or a clean little boy." I was, unfortunately, overly clean as a child—the fruit of a fastidious household. I shall try and make up for those years by doing my best to avoid becoming the former. Like I said, my timing—even without the daddyhood thing—was good.

It's all about the little girl. Because I am acutely aware of both her littleness (how could I be otherwise) and the fact that she's a blank page, her brain a soft surface waiting for the irreversible impressions of every raised voice, every gaffe and unguarded moment. The fact that she's a girl requires, I believe, extra effort. Dada may have, at various times in his life, *been* a pig, but Dada surely does not want to ever *look* like a pig again. This can't possibly be overstated. As the first of two boys, I can't even imagine what it must be like for a little girl to see her dad leering at another of her sex. This creature will soon grow up to be a young *woman* and that's something I consider every day.

I figure, I'm going to spoil the shit out of this kid for a while, then pack her off to tae kwon do as soon as she's four years old. Her first day of second grade and Little Timmy at the desk behind her tries to pull her hair? He's getting an elbow to the thorax. My little girl may grow up with lots of problems: spoiled; with unrealistic expectations of the world; cultural identification confusion, perhaps (a product of much traveling in her early years); considering the food she's exposed to, she shall surely have a jaded palate; and an aged and possibly infirm dad by the time she's sixteen. But she ain't gonna have any problems with self-esteem.

Whatever else, she's never going to look for validation from some predatory asshole. She can—and surely will—hang out with tons of assholes. Dads, I'm assured, can never hope to control that. All I can hope for is that she hangs out with assholes for her own reasons—that she is genuinely amused by assholes rather than needing them to make her feel better about herself.

I wish.

John F. Kennedy said something truly terrifying—guaranteed to make every parent's blood run cold: "To have a child is to give fate a hostage."

Something I wish I'd never read. I can only hope she's happy—even weird and happy will suit me just fine. She will feel loved. She'll have food. And shelter. A large Italian and Sardinian family—and a smaller American one. She'll have seen, by the time she's six years old, much of the world, and she'll have seen, as well, that not everybody on this planet lives—or can live—anything like the way she lives. She will, hopefully, have spent time playing and running barefoot with the children of fishermen and farmers in rural Vietnam. She will have swum in every ocean. She will know how to use chopsticks—and what real cheese is. She already speaks more Italian than I do.

Beyond this, I don't know what else I can do.

Soup du Jour

An unpublished short fiction, date unknown.

I cook. When I'm not cooking, I lie around the apartment with my wife. We don't wear any clothes, and when the phone rings, we don't pick it up. We listen to the phone-answering machine. When somebody calls, it rings, one time. Then there is a click, and we listen to the recording of my wife's voice prepare the caller for the loud beep that follows. "Good day or evening. No one can speak to you directly right now, so at the sound of the beep, please leave a brief message, as well as the time and the date that you called. Thank you. Bye." We lie in the extra bedroom, the room we call the "TV Room," and we listen to the messages. If we talk, we talk quietly, as if the voice on the other end might hear us. Some of the messages are brief and business-like. These people do not know us. They think we are not at home. Others call out our names. They know we are home, in the TV Room, listening to them, or maybe just asleep. They try to wake us. They call our names over and over. These are our friends.

My wife and I feel bad about it sometimes: hearing our friends' voices grow increasingly frustrated, then discouraged; the vindictive sound of someone hanging up. But we smile at each other. We say, if they are really our friends, they'll understand.

When I cook, I like to be the first one in the kitchen in the morn-ing. The cutting boards are all clean and bleached, the stainless steel sprayed and rubbed to a shine by the night porters. With no other cooks to get in the way, I can work on three or four projects at once: a batch of soup, a few sauces, the butchering of the meat and fish . . . I like making the soup best. I make enough for lunch and dinner, around ten or twelve gallons. I like to chop and peel. I like the hiss in the bottom of the big pot when I stir in the onions and garlic. When the Egyptian dishwashers and porters arrive, they put on coffee. My soup, the first real meal of the day, slowly overpowers the scent of coffee and morning cigarettes. One of the Egyptians sings softly in Arabic.

Once in a while, I visit my friends. They all smell like garlic and fish, even in their street clothes. I probably do too. It's the fingertips. No matter how much I scrub, my hands smell slightly of garlic and shallots. They are ugly, too. They look just like my friends' hands. Sometimes, when we're lying around the apartment, my wife massages my neck. Then I massage her, at the base of her spine. The muscles get all tense there, she says. She likes foot massages, too. I'm beginning to like them.

My wife asks, "Is this all right for tomorrow?" She stands in the doorway, hand on hip, modeling the dress she's thinking of wearing to work. I am lying on the bed in the TV Room, and I tell her she looks great. "Should I wear the belt with it or not?"

I say, "Belt."

"Really? I should wear the belt?"

I correct myself. I assure her that after thinking about it, maybe the belt isn't a good idea, that the dress looks much better without the belt, that she doesn't need the belt at all, that the belt sucks, that the dress looks much, much better without it. She disappears from the doorway for a moment and returns. This time I am paying attention. I think the gray pearls with the gray dress are too much, and I tell her so. She smiles.

Clothes all laid out for work, she joins me in front of the television. She runs her fingers through the hair on the back of my head. We watch a rerun of a situation comedy that we have seen many times before. She knows every line of this episode by heart. I do, too. But we are comforted by the familiar jokes, the canned laughter that follows. We lie there, our clothes in piles in the corners around us, naked, sleepy, and happy; truly happy. Happier than my friends. Happier than you.

III

Rage

It's an odd thing about the public memory of Tony that he's remembered very well for a handful of, well, passionately angry statements, when in reality he was very sparing with his ire. Or perhaps it felt that way to those of us who knew him, who could see the glint in his eye when he was enjoying skewering this or that authoritarian or this or that menu cliché. And he did enjoy it. If he weren't a writer, I don't know that he would have. It was in his writing—through his writing—that I think Tony made some things bearable for himself. This section contains both sides of his rage spectrum: both the frank and humane outrage on behalf of people suffering through no fault of their own, and the more cultivated and needling vitriol he poured on things such as sloppy brioche hamburger monstrosities.

Beat Henry Kissinger to Death with Your Bare Hands

An excerpt from *A Cook's Tour: In Search of the Perfect Meal*, originally published by Bloomsbury in 2001.

I flew Air Vietnam into Phnom Penh. At Pochentong Airport, a long desk of uniformed military men examined my passport, documents, medical certificate, and visas. All of them were in full parade regalia: leather-billed hats, mortarboards with tassels on their shoulders, chests festooned with medals. It looked like the Joint Chiefs had gathered to personally inspect every incoming visitor. The first guy gravely scrutinized my papers, handed them to the officer on his right, who read closely, made a tiny written notation, then handed them to the man on his right, who stamped them and returned them to the first guy—where the whole process began again. My papers made it all the way down to the last guy. Then, after some tiny incongruity was noticed, they were returned, once again, to the beginning of the line. Eventually, my documents made it through this ludicrously over-dressed gauntlet and I was in. Welcome to Cambodia. This is the last law you'll see.

Once you've been to Cambodia, you'll never stop wanting to beat Henry Kissinger to death with your bare hands. You will never again be able to open a newspaper and read about that treacherous, prevaricating, murderous scumbag sitting down for a nice chat with Charlie Rose or attending some black-tie affair for a new glossy magazine without choking. Witness what Henry did in Cambodia—the fruits of his genius for statesmanship—and you will never understand why he's not sitting in the dock at The Hague next to Milošević. While Henry continues to nibble nori rolls and *remaki* at A-list parties, Cambodia, the neutral nation he secretly and illegally bombed, invaded, undermined, and then threw to the dogs, is still trying to raise itself up on its one remaining leg.

One in eight Cambodians—as many as two million people—were killed during the Khmer Rouge's campaign to eradicate their country's history. One out of every two hundred fifty Cambodians is missing a limb, crippled by one of the thousands and thousands of land mines still waiting to be stepped on in the country's roads, fields, forests, and irrigation ditches. Destabilized, bombed, invaded, forced into slave labor, murdered by the thousands, the Cambodians must have been relieved when the Vietnamese, Cambodia's historical archenemy, invaded.

One look at the abject squalor of the capital city's crumbling and unpaved streets and any thought that Cambodia might be fun flew out the window. If you're a previously unemployable ex–convenience store clerk from Leeds or Tulsa, however, a guy with no conscience and no chance of ever knowing the love of an unintoxicated woman, then Cambodia can be a paradise. You can get a job as an English teacher for about seven dollars an hour (which makes you one of the richest people in the country). Weed, smack, whores, guns, and prescription drugs are cheap and easy to find. You can behave as badly as you wish. Shy boys on motorbikes will ferry you from bar to bar, waiting outside while you drink yourself into a stupor. You can eat dinner, then penetrate indentured underage prostitutes, buy a kilo of not very good weed, drink yourself stuttering drunk, and be driven safely home to your spacious apartment—all for under thirty dollars. Cambodia is a dream come true for international losers—a beautiful but badly beaten woman, staked out on an anthill for every predator in the world to do with what he wishes.

Phnom Penh's total population when the Khmer Rouge finished marching its citizens out into the countryside to dig irrigation ditches—

and executing most of them—was a mind-boggling twelve people. That's down from about eight hundred fifty thousand only a couple of years earlier. Most of the survivors returned to the city, to find their former homes in shambles; looted, waterless, powerless hovels, often occupied by equally desperate squatters. Armless, legless, limping, and crawling locals struggle still to scratch out a living making handicrafts for tourists. Or begging. The average wage in Cambodia is under a dollar a day. Four-year-old children wander the markets, begging, carrying their two-year-old brothers.

Where does one go in Phnom Penh? Just where you'd think the expats would go: the FCC (Foreign Correspondents Club), where you can have an American-style hamburger, and a cold beer, then retire to the rear balcony to watch the bats leaving the eaves of the National Museum at dusk—a nightly event where a stream of thousands and thousands of bats curls out and up into the purple-and-gold sky like fast-moving smoke. Then you can stumble into the street, where a crowd of skinny, underweight boys on scooters and motos wait, no doubt calling your name—as they know you and your predilections by now—brush by a few amputees, hop on the back of one of the boys' motos, and head off to "the Heart," local shorthand for the Heart of Darkness bar. After that, there are the nightclubs and brothels (a narrow distinction between the two), maybe some pizza seasoned with ganja, a bag of smack for a nightcap. With any luck, your Cambodian-made condom won't snap, you won't get rousted or shot at by the cops, and you won't run into any relatives of Hun Sen, the prime minister—any of which might lead to tragedy. If you do get into trouble, don't look to the law to help you out.

A story from the *Phnom Penh Post*:

> *Tha Sokha, 19, tried for the rape of a six-year-old girl, will serve only six months in jail for indecent assault because the rape of his victim "was not deep enough" said Kandal Court Judge Kong Kouy . . . After initially ignoring the girl's family's complaints against Sokha, district police brokered a compensation deal between the families of the victim and the perpetrator. The girl's parents thumb printed a contract in*

which they would receive 1.5 million riel in compensation for the rape of their daughter, but they never received the money. Upon taking the case to the commune police station on Jan. 11, the victim and her sister reported receiving death threats from a commune police officer named Lon if they continued to "talk about rape."

Another typical story from the *Phnom Penh Post*—same day as the above:

ACID MUTILATION A MISDEMEANOR: *The first case of a viciously mutilated acid attack victim pressing charges against her assailant has shocked legal observers by resulting in a two-year suspended sentence against the suspect. Kampong Cham Municipal Court Judge Tith Sothy dismissed a petition to upgrade the charges . . . Sothy justified the ruling on the grounds that [the perpetrator] had no intention of killing the victim but only sought to "damage her beauty because of jealousy."*

Getting the picture? So who is in charge? Hard to say. The easy answer is Hun Sen, the former Khmer Rouge officer who defected to the Vietnamese and then was "elected" prime minister, ousting his nominal competition by coup d'état. There's King Sihanouk, back again, installed in the palace after playing footsie with the United States, the Khmer Rouge, the Chinese—and everybody else. He provides a thin veneer of legitimacy and tradition to what is essentially a military dictatorship. There are the remnants of the Khmer Rouge and its allies—a loosely knit coalition of convenience among various unlovely private armies, organized criminals, former Vietnamese stooges, and extremist groups. The Khmer Rouge "defected" to the "central government" (such as it is), a while back, in return for amnesty, and was basically given control of its former stronghold and cash cow in northern Cambodia, free to pursue its traditional pastimes of gem smuggling and lumbering—and its new gambling ventures. Those in the Khmer

Rouge were given central government uniforms when they put down their guns, which means that nearly every male Cambodian of draft age, it seems, wears the same fatigues in one form or another, making it difficult to tell exactly who is robbing and extorting you on any given day. There are the much-feared private armies (everybody's got one), which act mainly as security for various despotic scuzzballs and their relatives—with attendant hit men—making it a dangerous matter if some drunken lout steps on your toe in a nightclub and you voice your displeasure too expressively.

Driving out by the airport one afternoon, my cabdriver pulled his car over suddenly, as did everyone else on the road. A police escort whipped by, sirens screaming, followed in short order by a spanking-new black Humvee with tinted windows.

"Hun Sen nephew," said my driver with distaste. Hun Sen's family and friends are the subject of frequent stories of drunken beatings, stabbings, and pistol-whippings, when one of them gets cranky during an evening out in the discos. There's a famous tale of the time one business associate arrived at Pochentong Airport on a commercial airliner. Told that the airline had misplaced his luggage, he is said to have disembarked, procured a gun from a waiting flunky, then begun shooting out the airplane's tires until his belongings were recovered. Needless to say, this behavior did not result in arrest.

Shooting things, if you have enough money in your pocket, is perfectly all right in Cambodia. Drinks are free at the Gun Club. Ammunition, however, you pay for by the clip.

My waiter, a slim, friendly Khmer, stood over my shoulder as I perused the menu. A tray of Angkor and Tiger beers sat in the middle of the table. Under the thatched roof of the long, open shelter, a few well-muscled soldiers in paratrooper camos from the nearby base sat at another table, unsmiling behind their sunglasses, drinking sodas and beer.

"I think I'll start off with three clips for the .45 . . . three clips for the AK-47 . . . followed by an entrée of five clips for the M16—can I have some grenades on the side?"

"You like James Bond?" asked my waiter, refilling my glass for me. "You like James Bond gun?"

"Depends," I said. "Sean Connery or Roger Moore? If we're talking Roger Moore, forget about it."

"Look!" said my waiter, dangling an automatic pistol in front of my face. "Walther PPK! James Bond gun! . . . You like?"

"Sure," I said, hefting the thing over a picnic snack of baguette and sausage I'd brought along. "I'll try it."

You've got to admire an establishment that invites its customers to get drunk and then fire automatic weapons indiscriminately. Next to the gun racks and the ammunition locker, at the Gun Club, there was a sign on the wall that said in big block letters PLEASE DON'T POINT YOUR WEAPON AT ANYTHING YOU DO NOT INTEND TO SHOOT. This being Cambodia, I thought the text left a lot of room open for interpretation. A Japanese businessman boozily pulling the pin from a grenade a few feet away gave a glassy-eyed look in my direction, smiled, and hurled the thing at a target about fifty feet away. Boom! Next time I looked over, he was playing with an M16, trying to jam a full clip into the rifle—backward.

I'd be lying if I told you I didn't have a great time. Firing bursts from heavy weapons at paper targets of charging Russians is fun. I did surprisingly well with the AK-47 and the .45, hitting center body mass almost every time. At one point, his hands over his ears to protect them from the racket of my discharging weapon, my waiter tugged my sleeve and asked, "So . . . whey you from?"

"New York," I said.

"What you do?" he inquired.

"I'm a chef."

My waiter looked at my target, which I'd pretty much shredded from neck to crotch, smiled encouragingly, and said, "You could be a killer!" That's what passes for a compliment in Phnom Penh, I guess.

Just Don't Smoke

An excerpt from *A Cook's Tour: In Search of the Perfect Meal*, originally published by Bloomsbury in 2001.

You can't smoke anywhere in California. Rob Reiner says so. Celebrity fuckheads who live in walled compounds and use words like *working class*—never having sat down at a bar for an early-afternoon shot and a beer with any such animal in their lives—say so. For them, the bar is a place where we stupid, lumpen, and oppressed blue-collar proles are victimized by evil tobacco companies that have tricked us with their clever advertising into killing ourselves and our neighbors. For me, the bar is the last line of defense. "It's an employee safety and health issue," explained Lucky. The state is protecting her fry cook (I could see him in the kitchen, picking at an abscessed track mark) from the pernicious effects of secondhand smoke. Now, I can understand why they don't want me smoking in restaurant dining rooms. If I'm enjoying a delicate pairing of seared foie gras and pear chutney, I probably don't want somebody puffing away on a jasmine cigarette at the next table. I'm considerate. I can find a way not to smoke in the dining rooms of decent restaurants. Though bitterly resentful that I can no longer enjoy a cigarette with my fucking coffee in most places, I've learned to live with it. But the bar? The *bar*! What these miserable screwheads are saying is that it's okay to kill yourself with bourbon or tequila at nine o'clock in the morning—just don't enjoy yourself when doing it. It's only a matter of time before some well-intentioned health Nazi busts into your bedroom and yanks that post-intercourse cigarette right outta your hand.

San Francisco is said to be one of the most "liberal" and "tolerant" places to live in America. That's a good thing, right? I'm avidly supportive of "alternative lifestyles." I'm "tolerant." But something's gone wrong here. It's a wildly expensive city to live in—even where I'm staying in the Tenderloin—too expensive for most people to afford. Yet San Francisco's acceptance of hopelessness, prostitution, and drug addiction as "alternative lifestyles" seems to have ensured that many of its neighborhoods are choked with hustlers, junkies, the desperate, and the insane. I haven't seen junkies in such great numbers since the bad old days of Alphabet City—and in such bad shape. They're everywhere—dirty, diabetic, their limbs swollen, chalky, covered with suppurating tracks and infections. West Coast skells make my old crew from the methadone clinic look like the Osmond family. San Francisco's main employment sectors, at a cursory glance, are the countless whorehouses, massage parlors, clip joints, live sex shows, and crummy-looking strip joints you see everywhere downtown. A great number of women in San Francisco seem to be sex workers, and while this is perfectly okay as a "lifestyle choice" in my book, there are so many of them, and they are so disproportionately Asian, it feels more like Cambodia than any American city. As rents are so high, there's nowhere to live—and the dot-coms ain't hiring like they used to.

With all their kind hearts and good intentions, San Franciscans, living in postcard-pretty houses atop high hills, seem to be sending a message: "It's okay to come here. If you are prepared to lap dance for us . . . and then sleep on our sidewalks."

Just don't smoke. That would be wrong.

Hypocrisy

An excerpt from *A Cook's Tour: In Search of the Perfect Meal*, originally published by Bloomsbury in 2001.

In every case, it appeared to me (in my jaundiced way of thinking anyway) that something had soured them on the world they'd once embraced—and that they now sought new rules to live by, another orthodoxy, something else to believe in. "Did you read about the PCBs in striped bass?" one whispered urgently, as if comforted by the news. "I saw online where they're pumping steroids into cattle," said another breathlessly, every snippet of bad news from the health front a victory for their cause. They seemed to spend an awful lot of time confirming their fears and suspicions of the world outside their own, combing the Internet for stories of radioactive dairy products, genetically altered beets, polluted fish, carcinogenic sausages, spongiform-riddled meat, the hideous Grand Guignol chamber-of-horror abattoirs and slaughterhouses.

They also seemed curiously oblivious to the fact that much of the world goes to bed hungry every night, that our basic design features as humans, from the beginning of our evolution, developed around the very real need to hunt down slower, stupider animals, kill them, and eat them. "Don't you ever wake up in the middle of the night craving bacon?" I asked.

"No. Never," replied every single one of them. "I've never felt so healthy in my life."

It was difficult for me to be polite (though I was outnumbered). I'd recently returned from Cambodia, where a chicken can be the difference between life and death. These people in their comfortable suburban digs were carping about cruelty to animals but suggesting that everyone in the world, from suburban Yuppie to starving Cambodian cyclo driver, start buying organic vegetables and expensive soy substitutes. To look down on entire cultures that've based everything on the gathering of fish and rice seemed arrogant in the extreme. (I've heard of vegans feeding their dogs vegetarian meals. Now that's cruelty to animals.) And the hypocrisy of it all pissed me off. Just being able to talk about this issue in reasonably grammatical language is a privilege, subsidized in a yin/yang sort of a way, somewhere, by somebody taking it in the neck. Being able to read these words, no matter how stupid, offensive, or wrongheaded, is a privilege, your reading skills the end product of a level of education most of the world will never enjoy. Our whole lives—our homes, the shoes we wear, the cars we drive, the food we eat—are all built on a mountain of skulls. Meat, say the PETA folks, is "murder." And yes, the wide world of meat eating can seem like a panorama of cruelty at times. But is meat "murder"? Fuck no.

Murder, as one of my Khmer pals might tell you, is what his next-door neighbor did to his whole family back in the seventies. Murder is what happens in Cambodia, in parts of Africa, in Central and South America, and in former Soviet republics when the police chief's idiot son decides he wants to turn your daughter into a whore and you don't like the idea. Murder is what Hutus do to Tutsis, Serbs to Croats, Russians to Uzbeks, Crips to Bloods. And vice versa. It's black Chevy Suburbans (which, more than likely, US taxpayers paid for) pulling up outside your house at three in the morning and dragging away your suspiciously unpatriotic and overopinionated son. Murder is what that man sitting across from you in Phnom Penh does for a living—so he can afford a satellite dish for his roof, so he can watch our *Airwolf* reruns, MTV Asia, and Pam Anderson running in slow motion down a Southern California beach.

Hide in your fine homes and eat vegetables, I was thinking. Put a Greenpeace or NAACP bumper sticker on your Beemer if it makes you feel better (so you can drive your kids to their all-white schools). Save the rainforest—by all means—so maybe you can visit it someday, on an ecotour, wearing comfortable shoes made by twelve-year-olds in forced labor. Save a whale while millions are still sold into slavery, starved, fucked to death, shot, tortured, forgotten. When you see cute little kids crying in rubble next to Sally Struthers somewhere, be sure to send a few dollars.

A Sandwich Is a Beautiful Thing

An excerpt from *Appetites*, published in the UK by Bloomsbury in 2016.

A sandwich is a beautiful thing—one of the great innovations of modern history. It freed us from the tyranny of the plate, the table, the knife and fork. Between two slices of bread exist near-limitless possibilities for deliciousness.

But no matter how tasty or outrageous, how juicy or flavorful, and no matter how engorged with meat, sandwiches remain a delivery system for their fillings. The purpose of the sandwich, like a hamburger, is to effectively deliver protein or other stuff into your mouth without a fork. Structure, texture, and proportion are as central to the success or failure of the sandwich as its taste.

That may be the very best chopped liver, but if the rye bread surrounding it falls apart, you may as well eat it out of a fucking trough. If there are so many ingredients on your deli sandwich named after a celebrity that you can't possibly fit the thing into your mouth in such a way as to include appropriate representation of each distinct layer in every bite, it's a failure. Your "Howie Mandel" may look like a tower of awesomeness, a teetering heap of pastrami, corned beef, brisket, slaw, Russian dressing, and sprouts—but if half the ingredients squirt across the table like the last shot of a Peter North film, what's the point?

It is for this reason that I declare the beloved American classic, the *club sandwich*, to be America's Enemy, a menu item that perfectly encapsulates all the principles of Bad Sandwich Theory.

Who invented the club sandwich, anyway? America's enemies, for sure. The club predates Al Qaeda—but it fits that group's MO. Mission: Destroy America. Method: Sap the will to live of ordinary Americans—by repeatedly fucking up their lunch.

Maybe it was the Nazis. Didn't they invent, like, methadone? And ephedra? The club sandwich was an even more evil idea.

What's wrong with it, you ask?

What's wrong with turkey or chicken breast, some crispy bacon slices, lettuce, and tomato on a sandwich? (And yes, adding a fried egg surely makes it only better.) How could any sandwich containing these delightful ingredients be a bad thing?

Where does the club go wrong? I'll tell you.

It's that third slice of bread. What's it doing there? It's the fifth column of sandwich elements, lurking silently and entirely uselessly, in the middle of an otherwise respectable sandwich—until it can strike.

The entire club sandwich concept is fucked from the get-go. It's a sandwich designed to look good on a plate—after you've stuck extra-long frilly toothpicks into it and cut it into quarters. It's designed for eye appeal, and edibility be damned. Because as soon as you bite into that fucker, your teeth crush into the top and bottom layers of bread, compacting together the meat layers and the lettuce and tomato layers and that stupid extra slice of bread and, like in a collapsing building, anything soft is gonna get squished. The slippery tomato, unmoored by Russian dressing or mayonnaise, is sliding right out of the party along with the bacon, leaving you with a soggy turkey sandwich, a disproportionately double-thick top layer of bread, and a plate full of broken dreams.

That third slice of bread was put there to *look* good. They don't care about you. But I do. So please: Continue to make your club sandwiches. Just leave out that third slice.

Escape Comix

A comic panel written and illustrated by Tony from an unpublished zine he cofounded called *ZILTZ*, date unknown.

Mauser

An unpublished piece of fiction, date unknown.

Everybody in the room looked like someone had just taken a shit on the rug when I took my Mauser out of my pocket. I was smiling. I couldn't help it, I felt so proud. It was a beautiful dream of a gun, a big chunk of black steel, dangerous, with a hand-tooled wooden grip. It seemed to growl under its breath at the other people in the room and they reacted with fear and astonishment. It was an unforgivable faux pas, I know, but it was worth it. They had invited me to the "little party" as I was an old classmate. An old college pal. They must have remembered me in some favorable perspective and made the mistake of inviting me, undoubtedly as some form of amusement for their jaded and bored friends. They had not reckoned with how jaded and bored I felt. Mutley Prince was the host of the affair. Though not himself a former student of my old university, he was the rich and retarded patron-boyfriend of Kathleen Bradford, who had at one time been associated with me in a peripheral sort of way. I deleted the two of them. Individually they were tolerable, once in a great while; I understand they could be pleasant to be with. But together, the spectacle of the groveling millionaire twit and the ambitious college girl was too nauseating to handle unprepared. So I expected the worst.

I had been watching television for around four months when the invitation arrived. It provided incentive for me to get out of bed and turn down the volume. I knew I'd need money so I wrapped up the television (my last remaining appliance) and took it downtown and pawned it. Then I took a bus to Forty-second Street to catch a few films. I saw *The Texas Chain Saw Massacre*, *Death Wish*, and *Lightning Swords of*

Death on a triple bill together for a dollar and a quarter. Feeling good after the movies, I strolled slowly downtown to Canal Street to check out an old friend. Michael was an old business partner in my days of dope dealing and cocaine promotion. He had returned from the Special Forces in Vietnam and had thrown in with me and my dreams of a new criminal empire. He broke the legs, I sold the coke. He set up the purchases and checked out new connections. In the lining of his green army jacket were a cheese cutter, two blocks of wood, and a length of piano wire, which he would playfully wrap around chairs at times and pull, with an unearthly grin on his face. His teeth would all grind together and his arms would expand until the wire sunk deep into the wood. Then he would laugh and kick the chair and it would fall into two pieces. He was a scream. I never saw him use the wire on anybody, but I could easily picture it.

Michael was deliberately quiet as usual when I went to visit. He had mastered the art of leaving questions unanswered, as if he didn't even hear them. The dangerous look on his face discouraged asking again and he would stare at the ceiling from under his wraparound sunglasses until that final second when I was about to ask again. I told him I wanted to buy a Mauser. He laughed but said he could do it.

That night we went all the way uptown to 180th Street in the Cuban neighborhood. Michael told me to wait in the car. I gave him the money and he ran into a four-story walk-up around the corner on St. Nicholas. A few minutes later he returned wearing an atypically big grin and carrying what I took to be the gun wrapped up in his army jacket. "Wait till you see what I've got there for you." When he finally unwrapped it, I could understand his exuberance. It was gorgeous. Nine-millimeter 1918 Mauser painstakingly converted to automatic with a detachable walnut stock and a scope. I was ecstatic. I had seen them use these on TV. Michael was very pleased with himself on such a find. "That sucker will blow people away like rotten watermelon." I loved it. I loved it. I felt a surge of power and adrenaline rushing through my veins and pumping into my brain. I couldn't wait to shoot it. I pulled ferociously on the trigger, emptying the custom thirteen-shot clip into the wall, blowing great holes in the plaster. Michael was amused at the spontaneity of my actions. I think he even appreciated the artistic statement, but the noise would draw cops for sure. So we hopped a quick cab uptown. I slipped Michael some money and left him to pursue his interests in Central Park. His old girlfriend had once suggested to me that he slept in trees in the park and would occasionally leap from the foliage and interrogate unfortunate passersby. I know no such thing for sure.

I checked into the Pierre, after which I put a stocking over my head and relieved my next-door neighbor of his money so that I could afford my stay as well as a few other necessities. I sent out for a tailor, at great expense, and had him make me a suitably conservative charcoal flannel suit for the party. Then I called Mutley and confirmed my plans to attend. As he spoke to me, I could hear him pause and put his hand over the receiver while he asked Kathleen for instructions as to what to say. I could hear her tell him and then him tell me the list of some of the more notable guests to be and I winced at some of the names, whom I had mistakenly assumed had mercifully disappeared from my life forever. The prospect of seeing them again amused me this time and I confess I slept that night with the Mauser under my pillow.

The next day my suit arrived, and I called in a barber to give me the works. He shaved off my beard and sideburns and gave me one of those styled haircuts with little wings over the ears, and when I put on the suit and looked in the mirror, I knew the other guests would never suspect me.

I blended right in. It was perfect. The "look" I had wanted exactly. Just another chump on the street. Joe Doakes, junior advertising exec.

I took a few buses aimlessly around town to check unsolicited reactions to my new appearance. It went over well, with not one person giving me a second look. It took me a while to realize that there was no longer a reason to feel paranoid when I stepped into a crowded place. I was now just a face in the crowd. I didn't know what I was going to do at the party. But I wanted to be prepared for any possibility. I took a cab to Chinatown and bought an arsenal of oriental weaponry: nunchaku sticks (at which I am very proficient), ninja stars, and two razor-sharp daggers, which I practiced with in my hotel room. I found a way to conceal all of these toys under my suit and the Mauser snuggled into my inside pocket, feeling wonderful under my left arm.

When the day of the party finally rolled around, I spent a few hours in the bathroom working on my appearance, combing my hair, something I hadn't done in years; polishing my teeth; and blasting my underarms with deodorant. Personal hygiene is a must for an important social event. I paid particular attention to my cuticles and nails as I had never previously given them much thought. I smoothed my eyebrows and slipped into my suit feeling like an angel. I pictured Ilsa Whiting with her bloated protégé hovering over an imaginary punch bowl trying to nibble discreetly at the hors d'oeuvres and inevitably dribbling caviar all over herself. I imagined her with a big red hole in her face the size of a hockey puck with only her eyebrows indicating her surprise. I intended to be merciful with Mutley. His crime was in being born and I would only want to put him out of his misery with one shot point-blank to the back of the brain. He would slump over like a bull and be dragged out of the room to wherever they put dead millionaires. I imagined him as the by-products they mention on the commercials for dog food, and I thought of a furry little poodle eating the dog food before it was viciously punted into Kathleen Bradford's lap. I would kill her quickly too as the thought of forcible sexual activity was too tempting. In the newspaper accounts to come I wanted no such simple motives suggested. Perhaps she would be left alive and unharmed, forced only to witness the grisly ritual. Her undoubtedly well-planned party would be an all-time bust as her guests were killed, humiliated, and crippled. This was the only thing to do and still show good taste and discretion. So I slid on my new Johnston & Murphy wingtips and took a rented limo over to Sutton Place, where the party was to be held.

The doorman opened the door and ushered me inside and I had to wait as he rang upstairs on the intercom. I was tempted to wrap the receiver around his neck and bounce his head into the buttons for the buzzer but I restrained myself and took the elevator upstairs. On the way up I wondered why they had ever invited me. Certainly our rapport at school had been one of convenience for them as they did not want me to burglarize their room or send rocks through their windows as was my custom at school. I remember the looks of suspicion that would greet my arrival at any school function, the way even their dogs would growl at me when I passed, and the clumsy precautionary measures they would take whenever I would come visiting, nonchalantly sweeping their exposed valuables into their pockets when I entered the room and concealing their drugs and cash. I always found them later.

Mutley greeted me at the door, gibbering enthusiastically for Kathleen to come and see me. She was obviously surprised at my new clean-cut look and she took me around to introduce me to the guests while Mutley fumbled with the record player, apparently knocking his brains for an acceptably cult favorite, Kathleen looked strangely strained; whatever expectations she had had previously were now revising themselves in her little peanut brain. She handed me a glass of champagne, which I sucked on for a while and then bit into, spitting pieces of glass into the cheese spread. Kathleen, to my surprise, looked delighted at my impromptu gesture, and giggling, she took a bite out of her glass and removed it from her mouth with a picking motion of her sculpted fingernails. I looked around the room and noticed some familiar faces. Faces that looked as blank and pasty as the last time I had seen them in the drugged condition in which I was usually found in my college days. Undistorted now by any drugs, the faces seemed just as distorted.

The crowd made lighthearted chatter with an occasional exclamatory shriek to describe a recent orgasm or a new variety of drug. Someone had brought amyl nitrate, and I could hear a frequent popping sound and smell the noxious odor. I declined when offered as I needed my wits about me on this night of nights. Chuck Flounder, who had lived across the hall from me at one time, cornered me by the fireplace and tried to involve me in some nostalgic great moments in dormitory living. I remembered only the unpleasantness. Vomiting in the halls, seducing women who under bar light looked delicious but under the fluorescent lights of the dormitory looked like fish, mouths opening and closing grotesquely. I had not remembered it as pleasant at all. But old

Chuck was beside himself with glee at seeing me after all these years. "It was all so funny, funny, FUNNY FUNNY FUNNY!" I wondered what my nunchaku sticks would do to his face.

Instead, however, I nudged a burning piece of kindling under his cuff and his polyester suit went up midsentence. Chuck ran screaming around the room, finally rolling on the floor while the guests dumped their drinks on him to extinguish the flames. When the flames went out it appeared that Chuck was unhurt, the only damage being to his Naugahyde suit, which had melted on the surface to a shiny wet look. Chuck excused himself and went home to change. As soon as the door closed the partygoers could not contain their laughter. Mutley asked me what had happened as he had been in the bathroom and then proceeded to bore me to tears with an extended interpretation of the hidden meanings in disco music, particularly Barry White. I tried to change the subject and we were joined by a small crowd of interested partyers, come to comment on the recent pyrotechnics. I remembered them from school. They all worked at places now like Gucci, Pucci, and such related enterprises. They were all so happy and successful. They were so pleased with themselves.

I withdrew a ninja star and sent the little disc flying across the room and into the Matisse in the foyer. There was a quiet as everyone looked to Mutley for a reaction, unsure as to the correct expression for their faces. He looked across the room to Kathleen, who laughed nervously, followed by the crowd, who chuckled appreciatively as Mutley tried to mimic my statement by hurling a potted plant at the torn painting. The plant and pot missed their mark by a few yards and crashed into the IV tube, which exploded in a blue cloud. I pushed aside the onlookers, grabbed a firm hold of the color console and, lifting it to my chest, toppled it into the French windows, out onto the balcony, and finally let it drop ten stories into the pavement below, a beautiful slow-motion spiral ending in a very satisfying crash. This was taken as some sort of cue by the guests, and they quickly followed suit, ripping up the carpet, breaking furniture, and carving designs into the wallpaper. I made a beeline for the dining room and sat in the corner, secure in a big mahogany chair. The guests were now on the rampage. Swilling down the alcohol at an accelerated rate while doing all sorts of damage to the room and each other. Mutley and Kathleen tripped together into the vegetables and deli food that had spilled from the toppled refrigerator. Like a hydrophobic dog, Mutley began to savagely dry-hump Kathleen from behind, smearing her face in the potato salad and spilling great quantities of guacamole dip all over himself. I watched from my chair as he pounded away at her; she seemingly enjoying it all a great deal, a line of spittle dribbling down his beet-red face. I walked over and loosened his collar, taking the time to remove a five-pound bag of chopped sirloin from the sink and then tossing it into the punch bowl.

I recognized the man who was punching holes in the loudspeakers with a jade letter opener as the wimp who used to sit across from me in English class and air his neo-Nazi opinions at great length, so I beaned him with a full jar of Kosher dills, after which he took a spill into the cocktail table. The place had become a demented playground as the guests struggled to satisfy their secret urges as quickly as possible before the fun stopped. Each member would turn repeatedly to make sure the other guests were indulging themselves as well and to confirm their approval. Mutley was now on the dining room floor; a short, stout Greek gentleman had him in a headlock. Some of the men had raided the powder room and were now wearing makeup, screaming and laughing like hyperactive children on methedrine. They had the water on in the tub and four or five of them were in together. Bob Reno, a former soccer player on the college team, squeezed into the bathroom and with a quick movement began to piss on the bathers. Soon they were all pissing all over each other and playing with the contents of the medicine cabinet, squirting shaving cream around and giggling naughtily when someone broke out the contraceptive foam. Unable to resist the temptation, I closed the door and leaned a dresser against it, grappling the wall inside until long after the novelty had diminished and they could realize what they were doing. There wasn't much left of the apartment. I expected the police to call soon as well, inquiring about the television set. So I reached into my jacket and whipped out the Mauser.

I held it up over my head pointing to the ceiling, so everyone could see it, then leveled it at the crowd and brought it around in a circle. Death. That ought to liven up this party. All the torn and half-naked people stood frozen in the room, all looking at the shiny steel animal in my hand. My suit was untouched by all the commotion, and they looked at me as some sort of alien beast. I placed the gun in the center of the floor and walked out the door. As I sauntered down the hall, I could hear the first *pop-pop* sounds as they slaughtered themselves like some big ugly lizard eating itself.

The Fish-on-Monday Thing

An excerpt from *Medium Raw: A Bloody Valentine to the World of Food and the People Who Cook*, published in the UK by Bloomsbury in 2010.

I was genuinely angry most mornings, writing *Kitchen Confidential*. An unfocused, aim-in-a-general-direction-and-fire kind of a rage only exacerbated by the fact that my writing "regimen" (such as it was) consisted of a five thirty or six A.M. wake-up, a hurried disgorging of sentences, reminiscences, and hastily reconstructed memories from the previous night (this after a ten- or twelve- or fourteen-hour day in the kitchen, followed invariably by too much to drink and a topple into bed). I'd spit whatever words I had quickly onto the page—no agonizing over sentences for me, there wasn't time anyway—then off to work again: Put on the sauces, cut the meat, portion the fish, crack the peppercorns, cook lunch, and so on. Three thirty, two quick pints down the street, back to Les Halles, either work the line or read the board, then off to Siberia Bar—or simply sit down with the remains of the floor staff for just one more—get drunk *en place*. Sagged down in the back right passenger seat of a yellow Chevy Caprice, legs twisted uncomfortably behind the bulletproof partition—that's where I did my best work, thinking about what I was going to write the next day. Window half-cracked and me halfway or fully in the bag, I'd think about my life as New York City rolled by outside.

As I lived then in Morningside Heights, on the Upper West Side, by the time I got home, my taxi would have passed through a near-comprehensive landscape of greatest hits, all my sorrows, all my joys—as I think the song goes. A densely packed checkerboard pattern of mistakes, failures, crimes, betrayals large and small. The occasional happy spot with good associations would make me smile weakly— before plunging me in the other direction as I'd recall how things got all fucked up, went wrong, or simply just came to . . . *this*. I was always glad to see the spot on Broadway where my then-wife and I had set up our books and records for sale, happy that I wasn't doing *that* anymore—and that there was no longer a need for either of us to adhere to that kind of unrelentingly voracious math. But I was still angry—in the way, I suspect, that mobs get angry: angry about all the things I didn't have and (I was sure) I would never have.

I'd never had health insurance, for one thing. Nor had my wife. And that scared the hell out of me—as getting sick was, on one hand, just not an option, and on the other, increasingly likely as we grew older. A sudden pain in the jaw requiring a root canal would hit the financial picture (such as it was) like a freight train. Total destruction. It would mean groveling. Beg the nice dentist in the filthy-looking office on the ground floor of a housing project to accept payment on the installment plan.

Car commercials made me angry, as I'd never owned a car—or so much as a scooter—and, I was quite sure by now, never would. Home ownership was a concept so beyond imagining as to be laughable. I was so far behind on rent, so ridiculously in arrears on income taxes, that on the rare occasion when I went to bed sober, I'd lie there in terror, my heart pounding in my ears, trying desperately to *not* think the unthinkable: that at any time, either landlord or government or the long-ignored but very much still-there folks at AmEx could take everything, everything away. That "everything" amounted only to somewhere between fourteen and four hundred dollars on a good day was cold comfort. It was only a combination of rent-stabilized apartment, a byzantine, slow-moving, and tenant-friendly housing court, and a wife who could work the system that kept a roof over our heads. And that streak of improbable good luck, too, could run out at any minute.

So, I was afraid. Very afraid. Every day and every night and every time I bothered to think about these things—which was a lot, because that's the way a responsible person with a job who *doesn't* have a drug habit was supposed to think about things: realistically. Frightened people become angry people—as history teaches us again and again. Facing "reality" after a lifetime of doing everything I could to escape it offered no rewards that I could see. Only punishment. No solution presented itself. I couldn't go back (that way was blocked for sure), and I couldn't go forward.

I'd quit heroin and I'd quit methadone and I'd stopped doing cocaine and stopped smoking crack—like everybody tells you to, right? And yet there I was, still broke and still frightened and in a deep financial hole I knew I would never climb out of.

And I was angry about that. Very angry.

I was angry with my wife—very angry, a long-festering and deep-seated resentment that year after year after year she didn't, couldn't, wouldn't *work*. Strong, smart as hell, with a college degree from a Seven Sisters school, solid white-collar experience, and she'd long ago just . . . stopped looking. In nearly two decades, after a promising start, nothing but a couple of short-term, part-time gigs stocking books and sorting in-house mail for near-minimum wage. It made no sense to me, and I resented it bitterly. To be fair, it consumed me out of all proportion, with the kind of smoldering, barely repressed passive-aggressive anger that poisons everything around it. And that, sure as shit, didn't help the situation. Waking up and going to sleep with this basic fact—and the way I then handled that resentment—was contaminating everything. I just couldn't get past it. I didn't get past it. And I made things worse—far worse—in all the drearily predictable ways. Underscore that sentence.

As partners in crime, we'd been—in my mind, anyway—a Great Couple. As solid citizens? Neither of us seemed to know how.

I was angry, too, that all my little-boy dreams of travel and adventure would for absolutely sure never come true—that I'd never see Paris as a grown-up or Vietnam, or the South Pacific, or India, or even Rome. From my vantage point, standing behind the stove at Les Halles, that much was perfectly clear. And, to tell the truth, I only became angrier when my boss, Philippe, sent me to Tokyo for a week to consult, because now I knew what I was missing. Which was—as anyone who's been lucky enough to see those places knows—*everything*. It was as if someone had opened a happy, trippy, groovy, and exotic version of Pandora's box, allowed me to peek inside, into another dimension, an alternate life, and then slammed the thing shut.

I'm sure that many middle-aged, divorced guys could describe a drunken snog with a female croupier in similarly lush—and even apocalyptic—terms. And any "epiphany" I had in Asia was, at the end of the day, already the subject of about a thousand not-very-good movies. I can only say that once I'd stumbled around Asia's impenetrably "foreign" streets, surrounded only by people whose language I would never understand, nostrils filled with strange and wondrous smells, eyes boggling at everything I saw, eating things I'd never dreamed could be so good . . . well . . . I was doomed. I would ultimately have done anything to get some more of that. (Not that anyone was offering.) I knew, too, somewhere deep inside, that sharing would be out of the question. That's a bad thing to learn about yourself.

I was angry, too, in the usual ways: With my mom for having me, for being stupid enough to love me. With my brother for not being a fuckup like me. With my father for dying.

And, naturally, I was angry with myself most of all (people like us always are, aren't we? It's a Lifetime movie almost anyone can star in) for being forty-four years old and still one phone call, one paycheck, away from eviction. For fucking up, pissing away, sabotaging my life in every possible way.

Five years earlier, after the kind of once-in-a-lifetime, freakishly lucky breaks that have been all too common in my life, the kind of thing most aspiring writers only dream of, I'd published two spectacularly unsuccessful novels that had disappeared without a trace, never making it into paperback. This, the general wisdom taught me, effectively finished me in publishing. About this—and maybe only this—I was actually *not* angry. It had been a nice ride, I'd felt, one on which I'd embarked with zero expectations. I'd kept my day job—never imagining I'd do otherwise. The whole enterprise had dropped in my lap, felt like a scam from the get-go, so I'd thankfully never suffered from any delusions of being a "writer." Two uninterrupted hours of sitting at an empty table in a Northridge, California, Barnes & Noble on a one-stop, crackpot and equally crack-brained, self-financed book tour had quickly disabused me of such notions.

When I sat down at my desk every morning to write *Kitchen Confidential* and began clacking away at the keyboard, I was both gloriously free of hope that it would ever be read outside of a small subculture of restaurant people in New York City—and boiling with the general ill will of the unsatisfied, the envious, and the marginal. Let it be funny for cooks and waiters—and fuck everybody else, was pretty much my thinking at the time.

Which worked out okay in the end, as I never could have written the thing had I thought people would actually read it.

So, the result was an angry book in a lot of ways—and, over time, that's what people have come to expect from me. The angry, cynical, snarky guy who says mean things on *Top Chef*—and I guess it would be pretty easy to keep going with that: a long-running lounge act, the exasperatedly enraged food guy. "Rachael Ray? What's up with *that*?!" (Cue snare drum here.) To a great extent, that's already happened.

But looking back at those hurried, hungover early mornings, sitting at my desk with unbrushed teeth, a cigarette in my mouth, and a bad attitude, what was I angry about that I'm *still* angry about today? Who, of all the people and all the things I railed at in that book, really deserved my scorn?

I certainly wasn't angry at Emeril. And the many dreamers and crackpots I wrote about who'd employed me over the years—whatever their sins—are certainly no worse characters than I'd been. In fact, I *loved* them for their craziness, their excesses, their foolishness—their shrewdness or guile, their wastefulness, even their criminality. In almost every case, their choice of the restaurant business as a lifestyle option had cost them far, far more than it had ever cost me.

I wasn't ever angry with any of the people who worked with me. Not in a lasting way. It was they, after all—all of them, heroes and villains alike—who'd kept me in the business all those years. I may have called waiters "waitrons" and joked about abusing them, but I had always believed that if somebody who worked with me went home feeling like a jerk for giving their time and their genuine effort, then it was *me* who had failed *them*—and in a very personal, fundamental way.

No. I instinctively liked and respected anyone who cooked or served food in a restaurant and took any kind of satisfaction in the job. Still feel that way. It is the finest and noblest of toil, performed by only the very best of people.

Okay. I *am* genuinely angry—still—at vegetarians. That's not a shtick. Not angry at them personally, mind you—but in principle. A shocking number of vegetarians and even vegans have come to my readings, surprised me with an occasional sense of humor, refrained from hurling animal blood at me—even befriended me. I have even knowingly had sex with one, truth be told. But what I've seen of the world in the past nine years has, if anything, made me angrier at anyone not a Hindu who insists on turning their nose up at a friendly offer of meat.

I don't care what you do in your home, but the idea of a vegetarian traveler in comfortable shoes waving away the hospitality—the distillation of a lifetime of training and experience—of, say, a Vietnamese *pho* vendor (or Italian mother-in-law, for that matter) fills me with spluttering indignation.

No principle is, to my mind, worth that; no Western concept of "is it a pet or is it meat" excuses that kind of rudeness.

I often talk about the "Grandma rule" for travelers. You may not like Grandma's Thanksgiving turkey. It may be overcooked and dry—and her stuffing salty and studded with rubbery pellets of giblet you find unpalatable in the extreme. You may not even like turkey at all. But it's *Grandma's* turkey. And you are in Grandma's *house*. So shut the fuck up and eat it. And afterward, say, "Thank you, Grandma, why, yes, yes of course I'd *love* seconds."

I guess I understand if your desire for a clean conscience and cleaner colon overrules any natural lust for bacon. But taking your belief system on the road—or to other people's houses—makes me angry. I feel too lucky—now more than ever—too acutely aware what an incredible, unexpected privilege it is to travel this world and enjoy the kindness of strangers to ever, ever be able to understand how one could do anything other than say yes, yes, yes.

I've tried. Really.

I can cheerfully eat vegetarian food and nothing but for about five days at a clip—if I'm in India. And I'm open to the occasional attempts by the opposition to make their case.

Unfortunately, those attempts don't always end happily.

A very nice, truly sweet guy, the boyfriend of a producer I was doing business with a few years back, went out of his way—as gently and as undogmatically as possible—to bring me over to the other side, making it something of a personal mission to get me to acknowledge the possibility of a delicious all-vegan meal. Let me repeat that this was a nice guy, who'd made his choices for what was, I'm sure, a visceral abhorrence for meat. When he saw a pork chop on a plate, I have no doubt, what he really saw was a golden retriever that had died screaming. I'd seen the genuine love this man had for his dogs—the way the poor guy would just tear up at the mention of some awful shelter on the other side of the country. I couldn't find it in my heart to refuse him. I went out to dinner at what was said to be New York's premier fine-dining vegan restaurant, a favorite, I was assured, of Paul McCartney's (not exactly a selling point—but a measure of how earnest were his efforts to get me in the door). The food was expensive and painstakingly—even artfully— prepared, and, admittedly, it did not entirely suck.

Over organic wines and much convivial conversation, I even passed on a suggestion (via my dining companion) to "Sir Paul" that I thought might be helpful in his very public efforts to save cute animals. I ventured that if he seriously wanted to see a *lot* of the rarest, most beautiful, and most endangered animals live longer, healthier lives— and maybe even multiply and prosper—he should, I advised, buy a few million dollars' worth of Viagra and Cialis, start spreading that stuff around for free where it mattered, with accompanying public service announcements, in the parts of Asia where they think bear's paw, rhino horn, and tiger dicks are good boner medicine. Unlike these stratospherically expensive traditional Chinese remedies—the end products of an enormously profitable black market that rewards the killing and even slow torturing of endangered animals—Viagra will actually make your dick hard, and for cheap. Hand out a few million little blue pills to middle-aged Chinese dudes—maybe even throw in a hooker, to boot—I suggested, and you'll see some changed hearts and minds. Break a centuries-old pattern of truly monstrous and extreme cruelty to what are often the rarest and most beautiful of animals! (I was later told that he'd actually passed this idea along. A conversation I would like to see a videotape of someday.)

After a surprisingly serviceable meal, I felt pretty good about things. I'd been a nice guy, I thought, had made an effort to be open-minded. The meal hadn't sucked. We'd even managed to find some common ground.

But then, months later, the poor bastard sent me an e-mail asking (innocently enough) for some statement of support—I think, for the Humane Society. Now, I *like* the Humane Society for the most part. I may disagree violently with their policy on—and activities on behalf of—anti–foie gras legislation, but I do like cats and dogs. (I've adopted one shelter cat after another for much of my life.) I'm supportive of any effort to stop dog fighting, to spay animals, and to prevent abuse of domestic animals.

I don't like circuses and, given the chance, would probably vote against the indenturing of elephants and lions and tigers, or any other animals they might want to stand on chairs or train to juggle. I frankly think Siegfried or Roy—whichever one of those guys got mauled by a tiger—got what he deserved. Tigers, to my way of thinking, *like* to maul people, they're certainly built for the job, and anything preventing them from doing that on the one hand—while tempting them with a German in a sparkly, cerulean-blue suit on the other—is clearly animal cruelty. Somebody who abuses an animal for the sheer joy of it—or solely for purposes of entertainment—should receive, at very least, equal ill treatment.

I'll go farther into PETA territory:

I would have preferred that Steve Irwin, "Crocodile Hunter"—regardless of his saintly conservationist prattle—had ended up as "Crocodile Chow." *That* would have been some rough but entirely appropriate justice. In my opinion, the loud, irritating little fuck was in the business of disturbing, poking, tormenting, and generally annoying animals, who would have surely been far happier had they never met him. And if Bindi Irwin lived in my neighborhood, by the way, I would have called Child Protective Services on her parents years ago.

So, contrary to my reputation, I'm like Saint Francis of fucking Assisi compared to what you might think—a friend to animals large and small, feeder of strays, adopter of runt kittens. A man who, though opposed to vegetarian orthodoxy, is still a reasonable fellow, willing, at least, to listen to the other guy's point of view.

Until, that is, I got back from Beirut, fresh from a war zone, to find in my inbox an earnest plea for support from my vegan dining companion. The urgency of his tone as he described what was happening to stray cats and dogs somewhere grated on me badly. As I read on, I found myself becoming angrier and angrier—soon becoming furious.

I'd just seen a city not very much unlike Miami bombed back twenty fucking years, I answered in a lather of righteous indignation. From a shameful distance, I'd watched, every day, as neighborhoods filled with people were smashed to rubble. I'd woken up and gone to sleep to the rumble of bombs and rockets rolling through the floor of my otherwise comfortable hotel room. And then seen, up close, the faces of people who'd lost everything—and sometimes *everyone*—in their lives: the fear and hopelessness and confusion of thousands of people, packed onto landing craft with the few possessions they could carry, off and away to uncertain futures. For nothing. For the "best" intentions, I'm sure—they always are, aren't they? But, ultimately, for nothing.

I had come straight from that—to this: this message filled with whiny, plaintive outrage on the behalf of the strays of Denver or something like that. There were strays in Beirut, too, I spat out, beginning what I'd intended to be a measured, sympathetic response. Surely, I suggested, where *people* were being bombed, and *whole fucking neighborhoods* knocked down to rubble, some doggies got hurt, too? I went on, warming (if not overheating) to my subject, venomously musing that when whole fucking families get crushed in their homes, abandoned pets can become a problem. Having just flown from the tarmac of a floating refugee camp, I now surfed deliriously on a wave of bile. Expanding the scope of my observations to include other places I'd been and other things I'd seen in my travels, I pointed out—any vestige of measured civility gone by now—that it was, perhaps, worth noting as well that *any place* where people were treated like animals—stacked in shantytowns, favelas, communes, and hutments—that animals suffered first and worst. Nobody gives a fuck about cute doggies or cats, much less a fucking dolphin or a white rhino, for that matter, when 90 percent of your diet is fucking bread—when you're lucky enough to get it—or pounded manioc gruel. Where charred monkey on a stick (in fur) is a lifesaving gift for a family, I spewed, all those neatly anthropomorphized animals we so love—like your fucking Yorkie (this was a low blow)—are seen as nothing more than bush meat. Sadistically putting the boot in, I gave examples of places where people are concerned that men in black vans might be coming at night to put hoods over their heads and take them away. Possibly for something they may have casually said, or a neighbor might have thought they casually said—or falsely reported they may have casually said.

I believe I might have mentioned Ceauçescu's Bucharest as an example. Plowing under an entire neighborhood and displacing its residents to build a pharaoh-scale palace, the megalomaniacal dictator had created an instant and frighteningly large population of abandoned dogs. Reproducing at an astounding rate, the desperate animals begat countless roving packs of terrifying and vicious feral dogs, wild, aggressive, and hungry predators who knew nothing but the streets. Parts of Bucharest became, particularly at night, a potentially dangerous jungle—with all the dog-on-dog, dog-on-man, and man-on-dog violence imaginable. Embarrassed by this all-too-visible phenomenon, the people's representatives were urged to deal with the matter. The dogs were eventually hunted down and exterminated in great number. If the death of the "Genius of the Carpathians" and his wife is any example (thoughtfully videotaped and broadcast), one can only imagine how gently the dogs were dispatched.

I believe I ended my bilious and cruel masterwork of an e-mail with the image of the gentle and beloved bovines of India, revered, protected by a population of people who worship them as life-givers, divine. Wandering freely through the streets, always and famously with the right of way, they were free as well, I thought my friend should know, to starve slowly to death, to eat garbage already picked over many times by equally hungry humans, often settling on the discarded plastic bags ubiquitous to impoverished communities where hope is almost gone and municipal garbage removal is a sometimes—if ever—thing. The plastic bags, of course, are indigestible, I explained, gradually becoming twisted and balled up in the cow's guts and eventually—after what is surely a long period of agonizing discomfort—killing them.

Leaving him with this awful image, I concluded that given the inconvenient and annoyingly complicated relationship between the conditions in which people live and his adorable animal friends, maybe he should start thinking about *people* first.

Granted, my reaction was on a par with suddenly taking a baseball bat to the barista who mistakenly used skim instead of soy milk on your latte, but I was really and truly angry. Not at my poor, unsuspecting friend, undeserving of such treatment (from whom I've never heard since). He just wanted to save a few animals, after all. It was just his bad luck that he'd asked *me* for help—and at a very bad time. I was angry at all the shit he made me think about.

And I'm still angry.

But I digress.

From the softer-edged distance of a changed and far more comfortable life, I've searched for a root cause, a common denominator that might explain my seemingly rote, instinctive, reflexive scorn for anyone cooking on TV (or in films, for that matter) whom I see, somehow, as unworthy.

What has Guy Fieri ever done to *me*? Why should I care if something Sandra Lee made on her show came from a can—or arrived held aloft by celestial virgins on a cubic zirconium–encrusted sleigh straight from Tuscany or Provence or fucking Valhalla? What does it matter if Rachael can cook or not? People *like* her! What's my problem? So *what* if the contestants on *Hell's Kitchen* are transparently delusional and hopeless? I shouldn't get mad about it, right?

But I do.

Here's what I'd like to think.

Back when I started cooking—back in the heady, crazy, admittedly lower-standard days of the early 1970s, when it was all about speed, endurance, attitude, physical toughness, and the ability to work through every variety of self-inflicted punishment—people handled food differently. The distinction between the way a "professional" and a home cook handled food was easy to spot: the professional cook was rougher with his food. (Obviously, I'm not talking about Lutèce or the Four Seasons or the better restaurants of the day here.) The fact was, cooks tended to slap their meat around a little bit more than was absolutely necessary, to drop portions of fish onto the cutting board with an audible panache that fell something short of delicacy. Looking like you didn't give a shit—while cranking out food with the speed and efficiency and consistency of someone who did—was something of the fashion. You saw it in the rough, easy familiarity with which professional butchers took apart a primal section, the too-cool-to-be-bothered expression that said, "I could do this in my sleep."

Simply put, neither I nor the people I worked with—or admired—particularly "respected the ingredient," as chefs are likely to call it these days. We were frankly brutal with our food. I don't know exactly when that attitude changed in me—somewhere, I'm sure, around the time I started putting on airs and spouting shit from the *Larousse*. But over time, without my realizing it was happening, my attitude *did* change, hardening, eventually, into a deeply held belief that doing bad things to food, especially when one does them knowingly—or wasting perfectly good food, or, in general, disrespecting it—is fundamentally *wrong*, a sin (if such a thing exists), a violation of a basic contract with decency, with the world and its citizens. In a word: evil.

Traveling has only reinforced that feeling.

I'm sure that I'm not alone in feeling an almost physical pain when I see somebody cut heedlessly into an unrested steak. Most people I know who have cooked for a living will react with a groan or a wince if they see someone committing an easily preventable crime against food. But most of my friends don't actually get angry when somebody who knows (or should know) better massacres a perfectly good dish on TV.

I do.

I don't dislike Guy Fieri, I realized, after many viewings of his cooking shows, much soul-searching at my personal ashram, and many doses of prescription hypnotics. I just dislike—*really* dislike—the idea that somebody would put Texas-style barbeque inside a fucking nori roll. I was, and remain, angry that there are genuine pitmasters who've made a calling of getting pork shoulder just right—and sushi chefs who worked three years on rice alone before being deemed worthy to lay hands on fish—and here's some guy on TV blithely smashing those two disciplines together like junkers in a demolition derby. A pre-chopped onion is *not* okay, the way I look at it—no matter what Rachael or Sandra tells you. The shit in a can is not anywhere nearly as good—and almost always more expensive—than stuff you can often make yourself just as quickly. It's . . . it's just . . . wrong to tell people otherwise.

It is, of course, ludicrous for me to be insulted on behalf of strangers who would probably find my outrage completely misplaced, embarrassing, and probably even deranged. I don't claim to speak for them and am unworthy, in any case, of doing so. I'm just saying that some of the shit I see some people doing to food on television causes a physical reaction in some deeply buried reptile part of my brain—and that makes me angry. It makes me want to say mean things. It probably shortens my life every time it happens.

One might expect Thomas Keller, who famously insists on storing his fish in their natural "swimming" position, to feel this way about food being mistreated. But me? Where do I get off? one might well ask.

It's more an affliction than the expression of any high-minded ideals.

I watch Mark Bittman enjoy a perfectly and authentically prepared Spanish paella on TV, after which he demonstrates how his viewers can do it at home—in an aluminum saucepot—and I want to shove my head through the glass of my TV screen and take a giant bite out of his skull, scoop the soft, slurry-like material inside into my paw, and then throw it right back into his smug, fireplug face. The notion that anyone would believe Catherine Zeta-Jones as an obsessively perfectionist chef (particularly given the ridiculously clumsy, 1980s-looking food) in the wretched film *No Reservations* made me want to vomit blood, hunt down the producers, and kick them slowly to death. (Worse was the fact that the damn thing was a remake of the unusually excellent German chef flick *Mostly Martha*.) On *Hell's Kitchen*, when Gordon Ramsay pretends that the criminally inept, desperately unhealthy gland case in front of him could *ever* stand a chance in hell of surviving even three minutes as "executive chef of the new Gordon Ramsay restaurant" (the putative grand prize for the finalist), I'm inexplicably actually angry on *Gordon's* behalf. And *he's* the one making a quarter-million dollars an episode—very contentedly, too, from all reports.

The eye-searing "Kwanzaa Cake" clip on YouTube, of Sandra Lee doing things with store-bought angel food cake, canned frosting, and corn nuts, instead of being simply the unintentionally hilarious viral video it should be, makes me mad for all humanity. I. Just. Can't. Help. It.

I wish, really, that I was so far up my own ass that I could somehow believe myself to be some kind of standard-bearer for good eating—or ombudsman, or even the deliverer of thoughtful critique. But that wouldn't be true, would it?

I'm just a cranky old fuck with what, I guess, could charitably be called "issues."

And I'm *still* angry.

But *eat* the fucking fish on Monday already. Okay?

I wrote those immortal words about *not* going for the Monday fish, the ones that'll haunt me long after I'm crumbs in a can, knowing nothing other than New York City. And times, to be fair, have changed. Okay, I still would advise against the fish special at TGI McSweenigan's, "A Place for Beer," on a Monday. Fresh fish, I'd guess, is probably not the main thrust of their business. But things are different now for chefs and cooks. The odds are better than ever that the guy slinging fish and chips back there in the kitchen actually gives a shit about what he's doing. And even if he doesn't, these days he has to figure that you might actually know the difference.

Back when I wrote the book that changed my life, I was angriest—like a lot of chefs and cooks of my middling abilities—at my customers. They've changed. I've changed.

About them, I'm not angry anymore.

I Quit My Job Yesterday

An unpublished handwritten short story about quitting a job, date unknown.

(1)

~~I~~ quit my job yesterday.
It was beautiful.

On a busy Sunday afternoon, in the
middle of ~~the shift~~ a boozy brunch. I took off my apron,
collected my ~~things~~ from my ~~office~~ desk, and
walked out the door, stopping only to collect
my pay from ~~the~~ my stammering boss. ~~the~~
~~tried~~ The sweaty little creep had ~~some~~ a hard pme
~~difficulty~~ counting out my last weeks pay,
~~keeping~~ ~~with~~ ALL THOSE crumpled twent~~ies~~ and at the same time
PARTING maintaining his composure. I ~~was leaving~~ LEFT
him neck deep in shit and he knew it;
but every muscle in his face and neck
strained together in a concerted effort,
at an expression of nonchalance tempered only
perhaps ~~by~~ by a slight disappointment at
~~my~~ the ~~sorrows~~ of the missed opportunities
I was leaving behind as I walked out
the door. ~~For~~ The benefit of the
waiters, cooks and counter people ~~who~~
~~all~~ all of whom watched from the
corners of their eyes, he shook his
head as if he was sorry for me,
and for ~~the~~ shortsightedness, the lack of
faith in his dream of epicurean elysium
fields franchised coast to coast he
did his best—but what he hoped to be
a kindly look of pity for the young
disbeliever who walked from grace out into
the cold world—was instead a shinny

taught mask of terror and disbelief ~~He too~~ He was looking over at the
rotire grill-man as I turned the
corner ~~as~~ wondering no doubt who
~~and how~~ would cook the thousands of
chicken orders that would soon be
yelled across the counter and through
the phones. Who would order the
chickens for tomorrow? From where.
Who would marinate them? and on
what and for how long. Who
would cut them? Who would do this?
And ~~how~~ who would get them
to do it for the ~~money~~ paltry sums
he was ~~prepared~~ to pay?

I ~~walked~~ Never did ~~that before I saw it~~ happen
~~I walked out the door~~ middle
of a shift. This was a first. Never
done that before though I had fantasized
about it a thousand times; dropping my
apron to the floor, putting on my
street clothes and walking out the
door leaving a busy kitchen and
a dining room full of impatient
customers to spin out into chaos and
hysteria behind me.

Afraid of the possibility of

an ugly scene in public, the
owner paid me with trembling, fat
little fingers. I shook his dead
fish hand, mumbled an insincere
apology — and headed straight uptown
in a taxi. I had 275 dollars
in my pocket and I was going
to spend every cent on crack
when I got to ~~85~~th and
Amsterdam. I had no money in
the bank. I ~~was~~ still owed AMEX
many thousands for my honeymoon,
and I had no prospects for
future employment I knew.
But a rash, impulsive and ~~grandiose~~
foolish gesture like this had
a grandiose, futile ~~esthetic~~
kind of a glory to it that deserved
no less than an even more
ill-considered and self indulgent
gesture to commemorate it.
    So two hours later I had
spent every bit of money I had
~~on~~ on a few off-white pebbles of
now long metabolized freebased. I
had smoked every crumb, scoured the
floor for any I might have

dropped, and had inhaled as well
every bit of black foul tasting scraping
from the carbon encrusted pyrex pipe.
Lying naked, sweating and ~~re~~ grinding
my molars ~~by~~ ~~tense~~ like a hyperactive gerbil
I squirmed and scratched on ~~the~~ my mattress
and considered those of my possessions
which might bring me ready cash at
this unlikely hour after 10 on
a Sunday night.
The telephone rang once and the
sound of ~~the~~ my taped voice on
the answering machine interrupted
my designs on the television. I had
already in my drug addled fervor
~~decide~~ ~~resigned~~ come to the conclusion
that by and large, I didn't really
need ~~the~~ most of my appliances.
And how often did I really listen
to records anymore? Not very often
I had to admit. And the records?
I'd played them all anyway....
And who needs a turntable if you
don't buy records? I certainly didn't.
The new music rarely tempted
me sufficiently to buy a record.
Didn't need the damn thing. Those old
records either.

So about now, the ^most pleasant prospect
I can think of for the next
few minutes/hours/days is to
~~pull~~ tear my teeth out, shave my head
with a rusty grapefruit knife and
go charging headlong through the window
in a final bleeding but graceful arc
onto Riverside Drive, six floors below.
Flop onto the pavement with a leaky-red
toothless smile, looking up at some blue-
haired pigeon-feeder with my dead,
glass-bunny eyes. Just the thought of
it feels ever so slightly... restful—
the painful frustrating buzzing in
my back brain turned off at last.
Plug pulled like an old appliance.
One of those noisy Christmas novelties,
all flashing lights and clever motion,
an egg-scrambler, smokeless ashtray,
~~foot~~-massager, electric toothbrush,
shoe buffer, used once, ~~largely~~ if
only for entertainment value, ~~then~~
consigned to its resting place in the
closet. Can't throw it out because of
the long forgotten sentiment involved
in its origin but too useless to
allow out of its box to buzz or spin,
or flash or hum till it ~~makes~~ demands
batteries, repairs or decisions as to its fate.

I used to think it was them. A ~~joke;~~
~~something~~ we'd call Restaurateur's Syndrome
~~when~~ ~~a few of chefs would~~ get together
and ~~talk shop.~~ We'd laugh ~~as one after~~
~~the other~~ we'd list the symptoms – each
~~new~~ one ~~met~~ recognized with more laughs
and often a spontaneous chorus of
voices mimicking the words of persons
who though never ~~met~~ – were the same
in tone, content, ~~and~~ ~~the~~ As we
talked of the scores of histories
of owners, each chef with a dozen
or more to mine for anecdotes, there
similarities grew more chilling, less
funny until ~~the~~ a unifying
force, one single ~~bundle of motivation,~~
affliction, ~~a~~ preying it seemed on
the nervous systems, brains, bodies
and souls of restaurant owners
everywhere, reared its head and made
itself known, with all its familiar
manifestations.
   Our bosses past present seemed interchangable,
all drawn to ~~all driven by~~ the same initial
vision of themselves as a white suited Bogart
in their own Ricks Café, signing checks
for vips. But largesse inevitably became
largeness. And as their dreams

deteriorated at ~~a rate~~ the same speed
as their livers, most signed checks were
for themselves as they sucked down more
drinks at their own bars than their
best paying customers – and then worried
~~to~~ and wondered who was stealing from
them. Surely they couldn't be drinking
all that booze. The disparity in their
inventories and projections surely was not
entirely their doing?

Tortured by the same questions – all of them
as they stand wringing their hands looking
up and down the street (is it the right street?)
from the front door on an empty rainy tuesday
in february...

"Why aren't they coming?"
"When are they coming?"
"Will they come if I put Chicken Hawaiian
on the menu?"
"Mr. X said we should have Osso Bucco?
Should I put Osso Bucco on the menu.
Will they come then?
Are the prices too high?"
Are they too low?
Is the bartender stealing?"
It's the chef. If I had the right chef
If I had the right food?
Should I add more Italian food?
Should we be an Italian Restaurant

"Is it the neighborhood?"
"Is American Food Peaking? Is it Over?"
"California, what is California Food."
"I'm getting an ulcer. There's blood in my stuff!"

We're washing food! We simply have to order less at a time - make sure nothing goes to waste - AND those food costs - those food cost forms the chef talked about during his interview Gotta Start USING THOSE!

IV

Being a Chef

Tony really didn't think of himself as a chef later on, and there are simple reasons for that; he stopped working in the kitchen at Les Halles by the early 2000s. But I suspect it's also because the more famous he got, the more he was able to encounter his hero chefs and see them in their element. He really admired innovative and exacting chefs of all kinds, and appreciated them with the flourish of a connoisseur. At the same time, his tastes never lifted him up so that he lost perspective, and his sense of camaraderie with line cooks and the unheralded stewards of the kitchen was unshakable. He wrote profiles of chefs he admired, but it was perhaps in his fiction where he was freest to dwell in the Dostoyevskian mindset of the man behind the grill, cooking up endless fish fillets for diners he detested. Did Tony feel that way? No, but he certainly enjoyed spending time in the mind of someone who did.

Gordon Ramsay

An excerpt from *A Cook's Tour: In Search of the Perfect Meal*, originally published by Bloomsbury in 2001.

Finally, there's England's greatest chef, or England's biggest bully, depending on which paper you're reading at the time—the fearsome and prodigiously talented Gordon Ramsay. I'd been hearing about this guy for years. Ex-footballer. Formerly with Robuchon, Ducasse, Guy Savoy, Marco Pierre White. A legendary wordsmith in the kitchen—famed for excoriating his crew, ejecting food critics, speaking his mind bluntly and undiplomatically. A while back, I was told about the cinéma vérité *Boiling Point* series, in which the beleaguered Ramsay was said to behave monstrously to his staff. Intrigued, I managed to track down a copy of the videotape series. To my mind, Ramsay was sympathetic from beginning to end. I rooted for him as he sweated out the beginning of a service period for a massive banquet at Versailles, ill-equipped, with only a rent-a-staff of indolent bucket heads to help him. I cheered when he summarily dismissed a waiter for guzzling water in full view of the dining room. *Pour décourager les autres*, I'm guessing. I suffered as he suffered the interminable wait for his much-hoped-for third Michelin star and was heartbroken when he didn't get it. (He since has.) Those who can't understand why a chef operating at Ramsay's level gets a little cranky, or appears to be operating at a higher and more self-important pitch than their boss, simply don't understand what it's like to work in a professional kitchen. They certainly don't understand what it takes to be the best in that world. It is not only how well you can cook that makes a great chef, but your ability to cook brilliantly, day in and day out—in an environment where a thousand things can go wrong, with a crew that oftentimes would just as happily be sticking up convenience stores, in a fickle, cost-conscious, capricious world where everybody is hoping that you fail.

Is he really such a complete bastard? Let's put it this way: On a recent visit to his restaurant in Chelsea, I recognized large numbers of staff—both front and back of the house—from *Boiling Point*. Years later and they're still there. When Ramsay walked out of Aubergine, the entire staff, service staff included—an incredible forty-five people—chose to go with him. That's really the most telling statistic. Does he still enjoy the loyalty of his crew? He does. No cook shows up every day in Gordon Ramsay's kitchen, works those kinds of hours, offers themselves up daily to the rigors of a three-star service period, toiling in a small, hot space where at any moment they could get a painful and humiliating ass reaming because Gordon Ramsay is the biggest bastard or the biggest bully in England. They show up every day and work like Trojans because he's the best. Because when they finally walk out that door to seek their own fortunes, they won't even have to write up a résumé. Say you worked for three years with Gordon Ramsay, and that's all any chef or owner should need to know.

There's another factor overlooked in the rush to brand Ramsay as rude, crude, brutish, and cruel. In the professional kitchen, if you look someone in the eye and call them a "fat, worthless, syphilitic puddle of badger crap" it doesn't mean you don't like them. It can be—and often is—a term of endearment.

Bottom line is, his food's good. After all, it is about the food, isn't it?

I had two meals at his restaurant in Chelsea, and both were absolutely world-class. A great chef at the top of his game. There's yet another overlooked dimension to Ramsay that doesn't fit with the depiction of an uppity, lower-class lout overly jacked on testosterone. Ramsay was trained as a pâtissier. This is significant—like discovering that a right-wing politician was a Bolshevik in his youth. Few chefs can really and truly bake. Most chefs, like me, harbor deep suspicions of their precise, overly fussy, somehow feminine, presentation-obsessed counterparts in the pastry section. All that sweet, sticky, messy, goopy, delicate stuff. Pastry, where everything must be carefully measured in exact increments—and made the same way every single time—is diametrically opposed to what most chefs live and breathe, the freedom to improvise, to throw a little of this and a little of that any damn place they want. Ramsay's food resonates with his training in pastry. It is precise, colorful, artfully sculpted or teased into shape (though not too teased). It is the product of that end point in a chef's development—the perfect balance of masculine and feminine, the yin and the yang, if you will.

What do I mean? Look at Roberto, my grill man. He's got a metal rod rammed through his eyebrow, a tattoo of a burning skull on his chest, muscles on his muscles. Rob Zombie and Metallica are his idea of easy listening. He's done jail time for assault. Not a guy you'd invite to an evening at the opera. But watch Roberto cook. He leans over that plate and delicately, carefully drizzles sauce from a favorite spoon, gently applies an outer ring of sauce, then sensuously drags a toothpick through it. He tastes everything. Looks at his plates with a decorator's eye for color and texture. Treats a fillet of fish as tenderly and as lovingly as a woman's erect nipple. Piles cute, girly little garnishes into high, cloudlike piles of gossamer-thin crunchiness. He's doing what everyone told him growing up that only women should do. (Ramsay's own father told him cooking was basically for poofs and that chefs were all ponces.) We work in aprons, for fuck's sake! You better have balls the size of jackfruits if you want to cook at a high level, where an acute sense for flavor and design, as much as brutality and vigilance, is a virtue. And be fully prepared to bulldoze any miserable cocksucker who gets in your way.

Both times I visited his restaurant, Ramsay was in the kitchen, supervising every dish that came out, riding his crew like rented mules. He wasn't gliding through the dining room, sucking up to his public. He's a cook in twenty-first-century England; that means he's an obsessive, paranoid, conspiratorial control freak. A hustler, media-manipulator, artist, craftsman, bully, and glory hound—in short, a chef's chef. That I found him polite, charming, witty, and gracious and am saying so here will probably be an embarrassment to him. For that, I apologize. His detractors should be so lucky as to taste the absolutely stunning braised beef and foie gras I ate at his restaurant—a dish so sumptuous that I am forced to use that word. A ham hock terrine of really extraordinary subtlety and flavor, a lobster ravioli with fresh green pea puree that revealed—as all food reveals its creator's true nature—a level of perception and sensitivity that can be a liability in the mosh-pit subculture of professional kitchens. Here's a guy who risked everything in his career, many times over. He walked away from a career in football when it was made clear he'd never play in the bigs. He endured a procession of stages in some very tough French kitchens. He bolted from his first restaurant, entangling himself in potentially enormous liabilities just when he was in sight of the mountaintop. He loudly announced he was going for three Michelin stars and then stayed on course until he got them. Rather than kiss the asses of all those people who might—under ordinary circumstances—be expected to be helpful to him, he has consistently kicked them in the teeth or even viciously sucker punched them. It's very hard for me not to like a guy like that. And every day those stars are sitting on him like six-ton flagstones, defying any who might choose to try knocking them off.

England's worst boss? I don't think so. England's worst boss is the boss who doesn't give a fuck, someone who's wasting his employees' time, challenging them to do nothing more ambitious than show up. Understand that in no-name pit stops and casual dining establishments, it's just a mistake when a cook forgets a single unpeeled fava bean or a tiny smudge of grease, but in a three-star restaurant, it's treason. In the cruel mathematics of two- and three-star dining establishments, a customer who has a good meal will tell two or three people about it. A person who has an unsatisfactory meal will tell ten or twenty. It makes for a much more compelling anecdote. That one unpeeled fava bean is the end of the world. Or it could be.

As most really good cooks or commis working in similar circumstances will readily tell you: Mess with the chef at your peril. It's his name on the door.

I've Seen Some Shit

An excerpt from *Appetites*, published in the UK by Bloomsbury in 2016.

During a dark period of my life, I worked in the twilight world of fly-by-night catering, usually under an alias (for reasons I'd rather not get into, as I'm uncertain about the relevant statutes of limitations). Later, I was the chef of a large nightclub and banquet facility in midtown Manhattan.

So I've worked a *lot* of parties. I've written menus and prepared finger food for many tens of thousands of fingers over the years. Probably hundreds of thousands.

I've seen some shit

I've also learned to hold certain truths to be self-evident

It is obvious, for instance, that when you're throwing a cocktail party with food that most of your guests will eat while standing up, you're expecting more guests than you have seats for, and therefore need to plan accordingly.

Here, then, are some basic rules. While not exactly the wisdom of the ages, these fundamentals will prove useful when planning a party:

* Ask yourself, when writing the menu, "Will my guests have to balance a plate on their knee? Will they need a fork? A knife?" If the answer to any of these questions is yes, re-write your menu. Otherwise, you are inviting a goat rodeo of spilled food, awkward conversations, and horrifying cleanup.

* Will my guests be able to pick up the food cleanly? Meaning: Will the structural integrity of the hors d'oeuvres enable your guests to eat them without dribbling all over their presumably expensive clothing?

* Can women with carefully applied lipstick fit said food items in their mouths without messing it up? And without distending their mouths or cheeks in a way they might believe to be unflattering to their appearance?

* Hopefully, some of your guests will be having sex after the party. Hopefully with you—but even if they're not, you need to consider the residual effects of the hors d'oeuvres you serve them. Excessive garlic, raw onions, lutefisk, and durian fruit

would all be, for this reason, inadvisable. Whether the hors d'oeuvres will leave hunks of food stuck between their teeth is also something you might consider.

✳   Will there be enough for everyone? Plan on 3 to 4 appetizers per guest if dinner will follow, and 6 to 10 appetizers per person, depending on the girth of your guests, if the appetizers are being served in lieu of dinner.

All that being said, the single most important lesson I learned over the course of many years, and many, many parties, is this humbling but inescapable fact: that no matter what you serve, no matter how beautifully presented, strikingly garnished, exotic in flavor, or expensive (I don't care if you're serving up tubs of beluga and fresh, still-steaming buckwheat blinis, or shrimp the size of a baby's arm), what everybody wants, what they will be all over like a swarm, every time, is commercially made freezer-case-sourced pigs in fucking blankets. It doesn't matter who your guests are. They will eat them, and they will love them. Whether this involves post-ironic posturing or just straightforward enthusiasm, they will love them just the same.

So the lesson here is this: **Always keep some pigs in blankets in the freezer.** They're the workhorses of the cocktail party. Did your guests hit the limited amount of crab cakes too hard? Afraid of running out? Send out a tray of pigs in blankets. They'll be delighted. Truffled larks' tongues in aspic all gone? No one will give a fuck once you send out those little doggies. And they'll think you're a genius.

The Program

An excerpt from *Bone in the Throat*, originally published by Villard Books in 1995.

The chef stepped reluctantly into the shower. The bathroom was filled with steam. It was a hot day, but he broke into goose bumps. The drain wasn't working well, and soon empty bottles of shampoo and conditioner were bobbing around him in the ankle-deep water, souvenirs of a long-gone girlfriend.

Teeth chattering, the chef turned off the water and wrapped himself tightly in a dirty towel. He stood shivering in front of the mirror.

His face in the bathroom mirror was pale and bloodless. Tiny pupils floated around in watery, bloodshot eyes. His thick brown hair was too long, sticking up at odd angles, and his sideburns were uneven. The chef opened his mouth and grimaced at himself, examining his teeth. One tooth was missing on the right side, but you couldn't see it; there was one crumbling molar on the left, also invisible to the casual observer, and a chipped eyetooth.

The chef moved his eyes down over his naked, bony chest: protruding ribs, the stomach that was showing the beginnings of a paunch. He examined his arms. There were no tracks to speak of, only a small, yellowish bruise in the crook of his left arm. He walked into the living area of his narrow apartment and put a CD into a portable player. He looked around the room.

The chef was suddenly struck by how little remained in the way of possessions from his previous lives. There was a mattress on the floor, a twenty-one-inch TV set, the CD player, a few CDs, the tiny speakers. A few cables lay useless on a bare shelf, left behind when he sold the tuner, amplifier, cassette deck, turntable, and big speakers. The records were gone too, sold off with most of his books. He'd actually stood there in the street, selling his treasured collection of cookbooks, the classic LPs from the sixties and seventies, many of them irreplaceable. The first Stooges album . . . that Yardbirds record that was only on the shelf a week before they pulled it . . . the Dolls records . . . that Nazz album, the one with the red vinyl. All gone. Sold for as little as a dollar each.

The Velvet Underground played "Sweet Jane" in the background while he dressed. He selected a long-sleeve three-button T-shirt from his closet, first sniffing it to determine if it was clean enough. He put on a pair of tight black Levi's, ripped in the knee; tube socks; and a pair of black elk-skin cowboy boots with damaged heels.

He rummaged around in the pile of unpaid bills and unopened mail on the top of his desk (not a desk really; just a sheet of plywood resting on cinder blocks and milk crates). Underneath a rent notice, he found the white pamphlet he was looking for. He folded it neatly and slipped it into his pants pocket. He took a last look at himself in the bathroom mirror, ran his hands through his hair, turned off the music, and let himself out the door.

He was sniffling and covered with a sickly sweat by the time he reached Cooper Square. He checked the address on the pamphlet and walked into an anonymous, municipal-type building through double glass doors. A security guard stopped him just inside the lobby.

"Who do you want to see?" demanded the guard.

"I'd like to see Mr. James, the director of Intake," said the chef.

"And your name is?"

"Ricard . . . Michael Ricard. I spoke to him on the phone."

The security guard stepped over to a small desk and turned down a clock radio playing Soca music. He pressed the intercom button and paged Mr. James to come to the front desk. There was a short wait. The elevator doors opened, and a stout black man with a shaved head and military bearing emerged, looking distracted and in a hurry.

"Mr. Ricard," he said, shaking the chef's hand like he was taking his pulse. "If you'd come with me, please."

They took the elevator to the second floor and walked down a long hall that smelled of disinfectant. The walls were painted institutional green. The floor was gray linoleum, worn through in spots. The chef noticed posters Scotch-taped to the walls, saying things like DO NOT LOITER IN THE NEIGHBORHOOD and REMEMBER TO THOROUGHLY CLEAN AND STERILIZE YOUR WORKS.

They passed a long line of identical cubicles. The doors were open, and inside each one, the chef could see a bored counselor sitting at a desk, with maybe a potted plant and a file cabinet. In each room, an animated junkie sat in a chair on the other side of the desk, spinning a tale of woe. The chef heard one loud voice, protesting an injustice. "I was jus' standin' there," said the voice. "I wasn't doin' no drugs. I wasn't lookin' for no drugs . . . They took my bottle off a me. Man said he was gonna put a cap in my ass! I said, 'Whassup with that?' Now you tellin' me I gotta go back to six-day? That's cold. Really cold . . ."

Mr. James led him down another hallway and into a large room, overlit with dirty fluorescent lights, where there were two badly formed lines of impatient and loudly complaining junkies waiting for the two bullnecked nurses at the counter to dispense methadone.

As each junkie reached the head of the line, the nurse put bright orange diskettes into a clear plastic cup, added hot water from a coffee urn, and handed it over. The person being medicated would add orange drink to the cup from the plastic pitchers on the counter and then stir the mixture with thin wooden stirrers. It was typically a swollen, puffy-fingered hand, covered with purple stripes and scar tissue, that would raise cup to mouth.

They drank greedily. Adding more orange drink to the cup, they would stir again, drink once more, the people on line behind them growing more impatient.

Mr. James led the chef back to a small office with a view of an air shaft. He motioned to a vinyl-backed chair, and the chef sat down. Mr. James took a clean file from his gray metal desk and sat down on the windowsill. He started by asking the chef for his full name, current address, and age.

"Mr. Ricard, how long have you been using heroin?"

"A little over three years, regularly," answered the chef.

"By regularly, you mean every day?"

"Yes."

"And how much heroin do you use on a daily basis at present?"

"Don't know, it depends. Three, four, five, sometimes six dime bags. Depends we're talking downtown bags or midtown bags. Two or three midtown bags will get me through."

"You shoot it?"

"Only in the last like six months. I just started. That's why I'm in such a rush to get on the program. Think, I know I've crossed some sort of line. I used to snort it. I got my habit snorting."

"You share your works?"

"Never," said the chef proudly. "I buy a new set every time. I never share."

"You're addicted to heroin?"

"I'm addicted to heroin," said the chef.

"Because that's not a lot. That's not a lot of heroin. Have you considered a seven-day detox?"

"I can't. I work. I still have a good job. I can't disappear for a week, a month. I got responsibilities. I've tried to kick on my own. It didn't work out."

"Three years is not a long time."

"Really?"

"Most of our patients have been using for much longer by the time they get here. Most of them ten years or more. Some have been using as long as thirty years."

The chef just nodded.

"Use heroin today?" asked Mr. James.

"Not yet," answered the chef. "But I'm sick now."

"Use any other drugs?"

"Today?"

"In general."

"Well," said the chef, hesitating.

"Cocaine?"

"Occasionally."

"What's occasionally?"

"One or two times a month."

"Crack or powder?"

"Powder. I've done the other thing, but mostly just powder."

"Depressants or hypnotics?"

"Not really. I'll score some Valium on the street sometimes if I can't get to sleep and I can't get any dope."

"Amphetamines? Speed?"

"No. Never."

"Street methadone?"

"A couple of times I've bought it when I can't get heroin."

"How about alcohol?"

"I can't. I can't drink when I'm doing dope. It doesn't sit in my stomach right."

"What about when you don't have heroin?"

"Like a fish. To excess. Whatever it takes to knock myself out."

"Marijuana?"

"Yeah. Every day."

Mr. James wrote something in the file.

"Prescription drugs. Are you currently being treated by a doctor for any illness or condition with prescription drugs?"

"No."

"Okay," said Mr. James, slamming the file shut. "Mr. Ricard, as you know, as I explained on the phone, there's a waiting list to enter this program. There are a lot of people who'd like to get in, and most of them have drug problems far more serious than yours. Many of them have been on other programs. Have you been on any other program?"

"No," said the chef.

Mr. James opened the file and made a small notation before shutting it again. "As I said on the phone, there's a waiting list."

"I had hoped, I like to think that I would be a patient with a good chance of success," said the chef.

"You say you're serious about rehabilitating yourself—" continued Mr. James, oblivious to the pleading tone creeping into the chef's voice.

"Very serious," said the chef eagerly. "I have to get out of the life. As soon as I can."

Mr. James continued as if he hadn't heard him. "You know this program, this clinic in particular, has been recognized by the state as the best, most effective in the country." He pointed to a state-issued license and a certificate of commendation in a frame on the wall. "You were sensible to come here."

"I'd like to know if—"

Mr. James cut him off. "You know what methadone maintenance is? You know what that means?"

"It means I get on and stay on, for an extended period."

"Exactly. You're sure that's the right option for you? There's counseling and various detox programs."

"Mr. James, I'm a chef. I can't get away and go to Minneapolis. I can't do that."

"You say you're a chef?"

"Yes."

"My son's a chef," said Mr. James, warming to the subject. "He's a garde-manger at the Sheraton."

"Oh, really?"

"He went to school for it, too. He graduated from the New York School of Restaurant Arts."

"Yeah? I've seen their ads on TV. They're supposed to be good," lied the chef.

"Once you're in the program—assuming the doctor sees you, I okay you—it's usually a long-term commitment. We encourage patients to stay with it, sometimes for many years. We have found that the longer a person stays on the program, the less likely he or she will return to heroin."

"I've read the literature," said the chef.

"So you understand."

"I'm a desperate man, Mr. James," said the chef, half smiling, trying his best to be disarming. He looked for encouragement in Mr. James's eyes, saw only zeal, a faraway look, like that of a religious fanatic. "I want to get off dope. I don't want to find myself, in a few months or a year, slipping back into it. I want to be sure. I want out of the life. I don't want to have to score on the street anymore. I want to stop having to look for dope every day. If that means staying on the program for life, that's fine. I don't want any chance, any chance that I could fall back. I don't want to risk it. I don't want to have to think about it." The chef looked Mr. James in the face. "I don't want to have to trust myself."

"You understand, once you're admitted, you'll have to give a urine sample on a weekly basis. Or more frequently if requested by your counselor."

"That's fine."

"That means no other drugs. If your urine comes up positive for any other drugs, then you're going to have a big problem. If it comes up negative for methadone, you'll have a problem. No messing around with your dose—you must take your medication every day. If we find the counselor assigned to you thinks you have misused your medication, you can be thrown out of the program. That means, not taking your methadone, selling your methadone, losing your take-home bottles, going on another program simultaneously. When you start here, you'll come in five days a week to be medicated. The sixth day you go to Saturday Clinic on 124th Street. They'll give you your Saturday dose and one take-home bottle. If your urines are clean, no other problems, your counselor can recommend a change in your schedule."

"What's the best schedule you can get?"

"One or two times a week, if it is felt that it's indicated, if it's approved by me. You screw around with your take-homes, we find out you're loitering in the neighborhood near the clinic, you have dirty urine, you go right back to a six-day schedule, or worse."

"I understand," said the chef.

"Okay, Mr. Ricard," said Mr. James, consulting a calendar and a sheet of paper in the middle of a clipboard, "I can schedule you a doctor's appointment here in three weeks." He consulted a desk calendar. "That'll be the third, ten o'clock in the morning."

Center of the World

An excerpt from the short story "Center of the World," originally published in *ZAT* magazine, issue number 3, in 1984.

The chef smiled and gazed out the streaked window. This had to be one of life's great sensations. The Checker cab rattled and shook its way down Ninth Avenue. The cool, night city air that blew in the window dried the wetness on the back of his neck at the hairline. It smelled of the river tonight, of Sabrett hot dogs steaming, of other nights and other places.

Out the window the dark silhouettes of midtown junkies darted from the shadows of doorways and shuffled and limped toward moving targets just beyond their reach. From his seat in the cab, head back, feet up on the jump seat, he could see some of the old faces illuminated for a second by passing headlights. The dark figures waited, as they always waited, rocking back and forth on legs that ached to the marrow. Out the window, on the street that slipped away behind him, swollen, elephantine hands fumbled for crumpled bills, hidden in an ancient sock.

The chef pulled hard on his cigarette and turned his gaze to the floor of the taxi.

The cab pulled onto Spring Street. Vladimir was waiting for him outside the restaurant dressed in full chef's whites, splattered with profuse amounts of the blood of many fish and six or seven identifiable fruit juices. He had been making sorbets. He twirled his mustache distractedly, eyes peering through his pince-nez down a long aristocratic czarist nose, over an imposing stomach, and down Spring Street the wrong way.

Michael pointed at the bloody abstractions all over Vladimir's uniform.

"You love it, don't you, you sick bastard? Standing here in the middle of the street right in front of your restaurant with your clothes covered in blood and viscera, gleefully horrifying the passersby."

Vladimir's eyes narrowed to slits as a great cat smile broke across his face. With the exaggerated mass of keys that hung perpetually on his belt, he let them inside the darkened restaurant. At the end of a long row of deserted bar stools sat Allen, in full uniform, a Coke in one hand and a copy of *Cuisine* in the other. Michael patted him affectionately on the shoulder. Allen smiled and nodded hello. His eyes were watery blue cartoon circles, pupilless, blind-looking. Michael chose not to comment.

"I had a very interesting Cuban meal last night."

"Do tell!" Allen sat upright and lit a cigarette.

"The place is called Hatsuhana, in the forties, midtown, east of Fifth Avenue. No round-eyes in the place. Crowded, but worth your soul to sample their squeaky-fresh fish. The rice is still steaming when they roll up your makis in front of you! Mimi herself gave them four stars just before she retired from the *Times*."

Allen sighed.

"I'll miss Mimi."

Michael protested.

"Not me. Now I can sleep at night. You know, she was the only food critic I ever gave a shit about. If she had ever suggested in a review that I hang up the apron, well, I would consider that cause to do some serious thinking."

Vladimir muttered to himself.

"Food critics are fucking nabobs! Someday a big red tide is going to come and wash them all away!"

The lights of Restaurant Isabel burned late into the night. The occasion for this meeting of para-culinary talent was a party to be held the next day, for which Vladimir, chef de cuisine of Restaurant Isabel, was duly responsible. Isabel was owned by Bobby Rosenberg, thirty-year-old restaurant mogul, and the party was to be a surprise in honor of his two years of successful ownership. He spent most of his time rolling around Manhattan between his various restaurants in a chauffeured cobalt-blue Bentley, puffing on a custom-made freebase apparatus in the backseat. None of them had really spoken to him for years, nor, to be accurate, had any of his employees. What little they saw of their lord and master was an occasional glimpse of the back of his embroidered silk bomber jacket as he ricocheted out the door after one of his two-minute visits.

Bobby was famous within the organization for these kamikaze raids. They referred to him as "the White Tornado" for, on these brief visitations, he would descend on the kitchen like a high-speed pinball, rocketing around, stuttering recipe suggestions, menu changes, High Concepts, and criticisms in a stream-of-consciousness machine-gun primal scream that was understood by few and ignored by all.

But, after all, it was the two-year anniversary of this chic, two-star eatery, and as Christmas bonuses were not so far off, it seemed like an opportune time for all concerned to do the Right Thing and throw a party.

Vladimir showed them through the swinging kitchen doors. This time of night was when restaurant kitchens were at their best. It was two thirty in the morning and the porters had just left, leaving behind gleaming expanses of stainless steel, bleached white cutting boards, and clean, shining, copper and steel utensils.

Vladimir indicated the battle plan for the party, listed on the kitchen blackboard in his peculiar, Germanic scrawl. A whole poached salmon, fully decorated and aspiced, was to be the centerpiece. Various pâtés and galantines of game and foul were needed. Vladimir had already completed the sorbets, the tricolor seafood mousse, the ceviche of sea scallops, and the vegetable marinades. Remaining to be made were a Parthenon of duck liver mousseline truffle, *bagna càuda* (a hot garlic and cream dip), and a Marsala zabaglione for the wild strawberries.

Allen volunteered to take care of the pâtés and galantines and immediately set about grinding meat and cutting and marinating tongue and liver for the center garnishes. Vladimir rasped conspiratorially to Michael.

"You come with me. We are going to create a monster. I have a plan."

He referred to the thirty-pound Atlantic salmon, fully poached, skin carefully removed, that lay curled defiantly on a raised metal decorating rack in the walk-in refrigerator. Allen shook his head fatalistically. The Russian was a notorious fanatic when it came to aspic pieces. His obsession with ornate and detailed tableaux was legendary. As Michael donned the traditional garb he was a bit apprehensive.

Together they assembled their mise-en-place to take with them into the cold room. For a piece of this size and scope it would be necessary for the two of them to do all the actual assembly under refrigeration. It was a familiar routine. They had spent many an evening bending over strange fish in faraway refrigerators. Vladimir lugged three large copper bowls of hot, amber-colored savory aspic into the walk-in. Then a box containing ladles, brushes, assorted paring knives, wooden skewers, and a tin of minute aspic cutters. Michael joined him a few moments later. He held two dinner plates on which he had collected a wide and numerous variety of cut and blanched vegetable shapes. Tiny bits of olive; hard-cooked egg; green leaves cut from leek tops; orange fleurettes, carefully trimmed from shaped carrots; geometric shapes of black truffle; and bits of pimento, squash, and anything colorful and edible that might prove useful.

From the tight expanse of white coat, Vladimir extracted a little bottle filled with white powder. Michael groaned.

"Oh no."

"Oh yes. And it's a real wiry, speedy, disreputable product. Just what we need under these circumstances: rocket fuel."

"More like Drano."

They emptied the bottle in two gluttonous snorts each, anxious to finish it before Allen became aware of its existence. Then with newfound inspiration and drive, Michael set to work, cautiously dipping the minuscule vegetable shapes into the hot aspic with a wooden skewer and paring knife. Then, one at a time, the shapes were affixed to the light pink flesh of the salmon, which Vladimir had thoughtfully coated with a thin transparent lamination of gelée.

Michael worked diligently at the tail end of the fish, laying down what became a spray of leaves interspersed with colorful flora and fauna. Two, maybe three, hours later he looked over to Vladimir's end of the fish to see what he was doing.

Vladimir was engrossed in one tiny detail. Even in the cold, beads of sweat studded his forehead. With a pimento and a slice of radish he had created a small representation of a mushroom, the size of a child's fingernail. As Michael watched, he painstakingly inserted the end of a plastic bar straw repeatedly into a slice of cooked egg white. He removed several microscopic white dots, which after much deliberation, he applied to the red hood of the mushroom. Michael inquired.

"What, may I ask, are you doing?"

Vladimir peered at him disdainfully and sighed.

"I am ensuring that these mushrooms here are identifiable as accurate representations of a species known as *Amanita muscaria*, recognized for their red and white spotted hoods and their recreational properties."

Michael shrugged and returned to his own garden. More hours passed. This time when he looked over at Vladimir he saw him to be at work on a number of human figures, engaged in what looked to be a biblical scene. This time he waited for the crazed and tortured Russian madman to volunteer the information. With surgical precision he was removing black olive circles from a dinner plate and transferring them to the salmon. He saw that there were two sizes, small black dots and smaller black dots. Vladimir grinned, proud of what was obviously a major effort.

"What we have here in the foreground is Moses and his Israelite companions. You will notice that I used the larger of the black dots for their eyes. Now here, in the background, are the Egyptians in pursuit of Moses, and of course, in the interests of perspective, for their eyes I used the smaller black dots!"

Michael just stared. The salmon was now a lush garden of dangerous botanical curiosities and religious iconry. They put it on a shelf and stepped back into the kitchen.

Allen lay slumped over the worktable, his nose resting in the center of a Greek temple of duck liver mousseline, his mouth open, snoring into the truffled dome.

When they had managed to bring him around he showed them the proud fruits of his labors; six intricately garnished pâtés and galantines, studded with ham, pistachios, livers, and tongue. Each slice was pink and perfect.

Vladimir screamed.

"YOU PUT NITRATES IN MY PÂTÉS!!?!!"

Allen protested. Holding up an empty packet of "Char-Rose," he barked, "This stuff is great shit! All the jet-set French chefs use it to keep their charcuterie rosy pink and fresh to the last slice!"

Vladimir was not entirely convinced.

"Are there any side effects, like with MSG?"

"A few minor incidents of skin rash, pressure vomiting, involuntary elimination, paralysis, sweats and chills, nothing serious. They'll love it! Trust me."

Vladimir revenged himself with frightening skill. He casually leaned over the pâtés, placed his nose to a slice, and took a long and dramatic sniff, a serious and intent look on his face. Then, as he had done successfully a dozen times, he rolled his eyes up into his head, dropped his shoulders despairingly, and sauntered slowly away, his posture that of a shattered and defeated man. As always, Allen was beside himself with agitation.

"Is it all right? What's the matter? Was the meat too old? Too much brandy? What? What is it?"

After a few minutes more of letting him sweat, Vladimir and Michael laughed and jeered at Allen and assured him that in fact, his labors had resulted in a fine display of product.

The party went predictably. Bobby Rosenberg had disappeared to his house in Saint Martin the night before. The ensuing festivities unfolded like a Pinter play. The guests stuffed their faces with abandon. The purposeless non-party became a free lunch for every hungry waitron, unemployed actor, and deadbeat in the company. The three tired chefs watched with philosophical detachment as their beautiful pieces were shredded and hacked at in a feeding frenzy of knives and forks, clutched in pudgy hands that stabbed and tore and pulled, locust-like, until nothing remained but a few melting aspic diamonds on the empty rental silver.

Vladimir turned away with disgust, tears in his eyes.

"I can't watch anymore."

Michael smiled affectionately.

"But it's always going to be like this. For us, it's all about those few seconds, before the locusts arrive, when the food is all laid out and arranged on the table, resplendent with fresh flowers, silver, crystal, and pleated Irish linen."

"You know, when you stand there in front of your salmon and you look at it and know you made it as pretty as you ever have made it, if not prettier . . ."

"At least we're never confronted years later by our lesser efforts," volunteered Allen.

"Fuck them all. They'd eat it just as quickly and like it just as much if the Colonel had catered this function. That one second when you look at your creation, and know that in a few more minutes, it will be indifferently and viciously destroyed, that's it; that's the Good Part."

That night at four in the morning, three chefs sat on the floor at Chin-Ya, a late-night sushi bar at Fifty-fifth and Broadway, in the back of a seedy hotel.

Allen nodded out in the corner, mouth slack and open. His head bobbed up and down slowly, like a deflating beachball. Vladimir was into his fifth sake and was hard at work on his third "Sushi and Sashimi Deluxe Combination," to the shock and amusement of the waiters.

Michael, twenty-eight years old today, smiled at his friends. It was good to be a chef, the sashimi was unusually fresh and tasty, he could feel a tangible protein kick from the fish, stimulating his endorphin production. The sake was warm in his stomach and comforting. The rest of the world slept in their apartments and their houses. But he was here. At the center of the world.

Chefs' Night Out

An excerpt from the short story "Chefs' Night Out," originally published in *Rovers Return*, published by Rebel Incorporated in 1998.

So, it was this lobster thing. I blame that for my unraveling. For my seemingly spontaneous, uncharacteristically violent reaction.

The steak had something to do with it. No question. But I'll get to that.

I haven't been any crankier at work. I was, and still am I think, a terror on the floor staff, an enigma to my boss, and "Dad" to my crew. Maybe I've been drinking a little bit more, but not during the shift, when I still confine myself to one shaker glass of margaritas, and two, maybe three pints of beer. I work in a fairly busy establishment, after all, even if it's a failing one, and one needs, in such circumstances, something to modulate one's natural homicidal urges. It would not do, as one of my fellow chefs recently did, to leap over the line in a rage, bury my teeth in a particularly slow-witted waiter's nose, and shake him like a dog. I never did anything like that, until last night. It's undignified.

No, I was managing to fall apart in private ways. Crying on the subway, for instance, on the way to work. The morning commute, I catch a glimpse of another commuter's newspaper, a headline that says, HERO CAT SAVES TWINS, or TOTS KILLED IN FIRE, and I start weeping. At home, sometimes, on my day off, I'm lying around, smoking a nice, fat spliff of hydro, watching the tube, and I start bawling over a car commercial, or a TV ad for long-distance telephone service. Those always get me. It's pathetic. A warning sign.

I haven't been answering the phone. I listen, on the answering machine, to the plaintive wails of my dwindling number of friends calling, and I lie there, immobile and terrified, like a trapped hamster, as their pleas to pick up, pick up, pick up . . . I know you're there . . . turn to frustrated, defeated droning. "Pick up, pick up, pick up . . ."

I never pick up.

I just can't. I'm too . . . fragile lately, in my off hours. At work, that's different. I can still bully a waiter or a line cook into tears. But at home, outside my kitchen, I'm five foot ten inches of exposed nerves, hurt feelings, suppressed rage, envy and fear. If they knew, these people calling, how I felt, believe me, they wouldn't be calling. At this point in my life, anything anybody has to say to me on the phone is *not* going to make me feel better.

Something good happened to you that you want to tell me about? Don't. Please. I hate you, am made miserable and unsettled by your relative good fortune. Your pride and happiness will only cause me to wish harm on you. Something gone wrong in your life? Don't tell me. My response will be inappropriate, inadequate, and will make me, on later reflection, feel guilty, will give me something *else* to regret. Best for everybody that I don't pick up at all.

You want to talk to me? See me at work. I know how to behave there.

Fucking lobsters. Cross-eyed, cannibalistic, dirty, carrion-feeding . . . You don't bind their claws with thick rubber bands, they'll tear each other apart. And they got me all fucked up.

It's gotten worse and worse, right up until last night. The chefs' night out, when what the police report refers to as "the incident" occurred . . . when a group of Manhattan's finest culinarians got together (as we often do), and bounced from one chef-friendly establishment to another, eating for free at one late-night bistro (oysters and nori rolls at 13 Barrow), then drinks at Bar Six, then more drinks and darts and some pool at the Stoned Crow, then more drinks and some cocaine, after-hours at the Nursery; finally ending up at the shuttered, but still open for business, Siberia on the Fiftieth Street subway platform: a grimy little corner of hell's rumpus room—six stools, a jukebox, some tattered posters of Lenin and Khrushchev, picture of Kim Philby in the bathroom over the urinal, bleary-eyed Irish bartender, a cum-stained couch. That's where the final conflict occurred between good and evil—where I resolved, in one brief, shining, and senselessly brutal moment, the eternal struggle, and cold-cocked that yellow rat-cocksucker with an ashtray, made myself the subject of restaurant legend for years to come.

There was me, Bobby, and my sous-chef Ricky. There was Ronnie, known industry-wide as the "Grill-Bitch"; Jimmy Sears with his cute new pâtissière (we were all sure he was fucking her); Laurent, a taciturn chef from the Gascogne; Maurizio, the Tuscan fundamentalist; and Alex, the master of Flintstones food. I remember hearing Maurizio mutter, "*Minchia!*" when Jimmy hit the floor.

We had been discussing other chefs. Chefs not present to defend themselves. You hang with chefs, you better know that about us— that when you leave the table to take a piss, we're gonna be talking about *you*. Like a cabal of small-minded, provincial grandmothers, or Alzheimer's-ridden retirees at some Florida compound, we'd rather gossip, duke it out over the last fruit cup, than chat about lofty culinary concepts over a snifter of Calvados.

By the time we hit Siberia, half-mad from tequila shots and endless pints, and the occasional sniff of Ricky's blow, the mood was even more mean-spirited than usual. Jimmy, I recall, was going on about Brendan Ford—nominally his best friend, mind you, a revered elder statesman of the NYC chef scene. Jimmy didn't think much of Brendan's new menu.

"It's *gay!*" he explained. "It's food for pussies! There's nothing . . . nothing to eat!"

"He's so pretty," said Ricky, sarcastically.

Brendan, who, on another night, would have been with us at Siberia, was known for his delicate herb-infused, elaborately garnished and presented plates. He was into weeds lately: grew them in his own garden, and his food tended toward items like Nearly Raw Fish in Sorrel Broth, Garnish of Lawn Clippings.

"Brendan. He is very talented," said Maurizio, always the diplomat.

"Cocksucker can't *cook*!" said Ricky. "Hasn't *cooked* in ten years! What's he *good* for? Walkin' around the dinin' room with a mother-fuckin' clipboard? Air-kissin' a bunch a dried-up old rich cunts? Fuck that bitch!"

"He can cook," said Laurent, weakly. "He just doesn't lately. He's at . . . he's at . . . another level now."

A few more restaurant types arrived: a saucier from the Hilton, looking to move up in the world, came over, started ranting about his broiler guy messing with his mise-en-place. He was fresh out of work, you could still smell Hilton food on him, and he was all jacked up, still, with adrenaline—eyes bulging, sweat running down his forehead. "Man stole my motherfuckin' kosher salt!" he shrieked. "Can you believe it? Right off my station!"

Two Ecuadoran pasta cooks from Le Madri came by, whacked out on aguardiente; one of them tugged my sleeve, roused me from my alcoholic torpor. "Chef chef . . . You need me, my frien', next week?" Next week there were banquets almost every day, and I needed the extra help. I tossed them each two shifts and watched them both stagger toward the pinball machine. A small group of waitresses and bartenders pushed through the door, fresh from Blue Ribbon, another late-night cookie and restaurant hangout. Somebody said they were hungry, and I saw Ricky pick up the phone. Ten minutes later, a porter from one of the hotel kitchens showed up with some stolen shrimps and a tin of caviar for us. We smeared fish eggs on potato chips, washed it down with Georgian vodka. People disappeared in twos to the bathroom, to pack their noses, handed off little packages, not so surreptitiously, under the bar. The music changed, the Cramps, and things started to shift.

I'm usually a happy drunk. A sentimental drunk. When I've had too much, I get quiet, then reflective, then sad. But this time, I could feel the evil genie slip out of the bottle. I knew, even before it happened, that something ugly was coming.

Sure enough, that was when somebody, maybe it was one of the recent arrivals, mentioned the review.

I flinched like a gut-shot dog. A palpable wince. Didn't say anything—just moved back and away, my balls scrambling up into my torso for protection, anticipating a boot to the crotch. I took another sip of vodka and saw that conversations had stopped, everybody looking now. Ricky, a perceptive young man, tried to change the subject back to pussy, but it was no go.

I heard, through the blood rushing in my ears, the words *"New York Times,"* a few choice excerpts—words burned into my brain weeks ago. I heard the word "steak." Then there was a pause. A long one. Even the waitress-bartender contingent saw that something was up, moved in closer, everybody sneaking looks to see how I was going to react. It was *me* they were talking about, after all. That fucking review, that motherfucking steak! *My* restaurant. *My* kitchen.

My comments were wordlessly solicited.

When I still said nothing, just knocked back my vodka and stared dreamily into space, focusing my gaze on a patch of mildewing acoustic tile on the low ceiling, that was when Jimmy, ill-advisedly, filled the silence with his own pithy, if rhetorical, question.

Addressed directly to me. So there was no avoiding it.

So, of course, I *had* to respond.

Which I did.

Truth:

I hate the general dining public.

I think people should be licensed to eat in a good restaurant. Yeah. That's right . . . A long and unnecessarily irritating process of testing and certification should be required of every would-be diner. To thin out the herd.

All the well-done-eating, low-sodium-egg-white-omelette-nibbling, crystal-worshipping, holistic vegan cocksuckers, the sauce-on-siders, the low-cholesterol, no-butter, no-cream, can-you-take-that-off-the-bone-split-for-two geeks, the slack-jawed, bed-wetting, mouth-breathing, fanny-pack-wearing scum pigs and rubes, with their Hard Rock T-shirts and their walleyed, no-necked, overfed monster off-spring in tow . . . they can get the fuck out of my dining room. *Now.*

The nauseating refrain "The Customer Is Always Right" is exactly wrong. The customer is rarely, if *ever*, right.

This is, it is said, a "service" industry. Jimmy says this all the time. Has no problem with it. Maybe that's why Jimmy is a success, and I, unfortunately, am not.

Serene, in his spotless, double-breasted chef coat, his name stitched in Tuscan blue over the right breast, Jimmy's got no problems administering roughage to the annoying foodies, trend-seeking Wall Street suits, blue-haired theatergoers, and all the rest of the waterheads and whiners who make up the great unwashed horde of the dining public.

I explained my plan once to him.

Vouchers, I said. You waddle into my restaurant, I said, and you present your papers to a trusted lieutenant. Should your papers not be in order—say you failed the "how to eat with a fork" part of your certification exam or got a low score on the seafood section—that's okay, I explain. We'll take care of you. You won't go hungry. You will be generously offered a voucher. For another kind of meal, to replace the one which you have been politely (if forcefully) refused. A nutritious and protein-packed sludge is yours, for reduced price, to be administered, say, in the rear loading area of the restaurant, out of view of the certified diners. Administered by trained nurses. Rectally.

I thought it was a modest proposal. Jimmy just snorted, scoffed. But then, he can afford to.

Jimmy, you see, is a brilliant cook. A theoretician, an innovator, a visionary, on the cutting edge of what the foodies call "Asian fusion," and what Ricky, my sous, calls "Pacific Rim-job." Give Jimmy a couple of coconuts, some frozen shrimp, a few sprigs of lemongrass, maybe a jar of red curry paste—he'll have half of Manhattan lined up to suck his dick.

I work for a living. I've got to work harder to get by. So much of what we do is a hustle, a con, that when honest, beautiful food, conscientiously prepared, is ignored, or worse, destroyed by some ignorant shit-stain of a customer, the pain is near unbearable. Bouncing from restaurant to restaurant, year after year, my motley crew of talented young thugs and hooligans in tow, I've come to feel like the *Flying Dutchman* of the professional cooking racket. Always arriving on the scene too late. Checks are already bouncing by the time I first put on my apron, button up my cheap cotton/poly-blend chef coat. No name stitched on my jacket.

When my crew and I arrive, it's like arriving at the scene of a car crash, the bodies already taken away, but the cars, damaged and nearly useless, are what we have to drive. My latest owner, always looking doom-struck and trapped, standing there, caught in the headlights, his entrepreneurial dream of empire circling the drain for the last few times. We're the pros from Dover, me and my boys, here to get you out of this mess, fix things up, get you back on track. But we know, Ricky and me. You're never getting back on track. There's no hope. Like the lobsters, chances are, you're dead—you just don't know it yet.

One silly, boneheaded fantasist after another. One more egotistical schmendrik with too much money and not enough brains—believed what his friends told him when they used to say, "You should open a restaurant!" Of course they don't tell him that anymore. They're not around. Now that the dining room is half empty and the deliveries are Cash On Delivery, and the owner stopped picking up their dinner checks, they don't come around much anymore.

After years of this . . . I *know*, from the moment we first shake hands, before the interview even *starts*, the place has no chance. Failure has a very distinctive odor, and I've become very adept at recognizing it.

I smell it on myself.

But, I take these jobs anyway. Shit, I need the money. Got to take care of my crew. That the latest ill-fated adventure will surely end in bankruptcy for my new master is completely beside the point. We're used to that, my crew and me. We can, at least, be counted on to per-form honorably, to go down with the ship. We give it our all, we re-ally do. Willingly suspend disbelief, work each day like this, this is the big one. We fight the good fight, every day, every night, in the face of certain defeat. Dien Bien Phu, seven days a week. It's what we do. It's what I do. Feed on the remains of dying restaurants, the last scraps of expiring dreams.

My latest boss—let's call him Squirrel Balls (it's what the floor staff calls him)—just last week, he's telling me his master plan to "turn things around." We're sitting over coffee in the empty cocktail lounge of his flagship restaurant-nightclub—the one that only a year ago was going to be the jewel in the crown of a chain of Squirrel Balls–conceived restaurant-nightclubs which would span the globe from Syosset to Samoa—anyway, he's sitting there bemoaning the weekend receipts, and I'm making the appropriate sympathetic noises, when he tells me about "Cabaret Night."

"There's a million unemployed singers, dancers, performers out there," he said, hopefully, "who'd just *love* a venue. Sort of a . . . a workshop, where they can work out new material, maybe get noticed . . . and we wouldn't have to *pay* them! I was thinking . . . I was thinking we could make Mondays Cabaret Night . . ."

I hear this, and I want to leap across the table, grab him by the hair, and twist a fork into his carotid artery. I've been through this part of terminal stage before, at other places. My last restaurant tried this knuckleheaded gimmick—invited a bunch of never-will-be performers to "entertain" our already diminished clientele. These hideously inept yodelers would open their stupid mouths, let loose with some nasally inflected medley from Andrew Lloyd Webber, and the dining room would empty like someone had just cracked open a vial of anthrax spores or let loose a cageful of Ebola-infected spider monkeys. "Check please," the customers would whimper, eyes looking longingly at the exits. "I forgot . . . I left the gas on," or "I forgot my medication . . ."

I hear this, and I *know* it's not going to work. Okay. Maybe I say, "Hmmmmmm," and try to look thoughtful as I fight the urge to projectile vomit. It's no use you see, trying to reason with Squirrel Balls. I *have* to let him live in hope, don't *want* him to give in to despair. I mean, let's face it—if he knew the truth—if he had any *idea* of the truth, had any sense at all—he would have shut the place down six months ago, cut his losses, stiffed his creditors, and run off to an Indonesian archipelago island with the few bucks left to him. Sad fact is: I *need* him to stay stupid. So I shut my mouth, swallow my rage and frustration. Later I'll have a margarita.

Now, Jimmy. My friend, my mentor, former patron, former chef—gave me my first sous-chef position, taught me everything I know about *huac nam*, jasmine rice, vertical food, infusions of herb . . . *that*

Jimmy . . . He owns. He gets equity in his place. His place will go bust too. His partners? They're gonna take it to the neck for some big bucks just like Squirrel Balls's partners. Difference is: Jimmy'll be fine. By the time the place goes down, he'll have raked off so much in skimmed cash, inflated salary, pilfered equipment, kickbacks, and "consultant" fees, he can take a year off. His partners won't mind a bit. They'll have gotten laid off their proximity to Jimmy's shining star. They'll have had a few good years playing Good-Time Charlies, buying drinks and meals for their pals, getting furtive blow jobs from the never-ending supply of waitrons. They'll have done a lot of coke, gotten a lot of flattering attention in the papers, had a good time. When Jimmy comes back from riding the waves in Hawaii or wherever, announces he's gonna open a *new* venture, right across the street, his old partners might even put up some *more* money. It's fun to be associated with a winner. And Jimmy, though he's never once shown a dime in profit, is a winner.

I told him so. Just before I hit him.

I said, "You're a winner, Jimmy. Everybody says so."

Then I cold-cocked him. Clubbed him upside the head with an ashtray, right there at the Siberia Bar.

He went down like a stunned rhino on one of those nature programs. You know the ones: "Zee rhino feels nussing as ze tranquilizer dart . . . ," usually delivered in heavily accented voice-over by some bucket-head in a safari jacket.

Afterward, I "went through the system," as the arresting officers called it.

When Squirrel Balls bailed me out, he wondered, on the way back to the restaurant, if "this could be a *good* thing. You know . . . for *us*. The publicity and all."

I had to say I didn't know.

"You could say it was a fight over principle," he suggested, always the optimist. "He stole a recipe or something. You could say that."

No way, I had to say. Unethical. Even for me. It was me, after all, who'd been stealing Jimmy's recipes for years. Over time, I'd seduced away his sous-chef with an offer of more money, stolen his best line cooks whenever I could. I'd even suborned one of his prep cooks, so he'd feed me information, regularly, on what was going on in Jimmy's kitchen. I wasn't going to step up and say Jimmy stole *my* recipes. That would be wrong. There *is* a limit. Plus, nobody would believe it.

The truth is, Jimmy said something to me that pissed me off. And I hit him. Hard.

Maybe too hard. I don't know. The way his head bounced off the bar on the way down, eyes blank . . . I don't know.

Information out of the hospital is pretty sketchy. They have him listed as "stable," whatever that means. My prep-cook source paid a visit, says that Jimmy, at least, is talking again, that he recognizes friends, is aware of the date, knows who the president is. That's good. As much as I enjoyed giving Jimmy a good whack—as richly as he might have deserved it—I wish him well in his recovery.

I am not a bad person. I'm glad I didn't kill him.

I'm glad I won't be grabbing my ankles for a crowded tier of Aryan Brothers at some upstate penal institution.

Even in a business where talking shit is an approved form of self-expression, Jimmy stepped over the line. And the threshold is pretty damn high. Verbal abuse, in our life, is an art form.

"I think I heard him say some shit about his mom," Ricky's telling someone else. "And Bobby's mom's got cancer, too. Can you believe it? Yeah. Stomach, I think. Damn *right*! I'd be pissed too. Shoulda seen Jimmy. He was cryin' like a little girl. Sayin', 'Not the face, not the face . . .'"

I have to make a face at Ricky when I hear this. My mother's fine. She lives in Florida now—and Jimmy didn't have time to say anything once I picked up the ashtray. Still, you've got to admire Ricky's creativity.

If I'd had time to consider things, when Jimmy said what he said. If I'd thought about it, had the strength, the resolve, to just let the remark pass, pretend I hadn't heard it, then carefully, over time, planned a prolonged and painful revenge, Ricky would have been the perfect instrument. He can be positively fiendish. One chef who pissed Ricky off,

Ricky started giving generous donations to an outfit called the North American Man-Boy Love Association in the poor guy's name, writing letters offering the services of the guy's restaurant to throw fundraisers for a group that advocates legalizing sex between men and male minors. Gave the guy's boss's office as a return address . . . I'm telling you, if Ricky had been working for Nixon, this would have been a very different country.

Waiting till the next day, tasking Ricky with the operation—that would have been the smart move. I'm sure it would have hurt Jimmy a whole hell of a lot worse in the long run than what I did to him.

But for instant gratification? Nothing beats a blunt object, delivered quickly and unexpectedly to the side of the skull. Take it from me.

I did not set out to be this way: a bitter, envious, aging crank—a journeyman chef with a record for assault. Since the lobsters started looking at me funny, I've gotten a little oversensitive, perhaps—a little thin-skinned. Abject humiliation tends to change a person. It changed me.

My early decision to become a serious, school-trained, European-style chef came after one particularly painful humiliation:

Nineteen seventy-three, Cape Cod, Massachusetts. I'd been working a summer job, as a dishwasher, my first restaurant. Elbow-deep in a sink full of dirty pots and pans, I'd look back over the line at line cooks, and envy them, swaggering, prideful young princes with a what-the-fuck attitude. They ate whatever they wanted, whenever they wanted it. They drank everything in sight, free of charge, fucked all the good-looking waitresses, stayed up all night shooting craps, playing poker, snorting coke, and getting involved in varied and occasionally freakish sexual adventures. They smoked expensive, seedless weed, filled their refrigerators at will with stolen sirloins, lobsters, boxes of shrimp, and champagne. They carried big, badass, razor-sharp knives (which I thought was *very* cool) in leather roll-up cases, which they slung over their shoulders like disgraced samurai, and they dressed in the height of outlaw style: artfully ripped jeans, faded Viet-vet type headbands, vaguely martial-looking double-breasted chef coats, casually spattered with gore. They were cool.

Compared to the squalid conditions of the professional dish-washer, they were gods.

So, the first time one of them went off on a bender and didn't re-turn, I stepped in, volunteered to work what was called the "berry station," or garde-manger. I happily cracked oysters on the half, made salads, plated desserts, filled champagne glasses with raspberries and strawberries. I bearded mussels, picked spinach, peeled potatoes and garlic and onions, and did the scut work for the big boys, the guys who cooked the hot food.

When the summer came to an end, when the regular crew began to fade away, off to work ski resorts in Colorado, charter boats in the Ca-ribbean, restaurants in the Florida Keys, I got my chance, and moved up for the last few weeks before closing for the season. I worked the fry station, dunking clams, shrimp, flounder, scallops, and french fries into hot grease for a while, until the broiler man got pinched for a parole violation and my moment arrived.

I was given charge of the broiler. The sheer pleasure—the *power* of commanding that monstrous, heavy iron and steel furnace, bumping the rolling grill under the flames with my hip, the way I'd seen others do—it was delicious. I couldn't have been any happier in the cockpit of an F-16. I felt like I could rule the world.

The next summer, my restaurant was bought by the owner of the better, larger, and busier restaurant across the street. Ciro, the new owner, was kind enough to allow those of us who'd worked the old place under its previous administration to audition for our old jobs. I was thrilled and headed up to the Cape from New York filled with hope and self-confidence, looking for that big-time broiler job, the big money, the position that would make me the studliest ass-kicking, name-taking, take-no-prisoners motherfucker on Cape Cod.

I pulled into town, I remember, wearing a spanking-new Pierre Cardin seersucker suit—color: light blue. I cringe now, remembering it. The shoes, too, were blue. Here I was, hitchhiking into a town that, for all intents and purposes, was a little artists' colony, a Portuguese fishing village, where people dressed unpretentiously in work clothes, cut-off denims, army surplus. And here I was, in some deranged early seventies bout of disco-inspired hubris, decked out in my batwing-shouldered Robert Palmer wear, come up from the city to show the local yokels how we did it in the big city.

I was so full of myself I could puke.

My audition took place across the street, at the usually jam-packed Ciro's. They were pounding veal in the kitchen when I arrived; the whole crew, on every horizontal surface, was beating on veal cutlets with heavy steel mallets for scallopines. The testosterone level was very, very high, like the locker room of a championship football team before the Super Bowl. My last crew had been adorable amateurs. These guys were pros, and they knew it. Everybody knew it. The floor staff, the management, even Ciro, the owner, visibly cowered when in their presence. Only I was too stupid to see how over my head I was.

I'd served a few hundred meals at a relaxed pace, in a not-very-busy joint in the off-season. These guys drilled out four, five, six hundred fast-paced high-end meals A NIGHT! Here it was: Friday, an hour before service, and I was informed I'd be working with Tyrone, the broilerman.

Looking back, I can't remember Tyrone as being anything less than eight feet tall, four hundred pounds of carved obsidian, with a shaved head and a prominent silver-capped front tooth and a gold hoop earring the size of a door knocker. While his true dimensions were probably more modest—you get the picture: He was big, black, fearsomely muscled, his size 48 chef coat stretched tight across his wide shoulders. A titan.

Unintimidated as only the ignorant could be, I started shooting my mouth off right away. Yapping about my old restaurant, what king-hell bad boys WE all were, back in the old days, regaling my new comrades with humorous anecdotes of New York City designed to shock and titillate, generally portraying myself as a street-smart, experienced, thoroughly professional gun-for-hire.

They were, to be charitable to myself, not impressed. Not that this deterred me. I ignored all the signs—the rolling eyes, the tight smiles—and plunged on, oblivious to the huge amounts of food the other cooks were loading into their stations. I missed the determined sharpening of knives, the careful arranging of side towels, favorite pans, ice, extra pots of boiling water, backup supplies of everything. They were like marines, loading up with ammo and sandbags, digging in for the siege at Khe Sanh, and I registered nothing, blinded by stupidity and self-love.

I should have seen the practiced choreography of their movements for what it was; understood the level of professionalism and experience that allowed these hulking giants to dance wordlessly around each other in the cramped, heavily manned kitchen, never wasting movement, turning from stovetop to refrigerator to cutting board with breathtaking economy of effort. I should have understood the terror in the eyes of the floor staff as we got closer and closer to service period, seen the way these cooks spoke to each other in high-pitched, femme-convict patois, calling each other women's names, for what it was—the end result of *years* working together in a confined space. They hefted three-hundred-pound stockpots onto the ranges, tossed legs of veal around like pullets, all the while indulgently enduring my endless, self-aggrandizing line of chatter without comment.

An hour later, the board was filled with more dinner orders than I'd seen in a lifetime. Ticket after ticket coming in, one on top of the other. Tables of ten, tables of six, deuces, three-tops, twelves, more and more and more of them, all containing dishes I'd never heard of with Italian, difficult-to-pronounce names. Waiters screaming ORDERING, food going out, more orders coming in, the squawk of an intercom, calling for food for an upstairs bar. Flames leapt out of pans three feet high, the broiler was crammed with rows and rows of steaks and veal chops, fish fillets and lobsters. Pasta was blanched and shocked and transferred in huge batches into colanders, falling everywhere, the floor ankle-deep in linguine, garganelli, taglierini, *spaghetti alla chitarra*, penne, and the heat was horrific. Everybody had sweated through their whites ten minutes in—the scratchy synthetic-blend whites inflaming wrists and necks so that everyone's skin was pink and inflamed. Sweat flowed into my eyes, blinding me.

I struggled and sweated, and spun around like a headless chicken, hurried to keep up the best I could, Tyrone slinging sizzle platters under the broiler, and me, ostensibly helping out, getting deeper and deeper into the weeds. On the rare occasions when I had a second to look up at the long row of fluttering orders, the dupes looked like cunei-form or Sanskrit—indecipherable. I was lost, thoroughly, totally lost. Tyrone, finally, had to help the helper.

Then, grabbing a sauté pan, I burned myself.

I yelped out loud, dropped the pan, an order of osso bucco Mila-nese hitting the floor, and as a small red blister raised on my palm, I foolishly, *oh*-so-foolishly, asked the beleaguered Tyrone if he had some burn cream and maybe a Band-Aid.

This was quite enough for Tyrone. It went suddenly quiet in the kitchen—all eyes on Tyrone and his hopelessly inept assistant. Orders, it seemed as if by magic, ceased to come in or go out for a long, horrible moment. Tyrone turned to me, looked down, smiling now, and said, "Whatchoo want, white boy? Burn cream? A *Band*-Aid?"

Then . . . then he raised his own enormous palms to me, brought them up close so I could see them properly, so I could see the hid-eous constellation of water-filled blisters, angry red welts from grill marks, the old scars, the raw flesh where steam and hot fat had made the skin simply roll off—they looked like the claws of some monstrous sci-fi crustacean, knobby and callused under wounds old and new. I watched, transfixed, as Tyrone, his shark's eyes never leaving mine, reached slowly under the roaring flames of the broiler, and with one naked hand, picked up a glowing-hot sizzle platter, moved it over to the cutting board, and set it down in front of me.

He never flinched.

The other cooks cheered, laughed their asses off. Orders began to come in again, and everybody went back to work.

I had been shown up for the loudmouthed, useless little punk I was. Identified as a pretender, and an obnoxious one at that. Humiliated.

Ciro ended up kicking me down to prep crew at my old restaurant—one step above dishwasher on the food chain—and I slunk home that night in my Pierre Cardin hoping I'd die in my sleep. After a day or two of sulking and self-pity, I resolved, out of sheer spite, to become a chef.

I would go to school. I would apprentice in France. I would let a procession of evil drunks, crackpot owners, sadistic sous-chefs work me like a Sherpa, until I became a chef. I would do whatever was necessary to become as good as, and better than, Ciro's crew.

I would have hands like Tyrone's.

Someday, somewhere, I would get to humiliate some other loud-mouthed little punk.

I would show them all.

So I became a chef because I'd been humiliated. I became a chef out of spite.

And I stayed a chef, for nearly two decades, until Jimmy Sears, for one brief second, made me a punk again.

*Whatever Squirrel Balls says, a reputation for violence is not a résumé-*builder. Not without three stars, anyway. Then it's okay. Three stars? Three stars, you can drink the blood of your enemies middle of the shift, stuff burning gerbils up a waiter's ass, parade naked and covered with brains and blood through the dining room, nobody gonna say boo. Not with three stars.

Me? With *one* pathetic star? Just getting through the fallout from this Jimmy situation is going to be plenty tough. The bastard could sue me. That would not be the good thing Squirrel Balls is looking for. In this tiny, incestuous, dysfunctional family we call the restaurant biz, you can't go around braining your peers. Not with one star.

One motherfucking star.

The steak.

The *New York Times* . . .

Let me explain. One star is a death sentence. Not an immediate death, mind you, it's a long lingering passing, a coughing, wheezing, blood-in-your-stool, gradual slide into obscurity and disrepute.

Finita la musica, papi.

See ya . . . Wouldn't wanna *be* ya.

Here's how it works:

Every Wednesday morning, every chef, sous-chef, restaurateur, cook, and serious foodie in New York City picks up the *New York*

Times. They don't start by reading the front page. Oh no. Armies of disgruntled former Soviet republics could be swarming across the borders of Europe, raping the livestock and enslaving the populace, Hezbollah suicide bombers could be lighting themselves up in Disneyland, Elvis Presley could have risen from the grave to feast on the brains of young children; it wouldn't deter anybody for a second. They—we, all of us, are going to do the same exact thing every Wednesday: turn directly to the Weekend section, second-to-last page—where the restaurant review appears.

We want to see if somebody we know got reviewed. We want that guilty frisson of pleasure that comes when an enemy, a rival, or better yet, a friend, gets trashed in the *Times*.

We know what to say if a friend gets a bad review. The usual platitudes: "Don't sweat it, man, nobody reads that shit," or "It's not *that* important," or "What do *they* know, anyway? Column's gone downhill since the last reviewer left," or "She's prejudiced against _____ food (fill in blank here), bro . . . Everyone knows that!" We've mouthed those words of hollow comfort many times—while snickering privately up our sleeves.

Fact is, of course, that everybody *does* read it. That it *is* that important. That she *does* know what she's talking about. If you get three stars in the *Times*, your business triples overnight. You get two stars—you dodge the bullet; you can go on as before, hold your head high, no fault, no foul.

But *one* star? One star: You may as well carve a swastika in your forehead and rub a nice steaming loaf of shit in your hair—'cause everybody you know, everybody you love, hate, like, respect, fear, is gonna read it, and laugh laugh laugh. If they're anything like me, they're gonna photocopy the damn thing, hang it in the kitchen, so their cooks can get a good laugh, too.

One star is a disgrace, a bad odor that will exude from your kitchen for years. Your cooks will look at you with shifty, worried, injured expressions, like sailors who, for the first time, have considered mutiny. Résumés will be secretly faxed. Other chefs will circle your staff like hungry buzzards, waiting to separate out the unhappy and disillusioned, pick off your sauté man, your butcher, your prep crew, your sous, even, one by one. Information will leak, hemorrhage out. Your currency on the job market, and with your present masters, will drop considerably. You may as well put on a paper Burger King cap and start stocking the fixin's bar for all the respect you're going to be getting. Truth.

So, imagine. Late one Thursday night, not too long ago, I open up the *Times*, and with shaking hands, turn the pages, see *my* restaurant's name on the second-to-last page, see *my* name, with *one* cancerous star above it. Just imagine how I felt, reading, "A hanger steak, ordered medium-rare, arrived rare . . . Returned to the kitchen for more cooking—when it came back, it was still under-done . . ."

Now, I remembered that order. I still do. I sure as hell didn't know it was the motherfucking *Times* critic: but, it wouldn't have mattered . . . I swear to *God*, on my eyes, on my firstborn male child . . . That motherfucking steak was *medium-rare*. It was medium-rare the first time. It was drop-dead perfect medium-rare the second time. And nobody, *nobody* is gonna tell me different. Escoffier himself could climb up my leg with a thermometer in his teeth, and I'm not worried. That steak was medium fucking rare.

How could it have happened? Why? Why? Why?

*Two paramedics arrived first, with two paunchy uniform cops right be-*hind them. Jimmy was loaded onto a gurney, hauled up the steps, bundled into an ambulance with flashing red and blue lights. I saw the little blond pâtissière follow them—probably intending to ride with her still unconscious chef to the hospital.

When the two cops began to take statements, I could see the unease on my friends' and drinking companions' faces when they asked the big question: "Okay. Who hit him?" Faces turned away, eyes drifted down to the floor.

Nobody wanted to be the first to snitch.

I made it easy for everybody, raising my hand weakly, a sheepish smile on my face.

The fatter of the two cops snapped on the cuffs, hands behind my back.

I remember how incongruously tender they were, the way they shielded my head with their hands as they shoved me into the back of the patrol car.

*It was the lobsters' fault. That look in their eyes—when I drove the skew*ers in . . . the way their eyes crossed. "Duhhhh . . ."

I think, in my mug shot, I had much the same expression on *my* face.

And that fucking steak. How I wish . . . what I would give for *that* not to have happened.

That didn't help at all.

*When I got out of the lockup, I went straight to work. Got a standing ova*tion from my crew. Ricky said all the right things, then got to work making some calls, doing what he could to fix things. He looked happy.

Ricky will dine out on this story for a long time. He'll get laid off of this story. He deserves to. His version, with any luck, will become the authoritative, the official version. By the time Jimmy gets out, whatever he has to say will seem like whining. I hope he's okay. I'd like to think he's making a full and complete recovery. And that he won't sue me.

I'm not a bad person. Really.

Things just got out of hand. I was vulnerable 'cause of what's been happening lately. Jimmy hurt me. I hurt him back. That's what happened.

Kappa

An excerpt from Tony's *Hungry Ghosts*, number 3, written with Joel Rose and illustrated by Sebastian Cabrol, published by Dark Horse in 2018.

THOSE OF YOU WHO KNOW ME, KNOW I CAME UP IN THE *OLD* SYSTEM.

THE *BRIGADE* SYSTEM.

THE WAY THINGS USED TO BE IN FRANCE UNDER *ESCOFFIER*...

"THIS SYSTEM WAS CRUEL."

"DESIGNED TO BREAK A BOY."

DON'T YOU KNOW HOW TO *DO* ANYTHING? YOU WILL *NEVER* BE A CHEF!

I MAKE *TWO* COOKS LIKE YOU IN THE TOILET EVERY DAY!

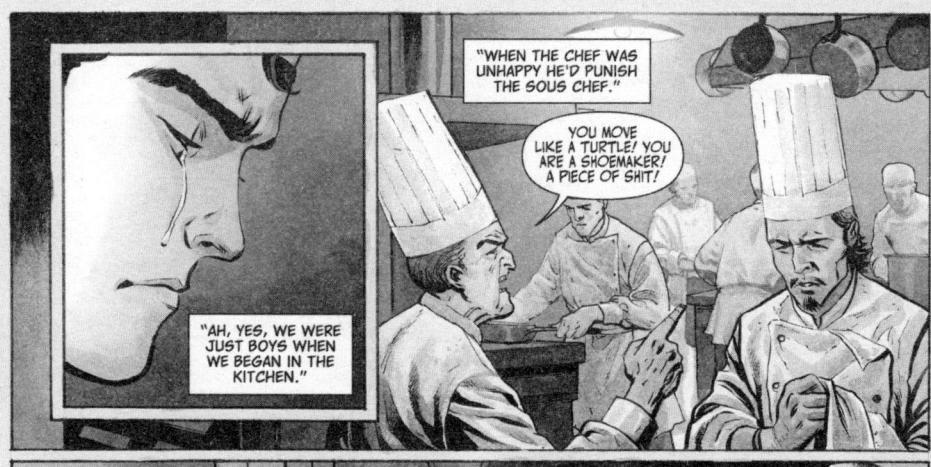

"AND WE, THE POOR APPRENTICES—BECAUSE WE KNEW NO BETTER—WOULD TORMENT AND PUNISH EACH OTHER."

YOU ARE *PIGS* AND *DOGS!*

PILE OF *DUNG!*

"OUR SUPERIORS, THE COOKS, WOULD CASTIGATE US FOR PUTTING THEM *DANS LA MERDE*. IN THE SHIT."

YOU! SLOW AND STUPID!

YOU! BACK TO THE FARM TO FUCK YOUR SISTER!

YOU! YOU STINK LIKE YOUR MOTHER'S PUSSY!

"PUNCHES TO THE SHOULDER, KICKS TO THE SHINS...THESE WERE COMMON."

"AND THEN, OF COURSE, THERE WAS THE GRABBING OF THE BALLS, THE SQUEEZING OF THE ASS."

"ALL CONSIDERED IN GOOD FUN."

HA!

HAHA!

HA!

HA!

"BUT SOME TOOK IT TOO FAR.

"I REMEMBER--HOW CAN I FORGET?--ONE CHEF IN PARTICULAR.

"HIS NAME WAS *GASPARD*.

"HE ABOVE ALL OTHERS WAS THE WORST OFFENDER. THE MOST CRUEL.

"HE TOOK SPECIAL RELISH.

"WHAT HE WOULD DO WHEN HE GRABBED THE ASS WAS NOT PLAYFUL. IT WAS NOT MEANT TO BE.

"HIS ACTIONS WERE NOT CARRIED OUT IN FUN.

"NOR WAS IT DESIRE."

"THIS MAN, THIS GASPARD, HE GRABBED, HE POKED, HE SLAPPED WITH A CERTAIN RAGE. A DESIRE TO DESTROY.

"WHAT HE DID WAS A COMPULSION MEANT TO CAUSE PAIN. TO HUMILIATE.

"THESE WERE EXPRESSIONS OF POWER, A DESIRE TO DOMINATE AND OBLITERATE THE YOUNGER AND THE SMALLER COOKS.

"MOST ESPECIALLY, ME!

"SADLY, I WAS THE YOUNGEST. AND I COULD NOT COMPLAIN.

"WE ALL HAD TO ENDURE IT. THIS WAS THE SYSTEM.

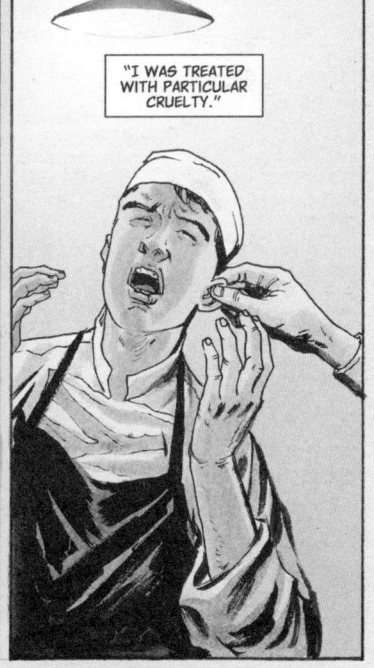

"I WAS TREATED WITH PARTICULAR CRUELTY."

"HE WOULD TARGET ME, ME AND ONLY ME, THIS MAN, THIS SOUS CHEF, THIS GASPARD.

"WHEN I WAS BENDING OVER THE PASS TO WASH THE VEGETABLES, HE WOULD TAKE EVERY OPPORTUNITY TO-- HOW YOU SAY?--GOOSE ME.

"BUT NOT JUST...

"HE WOULD PUSH HIS DIRTY FINGERS INTO THE CRACK OF MY ASS.

"ENTRE LES FESSES...BETWEEN MY ASS CHEEKS...

"...UNTIL IT HURT."

"ONE COOK TOOK PITY ON ME.

"THIS MAN WAS FROM A FRENCH-INDOCHINESE POSSESSION.

"HE GREW UP ON A PLANTATION IN VIETNAM OR LAOS OR CAMBODIA. I FORGET.

"FOR SOME TIME, HE WATCHED MY STRUGGLE.

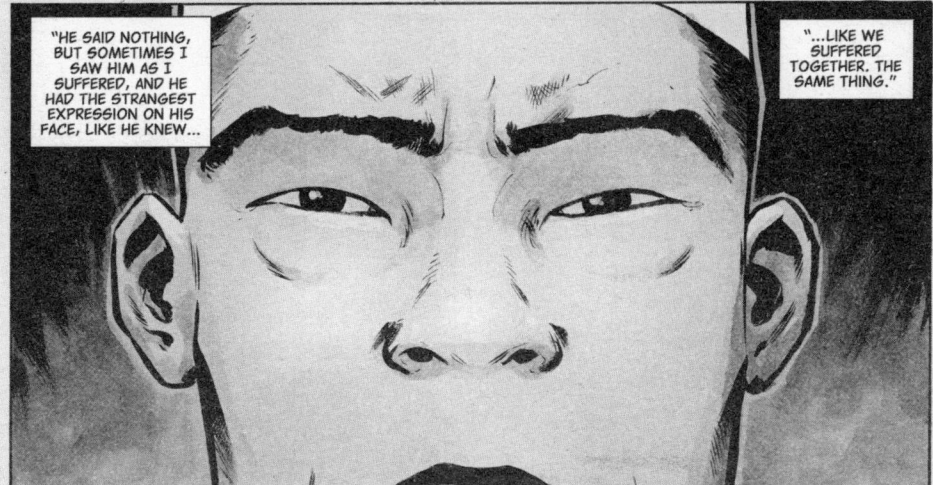

"HE SAID NOTHING, BUT SOMETIMES I SAW HIM AS I SUFFERED, AND HE HAD THE STRANGEST EXPRESSION ON HIS FACE, LIKE HE KNEW...

"...LIKE WE SUFFERED TOGETHER. THE SAME THING."

"ONE DAY HE TOOK ME ASIDE."

"'LITTLE ONE,' HE SAID."

LITTLE ONE. LOOK AT ME.

THIS MAN IS A BULLY. IN MY LIFE, I HAVE SEEN MEN LIKE THIS. THEY ALL SUFFER THE SAME CURSE. MEN LIKE THIS, THEY HAVE A SMALL *BALL* UP THEIR ASSES. TRULY! DON'T LAUGH! IT MAKES THEM VERY DISAGREEABLE.

BUT THERE ARE SPIRITS THAT *CRAVE* THESE SMALL BALLS. IN JAPAN THEY ARE CALLED KAPPA.

THESE KAPPA, THEY CONSIDER THE BALL A GREAT *DELICACY*.

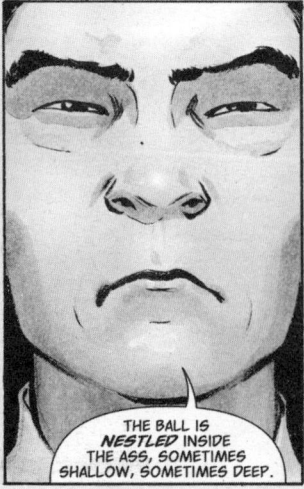

THE BALL IS *NESTLED* INSIDE THE ASS, SOMETIMES SHALLOW, SOMETIMES DEEP.

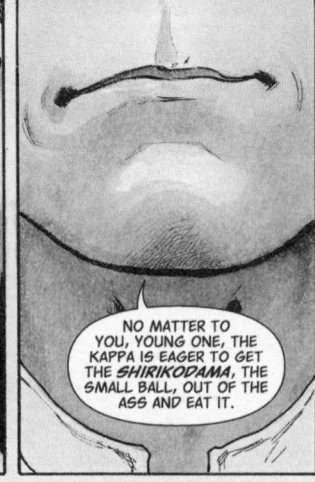

NO MATTER TO YOU, YOUNG ONE, THE KAPPA IS EAGER TO GET THE *SHIRIKODAMA*, THE SMALL BALL, OUT OF THE ASS AND EAT IT.

"THE KAPPA HAVE A *PREFERRED* METHOD OF EXTRACTION.

"A KAPPA LIKES TO COME FROM BELOW, EXTEND AN ARM UPWARDS, AND STICK IT UP THE ASS TO *EXTRACT* THE BALL.

"THERE ARE STORIES WHERE THE KAPPAS DON'T REACH UP WITH THEIR HANDS--

"--BUT INSTEAD ACTUALLY *SUCK* THE SHIRIKODAMA FROM THE BODY."

Sketch of a Chef

A sketch Tony did for *Kitchen Confidential*, originally published by Bloomsbury in 2000.

A Day in the Life

An excerpt from *Kitchen Confidential*, originally published by Bloomsbury in 2000.

Thanks to my bigfoot training, I wake up automatically at five minutes before six. It's still dark, and I lie in bed in the pitch-black for a while, smoking, the day's specials and prep lists already coming together in my head. It's Friday, so the weekend orders will be coming in: twenty-five cases of mesclun, eighteen cases of GPOD seventy-count potatoes, four whole forequarters of lamb, two cases of beef tenderloins, hundreds and hundreds of pounds of meat, bones, produce, seafood, dry goods, and dairy. I know what's coming, and the general order in which it will probably arrive, so I'm thinking triage—sorting out in my head what gets done first, and by whom, and what gets left until later.

As I brush my teeth, turn on the shower, swallow my first couple of aspirin of the day, I'm reviewing what's still kicking around in my walk-in from previous days, what I have to unload, use in specials, merchandise. I hear the coffee grinder going, so Nancy is awake, which leaves me only a few more minutes of undisturbed reflection on food deployment before I have to behave like a civilian for a few minutes.

I watch the local news and weather with my wife, noting, for professional reasons, any major sporting events, commuter traffic, and, most important, the weekend weather forecast. Nice crisp weather and no big games? That means we're going to get slammed tonight. That means I won't come crawling home until close to midnight. By now, half-watching the tube, and half-listening to Nancy, I'm fine-tuning the specials in my head: Grill station will be too busy for any elaborate presentations or a special with too many pans involved, so I need something quick, simple, and easily plated—and something that will be popular with the weekend rubes. The people coming to dinner tonight and Saturday night are different from the ones who eat at my restaurant during the week, and I have to take this into account. Saddle of wild hare stuffed with foie gras is *not* a good weekend special, for instance. Fish with names unrecognizable to the greater part of the general public won't sell. The weekend is a time for buzzwords: items like shrimp, lobster, T-bone, crabmeat, tuna, and swordfish. Fortunately, I've got some hamachi tuna coming in, always a crowd-pleaser.

As I walk up to Broadway and climb into a taxi, I'm thinking grilled tuna livornaise with roasted potatoes and grilled asparagus for fish special. My overworked grill man can heat the already cooked-off spuds and the pre-blanched asparagus on a sizzle platter during service; the tuna will get a quick walk across the grill, so all he has to do is heat the sauce to order. That takes care of fish special. Appetizer special will be cockles steamed with chorizo, leek, tomato, and white wine—a one-pan wonder; my garde-manger man can plate salads, rillettes, ravioli, confits de canard while the cockle special steams happily away on a back burner. Meat special is problematic. I ran the ever-popular T-bone last week—two weeks in a row would threaten the French theme, and I run about a 50 percent food cost on the massive hunks of expensive beef. Tuna is already coming off the grill, so the meat special has got to go to the sauté station. My sous-chef, who's working sauté tonight, will already have an enormous amount of mise-en-place to contend with, struggling to retrieve all the garnishes and prep from an already crowded low-boy reach-in—just to keep up with the requirements of the regular menu. At any one time, he has to expect and be ready for orders for *moules marinières*, *boudin noir* with caramelized apples, navarin of lamb (with an appalling array of garnishes: baby carrots, pearled onions, niçoise olives, garlic confit, tomato concassée, fava beans, and chopped fresh herbs), filet au poivre, steak au poivre, steak tartare, calf's liver *persillé*, *cassoulet toulousaine*, *magret de moulard* with quince and *sauce miel*, the ridiculously popular *mignon de porc*, *pieds du cochon*—and tonight's special, whatever that's going to be.

I've got some play here: Both leg of venison and some whole pheasants are coming in, so I opt for the pheasant. It's a roasted dish, meaning I can par-roast it ahead of time, requiring my sous-chef simply to take it off the bone and sling it into the oven to finish, then heat the garnishes and sauce before serving. Easy special. A layup. That should help matters somewhat.

By the time I arrive at Les Halles, I have my ducks pretty much in a row.

I'm the first to arrive, as usual—though sometimes my pastry chef surprises me with an early appearance—and the restaurant is dark. Salsa music is playing loudly over the stereo behind the bar, for the night porter. I check the reservation book for tonight, see that we already have eighty or so res on the book, then check the previous night's numbers (the maître d' has already totaled up reservations and walk-ins) and see that we did a very respectable 280 meals—a good portent for my food cost. The more steak frites I sell, the better the numbers will be. I flip through the manager's log, the notebook where the night manager communicates with the day management, noting customer complaints, repair requirements, employee misbehavior, important phone calls. I see from the log that my grill man called one of the waiters a "cocksucker" and pounded his fist on his cutting board in a "menacing way" when five diners waddled into the restaurant at three minutes of midnight closing and ordered five *côtes de boeuf*, medium-well (cooking time forty-five minutes). I sip my cardboard-tasting takeout coffee from the deli next door and walk through the kitchen, taking notice of the cleanup job the night porter has done. It looks good. Jaime grins at me from the stairwell. He's dragging down a bag full of sodden linen, says, "*Hola*, Chef." He's covered with grime, his whites almost black from handling dirty, food-smeared kitchen floor mats and hauling hundreds of pounds of garbage out to the street. I follow him down, walk through the still wet cellar to the office, plop down at my desk, and light my tenth cigarette of the day while I rummage around in my drawer for a meat inventory sheet / order form. First thing to do is find out exactly how much cut, fabricated meat I have on hand. If I'm low, I'll need to get the butcher on it early. If I have enough stuff on hand to make it through tonight, I'll still have to get tomorrow's order in soon. The boucherie is very busy at Les Halles, cutting meat not just for the Park Avenue store, but for our outposts in DC, Miami, and Tokyo.

I kick off my shoes and change into checks, chef's jacket, clogs, and apron. I find my knife kit, jam a thick stack of side towels into it, clip a pen into my jacket sideways (so it doesn't fall out when I bend over), and, taking a ring of keys from my desk, pop the locks on the dry goods room, walk-in, reach-ins, pastry box, and freezers. I push back the plastic curtains to the refrigerated *boucherie*, a cool room where the butchers do their cutting, and grab the assistant butcher's boom box from the worktable. Knives, towels, radio, clipboards, and keys in hand, I climb the Stairmaster back up to the kitchen.

I've assembled a pretty good collection of midseventies New York punk classics on tape: Dead Boys, Richard Hell and the Voidoids, Heartbreakers, Ramones, Television, and so on, which my Mexican grill man enjoys as well (he's a young headbanger fond of Rob Zombie, Marilyn Manson, Rage Against the Machine, so my musical selections don't offend him). I'm emptying the sauté station reach-in when he arrives. Carlos has got a pierced eyebrow, a body by Michelangelo, and considers himself a master soup maker. The first thing he asks me is if I've got snapper bones coming in. I nod. Carlos dearly loves any soup he can jack with Ricard or Pernod, so today's *soupe de poisson* with rouille is a favorite of his. Omar, the garde-manger man, who sports a thick, barbed-wire tattoo around his upper arm, arrives next, followed quickly by the rest of the Queens residents: Segundo the *vato loco* prep centurion, Ramón the dishwasher, and Janine the pastry chef. Camelia, the general manager, is last—she walks to work—and we exchange *"Bonjour!"* and *"Comment ça va?"*

Soon everyone is working: Carlos roasting bones for stock, me heating sauces and portioning pavées, filet mignons, *porc mignons*, duck breasts, and liver. Before twelve, I've got to cut and pepper pavées and filets, skin and slice the calf's liver, lug up cassoulet, caramelize apples, blanch baby carrots, make garlic confit, and reload grated cheese, onion soup, sea salt, crushed pepper, bread crumbs, and oils. I've got to come up with a pasta special using what's on hand, make livornaise sauce for Carlos, make a sauce for the pheasant, and, most annoying, make a new batch of navarin, which will monopolize most of my range top for much of the morning. Somewhere in the middle of this, I have to write up the specials for Camelia to input into the computer and set the prices (at nine thirty sharp, she's going to start buzzing me on the intercom, asking me in her thick French accent if I have "le muh-NEW").

Delivery guys keep interrupting me for signatures, and I don't have nearly as much time as I'd like to check over the stuff. As much as I'd like to push my snout into every fish gill and fondle every vegetable that comes in the door, I can't—there's just not enough time. Fortunately, my purveyors know me as a dangerously unstable and profane rat-bastard, so if I don't like what I receive, they know I'll be on the phone later, screaming at them to come and "pick this shit up!" Generally, I get very good product. It's in my purveyors' interests to make me happy. Produce, however, is unusually late. I look at the kitchen clock nervously—not much time left. I have a tasting to conduct at eleven thirty, a sampler of the day's specials for the floor staff, accompanied by detailed explanation, so they won't describe the pheasant as "kinda like chicken."

The butcher arrives, looking like he slept in his clothes. I rush downstairs, hot on his heels, to pick up my meat order: a towering stack of milk crates, loaded with plastic-wrapped CÔTES DU BOEUF, entrecôtes, rump steaks, racks of lamb, lamb stew-meat, merguez, saucisson de Toulouse, rosette, pork belly, onglets, scraps, meat for tartare, pork tenderloins larded with bacon and garlic, pâtés, rillettes, galantines, and chickens. I sign for it and push the stack around the corner for Segundo to rotate into my stock. Still downstairs, I start loading up milk crates of my own. I try to get everything I need for the day into as few loads as possible, limiting my trips up and down the Stairmaster as much as I can. I have a feeling I'm going to get hit on lunch today and I'll be up and down those stairs like a jack-in-the-box tonight, so those extra trips make a difference. Into my crates go the pork, the liver, the pavées, filets, some duck breasts, a bag of fava beans, herbs, and vinegar for sauce. I give Ramón, the dishwasher, a list of additional supplies for him to haul up—the sauces to be reduced, the grated cheese—easily recognizable stuff he won't need a translator or a search party to locate.

On my station (sauté), I've got only a six-burner Garland to work with. There's another range next to it that is taken up with a bain-marie for sauces and onion soup, the rest of it with stocks—veal, chicken, lamb, and pork—which will be reducing at a slow simmer all day and into the night. One of my burners during service will be occupied permanently by a pot of water for Omar to dunk ravioli in, leaving me five with which to work. Another burner, my front right, will be used mostly by him as well, to sauté lardons for frisée salads, to sear tidbits of hanger steak for onglet salad, for sautéing diced potatoes in duck fat for the confit de canard, and the cockles—which will leave me, most likely, with four full-time burners with which to prepare a wide range of dishes, any one of which alone could require two burners for a single plate. Soon, there'll be a choo-choo train of sauté pans lined up waiting for heat, requiring constant prioritizing. If I get a six-top, for instance, with an order for, say, two orders of *magret de moulard*, a *porc mignon*, a cassoulet, a *boudin noir*, and a pasta, that's *nine* sauté pans needed for that table alone.

Reducing gastrique (sugar and vinegar) for duck sauce while the Dead Boys play "Sonic Reducer" on the boom box, I have to squeeze over for Janine, who melts chocolate over the simmering pasta water. I'm not annoyed much, as she's pretty good about staying out of my way, and I like her. She's an ex-waitress from Queens, and though right out of school, she's hung tough. Already she's endured a leering, pricky French sous-chef before my arrival, the usual women-friendly Mexicans, and a manager who seems to take personal delight in making her life miserable. She's never called in sick, never been late, and is learning on the job very nicely. She inventories her own supplies on Saturdays, and as I hate sticky, goopy, sweet-tasting, fruity stuff, this is a great help to me. As I've said before, I greatly admire tough women in busy kitchens. They have, as you might imagine from accounts in this book, a lot to put up with in our deliberately dumb little corner of Hell's Locker Room, and women who can survive and prosper in such a high-testosterone universe are all too rare. Janine has dug in well. She's already managed to infuriate the whole floor staff by claiming she inventories the free madeleines we give away with coffee. I'm pleased with her work, making an exception in my usual dim view of pâtissiers.

Next to me, Omar, my garde-manger man, is on automatic. I don't even have to look over at his station because I know exactly what he's doing: loading crocks, making dressing, rubbing down duck legs with sea salt for confit, slowly braising pork bellies for cassoulet, whipping mushroom sabayon for the ravioli de Royan. I rarely have any worries about his end. I smell Pernod, so I know without looking what Carlos is up to: *soupe de poisson.*

Segundo is downstairs receiving orders from the front delivery ramp. I hear the bell every few minutes, as a few more tons of stuff arrive. He'll have my walk-in opened up like a cardiac patient by now, rotating in the new, winnowing out the old, the ugly, and the "science experiments" that sometimes lurk, forgotten and fuzzy, in dark corners, tucked behind the sauces and stocks. He's a mean-looking bastard. The other Mexicans claim he carries a gun, insist that he sniffs "thinner" and "*pintura*," that he's done a lot of prison time. I don't care if he killed Kennedy; the man is the greatest prep cook I've ever had. How he finds the time and the strength to keep up with deliveries, the nuts and bolts of deep prep, like cleaning squid, washing mussels and spinach, dicing tomato, julienning leek, filleting fish, wrapping and deboning pigs' feet, crushing peppercorns and so on, and yet still finds time to make me beautiful, filament-thin chiffonnaded parsley (which he cuts with a full-sized butcher's scimitar), is beyond me.

The last cook to arrive is our french fry guy. This is a full-time job at Les Halles, where we are justifiably famous for our *frites.* Miguel, who looks like a direct descendant of some Aztec king, spends his entire day doing nothing but peeling potatoes, cutting potatoes, blanching potatoes, and then, during service, dropping them into 375-degree peanut oil, tossing them with salt, and stacking the sizzling hot spuds onto plates with his bare hands. I've had to do this a few times, and it requires *serious* calluses.

I hold the waiters' meeting and tasting at eleven thirty. The new

waiter doesn't know what prosciutto is, and my heart sinks. I run down
the specials, speaking slowly and enunciating each syllable as best I
can for the slower, stupider ones. The soup is *soupe de poisson* with
rouille—that's a garlic pepper mayonnaise garnish, for the newbies.
Pasta is linguine with roasted vegetables, garlic, baby artichokes, basil,
and extra virgin olive oil. The whole roasted fish of the day is black sea
bass—that's not *striped* bass, for our slower students—crusted with *sel
de Bretagne*. The fish of the day is grilled tuna *livornaise*, asparagus,
and roasted potatoes. Does anyone need "*livornaise*" explained . . .
again? The meat special is roast pheasant with port wine sauce and
braised red cabbage. There *are* faux filets for two available (that's the
big hip-end piece off the sirloin, strip-carved tableside for fifty bucks).
Dessert special is tarte Tatin. It's not *too* bad a lineup on the floor today: Doogie Howser, "Morgan the part-time underwear model," Ken
the veteran (who has a maniacal laugh you can hear out on the street;
he's everyone's first choice for Waiter Most Likely to Snap, Shave His
Head, Climb a Tower, and Start Shooting Strangers), and some new
waiter, the one who doesn't know what prosciutto is. I haven't bothered to learn his name, as I suspect he will not remain with us for long.
There are two busboys, a taciturn workaholic from Portugal and a lazy-
ass Bengali; they should balance out, as usual.

My runner today is the awesome Mohammed, nicknamed Cachundo by the kitchen—the best we have. I'm lucky to have him, as
it looks like it's going to be busy, and the other runner, let's call him
Osman, tends to lose it when things get hectic and has an annoyingly
sibilant way of pronouncing the letter "s," making his calls for "musss-
selss," "meat sspesssiall," and "calvesss leever" particularly painful to
hear when you're under fire. Cachundo immediately begins picking
chervil tops, arranging garnishes, filling small crocks with grated Par-
mesan, harissa sauce, rosemary and thyme, gaufrette potato chips, and
picking out my favorite saucing spoons from the silver bins.

At various times during my labors, I manage to conduct two clan-
destine meetings out on the street: agent reports on the activities of the
previous night (after my departure). I'm investigating the grill man incident from the manager's log. Nothing earth-shaking. I have another

brief encounter near the liquor room with someone who gives me the latest gossip from our Miami store and a rundown of latest developments at Le Marais, our sister restaurant on Forty-seventh Street, as well as some speculation about imminent moves by upper management and ownership. Again, nothing I don't know or assume already. I like my bosses—and think they like me—so it's really only curiosity, not paranoia, that keeps me collecting and analyzing information from our distant outposts and conference rooms. Also, I like to hear different accounts of the same incident from different sources. It adds perspective and reveals, sometimes, what a particular source is *leaving out*, or skewing to leave a particular impression, making me wonder: *Why?* I like to tell selected people things in supposed confidence a few times a week, for fun. Later, when it comes back to me it provides an interesting road map of data transfer, a barium meal, revealing who squeals and to whom. There are a number of interesting variations on this practice—feeding *false* information to a known loudmouth, for instance, with a particular target in mind. A lot of what I hear is utterly useless, untrue, and uninteresting. But I like to keep myself informed. You never know what might prove useful later.

Twelve noon and already customers are pouring in. I get a quick kick in the crotch right away: an order for *porc mignon*, two boudins, a liver, and a pheasant all on one table. The boudins take the longest, so they have to go in the oven right away. First, I prick their skins with a cocktail fork so they don't explode, grab a fistful of caramelized apple sections, and throw them in a sauté pan with some whole butter for finishing later. I heat a pan with butter and oil for the pork, fling a thick slab of calf's liver into a pan of flour after salting and peppering it, heat another sauté pan with butter and oil for that. While the pans are heating, I take half a pheasant off the bone and lay it on a sizzle-platter for the oven, spinning around to fill a small saucepan with the port sauce to reduce. Pans ready, I sear the pork, sauté the liver—the pork goes straight into the oven on another sizzler—the hot pan I degrease, deglaze with wine and stock, add pork sauce, a few garlic confits, then put aside to finish reducing and mounting later. The liver half-cooked, I put it aside on another sizzler. I sauté some chopped shallots, deglaze the pan with red wine vinegar, give it a shot of demi-glace, season it, and put that aside too. An order for mussels comes in, with a breast of duck order right after. I throw on another pan for the duck, load a cold pan with mussels, tomato coulis, garlic, shallots, white wine, and seasoning. The mussels will get cooked à la minute and finished with butter and parsley.

More orders come in. It's getting to be full-tilt boogie time: another pheasant, more pork, another liver, and *ouch!* a navarin—a one-pot wonder but requiring a lot of digging around in my low-boy for all the garnishes. The key to staying ahead on a busy station is moving on a dish as soon as its name is out of Cachundo's mouth—setting up the pan, doing the pre-searing, getting it into the oven quickly, making the initial moves—so that later, when the whole board is fluttering with dupes, I can still tell what I have working and what I have waiting without having to read the actual tickets again.

"Ready on twelve!" says Carlos, who's already got a load of steaks and chops and a few tunas coming up. He wants to know if I'm close on my end. "Let's go on twelve!" I say. Miguel starts dunking spuds. I call for mashed potatoes for the boudins from Omar, give the apples a few tosses over flame, heat and mount my liver sauce, pull the pork mignons from the oven and clip off the strings that hold them together, heat potatoes and veg for the pheasant, squeeze the sauce for the pheasant between pots onto a back burner, move the mussels off the heat and into a ready bowl, calling, "*Papas fritas para conchas negras,*" to Miguel as I spin and bend to check my duck breasts. Sauce pot with duck sauce and quince, I'll heat those right in the sauce, no room now, the orders are really coming in, the printer chattering away nonstop. I'm sneaking peeks at the dupes while they're still coming off the printer, trying to pick out what I'll be needing, like a base runner stealing signals. The intercom buzzes and I pick up, annoyed.

"Line one for the chef," says the hostess.

I push the blinking green light. It's a salesman, wanting to sell me smoked fish. I answer all sweetness and light, lulling him into the bear trap in the Bigfoot style: "So let me get this straight," I say, after he's jabbered away about his full line of delicacies, me trying to sound a little slow and confused, "you want to sell me food, right?"

"Yes!" comes the reply, the salesman sounding encouraged by my interest and apparent stupidity.

"And in general, you'd say," I continue, "you have, like, a *lot* of restaurant accounts—in fact, you'd probably say that, like, you are in the business of servicing restaurants . . . and *chefs* in particular?"

"Oh, yes!" says the witless salesman, beginning a litany of the usual prestigious accounts, the names of other chefs who buy his fine smoked sturgeon, salmon, trout, and fish eggs. I have had enough and cut him off cold.

"So . . . WHAT THE FUCK ARE YOU DOING CALLING ME IN THE MIDDLE OF THE FUCKING LUNCH RUSH?!" I scream into the phone, smashing it abruptly into the cradle.

I catch the duck just in time, roll it over skin-side down again, and pull it out of the oven. I've got a *filet au poivre* on order—not on the regular lunch menu, but it's a steady customer, says Cachundo, and I'm set up for it anyway, so I start searing one off. Another pasta. I pour extra virgin into a pan and sauté some paper-thin garlic slices with some crushed red pepper, add the artichoke hearts, roasted vegetables, some olives. I don't know why, but I always start humming Tony Bennett or Dino—today it's "Ain't That a Kick in the Head"—when I'm cooking pasta. I *like* cooking pasta. Maybe it's that I always wanted to be Italian American in some dark part of my soul; maybe I get off on that final squirt of emulsifying extra-virgin, just after the basil goes in, I don't know. More *porc mignons*, the runner calls down to Janine, who's making clafoutis batter at her workstation in the cellar, and she comes running up to plate desserts . . .

We're doing well, so far. I'm keeping up with the grill, which is a faster station (unless a table orders a *côte de boeuf* or a faux filet for two or a whole roasted fish, which slows the order down). Omar is up to date with the appetizers, and I'm actually feeling pretty good, right in the zone. No matter what comes in, or how much of it, my hands are landing in the right places, my moves are still sharp, and my station still looks clean and organized. I'm feeling fine, putting a little English on the plates when I spin them into the window, exchanging cracks with Carlos, finding time to chide Doogie Howser for slipping that *filet poivre* by me without checking first.

"Doogie, you syphilitic, white-bread, mayonnaise-eating, John Tesh–ass wannabe—next time you slip a special order in without checking with me first? Me and Carlos gonna punch two holes in your neck and bump dicks in the middle!"

Doogie cringes, laughs nervously, and scurries out onto the floor, trailing muttered apologies.

"Chef," says Omar, looking guilty, "*no más tomates . . .*"

My jaw drops, and I see white.

I *ordered* tomatoes. I had thought that tomatoes had arrived—then remember I broke up the order between three companies. I call Segundo on the intercom, tell him to come up *ahorita*. I'm also furious with Omar for waiting until we're out of tomatoes to tell me there are no more.

"What the fuck is going on?" I ask Segundo, who slouches in the doorway like a convict in the exercise yard. "No Baldor," he says, causing me to erupt in a blind, smoking rage. Baldor, though a superb produce purveyor, has been late twice in recent weeks, prompting me to make some very uncivil telephone calls to their people—and worse, forcing me to do business with another, lesser company until they got the message and began delivering earlier. Now, with no tomatoes, and no delivery, and the rush building, I'm furious. I call Baldor and start screaming right away: "What kind of glue-sniffing, crackhead mesomorphs you got working for you? You don't *have* an order for me? *What?!* I called the shit in *myself* . . . I spoke to a *human*! I didn't even leave it on the tape! And you're telling me you *don't have my order?* I got three fucking produce companies! THREE! AND IT'S ALWAYS *YOU* THAT FUCKS ME IN THE ASS!" I hang up, pull a few pans off the flame, load up some more mussels, sauce a duck, arrange a few pheasants, and check my clipboard. I'm in the middle of telling Cachundo to run across the street to Park Bistro and ask the chef there if we can borrow some tomatoes when I see, from my neat columns of checked-off items on my clipboard, that in fact I ordered the tomatoes from another company, that I didn't order anything from Baldor. I have no time to feel bad about my mistake—that'll come later. After screaming at the blameless Baldor, my anger is gone, so when I call the guilty company, I can barely summon a serious tone. It turns out that my order has been routed to another restaurant—Layla, instead of Les Halles. I make a mental note to refer to my restaurant as "Less Halluss" in the future. The dispatcher at the guilty company apologizes for the mix-up, promises my order within the hour, and gives me a hundred dollars in credit.

More ducks, more pheasant, lots of mussels, the relentless tidal wave of pork mignons . . . finally lunch begins to wind down. I enjoy a cigarette in the stairwell while Carlos continues drilling out steaks, chops, and paillards, nothing for my station. D'Artagnan arrives, my specialty purveyor, bearing foie gras, duck legs, and an unexpected treat—a two-hundred-pound free-range pig, whole, which José, one of my masters, has ordered for use in pâtés and tête du porc by the charcutier. Now, I can lift a two hundred-pound, living breathing human—for a few seconds anyway—but dragging two hundred pounds of ungainly dead weight by the legs through the restaurant and down the stairs to the *boucherie* requires four strong men. The *boucher*, *charcutier*, dishwasher, and I wrestle the beast down the stairs, its head bouncing gruesomely on each step. I now know what it must be like to dispose of a body, I mutter. I do not envy the Gambino crime family—this is *work*!

The general manager sits down to lunch with the hostess. Two calamari, no oil, no garlic, a fish special, no sauce, a *céleri rémoulade*. Frank, my new French sous-chef, arrives. I have a list for him: dinner specials, mise-en-place, things to do, things to look out for. When he takes over the sauté station later, relieving me, I am grateful . . . my knees are hurting and the familiar pain in my feet is worse than usual.

José, my boss, stops by, wanting to take me to the Greenmarket. I quickly tie up a few loose ends, make sure Frank is briefed, and walk down to the market—about eleven blocks. We fondle, sniff, squeeze, and rummage through produce for a while, returning to the restaurant an hour later with pears, lemon verbena, some baby fennel, fingerling potatoes, and some turnips with greens, for all of which I'll have to come up with specials. The joke around Les Halles is that every time José walks in the door, the food cost climbs 2 percent. The man would have me mount all my sauces with Normandy butter and foie gras, garnish everything with fresh truffles if I didn't squawk—but he *loves* food, a good thing in an owner. José gets a dreamy look on his face when he hears about black truffles coming into season, or the first softshell crabs of the season, even at sixty dollars (!) a dozen, or anything seasonal, high-quality, classic French, gamey, or difficult to find. He wants to be the first to sell it, whatever it costs. It's a strategy that seems to be working. The backbone of the business may be steak frites, but our regulars are often pleasantly surprised to find fifteen dollars' worth of exotic food on a plate they're paying only twenty for, and little extras like that help develop a loyal clientele. Life with José means frequent surprise deliveries of very perishable and very expensive items, which I have to scramble to find outlets for, but what chef *doesn't* enjoy a load of Dover sole, still dripping with Channel water and twisted with rigor, falling into his clutches? Okay, my grill man won't be too thrilled—*he's* the guy who'll have to skin and bone and reassemble them to order—but that's just tough.

Back from the market, night crew suiting up in the locker room, I have just enough time to assemble the orders for Saturday. This is something I *enjoy* doing. My young gangster friend Segundo and I take a full tour of my walk-in and reach-ins. I've got two clipboards under my arm: one to assemble my orders (one page for Saturday, another to begin the Monday list) and a second for prep lists—my Things to Do Tomorrow list.

I break it down by company as I go along. DeBragga gets the Monday meat order. Schaller and Webber, the bacon. Riviera and Ridge get the produce—I'm too embarrassed to talk to Baldor right now. I see I need forty pounds of whitewater mussels, thirty pounds of squid, eight whole fish, and a new fish of the day for Saturday and Sunday. I call Wild Edibles and talk to Chris Gerage, who was also a chef for Pino at one point, and we discuss what's good for tomorrow. I go for some wild striped bass, some king salmon, and some baby octopus for appetizer special. Dry goods, I'm locked in for the weekend—no Saturday deliveries—but I start building a Monday list anyway. From D'Artagnan, I'll need some more foie gras by Monday, some duck bones, maybe some *magret*, and maybe I'll splurge on some fresh black trumpets and some chanterelles for a special—José will be thrilled—and since wild boar has been a big moneymaker for me lately, maybe I'll make up on the boar what I lose on the 'shrooms. I add two boar legs to my D'Artagnan list. Segundo knows exactly what I'm going to ask him and in what order—he's ready for me.

We go through the familiar list of items, in my inept but still useful Spanish:

"Mesclun?"

"*Veinte*," he replies.

"*Cebolla blanca?*"

"*Una.*"

"Shallot?"

"*Tres.*"

And so on . . .

Dairy has to be in early or they'll call *me*, which I hate. So I call the Monday dairy in right away: two poly milks, four fifty-five-pound blocks of sweet butter, one case of heavy cream ultra, a case of large eggs. Gourmand, another specialty purveyor, needs lead time—they ship out of Washington, DC, so I get that order together as quickly as possible: *haricots de Tarbe*, the expensive white beans we use for cassoulet (perfect absorption), *feuille de brik* for pastry, Provence honey for the duck sauce, white anchovies in olive oil for niçoise salad, escargots, flageolets . . . I'm already thinking about pot-au-feu for next week and will need plenty of the expensive gray sea salt for condiment.

Ramón, the day dishwasher, tells me he'll need the day off tomorrow to visit a relative in the hospital, but he's replaced himself with Jaime II, the night dishwasher who'll double for him. I'm grateful, as nothing causes me more grief than last-minute emergency scheduling, and I'm always pleased when my crew takes care of things internally.

Phoning my Mafia at home is a near impossibility. Most of them claim not to own phones. For those who do, their phones are answered by people suspicious of strange Norteamericanos asking questions, and are not likely to acknowledge that, yes, Mr. Pérez, Rodriguez, García, Sanchez, Rivera is actually in residence at said address.

Dinner-tasting for the floor staff is at five thirty, when the heavy-hitting veteran waiters have arrived. They fall on the family gruel and the tasting plates like rabid jackals. It's never pretty watching waiters eat; you'd think they had no money the way they dive into any available trough. Dinner-tasting is conducted in the kitchen, as there are customers in the dining room straight through lunch into dinner. It looks like a crowded subway car as I describe the evening's specials and present each plate. They tear at the four plates of food, ripping apart the pheasant with their hands, nearly spearing each other with forks as they gouge at the tuna, drag cockles to their greasy maws with bare hands, and quickly turn Janine's lovely tarte Tatin into a dark smear. I swallow some more aspirins.

At five forty-five, the downstairs is clogged with the nighttime lifer waiter crew, sitting on milk crates, folding napkins, smoking, and talking about each other. Who got drunk last night, who got thrown out of a mob-run after-hours club, then woke up in the bushes outside his house, who thinks the new maître d' is going to lose it tonight when the room fills up and the customers stacked up at the bar start screaming for their tables, who's going to win the World Cup, who thinks Heather Graham is a babe, who probably takes it in the ass *this* week, and how about the time the Bengali busboys got into a fight in the middle of the dining room and one stuck a steak knife into the other?

Dinner service. Overbooked as usual—with two whopping twelve-tops booked for prime time. I remain in the kitchen to expedite, hoping that maybe, just maybe, things'll slow down enough by ten for me to have a couple of cocktails and get home by eleven. But I know full well that the two big tables will hold up seatings by at least an hour; more than likely, I'll be here for the full tour.

By eight thirty, the board is full. Entrée tickets flutter in the pull from the exhaust fans. To my right, below the window, plated appetizers are lined up, waiting to get delivered to the tables; the window is full of sauté dishes, the worktable in front of the fry station a panorama of steaks of different donenesses. It's still Cachundo—he's working a double too—and he ferries the plates out by hand, four or five at a time. Still, I have to press-gang the occasional busboy or empty-handed waiter, separating them out from the herd at the coffee and bread stations and returning dirty plates and glasses, into delivering desserts. I don't want ice cream melting over the clafoutis, or the whipped cream on the chocolate mousses to start falling. Food's getting cold, and my voice is already blown out from calling out orders over the noise from the dishwasher, the hum of the exhaust, the whine of the Pacojet machine, and the growing roar from the dining room. I make a hand gesture to a friendly waiter, who knows what I want, and he soon arrives with an "Industrial," a beer stein filled with a margarita, for me. The drink manages to take the edge off my raging adrenaline buzz and goes down nicely after the three double espressos, two beers, three cranberry juices, eight aspirins, two ephedrine drinks, and a hastily gobbled hunk of *merguez*, which I managed to squeeze into a heel of bread before swallowing in two bites. By now, my stomach is a roiling hell broth of suppressed frustration, nervous energy, caffeine, and alcohol. The night garde-manger man, Angel, who looks like he's twelve but sports a tattoo of a skull impaled with a dagger on his chest (future wife-beater, I think), is falling behind; he's got three raviolis, two duck confits, five green salads, two escargots, two Belgian endive and Stilton salads, two cockles, a smoked salmon and blini, two foie gras, and a pâté working—*and* the sauté and grill stations are calling for urgent vegetable sides and mashed potatoes. I swing the pastry commis over to Angel's station to help out, but there's so little room, they just bump into each other, getting in each other's way.

Tim, a veteran waiter, is dry-humping Cachundo—to Cachundo's apparent displeasure. He's blocking the lane and impeding traffic in the narrow kitchen with his thrusting. I have to ask Tim nicely not to sexually harass my runners *during* service . . . after work, please. An order comes back for refire and Isidoro is *not* happy about it; it's cooked perfectly. I peer out into the dark dining room and see nothing except the dark silhouettes of customers waiting for tables at the bar, hear, even over the noise in the kitchen, the ambient chatter, the constant roar of diners as they shout over the music, the waiters describing specials over that noise, then fighting each other to get at the limited number of computer terminals to place orders, print out checks. "Fire table *fourteen*! Catorsayy! . . . That's *six, seven, fourteen*, and *one* on fire!" I shout, "Isidoro! You time it!" "I ready fourteen," says Isidoro, the grill man, as he slaps the refire back on a plate. Cachundo reaches around me and loads up with food, picking out plates seemingly at random, as if he's plucking daisies. I dry-swallow some more aspirins and duck back into the stairwell for a few puffs of a cigarette.

A whole roasted fish comes back. "The customer wants it deboned," says an apologetic waiter. "I told them it comes on the bone," he whines, anticipating decapitation himself. Isidoro growls and works on the returned fish, slipping off the fillets by hand and then replating it. The printer is going nonstop now. My left hand grabs tickets, separates out white copy for grill, yellow copy for sauté, pink copy for me, coffee orders for the busboys. My right hand wipes plates, jams *gaufrette* potatoes and rosemary sprigs into mashed potatoes, moves tickets from the order to the fire positions, appetizers on order to appetizers out, I'm yelling full-time now, trying to hold it together, keep an even pace. My radar screen is filled with incoming bogeys and I'm shooting them down as fast as I can. One mistake, where a whole table comes back because of a prematurely fired dupe, or a bad combination of special requests ties up a station for a few critical seconds, or a whole roasted fish or a *côte de boeuf* has been forgotten? The whole line could come grinding to a dead stop, like someone dropping a wrench into a GM assembly line—utter meltdown, what every chef fears most. If something like that happens it could blow the whole pace of the evening, screw up everybody's head, and create a deep, dark hole that could be very hard to climb out of.

"I gotta hot nut for table *six*!" I yell. There's a rapidly cooling boudin in the window, waiting for a tuna special to join it.

"Two minutes," says Isidoro.

"Where's that fucking *confit*?" I hiss at poor Angel, who's struggling valiantly to make blini for smoked salmon, brown ravioli under the salamander, lay out pâtés, and do five endive salads at once. A hot escargot explodes in the window, spattering me with boiling garlic butter and snail guts. "Shit!" I say, dabbing my eye with a side towel. "*Peenchayy* escargots!"

Frank's doing well, very well, keeping up. He did his apprenticeship with Robuchon, making food somewhat more elegant and delicately arranged than our Les Halles' humble workingman's fare, so it's a nice surprise that he's turned out to be such a line stud, cheerfully cranking out simple brasserie chow with speed and efficiency. He doesn't over-rely on the salamander, which I like (a lot of his French predecessors insist on cooking everything stone-rare, slicing and then coloring the slices under the salamander—something I hate to see); he makes minimal use of the microwave, which the cholo contingent has come to refer to contemptuously as "cooking French style," and I've only seen him throw one steak in the Frialator. All in all, he's worked out well so far.

"*Platos!*" screams Isidoro. The dishwasher is buried up to his shoulders in the pot sink, his prewash area stacked with plates of unscraped leftovers and haphazardly dumped silver. I snarl and grab a Bengali busboy, shove his snout into a plate heaped with gnawed bones and half-eaten vegetables. "Scrape!" I hiss menacingly, referring to the mess of unscraped plates. "Busy, Chef," complains the busboy, who, from what I've seen, has been wandering around with his thumb up his ass, taking out the occasional coffee, for hours. "I don't give a fuck if you're saving the world," I say. "Scrape the plates *now*, or I'll tear your booga off and hurl it across the street at Park Bistro!"

David the Portuguese busboy is making espressos and cappuccinos behind me, but he moves pretty gracefully back there, not bumping me or spilling. We're used to each other's movements in the narrow space we share, knowing when to move laterally, when to make way for incoming dishes, outgoing food, the fry guy returning from downstairs with another hundred-pound load of freshly cut spuds. I feel only the occasional light tap on the shoulder as he squeezes through with another tray of coffee and petit fours, maybe a whispered, "Behind you" or "*Bajando*." Fred and Ginger time.

Finally the printer starts slowing down, and I can see by the thinning crowd at the bar that the last seating is under way: white spaces opening up in the dining room, stripped tables waiting for customers. We've got 280 dinners under our belts already. I turn the expediting over to Cachundo, drag my ass down the Stairmaster for a final walk-through. I check the stocks cooling in plastic buckets outside the walk-in, the gauze-wrapped pigs' feet that will have to be painstakingly deboned tomorrow, the soaking *tarbais* beans that have to be blanched, the salt-rubbed duck legs that will have to be confited in duck fat and herbs, and I notice the produce that José and I bought earlier at the market.

I make a final swing through the dry-goods room, note that I'll be needing more peanut oil soon, more peppercorns, more sherry wine vinegar. I'm already working on an early draft of tomorrow's Things to Do list, tomorrow's order list. I've got striped bass already ordered, and baby octopus, I remind myself. José's got a hard-on for black mission figs—he saw some at the market—so I'll have to tell Janine to start thinking about figs for a special. I have weekly inventory tomorrow morning, which means I'll have to weigh every scrap of meat and fish and cheese in the store and record it, count every can, bottle, case, and box. There will be payroll tomorrow, making sense of the punch-ins and punch-outs of my not very computer-wise cooks and porters and dishwashers, all fourteen of them—and there's that extra shift for Carlos, who worked extra for me last week, and the extra half for Isidoro the night he covered Omar and Omar doubled twice to cover the vacationing Angel—and shit!—there's the overtime for that event at Beard House, and a promo party for what was it? A Taste of NoHo? Burgundy Night? A benefit for prickly heat? I have to record all the transfers of food from my stores to our outposts: the smoked salmon I shipped off to Washington, the flageolets I sent to Miami, the rosette and *jambon de Paris* I sent to Tokyo. I have to record all the stuff I gave to the butcher counter up front, and Philippe, my other boss, wants a list of suggestions for specials for the Tokyo chef. I peel off my fetid whites, groaning like a two-thousand-year-old man as I struggle into my jeans and pullover.

I'm on the way out the door, but Isidoro wants to talk to me. My blood runs cold. When a cook wants to talk to you, it's seldom good news: problem with another cook, minor feud, paycheck problem, request for time off. In Isidoro's case, he wants a raise. I gave Carlos a raise last week, so I'll have a rash of greedy line cooks jumping me for money for the next few weeks. Another note to self: Frank needs the sixteenth off, so I have to call Steven. I'm still buzzed with adrenaline when I finally push through the last waiting customers by the hostess stand and out the door, and wave for a taxi.

I'm thinking about going home but I know I'll just lie there, grinding my teeth and smoking. I tell the cabbie to take me to the corner of Fiftieth and Broadway, where I walk downstairs to the subway arcade and the Siberia Bar, a grungy little underground rumpus room where the drinks are served in plastic cups and the jukebox suits my taste. There are a few cookies from the Hilton at the bar, as well as a couple of saggy, bruised-looking strippers from a club up the street. Tracy, the owner of the joint, is there, which means I won't be paying for drinks tonight. It's one A.M., and I have to be in at seven thirty mañana, but the Cramps are playing on the jukebox—Tracy immediately fiddles with the machine so there's twenty free credits—and that first beer tastes mighty good. The Hilton cookies are arguing about mise-en-place. One of them is bitching about another cook nicking salt off his station, and the other cook doesn't see why that's such a big deal—so I'm gonna be involved in *this* conversation. The Cramps tune is followed by the Velvets singing "Pale Blue Eyes," and Tracy suggests a shot of Georgian vodka he's got stashed in the freezer . . .

Medium-Rare

An unpublished short fiction, date unknown.

So. His sixth or seventh cannelloni into the dinner rush, and the kid burns himself. And he turns to Alex, who's doing pasta station that night, and he asks him for a Band-Aid! Well, it's Friday, Saturday night, dupes coming in left and right, the sauté man is going ape-shit with the marsalas, and Alex just smiles, and holds up his palms for the kid to take a good look.

You know Alex's hands. Fucking lobster claws! All blisters and scars and burns and shit, not to mention the calluses, which beat even mine.

The kid takes a look at these fucking pink, oozing monsters, and Alex, with that row of gold and shit he calls teeth, grinning at him, and I think the dumb fuck starts seriously considering a new occupation right there, 'cause he shuts right the fuck up, and we don't hear a peep out of him for the rest of the night.

I don't know why Giro hires these dweebs out of culinary school in the first place. They all show up with, you know, those cutlery sets, in roll-ups, or those attaché cases, where the foam is cut so the knives fit right in, just like James Bond.

They come marching in the kitchen with their own set of whites, with the checked pants, and even those paper hats, the ones that look like coffee filters? And they all think they're Super Chef.

I'm telling you, not one of them is smart enough to pour piss out of a boot!

They can't hold a fucking French knife right! And right away, they want to do like Moses, parting the Red Sea, in aspic on the side of a bluefish. We call them all "Mel Carne." You know, like the Italian "*malacarne*," "bad meat."

It doesn't matter what their name is; we call them all "Mel."

But Alex, there's a maniac. You know he was in some crazy Russian Boy Scouts in New Jersey somewhere when he was a kid? Real junior commandos, they ran around out in the woods, doing maneuvers and shit, like preparing to march back to Russia and make like little czars and czarettes.

He showed up in P-town around ten years ago with his old lady. Like a lot of people around here, I think he came up for the weekend and stayed ten years.

One time, the kid asks Alex if he's lived in P-town his whole life, and Alex says, "Not yet."

Alex has two little girls by now, same old lady too. What's-her-name. He calls her the "septic cunt," and the girls, three and four, he calls them his "little slug-jockeys," "the rug rats," says they're just waiting for him to drop dead in the osso bucco with a brain hemorrhage.

Alex really started to get crisp around the edges last year at the "Pasta Pit." But he and the kid became big pals, a real Laurel and Hardy. Alex, this big whale, waxed mustache and all, and the kid, who looks like he has to run around in the shower to get wet.

The kid always gave me the creeps. His eyes, you ever see his eyes? Little black dots, like in the old Popeye cartoons, the black and white ones? And the long-sleeve chef coat. Middle of fucking August, steam table cranked all the way up on one side, flattops throwing off all that heat on the other side, and the kid still has the coat on.

I get a fucking rash just looking at the little geek. He has this look, like he's trying to look through your clothes and see what's in your pockets.

But him and Alex become like a real Dynamic Duo. Alex starts reading Escoffier, making little Jap garnishes, putting sauces under the fish. Soon the two of them are doing all of the private parties and buffets. The two of them, on cloud fucking nine, feeding lark's tongues in aspic and goose livers and shit to all those weasels from the Art Association and the Racquet Club.

Then they start catering freelance, on the side. Getting big fucking money too, for a lot of raw fish in vinegar and some kiwi fruit.

Every coke dealer and rich ex-wife on the Cape is shoveling the bucks at them.

The kid, he flirts with the wrinklers, and Alex, like his personal Frankenstein's Monster, makes all the actual food. And of course, he sneers, and rolls his eyes when the kid gives him the sign. One thing about Alex, when he puts on a clean white chef coat, he can make anybody feel like a ham and egger.

But the kid isn't shit without old Alex. They fight, in the kitchen, about like, what's the classic way to make *coulibiac* of salmon. Alex would just wag those scabby mitts at the kid and say how it all came down to "these."

They did some wild shit, I got to say. Seafood stew, in this coliseum of puff pastry, with a lid even. And the fucking aspics! They lock themselves in the walk-in refrigerator, hours and hours at a time, gobbling dexies, playing around with these fucking microscopic bits of olive and pimento.

But all the good stuff was Alex's.

Anyway, one night in the kitchen, Alex starts to get really weird on everybody. He grabs the kid's arm all of a sudden. He's got this look, like he just found out he's got cancer of the asshole, and he drags the kid over to the window and points at something in the parking lot.

It's a brand-new four-door station wagon. A Ford. Alex says to the kid that it's his station wagon, that he just bought it. He starts getting real loud, tells the whole kitchen, over and over, how he, Alexej Beria, owns a station wagon. A station wagon with four doors. Like he's going to drown in his own shit because he got a new station wagon!

He keeps looking out the window at the car, holding the kid's arm, like the kid is supposed to know what the fuck he's talking about.

The next day, Alex comes in to work, and he's shaved his head. Completely fucking bald. And to make it worse, he's got a real bad sunburn all over his scalp. So not only does he look like Alex, which is bad enough, but he's got this unbelievable peeling pizza dome for a head! None of the cooks would talk to him. You could not look at the guy!

Then Giro fires him. Supposedly for telling the bartender, who of course is a cousin, that he was going to pull his eyeballs out and skull-fuck him for sending him bar vodka instead of Stoli.

After that, no more Alex, no more kid. The two of them take a plane to New York. Alex leaves the old lady and the station wagon behind and the kids behind. Last thing I hear about Alex, he's gassing minks on a mink ranch somewhere.

So last week, he comes walking into the kitchen in his white Mussolini suit. He's all puffed up and beaming, like he just landed a nine-thousand-pound tuna, and he introduces us to the new chef.

You got it. It's the kid. I almost shit.

The kid's hands are nice and ugly now. I noticed that when he fired me.

He said I overcooked some food critic's filet mignon. Some mook from the *East Buttfuck Evening Star*, some one lung shopper news like that I don't know. Anyway, I'm out on my ass.

Maybe I don't know shit about newspapers. But I sure know what the fuck "medium-rare" is.

And that filet was medium-rare.

Mermaids Singing, Each to Each

An excerpt from the short story "Mermaids Singing, Each to Each," originally published in *ZAT* magazine, issue number 4, in 1984.

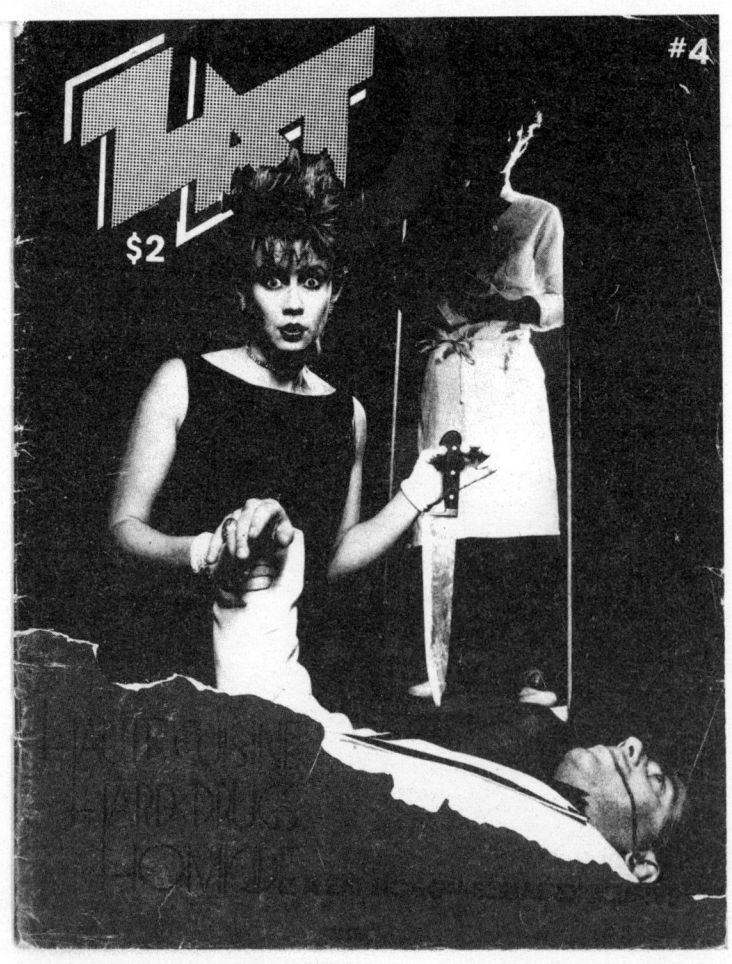

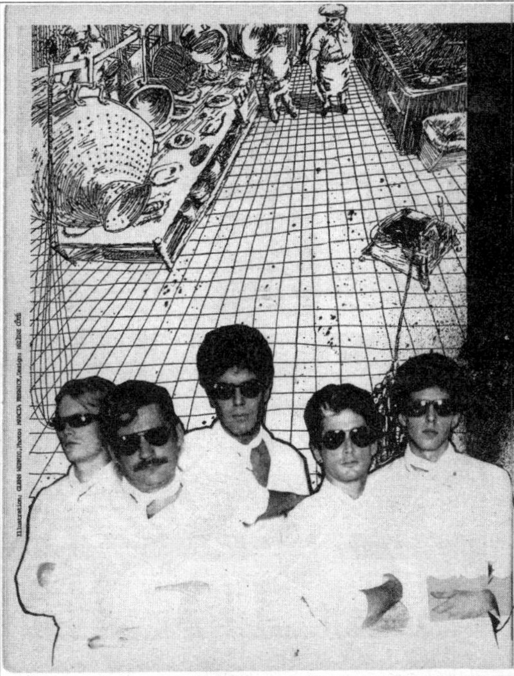

Mermaids singing, each to each

The kitchen was closed. The chef sat alone in his office surrounded by a pile of worn and splattered cook books. He stared at an old engraving of two cooks in Careme's time. They stared back at him defiantly from their comfortable place in culinary history, two young, slender figures, one leaning affectionately on the other, both with menacing, curved knives in leather scabbards that dangled from their apron strings. Their toques were of the soft cotton variety, pushed down jauntily to the side, an unusual pose for young cooks of the era.

His thoughts were interrupted by a half-hearted knocking at the office door. He reached over, unlocked it, and let it swing open, allowing a wave of hot, humid August city air into his air-conditioned bunker. It was Leonardo, the pasta cook, a rumpled figure in food-encrusted whites, wearing the evidence of a busy Saturday night behind the line. The chef looked sympathetically at the wilted young man in his doorway.

"Come in and close the door. You're letting the cold air out!"

The door safely closed, he motioned for the sweaty twenty-year-old, looking not unlike a short Ramone, to take a seat. Leonardo just sat there motionless for a few moments sucking up the air-conditioning. Finally he remarked with no small amount of pride, "We did over two hundred tonight! Must a' been over fifty pumpkin tortellonis! It was brutal!" The chef smiled at his apprentice.

"You did real good, Leonardo. You're really coming along."

"Even Q said I was slick tonight!"

"Yeah, yeah. Maybe we'll let you take a crack at the saute station one of these days. Is Q taking good care of you? You learning anything?"

"Yeah. We're getting along really well. He was telling me stories about you guys tonight, when you all worked together at Work Progress Restaurant."

"He was, was he? Yeah . . . we had a lot of fun in those days."

The chef called upstairs on the intercom and a few moments later a young, pear-shaped waitron-unit arrived at the door with a tray bearing a blender filled with frozen strawberry daquiris and two chilled pilsner glasses. The bartender, knowing where (or more likely from whom) his next meal was coming from had as usual taken good care of the chef. Leonardo gaped at the waitron's thighs, straining as they were at her Calvins. A purposeful look suddenly on his face, the chef turned to Leonardo.

Careful to bring the daquiris along, the chef led the way into the prep kitchen where his oversize chef's single knife sat waiting on the work table.

"Leonardo. Get thee to the walk-in and find six large spanish onions, ten pounds of squid, a couple of gallons of the freshest fish stock you can find in there, some garlic, and uhh . . . stop off by the dry goods area and get us two number ten cans of plum tomatoes (the spanish ones), a gallon of red wine, some ground cumin, some red pepper, and around eight medium size bay leaves. I'll get the salt pork and the potatoes."

Though it took a number of trips, Leonardo managed to accumulate the necessary ingredients, leaving them in a pile on the table and knocking over the daquiris in the progress. The chef shook his head and inspected the pile with exaggerated scrutiny. He selected a 12 quart stockpot from the ceiling rack and with both hands placed it on the range.

"First and foremost, the salt pork. Very important! We cut it into a very fine dice and render it slowly and gently in a bit of olive oil."

The little squares of fat melted slowly away in the bottom of the ludicrously empty pot. The chef peeled the six large onions of their skins, quickly, in one smooth motion each, then he brought down the blade of his knife six times to half the shiny white interiors, and hand gliding from one half to the other, made brief, measured cuts down into each half, then sliced steadily and a pile of perfect squares of onion fell away from the knife, forming a pile which grew rapidly to his right.

"We add the onions."

A loud hiss as the onions were angrily received by the hot fat at the bottom of the pot.

"And garlic . . ."

A smaller hiss.

"And the cumin and the red pepper and the bay leaves."

The pronounced and aggressive smell of young garlic and spices cooking licked sharply at Leonardo's nose. The chef turned the flame under the pot down to low, remarking, "As in all great dishes, it's essential that you understand and control the action of the onions."

Leonardo already knew this to be true. He had noticed this principle at work while watching Vladimir one day. Vladimir could coax more distinct and diverse flavors from a simple onion than Leonardo had thought possible. This remarkable faculty had made Vladimir a cult hero among all the cooks he knew. The humble root vegetable was smothered, pickled, carmelized, fried, and grilled by the talented czarist and the results were always as distinct from one another as they were delicious to taste. As the chef was careful to mention, "Vladimir

is the foremost authority on this subject. . . Just make sure in the Squid Stew that you sweat the onions till clear and soft."

They cleaned the squid together, cutting the tails into rings and reserving the tentacles. The chef reminisced about the old days. Soon the squid was all cleaned and cut and they began to peel the potatoes and cut them into a large dice.

"About five years ago (Christ is it that long?), Vladimir, Allen, Q, John, Mohammed and myself were all working together at Work Progress. We had been together there for about a year. Allen was the chef, Vladimir and I traded the title of sous-chef and banquet chef on alternate weeks.

"Anyway, right out of the blue, I got offered my very first chef's job up at Dick Waters, a theater and fashion joint on W. 46th Street. Needless to say I took it immediately. The lust for fame, fortune and personal glory were almost more than I could bear. I took along Vladimir as my sous-chef and was able to make Mohammed and Q more lucrative offers as well."

"About this time, I guess, some geek food critic from Manhattan-Life Magazine wrote the place up. Work Progress was featured in one of those artful retrospectives of Dining in Soho. Anyway, this slug-jockey was obviously so bored with his own prose, so tired of the same adjectives, the same rigid format, that even though he liked the food, he wrote a sort of stream-of-consciousness gonzo journalism piece. It was full of observations like, "The bar at Work Progress was redolent with the aroma of unsatisfactory Sex."

"Can you believe that? "Unsatisfactory Sex?"

"Well, New York's Dining Public didn't want to eat anywhere that smelled like unsatisfactory sex, or even of good sex, more than likely, and they stayed away in droves. Allen, like some sort of Captain Ahab, seemed determined to follow the White Whale down to the bottom of the restaurant ocean. Against all indications and our repeated warnings, he hung in there, staying on at the restaurant while I snatched every cook that jumped ship."

"After a month or so, the owners came to Allen and quietly informed him that the restaurant would close at the end of that week. They were pulling up stakes and reinvesting all their available assets in a Miniature Golf venture in Panama."

"Even though most of us didn't work there anymore, we all felt real bad when we heard that Work Progress was closing its doors. I don't think anyone actually ever made any plans for a gathering or a party or anything on the last night, but real soon it was apparent that that was what was shaping up.

"On the Sunday that it was to close, around 11:30 at night, taxis, filled with white-clad cooks and chefs, far-away looks on their faces, started to pull up in front of the restaurant and discorge their twisted cargo.

"By 11:45 there were more than twenty cooks standing silently in the small cellar kitchen waiting for the fateful Last Meal to go out of the kitchen. All the cooks, past and present, were there. You couldn't tell who was working and who wasn't, everybody lent a hand, flashing little jailhouse smiles at each other but not saying much. Hell, it was too sad. People were crying . . .

"It was great there, fulfilling our wildest pastry-wrapped fantasies . . ."

"At ten after midnight, the last order, two racks of lamb, medium rare, were taken from the kitchen by a very nervous looking waitron who took a look around and scampered the hell out of there. Somebody extinguished the lights and Allen grimly took his place by the stove. Vladimir started the tape one final time. When Jim Morrison's voice comes in over the sound of the choppers to sing *This is The End*, Allen poured two bottles of cognac over the stove. It made a beautiful flame. Everybody's faces lit up for a few seconds in the dark. We all just stood there watching the flames die down in what I guess was some sort of impromptu moment of silence.

"Right in the middle of this strange rite, Roland, the owner comes stumbling into the darkened kitchen. As his eyes adjusted to the dark, he peered out at this spectacle of twenty silent figures, all in white, some of them with what appeared to be blood streaked across their garments, and they're all staring at the flames with a scary look on their faces. He turned around and flew out of that kitchen so fast. . . Maybe he thought that a human sacrifice was forthcoming; it certainly looked like some sort of grisly burnt offering was taking place."

The chef poured the mass of squid, tails and tentacles, into the big pot with a hot splash and then churned it with a slotted spoon, grabbing the side of the pot with his free hand for leverage.

"Crack open those tomato cans . . . Has the fish stock reached a simmer yet?"

Leonardo crushed the plum tomatoes in his fists, returning the broken pieces to their cans. The chef grabbed them and poured them into the pot with the squid, following that with a gallon of not particularly distinguished red burgundy and finally the hot fish stock. As an afterthought perhaps, the chef added a spoonful of tomato paste and stepped back. When the stew had reached a simmer, they poured a prodigious amount of large diced potatoes in and then sat down to enjoy a second round of daquiris.

Gazing over at the simmering pot, the chef admired his handiwork.

"This is gonna be one motherfucker of a stew."

Leonardo grinned. The chef was rarely so enthusiastic about anything these days. Since his "rehabilitation" he kept to himself, spending long hours alone in his office, listening to the droning of his air conditioner, uninterested in the workings of the kitchen. Yet, at this moment, he paced exhuberantly about in front of the pot, wringing his hands impatiently and exclaiming, "It won't really be ready for a while yet. It's gotta marry up, the flavors have to develop. This here is one living Entity, evolving, metamorphisizing right under our noses!"

It did smell good. A rich, deep mosaic of smells and flavors issued from the purplish red stew. Leonardo hoped silently that the chef wouldn't make them wait too terribly long before they could sample a bowl. All this about flavors marrying was all well and good, but—

Q, dressed in his civilian clothes, burst into the kitchen.

"I smell Portugese Squid Stew!!"

"We didn't know you were still here."

"I was up at the bar. Can I get a bowl?"

Leonardo shook his head. "Not for an hour or so. It's gotta marry." The chef smiled. "I think we can sneak a bowl in an hour. We were just talking about Work Progress."

Q curled his six-foot frame onto the table, resting his enormous basketball sneakers on a case of potatoes.

"You tell him about what we did to Mark the manager?"

"No I didn't. Why don't you tell him."

"It was great. All night long we were setting the guy up. We'd go to him, each of us seperately, asking him if he had seen Vladimir. Meanwhile Vladimir is kept out of sight downstairs. All night long we're asking the manager "'Have you seen Vladimir? He was here before! Nobody has seen him! We're getting worried!"

Anyway, much later, when Mark comes downstairs at the end of the evening, Vladimir still isn't there and we ask Mark to get us some ice from the freezer. So he goes all the way into the shadows in the back of the restaurant and opens the chest freezer. Inside, is Vladimir, naked, wrapped in one of those transparent dry-cleaners bags with red food color running out of his nose and mouth and he's staring up at Mark with his best look of rigor mortis!"

"What happened?" Leonardo shrieked with laughter.

"Mark passed out cold. We had to get wet towels, raise his legs—the whole Boy Scout first-aid bit. Meanwhile, Vladimir's running around naked screaming "Let me Lance and Debride the wound!!"

The chef sighed loudly, a big grin crept across his face.

"Those were good days for all of us. We enjoyed the attentions of a sympathetic waitron staff, our own menu of our own drug-induced design, Roederer Crystale Champagne at cost, bar-tabs, credit, and newfound purchasing power for what were then considered to be exotic drugs."

Q laughed, adding, "I remember all of us standing in the kitchen trying to decide on a recipe for one dish or another, all of us waving our Larousse Gastronomiques at each other and arguing furiously about which was the "Classic" and "Correct" way to make it."

The chef interjected pensively:

"That's what made it so delicious. We were all so cocky, so filled up with ourselves and our creative liberties. Shit. We got away with murder! We intimidated the owners right out of their own restaurant. They stayed away rather than subject their staff to what we had assured them were an intolerable lack of social graces and sophistication!!"

Q added.

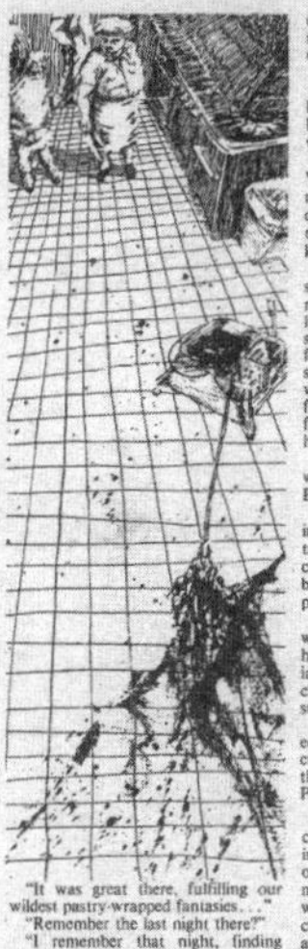

"It was great there, fulfilling our wildest pastry-wrapped fantasies . . ."

"Remember the last night there?"

"I remember that night, finding Allen sitting in his office with his coke grinder, alone. Vladimir had torn the doors off the hinges earlier in the evening, so it looked weird, him just sitting there in this nook. I felt bad for him."

"I resented Allen that night," said the chef, "or I don't know. I don't know if I was disappointed with him for going down with the ship, or disappointed with myself for jumping at the first port."

As they spoke, Q calmly removed a thick piece of white plastic from his jeans pocket and with a quick flick of the wrist, popped the lock on the dessert box. He reached into the dark refrigerator, feeling for something delicious to eat.

"GAA!! What the fuck is this!"

The chef and Leonardo laughed hysterically. Leonardo reached over to hold up the horrible object. The chef volunteered an explanation.

"I see you've found one of Vladimir's "Finger Sandwiches." He makes them out of sweet dough. Incredibly realistic. He likes to leave them out all over the restaurant. Never know when one is gonna pop up."

The workmanship was exquisite. A single finger, grotesquely torn from the roots, bits of scallion looking amazingly like bone splinters, a piece of onion skin serving as a perfect fingernail, red food-color caked about the stump, the sweet dough was colored and shaped with precision so that tiny shreds of flesh and viscera hung from the bone fragments. Q smiled and shook his head.

"That Russian is one sick puppy. No wonder they threw him out of Bavaria."

"They threw him out of hotel school in Bavaria, and subsequently the country, for doing the 'Twist' in the school cafeteria. That was considered lewd behavior in those days and in those parts, I guess."

The chef announced that the stew would not be ready to eat for almost an hour and the three agreed to meet back in the prep kitchen in an hour. The chef hobbled off to his office, his legs starting to ache.

Inside the office, the chef again gazed at the engraving of the young culinarians. They looked so sure of themselves. Like he had been at Work Progress.

Upstairs in the dining room couples crowded into the small outdoor cafe, interested in food only as sustenance, or tonight, as a hopeful prelude to mating. By the cappucino machine, the waitrons clustered together smoking cigarettes and speaking breathlessly of acting careers. An aging waitron talked in a cynical voice of "Bobby" De Niro, and "Marty" Sorcese; she'd served them drinks the year previous. Outside on Columbus Avenue, people with parrots, unseasonally jumpsuited, shoulders padded, looking like the Jetson Clan, sipped Perrier and White Wine and watched the passing crowd of designer clad musculature display their tans.

The chef was awakened by Q, bearing a bowl of the Squid Stew. He smiled at the chef.

"It's good. Really good."

And it was.

The Story of a Cook

An excerpt from *Typhoid Mary: An Urban Historical*, originally published by Bloomsbury in 2001.

Historically, to be a cook, to prepare food for others, was always to identify oneself with the degraded and the debauched. As far back as ancient Rome, and as recently as pre–Civil War America, cooks were slaves. Untrustworthy, unpleasant, and more often than not, unhealthy, cooks in early twentieth-century Europe and America worked in hot, unventilated spaces for long hours. They were underpaid, underfed, and underappreciated—their cruel masters despotic, megalomaniacal tyrants, parsimonious desk-jockeys, and brutish warders. Cooks tended—as they still do—to drink. And they died, usually at a young age, with their livers bloated by booze, their feet flattened, hands gnarled, faces ravaged, their lungs coated with the sediment of years of inhaling smoke, airborne grease, and bad air. Their brains were fried by the heat and the pressure and the difficulty of suppressing mammoth surges of rage and frustration, their nervous systems frazzled by mood swings which peaked and crashed with each incoming rush of business. They sweated and toiled in obscurity, cursed their customers, one another, their underlings, and their evil overlords. They cursed the world outside their kitchen doors for making them work like animals, for making them bend always to another's will. For existing.

And yet they were almost always proud. Cooks knew then, as they know now, that the people "out there"—the ones who lived outside those swinging kitchen doors, the ones who owned homes, who went out to dinner or to the theater on weekend nights, the ones who had holidays off and who saw their loved ones for more than a few fleeting hours a week—were different. Civilians, as all cooks know, take their pleasures in different ways and, just as significantly, at different times. The rules they live by are different too. And just as cooks are not understood, they don't, can't, and never have understood "them." The world of the nine-to-five worker, the property owner, the regular restaurant goer, the boss, is completely and maddeningly incomprehensible to those who've spent most of their lives bent over a hot range. As author Michael Ruhlman points out, cooks don't understand how others can live the way they live out there, in all that sloppy, unregimented luxury. It's messy. It's wasteful. It's scary and disorganized. *Out there*, things just don't seem to *work* the way they should.

For a cook, the well-ordered safety and certainty of the kitchen, however hot, cramped, and occasionally crazed, is a place of absolutes. The chef is the Absolute Leader. Food is always served on time. Cold food is served cold. Hot food is served hot. No one is late. No one calls in sick.

Let me repeat that: *no one* calls in sick.

The world outside the kitchen doors, to the mind of the cook, is imperfect—a constant source of disappointment, a place of thousands of tiny betrayals which threatens at all times to intrude into their own territory. Cooks are territorial creatures. No Serbian militia or feral dog defends its terrain more fiercely, and seemingly unreasonably, than a cook protects his station. Mise-en-place, the general sense of things being the way they should be—of being ready for anything—extends only to the exit. Outside, it's a strange and terrible place where things happen and don't happen in unpredictable and unforeseeable ways.

Mary Mallon, the woman who came (to her everlasting displeasure) to be known as Typhoid Mary, was a cook. Much has been written about Ms. Mallon over the years. There have been sensational newspaper accounts, plays, works of fiction, the predictable feminist reevaluations depicting her as the sad victim of an unfeeling, racist, sexist society bent on bringing a good woman down—her persecution and incarceration the result of some gender-insensitive Neanderthals looking for a quick fix to an embarrassing public health problem. And there is an element of truth in almost all these characterizations. She *was* a woman. She *was* Irish. She *was* poor. None of these, listed on a résumé in 1906, was going to put you on the fast track to the White House or a corporate boardroom or even a box seat at the opera.

Because, first and foremost, Mary Mallon was a cook. And her story, first and foremost, is the story of a cook. While that may not explain everything about some of the troubling aspects of her life, it explains a hell of a lot. Her tale has not yet, to my knowledge, been told from that point of view.

Little historical record of Mary's life can be depended on—and there are few recorded words or utterances from her own mouth. The accounts of the time, from others involved, directly or indirectly, with her case, are all too often self-serving, incomplete, sensationalistic, or plain wrong. Few, if any, take into account the worldview of the career cook.

There is one excellent, scrupulously researched, comprehensive, and insightful telling of Mary's story: Judith Walzer Leavitt's *Typhoid Mary: Captive to the Public's Health*, an absolutely indispensable volume which should (and did, in my case) serve as a road map to anyone interested in her life and times. But Leavitt's work focuses largely on the troubling public health and civil liberties issues raised by Mary's incarceration by health authorities, drawing a meaningful comparison to today's AIDS crisis, and the moral quagmire officials encounter when confronted with otherwise blameless people who can, through casual contact with others, cause illness or death.

That's not where I'm going here. I'm a chef, and what interests me is the story of a proud cook—a reasonably capable one by all accounts—who at the outset, at least, found herself utterly screwed by forces she neither understood nor had the ability to control. I'm interested in a tormented loner, a woman in a male world, in hostile territory, frequently on the run. And I'm interested in denial—the ways that Mary, and many of us, find to avoid the obvious, the lies we tell ourselves to get through the day, the things we do and say so that we can go on, drag our aching carcasses out of bed each day, climb into our clothes, and once again set out for work, often in kitchens where the smell, the surroundings, the ruling regime oppress us.

Going in, I knew only that she was a cook with a problem. Few, it seemed, knew her real name. "Typhoid Mary," the moniker she's come to be remembered by, is now an all-purpose pejorative, an epithet implying evil intent, willful contagion, shorthand for a woman so foul, so unpleasant, so infectious as to destroy all she touches. If you were to ask a passerby who Typhoid Mary was, you might hear that she was a plague carrier, someone responsible for infecting and killing thousands.

In fact, as I soon discovered, Mary's total body count—for all her career—as tabulated by her most fervent and least forgiving pursuer—came to thirty-three persons infected, with confirmed deaths of only three. Although, in all likelihood, there probably were a few more uncounted, undiscovered cases associated with Mary. God bless her, she often worked off the books.

So knowing nothing when I began this project, I soon found myself rooting around dusty collections, library stacks and archives. Research was fun, I have to say. I've been penned up in various versions of a twenty-five-foot-by-ten-foot professional kitchen (like Mary) for most of my adult life, so it was a very new experience for me to acquire knowledge in silence, seated. It helped that I was writing about a fellow cook.

The history of my profession has always fascinated me. Years ago, at culinary school, my fellow students and I loved the stories of Vatel, for instance, impaling himself on his sword over a late fish delivery. While we admired the seriousness with which he took his enterprise, we also thought, *What a punk! Who hadda cover for him the next day at work?!* Carême's edible monuments and minarets, his kooky ambition to marry architecture, fine art, and the preparation of food, inspired generations of cooks to all sorts of terrible and ludicrous excesses, nearly drove some insane trying to emulate his maniacal construction projects. We have—all of us professionals—worshipped at the altar of Escoffier, memorized his recipes, been drilled in his methods, heard and cherished stories of the Great Man, burned his image and the names of his dishes into our brains as deeply as any disciples of Chairman Mao or L. Ron Hubbard. We know the names of the greats like divinity students know the names of the apostles: Point, Troisgros,

Bocuse, Guerard, Robuchon, and so on . . . We know their progeny, the ones who came after—who begot whom—and in which kitchens—and we are comforted by knowing the names. It puts our own lives, our own toil, in perspective—it reminds us that we are a part of something, cogs, however tiny, in a great machine whose wheels have been turning for centuries. One of the best parts of being a chef or a cook is exactly that sense of belonging to something, of being made members of a large and secret society. It feels good knowing you are part of a long and glorious tradition of suffering, insanity, and excess. We may not have a secret handshake (though even brushing contact with the callused hand of another cook communicates, in an instant, scads of information) but we have a language, customs, tribal rituals all our own. There is a common structure, a shared understanding of the world, a hierarchy, terminology, and initiation with which we are all—whether flipping burgers in a Bora Bora beach bar or spooning caviar at the top of the World Trade Center—intimately familiar, and we take comfort in that too.

It has been until all too recently, however, a predominantly male club, this thing of ours. In exactly the reverse of the ignorant dictum that "Women Should Stay in the Kitchen—Preferably While Barefoot and Pregnant," in the hotel/restaurant kitchen it was always, "They're not strong enough to lift heavy stockpots!" (Hilariously wrong in that NO cook I've ever seen hoisted full stockpots without assistance—okay, one guy. We called him Hernia Boy.) Women, it was said, "can't take the pressure!" They're "too emotional!" You want to see emotional? Watch a table of ten's order come back for a refire in a busy all-male kitchen in the middle of the rush. You've never seen such weeping and rending of garments and tantrum throwing since you smacked your little brother and took away his favorite stuffed toy.

Point is, in the annals of professional cooking, there are precious few names of women. Catherine de' Medici comes to mind, but she didn't cook. She was, however, smart enough to bring along some Italian cooks when she moved to France. Had she not, the French might still be thickening their sauces with bread raspings—and tearing at their food with daggers and bare hands.

Not that women weren't cooking professionally. There were, all along, at any given moment, probably more women cooking than men. It's just that they were doing it in private homes, tiny bistros, Parisian pork stores, institutions. They stayed closer to the traditional role of professional cook of Roman times—which is to say they were slaves. Or darn close. They cooked, most times, alone. The domestic cooks of the nineteenth century and early twentieth didn't often work as part of a crew (a tendency tragically mirrored today with the predominance of the female pâtissière in the otherwise all-male kitchen). They didn't get to enjoy the yo-ho-ho camaraderie, the grab-ass hijinks of the restaurant kitchen. They did not enjoy the aid and company of sauciers, grillardins, entremetiers, poissoniers, garde-mangers, and plongeurs to assist them in their work. There were rarely chefs or sous-chefs to stand between them and their masters, no one to protect them from the caprices and unreasonable desires of their clients.

If Mary was part of anything, she was part of a very different movement, one forged in hunger, dislocation, and social upheaval, a sea change which pushed millions of women out of their homeland and away from their traditional roles, across the sea and into the lonely business of domestic servitude.

I have known, at various low points in my long and checkered career, what it feels like when one's pride in what one does—one's love of cooking, one's faith in one's ability—begins to fade, and I know the kind of sloppiness that can follow. Fortunately, in my case, those days are long gone. I got a second chance. Mary never did.

Bouncing from job to job, with lousy pay, no health insurance, no sick days, no vacation, miss one day at work and it's back on the treadmill . . . find another dirty, badly equipped kitchen . . . and no hope in the world. You endure simply so that you can afford to go on enduring. The small, simple joys of a perfectly made bowl of soup, a rustic stew, a lovely piece of fish cooked just right, disappear, replaced over time by a simmering forced-down resentment, bubbling up and choked down again and again like burning reflux. The small annoyances grow large: The way the boss smacks his wet lips when he tastes the soup, the acrid cloud from the steam table, the smell of old grease, the lingering odor of lamb fat—these become the nexus of all the evils and injustices of the world.

That you may have cooked good food in the past, worked in the homes of the rich, in great houses or great kitchens, seen the pyramids or danced naked on the moon, matters not at all. Nobody cares.

Where once you would have turned your head to cough, you turn no longer. Wash your hands after going to the bathroom? Maybe. If you have time, you're beyond caring. The people eating your food are abstractions now. Cough or no cough, you know they'll be back tomorrow, maybe for the Early Bird, the All-You-Can-Eat special. Unwashed hands, an errant cigarette ash, a roasted chicken dropped on a dirty kitchen floor and retrieved on the bounce . . . we've been there, you and me and Mary.

The central question when examining the career of Mary Mallon, cook, is always, "Why did she go on cooking when she had every reason to believe she was spreading a possibly fatal disease?" Many of you who've worked in greasy spoons, coffee shops, cafeterias, failing, not-very-good restaurants, institutional food services, know the answer already. I won't blame you if you don't care to admit it. But you know what the "three-second rule" is. Don't you?

Cooks work sick. They always have. Most jobs, you don't work, you don't get paid. You wake up with a sniffle and a runny nose, a sore throat? You soldier on. You put in your hours. You wrap a towel around your neck and you do your best to get through. It's a point of pride, working through pain and illness. And in the paranoid realpolitik world of the kitchen, it makes a great deal of sense. If you don't show up to work, someone else fills in for you—either an already overburdened fellow cook, who takes on additional tasks, or worse, an outsider, an interloper, a stranger who might well be considered to do a better job than you—or be less likely to call in sick in the future. When you are working in a kitchen that serves something less than haute cuisine, the likelihood increases that a strong back and the ability to endure are of the utmost importance, a chef or owner frequently passing over the superior technician for the more reliable one.

Mary, it should be pointed out, felt fine. She was strong. She was tough. She could take it—and she was proud of her endurance. She worked, and she went on—and when after a time they told her to stop, she ignored them and went on working. One finds oneself being defined by one's job. The job expiates us from sin. It excuses us, our excesses, and our lapses. That we are tired, or ill, or in extremis and yet persevere is all we have, sometimes, to sustain our image of ourselves.

Like Mary, I've worked for private clients. Briefly. Had I stayed on, had my boss asked me one more time for "an egg-white omelette—and no butter or oil in the pan," I would surely have grabbed hold of his skull, squeezed until his eyeballs popped out of his head like pachinko balls. Had I worked in the homes of the rich and silly circa 1906? I would have murdered them in their beds with the nearest available blunt object. I was never tough enough to put up with what Mary put up with. I'm "too emotional." I couldn't have "taken the pressure." I doubt very much I could have picked up heavy stockpots alone.

Mary learned her trade over time, the same way most of us learn. By watching, waiting, working our way slowly up from the bottom. By repeating the same tasks over and over again. It's a terrible thing—the worst thing, when a good cook, a proud cook goes bad. When pride and proficiency turn to bitterness and sloth. When outside forces corrupt the desire to do a job well and take pleasure in the doing. It's an awful thing to watch. It's awful when it happens to you.

It's what happened to the cook, Mary Mallon.

Try not to hold it against her.

V

The Low Life

If Tony had grown up in slightly different circumstances, either he would have written *The French Connection* or he would have actually been involved in the real-life French Connection. Luckily for us, his French connection was chiefly through food and travel (and his parents), and later on in life he was able to kick his heroin habit. Nevertheless, he was for a time a creature of downtown New York, when downtown New York meant something more than NYU and Soho sales. Of course kitchens provided him with an endless cast of characters, many of whom shared his youthful pursuit of sensation. The other thing that connected Tony to the low life was his lifelong fascination with crime fiction and crime stories more generally, and there's a reason his fiction is almost exclusively oriented around criminals and their desperate schemes to rise ever so slightly in the world.

Things to Do Today

An excerpt from *Gone Bamboo*, originally published by
Villard Books in 1997.

The man known as Kevin sat nursing a pint of Guinness at the
end of the bar. He was pale, somewhat overweight, in his early
fifties, and like the other men in the Shandon Green Tavern,
dressed in jeans, heavy work boots, and a denim work shirt worn over a
T-shirt. He wore a New York Mets baseball cap, and his face, as he had
been sitting there drinking since nine that morning, was lit with alcohol
and pink around the nose and cheeks.

It was like this between jobs: dreamland, a half-life of slurred
voices, stooped old men, barely remembered good intentions. Kevin,
for the ninth or tenth time that day, started a list in his head—"Things
to Do Today"—and again he could think of nothing.

The Jets were going down to another defeat on the silent overhead
TV screen, attracting little interest from the patrons at the bar. The man
sitting two stools down from Kevin was slumped forward, his face nearly
touching a half-finished plate of mashed potatoes, cabbage, and gravy in
front of him. A bleary-eyed harridan, with missing teeth and makeup on
sideways, loudly bemoaned her stolen welfare check on Kevin's other
side, her drinking companion, a wiry old man reading a racing form,
ignoring her. The stools next to Kevin were vacant. Even drunk, the
customers at the Shandon Green knew enough about him to be afraid.

People drank whiskey and beer. There wasn't a screwdriver, a sea
breeze, a margarita, or a mixed drink of any kind to be seen. Shots and
beer—serious drinks for serious drinkers.

Kevin let his eyes pass over the familiar row of framed portraits of

Joyce, Yeats, O'Casey, and other notable Irishmen behind the bar; the dusty commemorative bottles of single malt, the obligatory shillelagh, the clovers and maps of Ireland, the placards with clever sayings like YOU DON'T HAVE TO BE AN ASSHOLE TO WORK HERE, BUT IT HELPS.

The place stank of stale beer. The wooden bar sucked up spills like a sponge, year after year. Whiskey breath, the cigarettes that burned in every ashtray and dangled from the lips of the other customers, the pungent odors of pastrami, cabbage, turkey, and roast beef wafting from the long steam table near the front door—it all mixed into the particular hell-broth you found only on the west side of Manhattan.

Kevin signaled for another pint, and in a moment his glass was refilled, the bartender fishing two wet singles and a quarter out of the pile next to Kevin's ashtray without comment. One didn't make conversation with Kevin when he was drinking. The baby-faced psychopaths who came by once a week to collect the envelope, even they were respectful of the big man. That told you all you needed to know.

Somebody in the rear dining area dropped some quarters into the jukebox—a large group of stagehands were doing some midafternoon drinking—and Van Morrison came over the speakers, drowning out the ambient sound of street noise and disappointment.

The pay phone rang by the front door, and Tom, the bowlegged sandwich man, picked it up. He listened for a second, left the receiver hanging, and walked down to Kevin's stool, where he leaned in close. "It's a parson wantin' ta speak with you, Kev," he whispered.

Kevin slid carefully off his stool and picked his way, one foot after the other, down to the phone. He put the receiver to his ear and said, "Yeah."

"This Kevin?" asked the voice on the other end.

"Himself."

"A man wants to talk wit' you," said the voice.

"What man would that be?" asked Kevin. It wasn't Brian Meehan on the phone—the accent was all Brooklyn, and Kevin was feeling bilious and ill humored.

"You know the one," said the voice. "The man from the place . . . the place across the river there. The fat one. You know who I'm talkin' about?"

"Yeah. I think so."

"He wants to talk to you."

"Okay. Okay. So he wants to talk to me. I got that," said Kevin, the Guinness fogging his brain and a growing pressure on his bladder making it difficult to think.

"You know that place Rudy's over there? The one on Ninth?" said the voice.

"The place with the free hot dogs?"

"That's the place, that one. Okay? Be out front there at ten thirty tonight. Somebody gonna come by in a car and pick you up."

"Yeah? And just where am I goin' in this car?"

"Lissen," said the voice, "you want the work or not? The man talked to some people said you was available to work. You want it or not? There's other people he can call."

"He talk with my friend?"

"He talked with your friend."

"All right then."

"Ten thirty. In front a Rudy's."

"Right."

Kevin had a good piss in the men's room, retrieved his CPO jacket, his change, and his cigarettes, and lurched unsteadily out onto Ninth Avenue, leaving his latest Guinness untouched at the bar.

In his single room at the Globe Hotel on Eighth Avenue, Kevin took a long, cold shower and emerged from the mildewy stall looking for a towel. Unable to find one, he dried himself off with a T-shirt. He brushed his teeth and shaved, using the disposable razor the hooker he'd brought home the night before had used on her legs. He made a mess of his face, stanching the bleeding with bits of toilet paper, so many of them that the little red and white dots swam around in front of his rheumy eyes like stars when he tried to count them in the mirror.

He had something for his Things to Do list now, and he combed his thinning, straw-colored hair, scrutinizing his reflection with new purpose. It was not a terribly impressive sight, he knew. His swollen gut billowed out over his waist, pale and fish-belly white.

Climb Out

An excerpt from *Kitchen Confidential*, originally published by
Bloomsbury in 2000.

It is one of the central ironies of my career that as soon as I got off heroin, things started getting really bad. High on dope, I was—prior to Gino's—at least a chef, well paid, much liked by crew and floor and owners alike. Stabilized on methadone, I became nearly unemployable by polite society: a shiftless, untrustworthy coke-sniffer, sneak thief, and corner-cutting hack, toiling in obscurity in the culinary backwaters. I worked mostly as a cook, moving from place to place, often working under an alias.

I worked a seedy hotel on upper Madison, a place so slow that the one waiter would have to come downstairs and wake me when customers came in. I was the lone cook, my only companions the hotel super and a gimpy dishwasher. I worked a lunch counter on Amsterdam, flipping pancakes and doing short-order eggs for democratic politicos and their bagmen. I worked a bizarre combination art gallery / bistro on Columbus, just me and a coke-dealing bartender—a typically convenient and destructive symbiotic arrangement. I was a sous-chef at a very fine two-star place on Thirty-ninth, where I dimly recall preparing a four-course meal for Paul Bocuse; he thanked me in French, I think. My brain, at this point, was shriveled by cocaine, and I made the mistake of telling a garde-manger man that if he didn't hurry up with an order, I'd tear his eyes out and skull-fuck him, which did not endear me to the fussy owner-manager. I worked a deserted crab house on Second Avenue, steaming blue crabs and frying crab cakes. I cooked brunches in Soho; I slopped out steam-table chow at a bar on Eighth Street to a bunch of drunks.

For a time, I took another chef's job—of sorts—at a moment of need at Billy's, a combo sit-down/takeout upscale chicken joint on Bleecker Street. It was an operation that was to be the flagship of another planned empire, a chain of chicken joints that would stretch across the globe.

At this low point in my career, I didn't care if the place succeeded or not. I needed the money.

My boss was an older Jewish guy, fresh out of prison, who'd named the place after his youngest son, Billy, a feckless ne'er-do-well. He had been, in an earlier life, the head of the counting room at a Las Vegas casino, and after being caught skimming off millions for the "boys back in New York and Cincinnati," had been offered a friendly deal should he cooperate with the prosecutors. He had, admirably, declined, and as a result spent the last five years eating prison chow. When he got out, a near-broken man, his old buddies in New York, being Men of Honor, set him up with this restaurant—with promises of more to come—as a sign of gratitude for services rendered.

Unfortunately, while in prison, the old man had completely lost his mind. He may have been a stand-up guy, but he was absolutely barking mad.

This was not a classic bust-out operation, where the mob deliberately runs a place into the ground, using a front man / straw owner to run up bills, then pillage the place for merchandise and credit. I think that the wise guys, who from the early days of start-up were always around, really wanted the poor slob to make money and be a success. They made earnest efforts to help at every turn, enduring much nonsense from their visibly deranged partner.

It was, in retrospect, a useful experience for me, one I relied on for later works of fiction. I'd seen mobsters around before, of course, but I'd never worked in a place that was out-and-out mobbed up, where I came to know on a personal basis *real* wise guys, whose names I recognized from the papers. Everyone was astonishingly up front about their connections. My boss was fond of yelling into the phone when discussing prices with a purveyor: "You know who I am? You know who I'm *with*?!"

We did things differently at Billy's.

My cooks, for one: Every one of them came from the Fortune Society, guys who spent their off-hours in halfway houses, allowed out only to work. I was used to working with a fairly rough bunch, a lot of whom, at one time or another, had had problems with the law—but at Billy's, every single one of my cooks was *still* basically a convict. I can't say that it was an unhappy arrangement, either. For once I *knew* my cooks were going to show up at work every day; if they didn't, they went back to prison.

And credit was easily obtained. I knew, from previous experience, how difficult it is to set up terms for a new restaurant; even getting a week's credit with some of these companies was usually a lengthy process, involving credit applications, a long wait, initial periods of cash on delivery. At Billy's, no sooner was I off the phone than stuff was arriving, often on *sixty-day* terms. Produce and dry goods people who'd been loath to offer even two weeks at other places I'd worked were suddenly all too happy to give me all the time I wanted.

My boss spent a lot of time on the phone, investigating the serious business of horses and their bloodlines, and how well they ran in mud or on grass. Billy himself, at eighteen, was happy to drive his sports car around and chase girls. So my day-to-day was spent mostly with some genial gentlemen from an Italian fraternal organization. They helpfully told me where to buy my meat and poultry and how to meet the folks who would be supplying my linen, bread, paper goods, and so on. I had a lot of meetings in cars.

"The bread guy is here," I'd be told, and a late-model Buick would pull up out front. An old guy in a mashed-down golf cap would beckon me from the driver's seat and then get out of the car. The older guy in the passenger seat would slide over, indicating he wanted me to get in, sit next to him, and talk. We'd sit there in the idling car, talking cryptically about bread, before he brought me around to the trunk to examine some product. It was a strange business.

Yet some things were off-limits. Trash removal, I found, was a mysteriously prearranged division of labor. When I called around for price quotes, told them for whom I was calling, I was repeatedly quoted prices far exceeding the national debt—until I called the company I'd obviously been intended to do business with. "Oh yeah, Billy's," said the voice on the phone, "I was waiting for youse to call!" and quoted me a very reasonable price. I rang up a meat company, inquiring if they'd care to sell me tens of thousands of dollars of burger patties a year, and they gave me a flat "No!" They wouldn't even quote me prices. I was confused by this until years later, when I read a Paul Castellano biography called *Boss of Bosses*, and recognized the name of the meat company as a business operated by another family.

And there was the Chicken Guy, who also met me in a car, and showed me samples in a trunk. When I introduced him to my boss, the old man bitched about the price, telling the Chicken Guy, in his blood-smeared white butcher's coat, that the price was too high, that he could "just fly to fucking Virginia, buy the stuff direct," and "Do you know *who I'm with anyway*?!"

The Chicken Guy was not impressed. He spat on the floor, looked my boss in the eye, and said, "Fuck *you*, asshole! You know who *I'm with*?! You can fly to fuckin' Virginia and buy direct all you want—you *still* gonna pay me! Frank fuckin' Perdue pays me, asshole! *And you're gonna pay me too!*"

My boss was suitably chastened—for a time.

But he got wackier and wackier. When we finally opened, we were packed from the first minute. Orders flooded in over the phone and at the counter and at the tables. We were unprepared and understaffed, so the Italian contingent—including various visiting dignitaries, all with oddly anglicized names ("This is Mr. Dee, Tony, and meet a friend, Mr. Brown . . . This is Mr. Lang"), all of them overweight, cigar-chomping middle-aged guys with bodyguards and ten-thousand-dollar watches—pitched in to help out with deliveries and at the counter. Guys I'd read about later in the papers as running construction in the outer boroughs, purported killers, made men, who lived in concrete piles on Staten Island and Long Beach and security-fenced estates in Jersey, carried brown paper bags of chicken sandwiches up three flights of stairs to

Greenwich Village walk-up apartments to make deliveries; they slathered mayo and avocado slices on pita bread behind the counter, and bused tables in the dining room. I have to say I liked them for that.

But when my boss, inexplicably, showed up one day and told me to fire everyone with a tattoo on my staff, I was faced with a dilemma. Every one of my cooks was festooned with prison tats: screaming skulls; Jesus on hypodermic crosses, bound in barbed wire; gang tats; flaming dice; swastikas; SS flashes; *Born to Lose*; *Born Dead*; *Born to Raise Hell*; *Love*; *Hate*; *Mom*; portraits of the Madonna, wives, girlfriends, Ozzy Osbourne. I tried to put him off, explaining that we couldn't do without these guys, that the hardest-working, most indispensable guy we had—the guy who right now was loading trash cans with hundreds of marinating chicken parts in the cramped, stifling unrefrigerated cellar on his twenty-second consecutive double shift—was a goddamn Sistine Chapel of skin art. And where am I going to find a convict without a tattoo? The Watergate burglars weren't, to my knowledge, available.

Things only got worse. He came in the next day, obsessing about gold chains and jewelry. My grill man had the usual ghetto adornments of the day. "Where do you think that eggplant *got* all that gold?!" he raved, spraying food and saliva as he talked. "Selling *drugs*. That shit is *poison*! Mugging old ladies! I don't want that in my restaurant! Get him out!"

This was clearly impossible, and I sought counsel with one of the silent partners who, as my boss had become increasingly distracted and unpredictable, had grown noticeably less silent. He and his associates had started to attend management meetings. "You hear what he wants me to do?" I asked. The man just nodded and rolled his eyes, sympathetically, I thought.

"Do nothing," he said, and then, with truly dangerous intonation, added, "*Aspetta*," meaning "Wait" in Italian.

I didn't like the sound of that at all. He smiled at me, and I couldn't help picturing my boss, slumped over a dashboard after one of those meetings in a car they were all so fond of. When things came to a head a few days later, my boss openly screaming in the middle of a crowded dining room that he wanted all the tattooed guys and gold chain-wearers "out! Now!" I told him to pay me what he owed—I was leaving for good. He refused. The silent partner came over, peeled off my pay and an extra hundred from a fat roll in his suit pocket, and gave me a warm smile as he bade me goodbye.

I don't know what happened to Billy's. It certainly never developed into a worldwide chain as my crazed boss had envisioned—or even a second store. The next time I was in the neighborhood, a picture framer occupied the space where the restaurant had been. What happened to the old man and his dreams of a poultry empire for his son? I can only guess.

I worked at a Mexican restaurant on upper Second Avenue for a while, one of those places on the frat-boy strip with the obligatory margarita snow-cone machine grinding away all night and vomit running ankle-deep in the gutters outside. The place was owned by a very aggressive rat population, fattened up and emboldened by the easily obtained stacks of avocados left to ripen outside the walk-in each night. They ran over our feet in the kitchen, hopped out of the garbage when you approached, and, worst of all, stashed their leavings in the walls and ceilings. Every once in a while, the soggy, acoustic tile ceilings would crumble, and moist avalanches of avocado pits, chewed chicken bones, and half-eaten potatoes would come tumbling out on our heads.

I was reaching rock bottom, both personally and professionally. I got canned from the Mexican place, for which particular reason I don't know; there were plenty of good ones—alcoholism, drug abuse, pilferage, laziness—I don't know which of these unlovely traits actually did me in. But I didn't mind; the rats were really bugging me, especially when I was high on coke, which was most of the time.

I worked in an all-Chinese kitchen for a time, squatting on the floor with my fellow cooks, sharing their simple staff meals of rice gruel, pork broth, and fish bones each day, shoveling in my food with chopsticks and betting on how many plum tomatoes would be in a case in the day's delivery. I cracked oysters at a shellfish bar, watching as drunken customers gobbled jumbo shrimps without bothering to remove the shells—so pickled from booze they were beyond caring. I came to know actors, loan sharks, enforcers, car thieves, guys who sold false ID, phone scammers, porno stars, and a dope-fiend hostess who attended mortician school during the day. She came up to me one night at the shellfish bar, a blissed-out look on her face, and said, "We did a baby today in school . . . and it . . . like . . . aspirated in my arms, man. You could hear it sigh when I picked it up!" She looked happy about this. She had a fetish for Con Ed workers—something about the uniforms, I guess. And whenever they were doing electrical work or repairing a gas line in her neighborhood, she'd come in the next day singing the praises of the fine folks who kept our utilities running.

I got to know a steely-eyed Irish hood in his fifties who worked "with" the pressmen's union, sometimes. When he had a big tune-up scheduled, he'd recruit other regulars from the bar to go down to some warehouse or printing plant and smack some heads together. One night he came in with his right hand busted up terribly, the knuckles pushed back nearly to his wrist and a bone jutting horribly through the skin.

"Dude!" I said. "You should go to the hospital for that!"

He just smiled and ordered a round for the house, then a dozen oysters and some shrimp with that—and ended up drinking and dancing and partying until closing time, waving his bloody hand around like a merit badge. His pal James, who wore the same fatigue jacket he'd worn in Vietnam fifteen years earlier, liked to hang out by my shellfish bar, telling stories. James was a West Village celebrity, never, to anyone's knowledge, having paid for a drink. He lived off the generosity of others, throwing a well-attended rent party once a month so he could pay for the curtained-off illegal cellar cubicle he called home. James carried a mysterious stainless-steel attaché case with him wherever he went, hinting that it contained the Great American Novel, the Nuclear Codes, Unlimited Firepower. I suspected it was a few tattered copies of *Penthouse* and maybe a change of socks—but smelling James, I was less sure about the socks. He was a bright, sweet, apparently educated guy from a military family. He'd been eighty-sixed from half the bars in the Village, but the place I worked put up with him as long as the customers were willing to endure him. I admired his survival skills, his longevity, his staying power. He certainly didn't get by on his looks. He'd just learned how to hustle, instinctively—he didn't do it in a calculating way, he just did what was necessary to stay alive.

I saw myself becoming like him, and I didn't like it. Okay, I wasn't cadging drinks for a living, listening to a bunch of drunks in return for the occasional freebie, or throwing rent parties. I did have a job, and an apartment and a girlfriend who still, it appeared, loved me. But there was little good happening in my life. I was living paycheck to paycheck. My apartment was a dark, dusty cavern with paint peeling off the ceilings. Though I was no longer getting high at work, my off-hours were still revolving around the acquiring and doing of controlled substances—even if they weren't heroin. I was barely a cook. My culinary education, my early food epiphanies, the tastes and textures and experiences of my childhood in France and my rather privileged high school and college years were of little use to me behind a shellfish bar.

Something had to change. I had to get it together. I'd been the culinary equivalent of the *Flying Dutchman* too long, living a half-life with no future in mind, just oozing from sensation to sensation. I was a disgrace, a disappointment to friends and family and myself, and the drugs and the booze no longer chased that disappointment away. I could no longer bear even to pick up the phone; I'd just listen to the answering machine, afraid or unwilling to pick up, the plaintive entreaties of the callers an annoyance. If they had good news, it would simply make me envious and unhappy. If they had bad news, I was the last guy in the world who could help. Whatever I had to say to anybody would have been inappropriate. I was in hiding, in a deep, dark hole, and it was dawning on me—as I cracked my oysters, and opened clams and spooned cocktail sauce into ramekins—that it was time, *really* time, to try to climb out.

In the Face of a Jumpy Coke Addict I See a Dead Man

A piece Tony wrote for the *Los Angeles Times* about Robert Downey Jr. and addiction, originally published in 2000.

There is no one less sympathetic to the trials, tribulations, and humiliations of an addict than an ex-junkie. No emergency room triage is more immediate and unforgiving than the way an ex-junkie sizes up a still-in-the-grip former colleague.

I hear that familiar, whiny tone of voice. I see the pinned, cartoon eyes of the smack user or the jumpy, twitchy, molar-grinding, gibberish-spewing face of the coke fiend. I see a dead man. I'm not listening anymore. If I pay attention at all, it's to make sure they're not rifling through my coat.

Cold? Yes. But then, junkies are used to stone-cold logic. Life, for someone whose body, brain, nerves, and cell tissue require (rather than desire) his drug of choice in order to get out of bed in the morning, is actually a very simple matter. You have one job: Get drugs. There's only one thing you have to do each day: Get drugs. One's priorities are always straight. Simply put: Nothing else matters.

Those of us who have been addicted to heroin and/or cocaine (and I've been addicted to both) understand this better than anybody. You know, without question, that your best friend in the world will, given the opportunity, steal your drugs or your money or snitch you off to the cops. You know, without question, exactly how low you would be willing to go to get what you need. Chances are, you've been there already. More than once.

Stories about drugs and rehabilitation are boring—particularly when it's some Hollywood actor, grinning out from the cover of *People* magazine, yammering about Clean and Sober and his new project.

We've heard it all before. Some people live, others die. Who survives and who doesn't seems most often to have been determined long before the junkie enters treatment—when he looks in the mirror one morning and decides that he really, truly wants to live. If there's any question in his mind, before he even walks through the methadone clinic or rehab facility doors, about how badly he wants to turn things around and what he's willing to do to accomplish that, then lose my number. I know you in my bones.

The memory of the bitter taste of heroin in the back of my throat, the smell of burning candles, the taste of paint chips mistaken for a pebble of dropped crack, a whiff of urine and stale air from long-ago tenement drug superstores on the Lower East Side all came back when I watched Robert Downey Jr. being hauled off again in handcuffs. And this time, I actually cared a little.

This guy must really hate himself, I thought, reading of cocaine and speed allegedly found in his room. That he is, to my mind, one of the finest actors working in Hollywood matters not at all. That he's spent some time in jail was, if anything, a recommendation.

I'd hoped he'd be cast in one of the film versions of my books as he seemed to have the perfect résumé for the job. My first thought, though, was, *Cocaine and speed? That's not comfortable oblivion; that's pedal to the metal, headed straight for the wall.*

It's more panic, paranoia, the inevitable crash. If there is a faster route to the dung heap I don't know of it. It can't even be fun anymore. After years of having as much cocaine as you want, you find yourself just chasing that first pleasurable hit, looking to recapture that first pleasant rush. You never find it.

More than likely, you wind up squatting naked by the front door, listening for the tunneling probe microphones that aren't really there.

Ally McBeal can't have helped. If I was an actor of Downey's caliber, I can't say I'd be too happy with myself, mugging and lip-locking on that silly, faux heartwarming exercise in cynicism. I wondered immediately: *The guy's right out of the joint! Who let him work a job where he's going to have damn good reason to hate himself?*

People are very fragile when they leave rehab. For the first year, it seems like the pleasure centers of the brain have shut down for good, like your oldest and best love has died. This is not a time to acquire new reasons for shame, fear, regret; you've had plenty of that already. It's time to get away. Far away from old friends, old haunts, old temptations. In the jargon of rehab, "bottoming out" is mentioned frequently and annoyingly often as a prerequisite to treatment.

When life is at least as unbearable with drugs as without, when the thought of a fat stack of glassine envelopes or an eight-ball promises only more misery, some people make that hard choice to tally up the betrayals and the wreckage and keep living. It's not easy. Many—if not most—fail. Most times, you really have to do something terribly shameful, experience awfulness in previously unimagined degrees before you see a life without drugs as a preferred, even necessary, option.

Jail, in Downey's case, doesn't seem to have been enough. Hopefully, *Ally McBeal* was.

I'm a Chef . . .

A piece Tony wrote for the London *Times* about being a chef, which was not published. Date unknown.

I'm a chef. I've been a chef and a line cook—and before that, a dishwasher and prep drone—for over twenty years. As a chef, I always know how well or how poorly things are going: number of meals served, number and nature of customer comments, number of stars awarded, dollar amount of the night's receipts. These are the reassuringly constant parameters for what I do. Outside the kitchen doors, however, things are different.

In 1993, I was nearing the end of what I often jokingly refer to as my "wilderness years," a long middle period in my career, spent mostly in anonymous toil for a procession of one-lung mom-and-pop restaurants, Greenwich Village saloons, mob-run takeout joints, failing hotels, and soon-to-be bankrupt bistros. The eighties had been an exhilarating, if debilitating, time for me, and I was not yet ready to take the helm of another kitchen. I was in hiding, working under an assumed name, keeping my head down, trying to get well, and avoiding responsibility whenever possible. I was tired and broke.

So it came as a very nice surprise when my old friend, college roommate, and former criminal associate "Harold" called. Harold was in the licensing business. I still don't fully understand what that means, but back then, I gathered it meant that he parlayed certain recognizable name brands into other ventures, selling the rights, for instance, to the name of a well-known almanac to a publisher for use on calendars, coffee table books, amusing collections of anecdotes for bathroom reading. Harold had apparently been doing pretty well and had the ear of a few well-disposed editors. More important, he had had a recent epiphany: Sitting on a beach somewhere and reading a paperback copy of some fabulously successful legal thriller, he'd remembered me. Back in college, though I'd seldom bothered to attend class myself, I'd had a rather lucrative cottage business writing English papers and film essays for other students to plagiarize. Women customers in particular, it seemed, did very well with my material, their professors impressed by their sudden metamorphoses from aspiring Sylvia Plaths and Anaïs Nins to sardonic, wiseass stylists with somewhat more bone-crunching subject matter. Harold, as well as being a friend, had been one of my best customers and had me in mind when he returned from vacation and confronted an editor he'd worked with.

"I know a guy who can write better than this!" he boasted. Harold was fond of hyperbole. That he'd read nothing of mine in fifteen years did not deter him—nor did the fact that I had barely written a word in all that time.

I was breaking down chickens in a moribund saloon's kitchen when he called.

"Tony! I'll take you to an island. In Mexico. Cozumel," he said. "And I'll pay for everything. All you gotta do is write a hundred pages of a book for me to show this guy. When you finish, he'll read it, and if he buys it, I'll split the dough with you fifty/fifty."

Now, to any experienced writer—or even a novice writer—this might not have sounded like such a good deal. Fifty percent is a little higher than the usual cut for a representative of literary projects. But I hadn't been to a beach—much less a tropical beach—in ages. And I was breaking down chickens for chicken pot pie for Chrissakes! Nobody else was offering to take me to an island in the Gulf of Mexico for ten days. So I enthusiastically agreed. A few months later, I'd written the first few chapters of *Bone in the Throat*. Though pleased with the results so far, I had no expectation that it would ever be published. I was shocked when Random House bought it.

The action in the book takes place in a fictional version of an earlier period in my long and checkered career as a chef, a more hope-filled time, in the early eighties in New York's Soho, when I and a group of like-minded friends were hired to staff the kitchen of a formerly trendy restaurant which had fallen on hard times and been acquired by new owners.

We were young. We were ambitious. We were half-smart—almost good at what we were doing. And we were on drugs. It was the early days of food culture in New York, and we thought we were the only American cooks around who'd read the *Larousse Gastronomique*, who knew what nouvelle cuisine was about, who could reel off the names of our betters in Europe: Bocuse, Guerard, Verge, Troisgros, and the names of those who'd come before: Vatel, Carême, Escoffier. We were determined to make our mark, to scrawl our names—in blood if necessary—across the culinary firmament, and we were absolutely convinced of our greatness. We saw sex and drugs and rock 'n' roll as in no way divergent from the serious business of haute cuisine. We thought ourselves dangerous, trend-settingly debauched, and, of course, in no time at all, had made a serious botch of it all. The restaurant went under in less than eighteen months.

But even in 1993, post rehab and working in somewhat less ambitious circumstances, I retained a real sentimental attachment to those early, heady, hope-filled times. And a lot else had happened in the intervening years that helped inspire and inform the creation of the quasi-fictional subculture in *Bone in the Throat*. When I'd started out, organized crime was a much more prevalent factor in the restaurant business. You were told who your trash hauler was to be. Linen companies, seafood purveyors, poultry, meat and produce purveyors were often assumed to be joined at the hip with one of the five New York crime families. Accounting and labor practices were less regulated, to say the least. I'd worked for an overtly mob-associated chicken joint— where the boss, fresh out of jail, proudly surrounded himself with a cast of characters who would not have been out of place in a Scorsese film. My cooks at this place were all on work-release from prison. They'd show up at work, do their eight hours, and return to lockup at night. I had a lot of business meetings in cars with guys who called themselves "Mr. Brown" or "Mr. Dee." I took an interest, genuinely liking some of these fellows, and later began following some of their trials closely, reading the transcripts of wiretap recordings, keeping track of which ones were found in the trunks of abandoned cars, which ones turned state's evidence, which went missing, never to return.

I set *Bone in the Throat* in a restaurant very much like that Soho spawning ground years earlier, filling it with characters much like my chef and fellow cooks of the time. I made my good guys people with serious problems and conflicting loyalties and tried as best I could to make my characters sound like the people I knew and worked with. I never really believed the damn thing would be published—but if nothing else, I was determined that the cooks and chefs in the novel would talk like the cooks and chefs I knew and that the mobsters would sound more like the low-level organized crime associates I'd worked with than the kind of Homeric figures who populated *The Godfather.* I did not want any cooks or crooks of my acquaintance to read my manuscript and say, "Hey! I don't know anybody who talks like that! Who talks like that?" My cooks would have the same narrow, parochial concerns, the same hyperalert tunnel vision and paranoia we'd all had back then in the early eighties. And I wanted all that bad sex, bad drugs, hard rock 'n' roll, and occasional mortal terror to permeate the book's atmosphere as it had my life at the time.

If there are two central events in *Bone*, there is the "knife incident," where a chef finds that his much-loved and wildly expensive Japanese knife has been terribly misused by person or persons unknown. This remains a not unrealistic scenario—a chef getting hot about someone monkeying with his knife. We chefs are fiercely territorial about our tools. We don't like other cooks—much less civilians—messing with them. And then there's the "squid epiphany," where a young Francophilic sous-chef sees the threat of having to put a humble, Italian-style deep-fried calamari in tomato sauce on the menu as a precursor of the apocalypse. This is an accurate example of our worldview, then and now. We chefs like to think of ourselves as creative masterminds and innovators whenever possible. Our day-to-day responsibilities really have more to do with repetition and consistency than high-minded conceptualizing, and it's not too much of a stretch to imagine a young culinarian finding the thought of heaps of deep-fried squid rings drowning in red sauce to be soul destroying—a negation of everything he thinks he stands for. I felt that way. Once.

And of course, *Bone* being set in the early eighties, I couldn't help but describe the gigantic superstore of illegal powder merchants who'd set up shop on the Lower East Side of the time. Empty burned-out tenements had been converted by armies of criminal entrepreneurs into fortified rabbit warrens of steel-lined drug dispensaries, dark, candlelit labyrinths, where gun-toting steerers would guide hordes of new-generation junkies through unlit, water-filled hallways, up broken stairways, through punched-out walls, down into trash-strewn cellars; and I wanted to capture the fear and excitement of that criminal choreography, the movement through city streets and empty buildings of thousands and thousands of largely unnoticed and desperately needy young predators.

I don't know that I intended to make *Bone* funny—though I'm told it is. In fact, it is usually described as a crime comedy, or satirical thriller. That just happened. Criminals "talk funny"—and seem, even in real life, to get themselves into absurd and often humorous situations. Mobsters and lawmen, it appears, can't avoid the cruelly ironic in their daily work. And they seem at times, from what I can tell, to have a lot of fun exploring the soft and vulnerable spots in each other's natures, looking for areas to exploit. A wise guy looks to take advantage of some knucklehead restaurateur who finds himself overextended, seeing it as an opportunity to lend money at usurious rates, acquire food and property for resale, provide patronage jobs for cronies who need visible sources of legitimate income—or are too stupid to steal—and farm out business to associated criminal enterprises. Prosecutors and cops, on the other hand, are looking for an unhappy criminal—somebody passed over for promotion, under-rewarded by his masters for his loyal services over the years. They want to take advantage of his failings, his feelings of pride, bitterness, spite, or fear. They're looking for a bad guy in trouble to squeeze—someone with a long prison sentence hanging over his head, or a very real concern that one of these days, his best buddy is going to put a bullet behind his ear. The manipulation of sources and informants can be as cruel and as callous, and hopefully as funny, as the workaday business of loan-sharking, extortion, and murder.

As a chef, I am not entirely unfamiliar with the "handling" of informants. I work ten to seventeen hours a day in a smoky, claustrophobic kitchen, and my "reach" needs to extend beyond those four walls. There are things I need to know. I need to peer deeply into the dark hearts and minds of my crew of talented but frequently piratical thugs. So that dance—part bullying, part seduction—where one person tries to get another to betray a confidence or a friend is something I know well.

By the time *Bone* was published, my culinary career had taken a very nice upturn. I was, after a long absence, again a chef, a leader of men, this time as executive chef of a very swanky midtown nightclub / supper club. I had another novel in the pipeline, *Gone Bamboo*, which, though it took place in the Caribbean, was also populated with deeply flawed and occasionally homicidal New Yorkers. When *Bone* appeared on bookshelves, I had no idea what was in store for me. I had almost no writer friends, and no experience at book tours, television promotions, interviews. I had no clue as to how the book would be received and no idea how an author should behave. I'd spent the last decade in kitchens and was uncomfortable with dealing with the general public—I'd always had waiters and captains to do that. When *Bone* was favorably reviewed by the *New York Times*—and later named as Notable Book of the Year—I really didn't understand why. Sales were dismal. Though I got a lot of press, and a number of free meals out of interested Hollywood studios—and became semi-notorious in New York chef circles— the book itself sank into the landfill of remainderdom like another dead gangster. When my editor at Random House moved to another publisher, I was left confused, excited, and disappointed all at the same time. With an increasingly lucrative and high-profile chef's career to deal with, the "writing scam" felt more and more like a hustle— something a little shifty I did in my spare time. My cooks sure didn't think much of it. Outside interests don't count for much in my world. One is judged in the kitchen by one's performance as a cook and as a chef; someone manages to find a cure for cancer on their day off, they will be viewed only with suspicion and maybe even a little bit of contempt by one's comrades. This is an attitude I understand completely. I feel the same way. Nobody likes a dilettante.

Then, unexpectedly, my restaurant closed. In a rush of rage, frustration, regret, and lost love, I wrote a long, deranged poisoned valentine to the restaurant industry which I mailed blindly to the *New Yorker* magazine. They bought it. They printed it. And I became instantly and genuinely notorious, referred to in restaurant trade magazines as a "turncoat," as a "Benedict Arnold." The story itself, referred to as "that chef article," meant I was suddenly in demand as a writer again. That most readers missed the point of the article entirely, seeing my frank account of chefs' attitudes toward the general public and my mention of some less than appetizing food-handling practices as an exposé, didn't matter. Suddenly, people were calling me up and offering me money to write. I'm now in the eerily uncomfortable position of being a "memoirist." And there's something . . . undignified about still being alive when your life story comes out. I can tell you that it's a good thing my bosses at my restaurant have a sense of humor, 'cause this project is definitely going to finish me in the business. I don't want to be out on the street looking for work with this particular project at the head of my résumé.

I still have no idea what I'm doing. Like I said, I'm still a chef. I know how to behave in my very busy kitchen, presently a classically old-school French brasserie on lower Park Avenue. The ebb and flow of hungry diners, the movements, moods, and psychotic episodes of my crew of cooks, are warm and familiar to me. I know chefs and cooks I can trust. I don't know of many writers I wouldn't subject to a frisk after a stay in my home. If my circumstances change, and I find myself sticking up liquor stores for a living, I won't be asking any writers to drive the getaway car.

In March, I'll be visiting the London Book Fair, putting on the black pullover and the writer jacket and flogging my books around the UK. But tomorrow? Tomorrow, I'm cooking choucroute garnie for three hundred people. I'm serving smoked duck breast and foie gras and runny stinky cheeses to a horde of the hungry, unseen public. I'm hauling crates of veal bones and shell steaks up and down the stairs with my crew of heavily tattooed and brilliantly talented Mexicans and Frenchmen, a lovable band of roughnecks whose every foible I find adorable and endearing. I'm making cassoulet, *boudin noir*, rillettes, whole roasted *dorade*, demi-glace, basil oil, *terrine de lapin*, and *saucisse de poisson*. I'm slinging pans and roasting ducks and terrorizing waiters and calling out orders over the clatter and din of a busy kitchen.

I like writing. I like telling stories. In the kitchen there is a long and distinguished oral tradition, and I enjoy trying to capture that multilingual, unbelievably obscene patois on paper.

But I'm not entirely comfortable as an "author." I know I can cook. Five hundred people coming to dinner? No problem. I know what to do. This writing thing? It's shifting sands.

Crime

An excerpt from *The Nasty Bits: Collected Varietal Cuts, Usable Trim, Scraps, and Bones*, originally published by Bloomsbury in 2006.

I love reading about crime. I like *writing* about crime. I like listening to wiretap recordings of gangsters, hearing the marvelously loopy, repetitive, elliptical, and wildly profane patois of two semiarticulate career criminals who think they just *might* be being recorded by the FBI, but have business to conduct anyway. It's poetry to me.

In my apartment, Court TV, the twenty-four-hour criminal justice cable network, is always on; the sounds of badly miked witnesses, recorded emergency calls, droning coroners, and preening lawyers are the background music to my leisure hours. While I sip my morning coffee in bed, friends are betraying friends on the stand, pathologists coldly recite the particulars of damage to bones and tissue, stone killers affectlessly describe the circumstances leading up to murder, dismemberment, arson . . . and worse. Lawyers aggressively examine and cross-examine, shrieking with feigned outrage, while outside my windows, car alarms whoop and wail—the occasional urban percussion of shattering safety glass when yet another young entrepreneur makes off with a car stereo. It's like jazz to me, and I miss it when I'm away. The familiar criminal sounds are almost comforting.

A lot of crime buffs favor the lone sociopath, the serial killer, the pathological narcissist. They like maladjusted teens who listen to Metallica, shave their heads, and then go on killing sprees, or former bed wetters who kill their mothers, then describe how they could still hear

Mom's voice, chastising them as they flushed her vocal cords down the food disposal. They thrive on the special little moments in criminal trials when, for instance, the best friend of this month's latest juvenile mass-murderer balks at admitting on the stand that he saw his buddy cry—this just after cheerfully implicating him in the slaughter of ten of his classmates:

> LAWYER: So, after emptying his weapon, am I to understand that Mr. Sprewell adorned his person with the blood of his victims? Is that correct?
>
> WITNESS: Huh?
>
> LAWYER: His face . . . he put blood on his face after killing them?
>
> WITNESS: Oh, yeah. He, like, smeared blood on his cheeks . . . like an Indian, you know? Stripes like. He said it looked cool.
>
> LAWYER: And later . . . after you say you both went back to the defendant's home to play video games and kill his parents . . . did the defendant at any point cry?
>
> WITNESS: Cry? I don't know. I don't know if he, like, cried. He was . . . you know . . . upset.

Me? I'm bored by the lone nut and the sexual psychopath. I don't care to what degree Metallica recordings played a role in young Timmy's transition from honor student to thrill killer. I don't care "who dunnit" . . . or even "why he dunnit," and my tastes in crime fiction reflect that attitude: I'm interested in professional criminals. I'm interested in crimes where you know from the get-go *why* they did it: because it was *their job* to do it. As in the case of the mob-style execution of Gambino capo Paul Castellano, shot to death out front of a popular midtown restaurant. It's the little things I want to know about. Before the killers loaded their weapons and dressed themselves in identical raincoats and hats, before they set out separately from their modest family homes in Staten Island and Queens, did the killers kiss their children, jot down brief shopping lists of groceries to bring back on their return? (One box Cheerios . . . half gallon milk . . . dozen eggs . . .

tampons, large . . . two cans tuna, chunk style.) Did their voices tighten at all at the breakfast table when they told their wives that they might be a little late tonight? Did they program the VCR to tape their favorite sit-com? And what sitcom was it? It's the jargon of crime—the characters, the rituals, the workaday details—that fascinate me.

Crime is hard work, after all.

As a red-blooded American child, I always wanted to be a crimi-nal. My heroes, like those of so many American children, were an unlovely assortment of back-shooters like Billy the Kid, bank robbers like John Dillinger, racketeers like Legs Diamond, capitalist visionar-ies like Bugsy Siegel, and innovators like Lucky Luciano. These were guys who did what they wanted, *when* they wanted, said whatever the fuck they felt like saying, and, in general, avoided the restrictions of societal convention—attractive qualities to a young kid weaned on the MC5 and the Stooges. Later, when I actually *became* a criminal of sorts, trying to support myself through a variety of harebrained drug-dealing schemes, sneak thievery, petty burglary, and fraud, I found to my dis-may that a life of crime was difficult and unglamorous. It required that most dreaded trait, discipline, as well as a closed mouth and a lot of downtime, where money was going out and none was coming in. My coconspirators at the time were an unreliable lot, either talking too much or making dangerously stupid improvisations on our carefully hatched plans, and in my case, anyway, our few ventures into felonious activity were at the end of the day decidedly unprofitable.

Which is how I became a chef.

But that's another story.

Suffice it to say, when I finally buckled down to a life of legitimate toil in the restaurant business, I began to meet some *real* criminals, guys connected to organized crime, and I recognized right away that while *they*, apparently, had what it took to live a life outside the law, *I* did not. And I was curious about the differences between myself and these full-timers. What remained with me from my early, heady days of surreptitious entry was the love of conspiracy, an appreciation of clan-destine meetings, the comfortably familiar phrase book, long ago codi-fied and set down in Hollywood films, of the hard-core, professional bad man. La Cosa Nostra and, to a lesser extent, espionage became obsessions. I wanted to know, for instance, how Kim Philby kept his mouth shut for all those years. How could a kid in his early twenties, still in college, keep quiet about his true loyalties? Especially when he was doing something as exciting as spying for the NKVD? How could he *not*, after a few beers, blab to his friends about his secret work for the Workers' Paradise, especially when he'd been loudly espousing unpopular political views to all and sundry? How could young Kim *never*, while trying to bed some breasty Marxist sophomore, have boozily confided, "All this right-wing twaddle is a *sham*, baby . . . I'm down with the International, bitch. And doing some serious motherfucking undercover shit! Now take off those panties!"

Guys who wake up every morning, brush their teeth, shower, shave, then go to work at the serious business of committing felonies, these are the characters who continue to dominate my reverie and my fiction. Bank robbers, spies, enforcers, contract killers, loan sharks, confidence men, and racketeers . . . it's their consistency over time, their relentless adherence to the requirements of the job, that makes me, in my way, love them. Take a guy like Vincent "the Chin" Gigante, the former boss of the Genovese crime family, whom I used as an inspiration for a character in *Bone in the Throat*. Here's a guy who, for *thirty years*, played the public role of a doddering, schizophrenic old man, appearing on the street for walk-talks with his soldiers in bathrobe and slippers, talking to himself, behaving erratically, moving his eyes and head in such a way as to indicate insanity, and all the while was running with an iron grip the largest and most ruthless criminal enterprise in the country. This crazy act kept him out of jail for most of his life—though the Feds did catch up with him in the end. You have to admire that kind of work ethic. They never caught the Chin on tape, telling a subordinate to "whack somebody out" or "put a rocket in his pocket." You never heard the Chin's voice playing over the courthouse speakers, talking about how he was going to "sever [somebody's] motherfuckin' head off" (one of my favorite Gotti-isms). The Chin played his part to the end.

Gotti, to his detriment, surrounded himself with those other fascinating creatures of the criminal netherworld: informers. Listening to recordings of the embattled don in his Little Italy social club, berating his crew, bemoaning his gambling losses, contemplating the machinations and intentions of his rivals, there's a poignancy to the experience: Not only was the poor bastard being secretly recorded by the FBI, but sometimes three out of four of the close associates in the room with him were, or later became, government informants. It's hard these days, it seems, to get good help.

So for purposes of fiction, organized criminality offers plenty of drama, plenty of situations in which characters find themselves in extreme circumstances with presumably difficult choices to make: Should I shoot my best friend today? What happens if I don't? Can I trust Paulie? After I kill him, when his kids come over to play with my kids, what should I tell them about Daddy's disappearance? Should I cooperate with the prosecutors? Can I survive the rest of my life eating jail food? These are the Big Questions in my kind of crime fiction.

And of course, crime can be funny.

The line between crime fiction and real-life crime becomes fuzzy, often hilariously so. All the real gangsters have *seen The Godfather*, One, Two, and maybe Three. They've *seen Goodfellas*. And these films made a powerful impression. Recently I visited my favorite website, Gangland.com—an online repository for up-to-date organized crime arcana—to find a transcript of New Jersey's DeCavalcante crime family members enthusiastically speculating on which among their number had provided inspiration for the Tony Soprano character on *The Sopranos*. Real-life gangster "Crazy Joe" Gallo, prior to falling down dead into his linguine with white clam sauce, is said to have practiced his Tommy Udo imitation in front of the mirror every morning. (You remember Tommy, the Richard Widmark character in *Kiss of Death*? The famous scene in which the giggling Widmark binds and gags an old lady into her wheelchair, then pushes her down a flight of stairs? "Heee-heee . . . heee . . . heeee"?) And there *must* be scores of aspiring Joe Pescis out there, taking the occasional break from the daily grind of extortion and murder to do dead-on impressions of Joe: "What? I *amuse* you? I'm a clown?"

There is a powerful element of pure comedy, of classic shtick, in the business of crime. With so many natural wordsmiths, mimics, movie fans, and practitioners of a century-old oral tradition, is it any wonder? And as Monty Python so astutely demonstrated many years ago, the basic elements of comedy *all* come down to the unexpected head injury, repeated blunt-force trauma to the skull. Whether it's Oliver Hardy getting a good smack upside the nut with a mishandled ladder, or a Colombo loan shark getting his brains spattered all over the dashboard of his shiny new Buick, the principle is the same and it spells *funny.*

Joe Pesci, thinking that today he's gonna be a "made guy," looks down at the floor, sees that the carpet has been rolled up, and has time only to say, "*Oh shit!*" before getting two behind his ear. Classic. Just like Oliver Hardy *should* know that a ladder will soon be bouncing off his face because it bounced off his face in the scene before, and in the scene before that—Pesci's character *should* know that when a close personal friend invites you to a sit-down with the bosses, or says that *you* can have the front passenger seat ("That's okay . . . you sit in front"), there's every likelihood that a fatal head injury is imminent. There's a historic inevitability to both comedy and organized crime, and the punch lines are often the same.

Times, sadly, are changing. Traditional criminal groups like New York's Cosa Nostra, Boston's Winter Hill Gang, Chicago's Outfit are being replaced by newer and less amusing stylists, clever mobs of ruthless Russians, Serbs, Israelis, Asians, Jamaicans, Colombians, and Nigerians whose appreciation of the classics seems lacking. Their crimes, for the most part, are so sophisticated and so *boring* that simply reading about them induces coma. Notoriously closed-mouthed, even by professional standards, these recent arrivals to America's shores are less likely to provide the kind of recorded admissions that thinned the ranks of their predecessors and entertained generations of readers and moviegoers. Some of these guys, I don't even know if they've seen *The Godfather*—much less *Mean Streets* or *Goodfellas*! I doubt sincerely whether they will honor the tradition of amusing movie audiences.

The bad guys of the future will probably look and sound and act more like Bill Gates than "Fat Tony" Salerno . . . and the world will be a bleaker place for it. No more "Gentleman Jimmy" Burkes hijacking loads out of Kennedy airport. Tomorrow's criminals will simply move tiny blips from place to place on their computer screens, theoretical felonies that take place somewhere in the ether. Monies from the Bank of Smerzsk will somehow find their way to another account in the Grand Caymans, or to a shell corporation in the former Soviet republic of Torporistan. And the man who presses the "enter" key will have all the seething menace and dangerous charisma of a certified public accountant.

So I'm looking elsewhere these days. Crips, Bloods, La "M," the Aryan Brotherhood, El Rukn—they just don't do it for me. They kill like sharks, as remorselessly and predictably, for reasons as silly as choice sneakers. Our secret services, particularly the CIA, have such a long history of incompetence at the manly arts of assassination and as organizations have come to resemble nothing more than midwestern cow colleges that there's little hope of returning to the fun-filled days of pragmatic killers, ideologically driven cold warriors, and Yalie pranksters. While the Israeli Mossad still provides the occasional item of interest (I particularly enjoyed the exploding cell phone gag), recent developments do not bode well for the future. The remnants of the KGB seem too preoccupied with stealing the silver and pilfering what's left of their former empire to actually whack anybody, so there's no help there either. As the modern-day ranks of the Five Families increasingly emerge from the shallow end of the gene pool, we see fewer and fewer instinctive funnymen like Gotti or Sammy Gravano (or even that kooky, kuh-razy Brit comedy duo the Kray twins), and it gets harder and harder to imagine a modern-day Cosa Nostra killer with the wit, charm, and cold competence of *The Godfather*'s Clemenza, instructing his accomplice after murdering an incompetent and possibly treacherous coworker, "Leave the gun. Take the cannoli."

As John Gotti said, complaining (on tape, naturally), about people talking too much:

From now on, I'm telling you that if a guy just so mentions
"La," and he goes . . . I heard nine months of tapes of my life [in
court]. I was actually sick, and I don't wanna get sick. Not sick
for me, sick for "this thing of ours," sick how naïve we were five
years ago. I'm sick we were so fucking naïve.

I empathize with John. His underboss, Sammy, to whom he made the above comments, turned cooperating witness and put John in the can for life without. The government generously rewarded Sammy by forgiving him his part in *nineteen* brutal murders, a small price to pay for his testimony and for a very revealing, very funny book.

For a while, I had an ex-mobster friend named Joe "Dogs," who, after his best pal tried to kill him, also became a government witness. He called from time to time, late at night, wanting to talk about nothing in particular: the city, restaurants he used to be able to go to. He liked to gossip about recent arrests of old friends, wonder aloud about book deals as he too has a second career as a writer. I think it's the New York accent he missed most, that he couldn't talk with anyone where he was now the way he used to talk when he was a functionary for the Gambinos. He missed the good old days.

I know how he felt.

Gumshoes

An unpublished script, date unknown.

ACT I

The scene is Fat Rudy's bar, somewhere on the Lower East Side. Sam and the Op enter through main door and approach bartender. The few customers disperse.

SCENE I

RUDY: Gumshoes?

SAM: Maybe.

RUDY: What can I do for you fellas?

OP: We're looking for a friend of ours. We think maybe he might show up here.

RUDY: I'll be closing in half an hour, but you're welcome to hang around till then . . . Drink?

SAM: Bourbon and ice.

OP: Whiskey.

RUDY: How do you want that?

OP: In a glass.

RUDY: Okay, okay. Long time since I seen any of you boys around. Private Ops?

SAM: Retired.

RUDY: This guy you're waiting for . . . business or pleasure?

OP: I think maybe you ask too many questions.

RUDY: No, no, don't get me wrong, I want to help. Maybe I know this guy. What does he look like?

OP: Look, buddy, I don't mean to be rude but guys with a curiosity like yours have a habit of losing teeth.

SAM: What if I were to tell you we were waiting for the Iceman.

RUDY: The Iceman, the Iceman. Oh I get it, the play. Yeah, I read that. Very funny. I like you guys. I don't get to talk to many guys like you.

SAM: Another.

RUDY: Comin' up . . . On the house, gents.

As Sam and the Op are off guard, Rudy pulls an ice pick. The Op slams his fat body against his arm and wrestles away the ice pick. Sam grabs Rudy's collar and pulls his face over the bar.

SAM: All your friends carry ice picks too?

OP: Lovely habit. You're a real sweetheart.

SAM: Give him a couple a knocks in the noodle. I wanna ask him a few things.

The Op grabs Rudy by the hair and smashes his face repeatedly against the bar.

OP: Okay. Give me the rumble or I'm going to have to get very unpleasant. I'm usually a very lovable guy. But when people get mad, well sometimes I just can't control myself.

SAM: It's true you know.

OP: Despite my kind face I can sometimes be very cruel.

SAM: Oh, that's really true . . . that poor guy's ribs in Vegas . . .

OP: —and remember that sucker who tried to blip me with a baseball bat?

SAM: Really brutal. . . . What a mess.

RUDY: All right, all right . . . what do you want out of me?

OP: The Iceman! He put you up to this. Where is he?

RUDY: The Iceman? The Iceman? What kind of—Nix on that, friend. I don't know any Iceman. It's only a play.

OP: Don't be a sap. The Iceman. Where is he?

The Op slaps Rudy across the face a few times.

OP: Come clean, fat boy. Where is he?
RUDY: No. Let me go. I don't—
SAM: Let me play with him for a second . . . (*to Rudy*) C'mere for a second.

Sam whispers in Rudy's ear for a few seconds. Rudy appears very shaken.

RUDY: All right . . . all right. I don't really know anything. I just spoke to somebody over the phone. I was paid in advance. I don't know anything else. I don't know any Iceman.
SAM: The guy on the phone. What did he say to you? Spill it, pal.
RUDY: He just says two old gumshoes are gonna come in my place tonight. He tells me to jump you guys. Paid me a big one. Cash in the mail.
SAM: Anything else?
RUDY: Yeah, it was kind of funny after the grand and everything . . . but he says to me that if things don't go right I should tell you guys to stay here and wait. He said you should expect an old friend to drop in.
SAM: Okay. It sounds on the level to me. What do we do with him?
OP: Let him go. He's finished his job. I don't think you're going to bother us anymore, are you? Good. If you're not outta here in ten seconds I'm going to blow your kneecaps off.

Exit Rudy.

SCENE II

OP: It's not all fat. I've managed to keep busy all these years . . . What are you smoking?
SAM: Bull Durham, roll-ups, remember? Want one?
OP: Whatever happened to Fatimas?
SAM: They discontinued those stinkweeds around '49. Where you been?
OP: Hell, I been out of the country. Been to Hong Kong, Taiwan, East

Germany, Cuba, all over. Muckin' around with the Feds. Worked with
Interpol for a while, CIA, FBI. Did some freelance in South Africa, off
the record . . . Yeah, give me one of those. Never really got the knack of
how to roll one of these buggers.

SAM: Let me—

OP: No, I can do it.

SAM: Think he's going to show?

OP: I don't know.

SAM: He's gotta show. He said he would. He sent us a message. I figure
he knew Rudy would botch the job. He used him for a finger without
him knowing it. Rudy was just a patsy. His job was to establish our
identities. He was expected to bungle and was allowed to pass on the
message. I think he'll be here. He has to. How can he resist?

OP: Maybe he just wants to talk over old times. It's been a long time.
Maybe he's just another broken-down old geezer by now.

SAM: He still makes my skin get all horny thinking about . . . Well,
strange things have been happening to me lately. Like, people are
listening to me. Somebody has been watching me. Sometimes late at
night I think I can actually hear them breathing out there. Makes me
feel like a piece on a chessboard or something. I don't know.

OP: You just got a case of the willies. Spooks.

SAM: No. I've been finding little bugs around my apartment; I hear
funny noises at night, like people pushing buttons. Plays real hell on
my dreams. I don't sleep much lately, got too much to do. But when I
finally make it to something warm and flat I get bad dreams. Some of
them are real nasty. I have this one in which I'm in this big white room
with a glass ceiling and people are trying to stick wires in me and I
can't eat because there's poison in the food. People trying to cut me,
stick all these tubes and wires into me, and I can't get out. Really gives
me the heebie-jeebies.

OP: Probably means you always wanted to fuck your mother or
something. Psychology, you know.

SAM: Yeah. I think he uses that stuff. Psychology. We've both had some
bad breaks lately and sometimes I wonder if—

OP: Yeah, the Iceman's behind it all, right?

SAM: Sometimes I think so. I met him face-to-face once, remember.

OP: Listen, you weren't dealing from a full deck after that one. How can you be sure that half of it wasn't a—

SAM: A dream? A dream? I'd like to think so. I really would. I'm slowing down . . . I got a real treat for us.

OP: What's that?

SAM: Seventy-five milligrams of pure energy.

OP: Looks like dope.

SAM: Well, kind of. It's methedrine, my friend, and it keeps me awake and alert for nasty nights like this one. It takes care of me. I can work for a week with a little help from this stuff, and no time wasted on sleeping or eating or any of that.

OP: Well, I think you look like hell. I never thought you'd end up some sort of hophead.

SAM: No, it's not like that. This stuff is a boon to our profession.

OP: Well, that's all dandy with me, Sam, but I'll pass it up. You can reach back there and snag me a bottle and it would be swell.

SAM: The juice. That muddles your mind. You've got to have a clear head for this work.

OP: Swell. What kind of a heater are you carrying around with you?

SAM: Beretta.

OP: Nice. Nice. But what kind of damage can you do with it?

SAM: Enough.

OP: This thing'll turn somebody's head to coleslaw. Splatters lead all over the place. Puts a hole in you you could put your fist through.

SAM: I'm still a little shaky. When's this guy gonna show?

OP: He's playing it smart. He's gonna let us stew for a while and then he's gonna make his move. The Iceman's probably no patsy, he's not going to just walk in here and sit down for a snort with us.

SAM: He's probably watching us and waiting for the right time.

OP: The right time for what? Maybe he just wants to talk. You get a certain respect for a guy who can be a pain in the ass for thirty years . . . cigarette?

SAM: Yeah . . . Yeah. But what if he's mad? You messed up a lot of his playmates a few years back. And I'm sure he's not too happy about Nick the Gimp either.

OP: What happened with the Gimp?

SAM: I was working the hole one night on a missing persons and Nick tried to ventilate me. Blew a hole in my shoulder. I couldn't believe it was him after all these years.

OP: What happened to him?

SAM: I blipped him.

OP: So?

SAM: They say that the Gimp used to be like this with Laughing Boy.

OP: The Iceman always moved in good company. Remember Frank the Smell?

SAM: Yeah. Yeah. He was in with Redpoint and Big Babe. That whole crowd rubbed each other out a long time ago.

OP: Yeah, but I made things pretty hot for them until they all got wasted.

SAM: You ought to slow down on the juice. They're gonna have to bury your liver in a separate coffin.

OP: Since when are you my fuckin' mother?

SAM: Forget it. Get blotto. When the Iceman shows I'll just sit here and watch while he slips that steel in between your ribs like a hot knife through butter. You'll look like a Thanksgiving turkey.

OP: No. The Iceman's usually pretty neat. Just one little mark, usually in the back. Somebody once told me he was cleaning up after himself lately. Likes to clean the wound and prop 'em up in a chair with the eyes open, so they don't even look like a stiff. Little joke, you know.

SAM: He's a real comedian.

OP: And a nice guy.

SAM: So where the fuck is he? I want to pop that guy. I want him out of my hair for good. I want to stop worrying about him and his friends and all his little toys. I want to see him right in front of me and blow his head clean off so I know he's dead.

OP: The guy really has got the screws in you.

SAM: I want to pay him back for something. I want to pay that guy back in spades, because I owe him.

OP: That dame?

SAM: I don't want to talk about it right now. Maybe later. Give me a drink.

SCENE III

OP: Jesus, I'd like a Fatima right now.

SAM: You can roll up another one of these.

OP: Sheeeeeeit.

SAM: If you don't like 'em you can run around the corner to Pearl's and get some Chesterfields.

OP: No, I'm going to wait right here. I wouldn't miss this little party for the world.

SAM: You know, I get the feeling I've been in this dive before. Maybe it was a speakie back then. Yeah . . . yeah. I remember this joint. I was here once with the Shivering Kid.

OP: The bulls got the kid, didn't they?

SAM: No, I did.

OP: . . . Back in the old days they were dropping like flies. Every Tom, Dick, or Harry I saw in the street would end up pulling a gat on me. And look . . . look, see these knuckles? You know what made them like that? Thirty years of popping guys in the chops.

SAM: Yeah. Yeah. Things were okay. The dames looked better. The crooks were easy to catch.

OP: Yeah, the skirts were certainly a cut above what's running around lately.

SAM: Broads.

OP: I don't have much use for any dizzy broads gumming things up.

SAM: You never did. I'd like to know when we can expect him.

OP: Let me tell you a story.

SAM: I don't know if I'm in the mood for stories.

OP: No, it's a good one. About the Iceman and me. It was in the early fifties. I was still working for the agency. The Old Man had kicked off and some hot-shit new mugs from the East Coast had taken over the place. I'd been assigned the Iceman's case before the Old Man kicked, so I was still working on that when the new boys took over. They thought it was okay that I keep working on it, though they weren't too sure about the existence of this Iceman guy. But they put me on an account and gave me a couple of other operatives and sent me off to Hong Kong.

As soon as I got there I looked up our Hong Kong Op. He lived in a sleazy little hole over a mah-jongg casino.

OP: So let's have it. What's the scoop on the Iceman?

SAM: He's here.

OP: In Hong Kong?

SAM: Yes. Yes. But he has some new friends. It is said that he is working for the Yakuza.

OP: Yakuza. Shit. This is going to be a real messy case, I can smell it from here.

SAM: This Iceman? Who is he? What has he done?

OP: He's not a nice man.

SAM: I don't know if you've ever messed with the Yakuza. But I can tell you I'd rather an Anastasia contract out on me than have those yellow devils mad at me. A Japanese version of the Mafia. They employ all these fanatic samurai types, assassins. They run all the gambling, prostitution . . . contracts. But they're the type of buddies that the Iceman would get along with.

So I started hanging around some of the Yakuza-controlled dives. Opium dens, gin mills . . . Hoping I'd pick up some word. I tried to bribe one little slope and the next thing you know, somebody cracks a stick over my noodle. Asking too many questions. So I turn and pop the little guy behind me right in the nose, only it never connects. You know, he was fast. Really fast, and he pulled all sorts of weird Chink moves on me, almost like he was dancing. I pulled my rod and he snaps my wrist like a piece of cardboard. After that I didn't feel too argumentative and they tied me up real tight and put me on a table.

I always hated it when they did that. You feel real helpless just lying up there like somebody's dinner that hasn't been eaten yet. I remember lying there in the dark and wondering about the Iceman. What he looked like and all that. You know, I'd heard a lot of stories . . . So I'm just waiting down there when I heard a noise. I musta been in a cellar or something. My head started to feel funny. The room had this smell too, like flowers, and my head . . .

SAM: Did they hurt you?

OP: They tried. Yes, they hurt me a lot. For a long time. They were real good at hurting people I'd say. They made me scream and I don't do that much.

SAM: A lot of people have tried to hurt me. A lot of people are still trying I think.

OP: They had a lot of laughs with me on the table before they let me go.

Pantomime of Op being tortured.

SCENE IV

SAM: What do we know about the Iceman aside from the fact that he has some nasty habits and rough playmates?

OP: There are a lot of stories. I don't know how many of them are true. But there are some good stories.

SAM: Tell me stories.

OP: None of them are too pretty and they all have the same ending.

SAM: In which the Iceman gets away clean and somebody's left with an ice pick in their back.

OP: You got it. He's a clever one. I think he must be crazy. Nothing he does ever seems to make much sense. But I heard one story once in a speakie in the twenties. Three-Fingers was telling it to me. Said he got it straight from the Iceman when he was drunk.

As the story goes the Iceman was just getting his start in Chicago working for Capone. He had to leave the country for some job in Sicily. So he gets back and he hears that his dame is hotsy-totsy with Angel Vance. He drops out of sight and as the story goes, Angel and the lady both get letters in the mail, signed like the ones we got, except the letters say "You are dead."

Now, Angel was Big Stuff in Chi back then and everybody had a big laugh at the Iceman's expense that he was going to try to waste the Angel. But they found the Angel in his bed looking real peaceful and very cold and stiff the next morning. So the lady involved starts to get sweaty around the asshole. She hocks all her ice and rents a bungalow out by the lake. So she was hiding out there for a week and maybe beginning to feel not so scared anymore when she hears funny noises from upstairs.

Three-Fingers was pretty detailed about this part of the story. I'll tell it 'cause maybe it shows something about our boy. But as I heard it, the dame turned off all the lights in the house except for in the kitchen and goes snooping around upstairs to see about the noise. So she pokes around the whole house in the dark and she must have been real scared by this time, bumpin' around in a dark house like that, and finally after she can't find nothing goes back to the kitchen. And it's all lit up like when she first left it, except that the Iceman is sitting at the kitchen table with a big smile on his face and holding an ice pick.

So she makes with the screaming and everything but it doesn't matter 'cause they're out in the middle of nowhere. And the Iceman slaps her up against the refrigerator and gives it to her a couple of times with the pick. Not his usual neat job either. He was real careful to give it to her in the stomach so it would take her a little while of crawling around on the floor and moaning before she stiffened out.

Now, here's the good part of the story. So the Iceman's all finished with the carving, right, and the broad's on the floor moaning and spreading the red stuff all over, so the Iceman just sits down at the kitchen table and makes himself breakfast. Just sat there stuffing eggs in his face while his ex was twitching on the floor. According to Three-Fingers, he even remembered to wash the dishes.

SAM: You believe that story?

OP: Doesn't matter. Iceman's done some weird things. Who cares which ones are true and which aren't at this point. I heard he was a big man with Murder Incorporated.

OP: Some of 'em say he was brought up in a cathouse near an ice-packing plant. They say he got bored watching his mother get plugged by bums every day and had to find some new toys. Started messing around with an ice pick.

SAM: He split with those boys two days before Anastasia got his last haircut.

OP: The Iceman is smart.

SAM: Yeah, that's probably it. Maybe he's got his own racket all set up. He could do it. All the mugs used to look up to him. You ever try to make one of his little buddies sing for you? They shut up like clams. Rather be dead than squeal on the Iceman they say. My guess is he's got his own setup. Got people working for him. Same angle probably, only big-time. Traveling around the world stickin' ice picks in people. I'll bet he enjoys it.

OP: Maybe so. Why not? He must like his work, he's been at it a long time. He's a success.

Maybe we bother him. Hell, he's bothered us all these years, maybe we've succeeded in bothering him just a bit. Or like I said, maybe he just wants a few laughs with some of the old crowd.

SAM: But I never even saw him or spoke to him. Until I got that letter I wasn't sure this guy really existed or whether he was some sort of sick bad dream. I mean I was pretty sure, but . . .

OP: You've never seen him? Even from a distance?

SAM: Never. A couple of almosts I think but never face-to-face the way I wanted.

OP: I've seen him.

SAM: I know, but close up?

OP: Yeah, real close up. But it was kind of funny, I was so wacked out and beat up and hurting so bad I couldn't see his face even though he pressed it right up against mine.

SAM: Why didn't you . . .

OP: Let me tell you about it. It's kind of funny.

You see, I caught up with the Iceman in Tangiers. Or maybe he caught up with me, in any case it doesn't matter. I'd been flopping in some dive with a bunch of Arab kids, you know, and I was pretty far into a bender. I'd been chasing this goose around the world so long

I was punchy. Began to think like you that maybe he was a figment of my imagination or something. All the money the agency had given me was gone on booze. For a while I was a real good-time Charlie with the Arab boys, who weren't bad company. I couldn't write the agency for more scratch 'cause I had absolutely nothing to give them. Then one day, Mufti, the landlord, kind of gives me the word that there's an American in town to swing a big dope deal. So I tried to straighten myself up a bit and got out of the suit I'd been sleeping in, put on my old pinstripe, and went down to the market to ask a few questions.

[BEGIN FLASHBACK]

OP: My friend. Maybe you can tell me something.
ARAB: Yes?
OP: There's an American in town. To buy junk. You understand? Where do I find him? Where would he go to?
ARAB: You have money, American?

The Op grabs him and hits him across the face.

OP: Listen, you greasy little wog . . . I've been all over the fuckin' world looking for this goose and I want to know where I can find him. I want answers. Understand? Now spill it if you want to breathe right!!!
ARAB: I don't know of any American. But for drugs you must see Hassan. He lives on the hill. To see him you need someone to introduce you.
OP: Yeah, yeah. He'll speak to me.

[END FLASHBACK]

OP (CONT'D): So I was real gung-ho about the whole thing and I went charging up the hill to see this Hassan. I must have been still pretty juiced up 'cause I just busted in the front door and demanded to see the Big Cheese. I was in a bad way. I started waving my gat around and giving orders, screaming to high heaven to let me see the Iceman. Some big spade tried to cut my head off with a scimitar and I dropped him right away. Then things got pretty serious. Suddenly it was wall-to-wall muscles with guys crawling all over me banging my head on the floor.

I woke up a bit later. I was feeling real sick and couldn't see so good. But I could tell that I was in a back lot somewhere and I could just about make out somebody's shape standing around ten feet in front of me.

[BEGIN FLASHBACK]

ICEMAN: You're a real prize, you are, yes.

OP: Are you talking to me?

ICEMAN: Yes, you. I'm talking to you. You fat, disgusting old fag.

ICEMAN: You think you're so tough. You always thought you were tough. I don't think you're so tough, fat man. Fat old man. You must think that you've been causing me a lot of grief, running all over the globe trying to find me. But do you want to know something, faggot? You don't bother me in the least. I think you're funny. Funny! Lying around on your fat ass, spending your agency's money on drinks for you and your little pretty boys. How long do you think they'd hang around a fat disgusting pervert like you if you didn't have that expense account, little man? You ever think about that?

OP: You, you—when I get up, I'm going to blow out your liver.

ICEMAN: You are funny. Funny. No, pitiful. You know what, fat man? I'm going to let you live. I'm going to let you live. Do you know why? Because you aren't worth killing. Why should I bother when you're going to save me all the trouble and mess by doing it yourself? Why should I deny myself the pleasure of seeing you stumble over your own fat feet on your way to the morgue by killing you now? You are too pitiful to kill, fat man! You are old, smelly, and repulsive. This is probably the only place left in the world where you'll find little boys who will let you paw them with your sweaty hands for a dollar or two. You are finished, Fat. Finished.

[END FLASHBACK]

SAM: So what did he say to you?

OP: I can't remember any of it except that I knew it was him.

SAM: So what happened?

OP: Well, he got away of course. I tried to get myself straight again with some success, though the agency dropped me. I went on the wagon for a few months, started going to gyms, finally got a private practice together in the city. And you know.

ACT II

SCENE I

[BEGIN FLASHBACK]

SAM: All right, so maybe you didn't do it. Maybe you did. It all seems upside-down right now.

GIRL: I swear, I swear I didn't do it, Sam. I love you, I wouldn't lie to you.

SAM: Maybe, I don't know. How can I be sure? I don't know, sweetheart, I like you, but I don't know that I'd turn my back on you.

GIRL: How can I convince you?

SAM: You'll have to be patient with me, sister, I'm just having a little trouble forgetting that stupid look on your husband's face with the ice pick just—

GIRL: Stop, don't . . . please.

SAM: Don't pull the crybaby act on me, sugar, you weren't crying when you put that slug through Rico and you weren't crying when you stuck that ice pick in your husband.

GIRL: No, no.

SAM: I couldn't forget that stupid look on his kisser when we found him. Like he'd been surprised, genuinely surprised when that piece of steel slid between his ribs. All those people with a motive to croak him and he ends up stiffed by his own wife. That's what put that stupid look there. You killed him and set Rico up as the fall guy. He was so in love with you he wouldn't even sing for the wrecking crew downtown. He sat there under the rubber hose all night to cover for you.

GIRL: No, it's not true. I mean . . . yes, I killed my husband. But he was a monster. He was a monster. You can't imagine.

SAM: He never had too many friends.

GIRL: Please. Please. I love you. Can't we forget this? If we let things lie the way they are, it will be like nothing ever happened . . . please . . .

SAM: I'm going to let you go free to maybe put a hole in me?

GIRL: You don't really believe that. You can't.

SAM: All right. All right. I've sent a lot of people to the cooler in my time. So maybe your husband was a monster. Maybe you had to kill him. Maybe it was right. But what about Rico? Why did he have to die?

GIRL: I had nothing to do with that. I swear it.

SAM: You'd swear to anything right now to get out of the chair. That's where they put people like you.

GIRL: People like me?

SAM: That's where they put murderers. The chair. The state fries them. You're a murderer, the law says I should put you in the chair and watch you fry. I don't know whether I can do that.

GIRL: No, you can't. Please, stay with me.

SAM: You're a murderer, I don't know if I can sleep next to a murderer. It'll give me bad dreams.

GIRL: Sam.

SAM: You know I can't do it. You know I can't do it. That's the part that I don't like. But I can't.

GIRL: Please, Sam, just hold on to me for a second.

SAM: I don't know whether we can get away with it. I don't know if it'll work. I know what I want to do. I want you so bad I can taste . . . but my brain is telling me to call the bulls and kiss you goodbye. But I can't do that, can I? Maybe you're too smart for me.

GIRL: You think too much, please.

SAM: I love you. I'm going to let you go free because I can't help myself. I'm weak and I'm always going to hate myself a little for it, but if you can live with that, maybe I can.

GIRL: I love you, Sam.

SAM: And I love you, but if you ever betray me . . . If you ever play me for the patsy I feel like I am . . . If you betray me, I'll kill you. And if I die first, I'll come back and haunt you. Now come here.

[END FLASHBACK]

SAM: So she kind of moved in. I guess I was in love or something. But after all the floozies and nickel-and-dime whores, somebody to scratch my back was a tasty proposition. I don't know. I must have been real happy 'cause I started getting real slow in the brain department. People get kind of sluggish when they're happy, and somehow I must have been happy. I don't know why I let her get away with it. It still makes me crazy to think about what a sucker I was. But I was sold on the dame and she knew it. We spent around a month getting pretty blotto—she could really drink—and lying around fucking all the time. My brains must've been mush 'cause one day we get into the bath. I can remember it real clear. She was looking real pretty with this kind of pink flush. I was sitting in the bath and she comes into the bathroom. She was naked, holding a bunch of towels, and she put them next to the tub and got in. I was sitting there with a stupid smile on my face, watching her get in. So she leaned toward me and kissed me and I hugged her, and she put her left arm around my neck and started to play with my hair and with her right arm she stuck an ice pick in my back.

I remember feeling it go in all the way and looking at her. Everything started swimming and all I could see was her standing naked in front of me with a big smile on her face like she was a little kid who'd just gotten a good report card in school. And she was smiling and I looked at her angry like and she said, "The Iceman," and then I passed out.

OP: She worked for the Iceman?

SAM: I don't know, I never . . . I want to find out tonight.

OP: What happened to you after—

SAM: Well, the bulls found me after a couple a days, lying in a bathtub full of my blood with a shit-eating look. I was in the hospital for a while for the croakers to put me back together. Never really knew what hit me. Christ did I feel like a palooka. Letting an ice pick killer in my bathtub. Tonight I want to find out.

OP: So all this Iceman business with you is just 'cause some dame played you for a sap thirty years ago?

SAM: I suppose so, yeah. That's it.

OP: You ever see the dame again?

SAM: No.

OP: You always were a softie.

SAM: Maybe so. I never did like to think so. Thought they'd walk all over me. My old man used to say that. He'd say, "Never let anybody take advantage of your better instincts, they'll walk all over you in the end." I was never really sure if he was right or just a cynical old fart. I guess he must have been right.

OP: Maybe so. Getting old may not be so bad. You get kind of crusty after a while. Learn control. You don't let your dick get in the way of good sense.

SAM: Still have a scar the size of a quarter over here. Want a look?

OP: I seen enough scars, thanks.

SAM: Scars are okay. When I look at a scar on me somewhere I learn something. I remember how I got it and remind myself not to make the same mistake twice.

OP: You know in forty years how many people have blown holes in me, stabbed me, hit me over the bean, sliced me up, and slipped me Mickey Finns? I wouldn't want to try to count.

SAM: But you learn something real basic. Like you know when you're tangling with somebody and you're throwing fists all over the place, each time a punch lands it's like the ring of truth. BAM—TRUTH. I like to think I learned something in all those years.

OP: You learn a lot about human nature for sure.

SAM: Too much about human nature. I frankly don't think too much of human nature lately.

OP: You know what I could never stand? The wise guys who can look you straight in the face and hand you such a load of bullshit and actually expect you to believe it. I always took it as a real insult to my intelligence. I mean all those lies, little white ones. The Big Lie. Hell, I heard so many stories I kind of geared myself like they were lying until proven otherwise.

SAM: It's all a big lie. Supposedly everybody is real nice and it's the sick ones, the bad guys, who lie and cheat and steal. I sometimes almost think it's the other way around.

OP: Ahhh. It doesn't really matter. I just always tried to keep them outta my way.

SAM: Keep them out of your brain, friend. You have to keep them out of your brain. Once they're in there they can mess you all up. Throw you off balance.

OP: I knew this beatnik hophead a few years ago. Would give me the rumble for a fin now and then. He said to me once, "All you got to do is keep your cool. You lose your cool and you blow the whole thing."

MISSING PAGE 5

OP: We've got to keep our cool tonight, pal.

SAM: I used to like to think she was a hophead. That she had to do it for a bang. Maybe she was crazy like and needed a shot. Hopheads, you know? She had to bump me off to get the stuff.

OP: Forget it.

SAM: Yeah, I'd like to.

SCENE II

SAM: Funny thing about Mike.

OP: What's that?

SAM: Him going and kicking off like he did.

OP: Car crash. Not the Iceman's style if that's what you're driving at.

SAM: Did you go and take a look down at the morgue?

OP: Yeah.

SAM: Hmmm.

OP: What's that supposed to mean?

SAM: Just hmmm.

OP: I think you're seeing spooks where there aren't any.

SAM: Mike helped me bust up that kidnapping racket in Canada.

OP: I didn't hear that one.

SAM: It was a missing-girl case. Old bird hired me to find her niece. Was taking her for a tour of the amusement park when the kid got snatched. So I went down there and started poking my nose around.

[BEGIN FLASHBACK]

BARKER: Come right in and see a horse as small as a dog, a dog as large as a horse. They're in here alive. If not alive we will pay you one hundred dollars. Step right in. The Giant Rat of the Amazon.

SAM: Hey, friend, maybe you can help me.

BARKER: Cop?

SAM: No, just a curious citizen. I'm curious about a little girl eight years old. She disappeared here last night. Her family misses her. I wonder if you can help me.

BARKER: No, I don't think so. I don't know anything about this, mister. Sorry.

[END FLASHBACK]

SAM: Everybody I asked a question would clam up right away. It was getting close to impossible to get any answers. So I went to see the fortune teller kind of as a joke.

[BEGIN FLASHBACK]

SAM: What can you tell me about a missing girl?

GYPSY: It is expensive to know such things.

SAM: Here's a ten, that's all I got. If you know anything spill it.

GYPSY: You want to know about missing girls?

SAM: Yeah, a blonde, eight years old—

GYPSY: There are a lot of missing girls. They seem to like to disappear at this carnival.

SAM: Where do they go?

GYPSY: I don't know. But trucks come and go late at night behind the fun house.

[END FLASHBACK]

SAM: If you're ever looking for a case of the crawlies, try hiding out all night in a drainpipe behind some dump of a carny fun house. I did, and around three in the morning a truck pulled up and gave a flash of the lights to somebody in the fun house. Some guy with a limp came out to the truck leading the little girl. I slipped up to the truck quiet like and got my ass in the back. The truck started and I got mentally prepared for a long ride. After a while I must have fallen asleep.

I woke up with my head spinning and my arms and legs tied down. I was in a big black room that was damp with all sorts of dripping noises and I could hear rats if I listened. Some old guy dressed up like a croaker was standing over me and smiling.

[BEGIN FLASHBACK]

SCABES: Hello. It's good to see you're still with us after such a long ride. Hit him.

Thug hits Sam in the face.

SCABES: You've complicated things a bit, by your unexpected dropping in, Mr. Detective. But things are not too far awry. They can still be tidied up very nicely, but I'm afraid you will have to be killed.
SAM: Listen, pal, I don't know who you are, but if you think—
SCABES: Hit him again, please, George.

Thug hits Sam again.

SCABES: Do you have any idea what you've stumbled onto, my nosy friend? Do you have any idea? How could you?
SAM: It's got something to do with a lot of missing little girls.
SCABES: Yes! Yes!! That's very good. Very good. But do you know what we do with all those little girls, Mr. Detective?
SAM: Tell me, I'm just dying to find out.
SCABES: We change them. We make new and exciting playmates out of our little girls. We change them. Sometimes ever so slightly; sometimes a lot. It all depends on what the customer wants. The customer comes first here. Hah hah.
SAM: Are you some kind of doctor?
SCABES: Yes. Yes. I am a doctor you might say. I prefer the title of artist. I am an artist. I make beautiful things out of ordinary materials.

We have all the newest facilities here. I'm very proud of them. We can perform transplants, skin grafts, plastic surgery, and mental conditioning here in our own little refuge.

SAM: Sounds lovely.

SCABES: I'm so glad you think so. You see, you are about to meet the little girl whom you were sent to find. She's a little different from when we first found her, but I'm sure you two will be good friends.

George, please bring her in. That's right, this way. See, she's actually very cute, don't you think?

. . . Wonderful . . . right over here, sweetheart . . .

[END FLASHBACK]

SAM: You know, the little kid was holding an ice pick and she had a grin on her face like she'd just gotten the biggest lollipop you could give a little kid . . . She looked different, like a retard kind of, with this dumb stare like she didn't really know. And she started walking toward me waving that pick around and smiling and she was getting closer and I could see the stitches. She probably would have stuck me in the chest.

OP: What happened?

SAM: I kicked her in the face. Killed her right away, and the old croaker started screaming and crying. Then the bulls busted in and carted the whole bunch off . . . not a very pretty scene at all, you know, what with all these twisted little kids . . . and you can be sure my client wasn't too happy about the kid.

Anyway, Mike was in on it in that he trailed me up to Canada and got the Feds in on it.

OP: So it doesn't have to tie in with the Iceman just because you got scared by some twinkle-twat with an ice pick.

SAM: I just think so. I have reasons.

SCENE III

SAM: In another ten minutes I'll be on the nod.

OP: Shooting that stuff is fine with me but don't make me watch.

SAM: You can take it, tough guy. You've seen it before.

OP: I didn't like it then and I don't like it now.

SAM: You go for the sauce in a big way. Well, this is my poison. It's my brains.

OP: You're wacko. That shit makes you nuts.

SAM: Listen, pal, you want me alert and fresh as a daisy when the Iceman shows, right?

OP: Shut up and do whatever you have to do.

Sam injects methedrine.

OP: It's not a pretty sight.

SAM: A lot of things aren't pretty, but you've got to learn to like them. I'm telling you you should really try this shit. One bang and I feel like a goddamn kid. Really. The stuff is incredible.

OP: Makes you nuts.

SAM: This waiting's getting to me.

OP: You're just wacked out on that shit.

SAM: No, no, it's not that at all. What's that?

OP: It's him. He's here.

SAM: Where?

OP: Look.

ICEMAN: Good evening . . . Good morning, I should say, gentlemen.

SAM: Come in the light where we can see you.

ICEMAN: I'll stay right here, thank you.

SAM: I said—

OP: Shut up.

ICEMAN: You know, I don't like either of you gentlemen, never did. But I had to come.

SAM: Get to the point.

ICEMAN: The point?!? The point! There's no point really at all. You'll get the point in time, friends.

SAM: I'm not your friend, laughing boy.

OP: What do you mean? We're all good pals.

   Why don't you sit down and have a drink?

ICEMAN: No, no, thank you, really, but I prefer to stand if you will. I just wanted to see you both, couldn't believe it when I heard you cranks were still walking around. And I was even more amazed to hear that you both seemed to have an interest in ice picks.

An ice pick lands with a thud in center of table.

SAM: Do that again and I'll drop you.

ICEMAN: You will find that neither of your guns are operatable, so why not just sit down and relax. Let's talk. Let's be friends. All I'd like to do is have a little chat and I'll be on my way. Wouldn't you pitiful specimens rather be dead.

SAM: Fuck you, buddy.

ICEMAN: Oh . . . you don't like me. I'd so hoped that you could be civil long enough for a little chat. You just don't like me because you're jealous and frustrated. Particularly useless feelings to leave about cluttering things up, yes? They get in the way of communication. Now, how can I ever relate to either of you gentlemen if you persist in feeling so hostile toward me?

SAM: You're a murderer and a particularly sadistic form of crook. You're no better than a lizard or a snake. You're worse. You like killing people. You like to hurt them, see them suffer. That's worse than the worst kind of monster. You belong in the sewer with the other filth.

ICEMAN: Ha ha ha . . . I am a murderer. I admit it freely, gentlemen, never denied it. But how many two-bit thugs and unfortunate grifters, blackmailers and bank robbers have you dispatched with those forty-fives in your decades of collective crime fighting? You like to kill people. Why are you detectives?

OP: Maybe because we like it. It's a job.

ICEMAN: Well, I have a job as well . . . I kill people for money. Large sums of it. The more difficult to arrange the death, the more money I get. I like my job too, my friends, it's a challenge, and there's room for advancement. I find my job much more practical than setting myself up as a clay pigeon every day of your life.

SAM: Didn't you . . . don't you ever feel the slightest bit for all the poor suckers you've hung on your ice pick? Doesn't it bother you, ever?

ICEMAN: No, never, not at all. I can only do what I was born to do. I accept the path chosen for me by my chromosomes. And I don't mind a bit . . . What does it feel like to kill someone with whom I have no grudge? I don't feel it at all. I thought at one time I might. But I chose to believe that if the tree falls in the forest and no one is around . . . well, who's to know? People only feel guilty when they're caught. Guilt only comes when they slap you up against the wall and look you in the face and say guilty guilty guilty. Getting caught is the only crime. And I have not been caught. I dispatch people quickly into the next world. They just disappear from the ranks of the living. No connection with me whatsoever until that one final second. Bingo!!! If no one is around to observe that final second, well, who's to know? Who is to know?

So I shorten a few lives. But not really if you gentlemen are fatalists. I am one factor in the fate of many different people. The final factor. Just like the bus that might hit you in the street tomorrow or the fatal disease that you've had all your life and suddenly stops your heart. I can only exist and treat myself well until somebody stops me. And I'm not going to allow anyone to stop me.

SAM: I think you're wrong. Somebody is going to stop you. One day somebody is going to walk up behind you with a rod and paint the street with your insides. You may be a smart cookie, smarter than most, but you aren't that smart. Someday you'll be lying on the ground with a hole in you watching your blood spill out and you're going to want to live. No case of the smarts is going to help you. No ice pick made is going to put the blood back in the hole again. I might be the one to put that hole there.

ICEMAN: Oh . . . you want vengeance. The girl, the girl, I forgot. He's the big fag and you're the Humphrey Bogart of the duo.

OP: Why don't you shut your filthy clam before I shut it for you!!!

ICEMAN: You both disappointed me terribly. You bore me.

Pulls a gun and shoots them both.

A Strange and Twisted Adventure

An unpublished short story Tony wrote for an English class in 1974.

A six-page story of sex, drugs, and two abnormal American teenagers and their search for something significant.

The behavior mentioned in this true story does not reflect the present attitudes of any of the protagonists, should this document fall into the hands of certain parties, notably, parents, doctor, school administrator, it would certainly mean my instant confinement to a state institution or similar establishment.

ANTHONY BOURDAIN, ROSENTHAL / ENGLISH . . . 1974

In my early days of manic teenage sex, drugs, and other zany pubescent antics, I had an adventure. It was a planned adventure, with a clearly defined program and goal, but it turned out stranger than my wildest dreams or darkest hallucinations. My friend Alfred and I decided to take a voyage to the Edge. The concept of the Edge was created by Dr. Hunter S. Thompson, and is best defined as the thin, savage line separating behavior considered socially acceptable and permanent Insanity. To walk the Edge, one must tread that line, pressing oneself to the limits of physical and mental endurance. One might ask, "What is the point?" To those persons, I would say what better way to define one's own boundaries, test the realm of "reality," than to experience insanity firsthand, an expedition into the world of the twisted and the bizarre. To achieve this state of mind and body,

Alfred and I set off one day for Monticello, New York. Alfred commandeered an expensive Japanese auto, and I sat in the passenger seat reviewing our provisions. The two of us were headed for Kutscher's resort. Disguised as press agents in brown double-knit suits, we would infiltrate and observe, gaining occasional refuge with some musician friends who were employed there. No one would suspect that beneath our cool, sophisticated exteriors lurked two drug-crazed teenagers on a mission of celestial significance.

After a few hours of high-speed cruising, we checked into the Holiday Inn of Monticello. Glen Miller's band was sharing our floor, and the halls were filled with extra mattresses to be moved into the rooms. We locked ourselves into our suite and set up our equipment. A tape recorder with a condenser mike was plugged in to preserve whatever happened for future posterity. Ice was poured in the sink to chill the case of Maximus Super and bottle of Gordon's dry gin. Our press cards were scrutinized for flaws. And the kit bag was opened, letting loose a galaxy of Bizarre and Dangerous Drugs. LSD, cocaine, methaqualone, Thorazine, mescaline, and marijuana were spread over the dresser and rapidly consumed. We would be in Monticello for twelve hours and we figured the drugs would last. I felt the LSD grab a firm hold of my brain as Alfred quietly sat down and snorted some cocaine while watching *Gigantor* on the TV. A knock on the door and I soapily stumbled over to open it. The towel lady offered me some washcloths. Her face was fluctuating with grisly images of pig snouts and red skin lesions creeping across it. I slammed the door. I quickly called to mind a Thompson quote to the effect that LSD users must learn to cope with visions of their "dead grandmother crawling up their leg with a knife in her teeth." It did not help. "Christ, that woman had cracks in her face, Alfred!"

"Calm down, Anthony, it's the drugs, don't let the swine bother you."

"But, but, that thing was a mutant! Radiation! Don't you understand, we're contaminated! They sent her to poison us, the running dogs!" I ran into the bathroom to decontaminate myself under the ultraviolet lamp, pausing to pour beer down my throat and over most of my body.

We sat around for a while and finished all the drugs except for the cocaine, which we put back in the kit bag. A quick snort off Gideon's Bible and we jumped in the car and cruised toward Kutscher's. Alfred squinted through the windshield and rearranged his long fingers on the wheel. "Anthony, there are some hitchhikers up there and they appear to be of the opposite sex." I peered through the translucent panorama of hallucinations on the hood and made out two female figures on the side of the road. "Pick them up, they don't look dangerous." The two girls got in the back of the car. One of them I can't remember anything about, she was let off around a mile up the road. The other was around twenty-five years old with bright red hair and a very developed body. She was scrutinizing us from the back seat and noticed my camera case and brown double-knits.

"Are you a photographer?"

"Yes, this is true, I am a photographer."

"Will you take some nude pictures of me?"

"Certainly, my services are for sale."

"Where are you from?"

"My associate and I are from Topeka."

"Kansas?"

"Yep, we're on assignment for *Rolling Stone*. We're Doctors of Journalism."

"Would you guys like to get high?"

We brought the girl to her apartment. Her name was Panama Red. She was from Las Vegas. She lived behind the Pussycat Lounge, where she worked nightly as an exotic contortionist / topless dancer. Her room was a small affair with a sink. A small, furry, pink object scurried out of the closet and across the vomit-green rug. This was Pinky, I was told, Panama's dog. I sat in a chair next to the bed; Alfred perched himself behind the sink. I could see from the desperate look in his eyes that he was having a hard time separating reality from hallucination. The poor bastard. You take LSD and it just happens to be the time you pick up an exotic contortionist. Alfred was chain-smoking Black Russians with sweaty fingers, looking first at Panama, then me. I clutched the chair and assured myself that it existed. Working from that basic premise, I re-created reality, step by step. Panama showed us some pictures and belted back a whiskey and soda with two pills she had pulled out of her drawer. Jesus. Rover 714s; the most powerful quaalude made. This girl was asking for trouble.

Allow me a slight tangent. Quaaludes are ugly drugs. They are also fun to take. The user bops around all night feeling no pain, friendly, happy, warm, with an inhuman urge to fuck anything that walks. To observe the user is another matter. People on soapers are usually draped somewhere over a chair telling everybody how much they like them. They often vomit and, inevitably, pass out. There is nothing more grotesque than a horny geek on quaaludes telling you his life story. Panama started to move slowly. She reached under the bed and showed us pictures of her friends from Vegas. "See this one?"

"Yeah."

"Silicone."

"Hmm, bulbous, very, mammaries . . ."

"Are you guys stoned?" I lit my tenth Black Russian and tried to deal with this person. She went into her closet and took out her stripper clothes. Oh no, a soaped-out contortionist.

She took off all her clothes and started modeling her various stage outfits. "I like this one, you like it?" Alfred and I just sat there in the room. I was a young person at this time and my addled brain raced to absorb the twisted Information which was pouring into it. Is this life? She sat down and lit up a joint. "I'm really a nice person. All I want is for you to smile at me. You know, I was working the other night and I danced over to this guy's table and gave him a little attention so he'd give me a big tip. Well, the guy puts down a fifty."

"A fifty?" Incredulous.

"Yeah. You know, now I let guys get away with a lot, especially for money, but not this time. I'm lying up here on my bed and the bastard comes in and starts trying to fuck me. I told him to fuck off and he wouldn't, so I reached over and grabbed a bottle off the night table and smashed it across his face. He got out fast, but I cut the shit out of my hand. Look, you can still see the scars." Scarred contortionists weaving obscenely around the room. Too much. Christ, I'm only fifteen. She leaned over the sink and puked watery vomit. Alfred stood up to help her and she fell over onto the floor. Her foot went through the plastic cup holding Pinky's water. She didn't move. Alfred stared over at me. I looked at him. We had a quick mental conversation standing there mutely on either side of her body.

"What will we do?"

"Erase the fingerprints!"

"Check the ashtrays for butts and ashes!"

"Escape!"

Visions of Jack Webb kicking down my door came quickly and horribly to mind, snarling Dobermans chasing me through the Catskills, accessory, crimes against nature, violation of the law. And the trial. My parents sitting there watching me in the witness box as the defense asked the questions, "How was it, Mr. Bourdain, that you happened to be in the room of the deceased, a Miss Panama Red, contortionist, on said date? And according to our lab report here, you were found under the influence of the following Illegal Drugs . . ." It was too horrible to imagine. She started to move. We helped her to the bed when she said, "Guys, why don't you come back at three o'clock for an orgy. I have to go to work."

"No thanks, we have to leave for Topeka immediately."

"Really? Well, listen, before you go, snort a little coke." So Panama laid back spread-eagle, naked on the bed, and filled up her navel with cocaine. And, dear readers, Alfred and I approached and snorted deep without a second thought. I think it was at this point that we achieved our goal, the Edge. Any more and we would have cracked, walked around for the rest of our lives thinking it perfectly normal to pull up someone's shirt, stuff cocaine in their navel, and snort it out, grasping their thighs and whirling about in a psychotic little dance and then taking off. The two of us jumped into the car, Alfred content to sit catatonic in the passenger's seat while I drove homeward on the dark mountain roads.

Wet Affairs

An unpublished short story Tony wrote in 1985. Portions of this later appeared in *Between C & D* magazine and *ZAT* magazine.

A cool, sustained breeze came in off the bay, lifted the chef under the armpits, and dried the wetness on his neck and forehead at the hairline. Another breeze wrapped itself around him for a second, tugged at the back of his knees to follow it, and then disappeared down Commercial Street. He could see the charter fishing boats heading for port in the orange-streaked Cape Cod twilight. Chattering seagulls trailed behind the boats and dove for the bits of Cheez Doodles and Wonder Bread thrown out on the water by sunburned tourists.

The chef walked down the narrow path to the old pier at the water's edge, seashells crunching under his feet with each step of his food-encrusted paratrooper boots. He sat down, hung his legs over the splintered wood, and began to unravel the crisscross of soggy yellow and maroon bandages from his hands. One by one the bits of tape and gauze were gingerly removed, rolled into little balls, and flicked into the black water of the bay, where they bobbed on the surface.

It smelled of salt air and restaurant kitchens. From screen doors and exhaust fans across Provincetown the collage of cooking smells filled the evening with hints of the Portuguese, Italian, French, and New England dishes being prepared. The chef smiled as he recognized in the occasional waft of air, the flippers frying at the bakery, mussels steaming in garlic at Ciro's, fudge from the wharf, veal piccata at Sal's, and the unmistakable scent emanating from his own place of employ, the "HMS Dreadnought," a bitter cloud of steam that signified the demise of yet another score of lobsters, red bodies stacked in the steamer, waiting for pink and blistered hands, cooks' hands, to stuff them with crabmeat and prop them up in oval gardens of parsley and lemon wedges, a goblet of clarified butter grasped protectively between dead claws.

The chef held up his hands and looked at them, turning them slowly. He scrutinized the constellations of splatter burns and tiny fading punctures, bisected by a road map of raised lines, some straight, some curved and lagged. Cooks' hands. His red badge of courage. The hands felt good open to the night air. He was proud of these scars, and of the kitchens where he had acquired them in this little Portuguese fishing village, this Times Square by the sea.

From the pier, he looked at the Dreadnought. It jutted out into the choppy water, waves slapping against the wooden pylons that held the restaurant out over the bay. Built from the wrecks of wooden ships, the dining room was a dark maze of hanging and swinging objects of marine memorabilia. Through the window screens and fishnets, the chef watched the first customers file into the restaurant. The yellow ships' candles that glowed on every table flickered as the pudgy silhouettes waddled past, intent on the ritual consumption of fried seafood and raw clams.

He pulled himself to his feet and started up the path back to the kitchen, could hear the hiss and spray of the dishwasher grow louder and the laughs and curses of the cooks.

At the garbage stacked by the kitchen door, he stopped and glanced across the street to the pizza shop where Christine stood each night spinning pies and serving slices. A single picture window faced out onto the street, and he could see her framed in the light. He turned to watch. She stood there, tossing a big, beige circle of pizza dough between her two hands, sent it spinning confidently skyward, and for a long second, out of the frame of the window and his line of sight. Then it dropped, seemingly from nowhere, back into her outstretched arms. He watched as she ladled on the tomato sauce with a quick circular motion, smiling as she sprinkled grated cheese over the top.

She turned, lifted the pizza to a favored spot in the top oven with a large wooden spatula, and with an expert jerk of the left arm, whipped the spatula out from under, closed the oven door, and turned again with a quiet look of satisfaction. Her blond hair was tied back in a faded pink towel, but a single straw-colored strand escaped out over her eyes. He smiled at her. She couldn't see him in the dark beyond the window.

Down dark tree-lined suburban streets, young Michael, blissfully unaware of any culinary campaigns in his future, lay flat on his back in the yard. The sky was smeared with purple and orange. Any moment the streetlights would come on. Michael lay in the dusk, feeling the bristly green carpet through his T-shirt, looking up at it all. The thick smell of freshly cut grass seemed ever present in the air that hinted also of distant barbeques and burning leaves. The barking of a lawn mower interrupted the silence, starting, stopping, and then droning onward, changing in pitch as it gobbled up thick patches of lawn. Water hissed in the neighbors' kitchen sink and a screen door banged shut. Michael heard laughter through the hedges.

Children in molded plastic army helmets stalked each other through the heart of darkest rhododendron. Moths fluttered noisily about the orange light on the front porch, scattering shadows on the columns and white stucco walls of the old house. Beyond the hedges and the cyclone fence that ringed the property, Allen and Nelson waited for Michael under the yew tree, where each summer night, they met to plan their destructive forays. Michael hoped that Allen had fireworks. He walked down the crooked cobblestone sidewalk (careful not to step on the cracks), head filled with visions of cherry bombs and M-80s.

Young Michael crouched in the darkness. His cohorts, Nelson and Allen, peered over the fence next to him. The dark, and the tall grass in the deserted backyard, hid their fumbling efforts to ignite a particularly nasty firework.

Across the street, a young couple strolled past the Dutch colonial houses, laughing and smoking. The bottle rocket screamed downward and upon them, an orange-sparkling, spiraling trajectory that ended with a loud bang that echoed through the town.

The girl shrieked. The young man, a brawny footballer with a letter jacket, caught a glimpse of the three aspiring hoodlums beyond the fence. A few strides and a leap, and the vengeful jock was after them.

The young guerillas ran terrified through the bushes, lumps in their throats, cold sweat breaking out under their T-shirts.

Michael took ten short strides, a hard right, and flung himself to the ground, flattening his small and skinny body in the tall untended grass. He felt the ground rumble around him as the growling bulk passed him by. Nelson and Allen ran a straight and ill-considered route homeward. Michael could hear it when the footballer caught up with them. The side of his face pressed in the earth, he could see only the moon, held in the suburban sky over the empty wood-frame house that stood in the center of the lot. In the distance, the sounds of slapping, and short, angry accusations, the shrill cries of Nelson and Allen, and then only their whimpers as the avenging shadow passed him by once again, missing him by inches.

He waited for a good ten minutes before he rose from his hiding place and sought out his partners in crime. He found the hapless pair sitting together on the corner. They stopped weeping when they saw Michael. Their chests rising and falling convulsively as they gulped back the tears, their faces struggled to remain stoic though puffy and pink. They were determined to extract some manner of delinquent glory from the frightening and unpleasant experience.

Michael had been afraid. But as badly as he felt for his scraped knees and bruised comrades, he felt a strange and new substance begin to creep into his brain, secreted from some heretofore unknown region of his network of electric charges and synapses. It was to this mysterious substance that he would, from this time on, remain hopelessly addicted.

The leather seats of the Mercedes sedan squeaked as it rounded corners. The baby slept silently in Nelson's fur-swaddled arms. The passengers (Allen at the wheel, Nelson, Christine and baby in the back seat, the chef in the front passenger seat) were silent, thinking, no doubt, of the same thing. Allen made a half-hearted attempt at humor, saying something about the road to hell needing repaving. They all laughed, a hollow chortle that trailed off into sneers and shrugs.

The chef smelled it all from blocks away. He had hardly felt a blast of air that opened his every pore with the dank bite of stale piss and burnt candles, the smoking, the embers of the bits of wood and insulation that warmed the unseen lines of impatient junkies who scurried insect-like through the maze of burned-out tenements. Each building that whipped past the windows of the car reminded the chef of an ugly memory; each one remembered as a name as it disappeared behind them: "Tri-Zone," "Alcatraz," "Laredo," "Maze," "Poison," "357," "BI," "Nova," and "Toilet."

Their destination tonight was "Executive." When the car turned onto Avenue A, the chef directed them to give him the money and to meet him at the agreed-upon time and place. Allen put six hundred dollars in bank-fresh twenties in the chef's hand. Allen was shaking and his eyes were wet.

"Please, please . . . try not to get beat or ripped off."

"Believe me, I'll do my best," the chef replied contemptuously. He walked down Fourth Street toward Avenue D, could hear the approaching cries in Spanish, the names of the brands, cries of warning, offerings of drugs and death of all varieties.

"BA HONDO . . . BA HONDO!!"

"FAO . . . FAO . . . FAO!"

"Executive is OPENNNNNNN?!"

"GATO!! GATOOOO!!!"

Halfway down Fourth, he took a quick look each way, exchanged nods with the sullen lookout, and ducked into the maze of sheet metal and planks, crawling on hands and knees into the dark, abandoned building.

He had been here before. It was, by neighborhood standards, a reliable operation, servicing the community for over six years in the same location (across the street from a grammar school). The chef stood inside the doorway for a moment, waiting for his eyes to adjust to the lack of light, the smell of candles, and other people's endorphins engulfing him like Mom's apple pie. He slogged down the hall in ankle-deep water. A big Cuban in a hooded sweatshirt and a Walkman shoved a flashlight in his face and barked—

"Show tracks, bro!"

The chef pulled up his left sleeve. The old marks had faded. The sentry scrutinized the arm with unconcealed disdain for the expanse of unblemished pale flesh.

"You gotta have tracks to get in, homeboy. I don't see no kinda ID."

The flashlight pointed to the exit. The chef started to perspire, he heard himself, watched almost, as the old junkie whine crept back into his voice, the irritating and shameless pleading and cringing.

"I used to come here every week, man! You don't remember me? I'm Mike: I came here every day for years, dropped thousands . . . Thousands in this place! I just been on the Program for a while is all. Look, look! There're tracks there! They just old is all 'cause I been on the Program."

The Cuban must have been impressed by what was obviously a bona fide Junkie Whine. The flashlight pointed up the steps.

"OK, B. There's a long line up there. You want express for five dollars? I take you right up to the hole, no waitin'?"

"No thanks . . . don't have enough cake for that, thanks."

The Cuban smiled.

"Watch the steps, homeboy."

The busted stairs were illuminated by only the occasional candle, melting over the banister. The chef climbed carefully, feeling with the tips of his toes for missing steps and any holes or booby traps left for the cops and the careless. On the second floor he followed the trail of candles down a long hall and through more puddles and dark rooms. A hole had been bashed through into the next building, and the trail of tiny flames led him around until he arrived at a second stairwell where two workers lined the customers into groups of ten and then up the steps to the hole. The workers swung their long, black-taped flashlights like billy clubs, herding the limping and compliant crowd like so many cattle.

"NO TALKIN' ON THE LINE!"

"HAVE YOUR MONEY OUT THE LONG WAY! NO SINGLES!"

"Stand up against the wall and NO TALKIN'!"

"You be talkin' an' you don't come here!"

Discreetly, the chef examined the faces around him on the line. In front of him were two blond girls who looked as if they might have at one time been pretty; now they were skinny, bent creatures with sunken eyes, bitter mouths, and spandexed drumstick legs that rocked back and forth impatiently. Swollen, elephantine hands protruded from the sleeves of the tattered old man behind him. A hospital bracelet still adorned one puffy limb, the other held a few stolen belts which the aging schmecker had no doubt been trying to sell all day. Three anxious young kids from the suburbs, all looking as if their mothers still dressed them, giggled and complained; their friends probably waited for them in a Camaro, idling conspicuously on a nearby corner. There were overdressed Frenchmen and assorted Eurotrash, punks, skunks, ex-models, ex-musicians, old-timers, and the occasional tuxedo, all lined up like obedient walking wounded, listening to the relay of shouts from the streets and the rooftops.

"GATOOOO . . ."

"FAOOOO . . ."

The line moved quickly. Soon the chef stood before the hastily constructed plywood wall at the top of the steps. He pressed six hundred dollars through the small hole in the center of the board and whispered the number of bags.

"Sixty."

He could hear them inside the hole, counting his money. A few seconds later, six bundles of tightly banded glassine bags popped through the hole back at him, held between the thumb and forefinger of someone he couldn't see. He put the six bundles into his front pants pocket; the little packets of hard drugs felt all snuggly and wonderful inside his jeans. Retracing his steps through the black and leaking maze, he hurried out to the street and half-ran, half-walked the three blocks over to the corner of A where the expensive automobile awaited him. Behind the windshield, he could see his friends and loved ones searching his face for an indication. Cruelly, he kept his face expressionless and watched their eager gestures. Then he smiled. Mission accomplished.

When the car had crossed Fourteenth Street, the chef began to relax. He had gone to the well much, much too often, and yet, once again, he had survived. He boasted to the others, reveling in his proud familiarity with the criminal element, with the great Underbelly.

"New York City! . . . Greatest City in the World!!"

Christine looked knowingly at the back of Michael's head as she sank back into the leather upholstery. She knew how he felt now, like Nick Charles, Super Chef, John Garfield.

The chef turned and beamed stupidly at his Nora.

*Allen called the restaurant from a pay phone on Eighth Avenue and re-*minded his saucier to pull out the seafood pâté he had left in the oven. When he hung up, he felt a sudden paranoia coming on like a cramp. The bag of meth he had just bought on Forty-ninth Street had hit him hard, harder than he had expected for a midtown bag. He was delightfully, blissfully, helplessly high, nodded and nodding as he tried to negotiate traffic on wobbly legs that he could barely feel. Ten minutes ago, the legs had hurt him, sore from standing long hours in the kitchen; now he stumbled along painlessly as if skipping on cream cheese.

Some remnants of Allen's conscious mind alerted him to the all-too-obvious spectacle that he was likely to make of himself. He sleep-walked across Times Square, mouth hanging stupidly open, his eyelids drooping, closing, irresistibly. The passing cars that honked their horns at him seemed distant and laughable. He made for the nearby doors of the Pussycat Club. A handful of tokens was exchanged for his twenty by an oblivious cashier. Allen staggered up brightly painted steps lined with Christmas lights and was swallowed up by the blare of the music. He felt safe and anonymous among the averted eyes and turned faces of the gray businessmen who milled about among the booths and magazine racks. Allen felt far from the street and any pursuers, real or imagined.

He noticed a girl looking at him. She stood out among a threatening lineup of gaudily clad women. She was short, wiry, and intense looking in a way that he found attractive. She gave off a junk smell that Allen found sympathetic. He hardly noticed the ludicrous ensemble of tit-lifting, crotch-revealing lingerie that she was wearing. Her hair was short. He liked that. She looked to be a bit hard, a bit soft, a solitary compelling figure among the stony-faced, unsympathetic mannequins who sagged into their underthings on either side of her.

He followed as she beckoned him into a short passageway with a movement of her head, the corner of her mouth turning up slightly. She guided him with a touch on his elbow around and into the other side of her booth and pulled the curtains closed.

She stared into his eyes through a thick plexiglass wall that divided the booth from floor to ceiling. It looked bulletproof. She motioned to him to pick up the phone to his right and picked up hers. Visiting day at Sing Sing. He dropped some tokens into the slot by the phone, and her side of the booth lit up with pink light, and he could hear her voice in the receiver.

"Hi, honey. You look nice. What's your name? Mine's Candy."

"David . . . name is David." He lied.

He noticed now how nearly naked she was and felt embarrassed. But she continued to look at him dispassionately with nurse eyes, tilted her head like a marionette, spoke to him, a disembodied voice through the plastic receiver.

"What do you like, honey? What can I do for you? You like this?" She moved her gaze down to below his navel and looked up expectantly.

"I want to see you. Let me see it. I want to see what it looks like."

Allen, not wanting to be difficult, compliantly unzipped his pants and flopped his limp and disinterested member out into the air. Pleased apparently, the girl kept things moving. Her accent confused him. He couldn't tell what country she could be from, or to what degree the French accent was faked. On the other side of the plexiglass, she moved in the pink light, looking back at him performing a series of classic, self-involved poses, fondling herself mechanically, tweaking nipples that she then proffered to the bulletproof barrier.

"C'mon, honey . . . Let me see you come. Come for me."

Her half of the room went frighteningly and abruptly dark, leaving him alone, inglorious and illuminated, his cock hanging out of his pants, vulnerable and cut off from the voice on the phone. Craving darkness, he loaded more tokens into the box and just as suddenly, all was as before.

It gradually dawned on Allen that his unenthusiastic dick was the object of her attentions. He began slowly to jerk himself off with his right hand, anxious to accommodate the abstraction that spoke to him on the phone from her pink and plastic cage. She was just inches in front of him. Yet she skipped and jumped and flickered like an old and blurry eight-millimeter loop.

And though it was becoming, with each token, a thoroughly pathetic little melodrama, Allen started to feel the comforting megalomania of Junk Power coming to his aid. The junkie in his head purred admiringly, with curiosity and appreciation, measuring great irony and tragedy in the extent of his degradation. He met the girl's increasingly animated contortions with movements of his own, hips forward, clutching an increasingly cooperative hard-on, cheered on by the narcissism that only heroin can sustain. He wordlessly defied her to culminate their business, and with admiration for his own unrestrained exhibitionism, stroked his dick like a monkey. Allen was determined to not be remembered as one of the thousands of petulant and perspiring children that the girl no doubt knew as the male sex. She was working, working harder with each drop of a two-dollar token. For him.

He looked into her eyes and, defiantly as is possible in such circumstances, ejaculated onto the plexiglass. She hopped onto her knees and with a final theatrical flourish, followed the hapless stream on its voyage downriver, pantomiming at it with flicks of her tongue as the stream diverted into tributaries and joined the sticky ocean on the cement floor.

The lights came on. The voice on the phone beeped off for the last time. Allen congratulated himself on his timing; there were no tokens left to hide from Helen. Zipping up, he felt once more capable of simulating normal public behavior. Without looking at the girl, he pressed a five into her hand.

Across the booth-lined room, two men were arguing in Spanish. Allen couldn't hear what they were saying over the loud music and the amplified rasps of the barker, inviting one and all to "live sex onstage." The two men faced each other, the larger of the two men with his back to Allen. The man facing saw him, seemed to recognize him. The other man, responding, it seemed to something the other said, turned and met Allen's eyes with his own black shark gaze, and smiled. It was Georgie.

They found Allen three days later. He was stuffed down an air shaft in an empty tenement on Third Street (where they used to sell the Tri Zone). His throat had been cut, and he had been stabbed a lot. The chef read about it in the *Post*. We read it on the subway on the way to work, stood between cars and sobbed over the clatter and squeal of the number 1 train as it banged its way down Broadway. They printed Allen's high school graduation picture, naturally. Too bad, thought the chef, that Allen hadn't been an Eagle Scout, he would have made the cover.

The article indicated that "Ivan Rodriguez," apprehended in connection with the case, had dropped a dime on a "Jorge Riviera." It was a name the chef knew.

As planned, the chef swallowed the last forty milligrams of amphetamine sulfate. It was a slow, long drive to Avenue D and Fourth, and by the time Vladimir's Land Rover crossed the sun-drenched intersection at Houston, the speed was pumping homicidal fury through his veins, evil adrenaline. Through clenched teeth he told Vladimir where to pull over, coming to a halt at the uptown corner of D on the west side by the projects.

The strip was in full attendance. All the old faces stood in their faded and tattered clothes (schmattas), heads turning uptown and then downtown and then uptown again. Across the street he could see Vinnie and Joyce and Frankie conferring in a doorway, probably discussing the financing involved in getting down on a bag. Everybody was waiting, with little or no success, pinched, hopeful expressions on their pained and anxious faces. Shari, the little blond hooker with the acne-scarred face and pink halter top and hot pants (wedged in the crack of her ass), noticed him across the street and discreetly nodded her greeting.

And there was Georgie. He stood with his powerful legs slightly apart, arms folded across his chest, perched on the corner by the mailbox. Like the figurehead of a ship, cutting through the scenery by the sheer force of his immeasurable capacity for destruction. He looked out across the square where street met avenue, not looking at anything in particular, more a heroic posture, white cane in fist; Napoleon survey-ing his conquered city, not seeing the carnage in front of him, surround-ing him—rather peering into future campaigns, envisioning (perhaps) some like this. Georgie posed: a Goya painting but apocalyptic victory gone mad. King of the Cell Block, baddest motherfucker on the avenue, fearful of no man, possessor of all he surveyed.

"GATO!! GATO!! GATO TATO!!"

The chef stepped out of the car with a trench coat and hat held in his left arm, a bottle of Dom Perignon brut in his right. He was in full uniform: checked pants, white double-breasted chef's coat, and apron. Georgie spied him immediately and smiled, amused. The chef made a straight line for him, diagonally across the avenue. Georgie looked curi-ous, still smiling, showing large white teeth, an ancient Aztec smile that said DEATH DEATH DEATH.

Visibly trembling, the chef extended the bottle of champagne, care-ful to affect the proper whine in his voice.

"Georgie, listen . . . I'm sick, really sick. I couldn't score any cash, but I stole this from my restaurant. It's champagne, Dom Perignon. You know, Dom fucking Perignon! I'll give it to you if you hook me up with just one bag of D. If you can even just get down on a bag with me fifty-fifty, that would be chill, I don't care . . . I just gotta get somethin', I'm hurting bad . . . What do you say? It's a good deal. Can't you give me some play for the bottle? It's worth ninety bucks!"

Georgie's smile broadened horribly, spreading across his face, a threatening, blinding chasm of piano teeth.

"Give it to me."

With apparent uncertainty, the chef held the bottle up to him. Georgie snatched it from his grasp without hesitation and held it close to his chest, glowering with indisputable ownership.

"Get the fuck outta here."

"What about the bag?"

"Get lost, *puto, cabrón.*"

"C'mon, man, that's a ninety-dollar bottle a bubbles! You make out great on the deal!"

"This way I make out better. Now get the fuck outta my face. Beat it! You wanna fuck with me?"

The chef moved crablike backward on the sidewalk, stumbling clumsily off the curb and into the street. Turning, he beat a whimpering retreat up Avenue D and hailed the Land Rover, muttering loudly to himself all the while.

The Young Caremians

Originally published in *ZAT* magazine, issue number 2, in 1984.

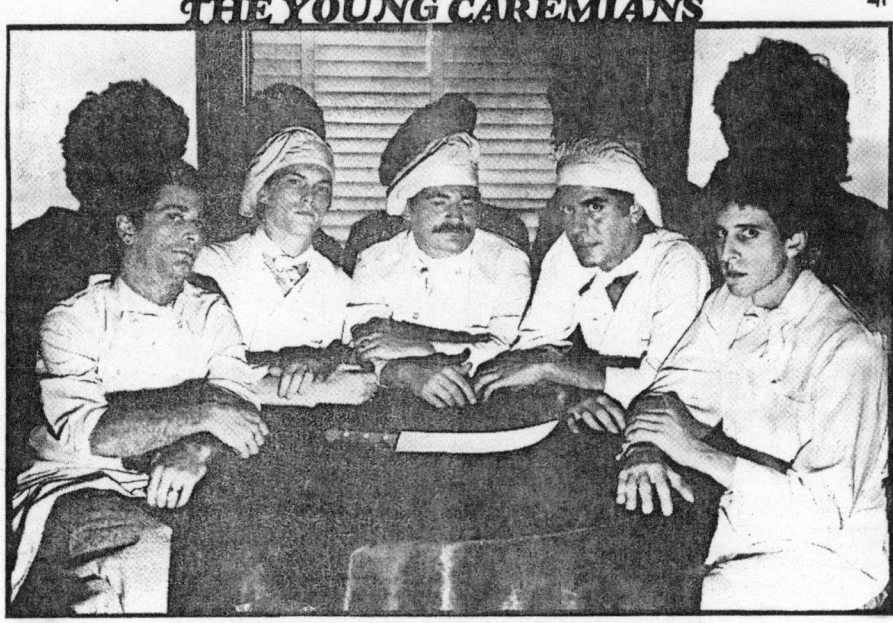

Anthony BOURDAIN

"The Young Caremians" met each and every Thursday night at "Le Mec," a little french restaurant in the East Village with a sympathetic owner-chef named Raoul. At eleven o'clock, when dinner service had ended and any customers who might possibly be offended had long since gone home, he opened the small, slightly sleazy room to the Caremians.

The group consisted of six chefs. There was Michael, who even the other chefs referred to as "Chef"; Allen, who worked in a trendy nouvelle place in the West Village; Vladimir, the father figure, a forty year old Russian-German Cape-Codian with a handle-bar mustache and the only belly among them that truly befitted a chef; Johnny, a quiet, intense young man who Vladimir had brought up from dishwasher; "Q", a gangly, brilliant kid with a face out of an old Fleischer cartoon; and Mohammed, a silent, enormous Egyptian who revered the lot of them. They had trained him to cook, kept him steadily employed, married him off to keep him in the country, and one time, recovered his wallet, filled with two weeks pay,

when a shifty waiter had stolen it. He had given them each an inscribed Arabic-English volume of the Glorius Koran. It was understood that he would gladly step in front of a bullet for any of them, if necessary.

It would be difficult to define a common creed. What they did have in common was an interest in exotic cuisine, drugs, neomilitarism, Scorcese, Coppola, Schrader and New England Portugee food, particularly Squid Stew.

As they had come together on Cape Cod many years ago, it was perhaps to be expected that half of them were rabid Yankee fans, and the rest, honor-bound to follow the Boston Red Sox to their inevitable yearly destruction.

Their get-togethers were marked by heated tirades about the latest jet-set chef's gourmet pizza or kiwi grilled over mesquite. Plans were made to descend on enemy restaurants, burst in the kitchen screaming, "DROP THOSE KNIVES!!CULINARY COPS!!!", and then prosecute on the spot for crimes against food.

Advocates of so-called "Nouvelle American", or worse, "Nouvelle Californian" were frequent objects of derision and ridicule. Gossip was exchanged. A particularly influential and corpulent food critic for a glossy Manhattan magazine was often the topic of wide-eyed discussion. She was legendary for providing four-page color photo spreads and complimentary puff-pieces in return for marathon cunnilingus as administered by hopeful and ambitious young culinarians. She was said to have a notorious male porno star on permanent retainer, and the quality of services rendered determined the choice of adjectives use in her articles. "Succulent", "intoxicating", and "innovative" all in one article meant that some hapless young cookie somewhere was probably still nursing his sore jaw and walking with a slight limp.

As the evening wore on, it was inevitable that someone would slip on the taped soundtrack to "Apocalypse Now." A dreamy look wafted across the faces of the white-clad, angry young men, and as the sound of distant choppers rose to meld with Wagner, one would usually mutter, "I jus' wanna fuckin' cook, man, . . . just wanna fuckin' cook . . . Never get off the boat. NEVER get off the boat.." For a few seconds they would share an exhilirating vision. Screaming F-14 fighters, manned by white-clad chefs wearing headsets, kicking in the afterburners, showering death on the bad restaurants, ignorant diners, waiters, and insensitive restauranteurs that dissolved below in a hurricane-wind of phosphorous and napalm that swept out from their cocks, and for one beautiful second, disintegrated their enemies.

In post-coital bliss, they would eat and drink and tell good stories and better lies. They were the chefs of the future. "The Para-Culinary Elite." The Young Turks, on the brink of wiping away, by force of their sheer collective genius and originality, the Moustache Petes of the tired Frog Ponds, bland Nouvella Cucina, Fake Tex-Mex, and everything that was over-precious, over-mesquited, over-done, over-trendy, or overly successful.

As far as a plan for the brave new world of the future, they were split down the middle. Michael was a proponent of "Neo HoJo," while Allen and Vladimir promoted what they called "Retro-Institutional."

Michael envisioned leading an assault on established cuisine with a whole style based on the fondly remembered full-color photos on the old Howard Johnson menus. Those oval plates, overburgeoned with checkered steaks, electric colors, huge portions and cubist garnishes; this, he felt, was the right way to go as a group. Allen and Vladimir loved nothing more, though, than to painstakingly recreate, with the finest and most expensive ingredients, the institutional favorites that festered in the steam-tables of long-ago cafeterias.

When Vladimir had the rare opportunity to make such high-school cafeteria classics and "Chicken Hawaiian," "Shepherd's Pie", or "Tuna-Noodle Casserole", tears would come to his eyes from the sheer pleasure of it all. And even Michael had to admit, the results were always wonderful. Often, when Vladimir worked the day shift, Michael had to run to work, anxious to sample his Chicken Pot Pie or his Meat Loaf. When Vladimir had been his sous-chef at "Dick Waters", a theater restaurant on 46th Street, he loved arriving at work to find the Mad Russian, beaming over a hotel pan of Baked Macaroni and Cheese, eyes twinkling . . ."

"Looks just like the real thing, huh?"

Even Chicken Hawaiian, possibly the most loathsome, unlikely, tasteless dish in the annals of cuisine, became an exotic and guilty pleasure with Vladimir's talented ministrations. And it was inarguably "authentic", right down to the maraschino cherries.

Michael quietly worshipped Vladimir. They all did. He was the natural of the group. Just watching him take pleasure in the simple wiping of a finger through some excess pate fat, or nibbling on a bit of fish aspic, it was clear to all that he was somehow the genuine article. While the rest spent their free time at the beach, nodding out in after-hours clubs or chasing spandexed bartenders, Vladimir went home to his vegetable garden where he tended to his herbs, his beans, his cucumbers, his basil and his mash. Dinner at Vladimir's was better than and rarer than Christmas. The last one, two years ago, was still remembered, rehashed and revised until it neared legend.

On this particular evening, Raoul stood behind the tiny zinc bar, wiping in circular patterns with a damp bar towel. The Velvet Underground Banana album was on the system, "Sunday Morning" to be exact, and it had been decided already that they would not, definitely not, play poker owing to the lack of funds in some corners. Michael noticed that the ones drinking Coca Colas were the ones with no money. Not surprising. He was relieved anyway that the game was off; two, maybe three less bags tomorrow would be an inconvenience at best.

"Q" looked like he had something to say and had been holding it in till ready to near burst. His eyes twinkled, glazed, the corners of his mouth struggled to form a straight line. Big grin,

"I gotta tell you this one. You guys'll just love this! It happened at my restaurant tonight, at "Al Dente", Picture this; a quiet evening in fashionable Soho. Upscale young Aryans in pastel-hued designer clothes are eating pumpkin tortelloni and porcini mushrooms in our peach-colored dining room. Pat Metheny is playing softly in the background . . . Well, two well-dressed customers at a center table are starting to have words. They're getting louder and louder in some foreign language, Slavic, maybe. Anyway, one of them stands up and starts pointing at the other guy. The other customers are getting nervous now, but they like slump over their pasta and pretend not to notice these two guys screaming at each other in the middle of the room!! Then, one of the two guys reaches down and comes up with his steak knife, I guess he was having the Tordimatti; anyway, he comes up with the knife and drags it right across the other guy's throat!!

"Well, you wouldna believed it! I mean Sam Peckinpah never did anything like this!! The guy starts doing a jig, hopping up and down and turning, kinda jerking around. The blood is pumping up outta his neck like SQUIRT! SQUIRT!! and he's hosing down the whole room with blood. I mean, picture all these genteel diners' faces as they're being showered with blood. It was fuckin' unbelievable! For the first few seconds there's total silence. The guy with the knife just sorta walks out the door real fast, the customers are like . . . nobody is moving except the guy in the middle who drops into his fettucine and stops moving. Then they start screaming. And then they look at each other, believe me — a real sight, and start screaming louder. The cops come, and the meat wagon, and the paramedics. We closed two hours early!"

They all liked the story. Vladimir said, "Real Grand Guignol, I like it." Allan inquired. "Did everybody have to pay for their dinners?" Q laughed, "Yeah! Yeah! They paid, the waiters started threatening a walk-out as soon as management even hinted that it might be the right thing to do."

Allan leaned back and put his glass down on the table in a way that indicated he had a good story. He put on his "wise" look, letting his eyes get hard and old-looking and began.

"This was last week, and if anyone breathes a word of this story to anyone, especially my girlfriend, you're dead."

They all exchanged looks. This was the standard introduction to all of Allan's stories.

"I was on the 104 bus sitting in the back corner seat. By chance, instead of my usual New York Post, I was reading a paperback collection of Elliot poems. I'm sitting there, the bus is real crowded, and from next to me I hear a very nice voice ask, "Is that 'Love Song of J. Alfred Prufrock' you're reading?" It was and I said so. She was beautiful. Twenty, twenty-one, slim, long black hair, and intelligent, in a visible but very attractive way. A tall Isabel Adjani. She says, "That poem is like a ride on a roller coaster; it excites, surprises, amuses, saddens, and thrills." Nervous really now, I can't think of anything literate or bright to say, so I just smile at her. Meaningful-like."

"Then she says, 'are you reading it for fun?' Later, I figure out she must of thought I might be reading it for some school or something, I didn't really know what she meant but I say, 'Yeah . . . fun.' She gives me a real long look like I'm going to be dinner in five minutes, and then she says, 'Thrill me.'

So we get off at the next stop. By now I'm like not in control. Somebody on Mars is controlling my behavior. Saying practically nothing, I take her to the nearest hotel, turned out to be the Woodward on Broadway, the one with the 24-hour sushi bar, and we take a room. She fucks the living shit out of me. Then she gets dressed, fixes her face, and says, "What do you do?"

"I tell her I'm a chef. I tell her where I work. I tell her I think she is intoxicating. She leaves."

Michael leaned across the table with the look of a detective on a case.

"You think she'll see you again?"

"I don't know. I'm a little afraid. I mean, she's too perfect. She's incredible, like somebody sent her to get me to detect or something. I kept thinking, "What does she want from me?"

"Hey, all that dope makes you a good fuck. She must have loved it, a guy who just fucks and fucks and NEVER comes!"

"Yeah, but it was more than that. I think she wants my brain for agents from Outer Space. I mean . . . I have a girlfriend. I'm happy. I'm in love. Maybe she was custom designed to destroy my life."

"Sounds like she could."

Vladimir looked down his nose, through his specs at them disapprovingly.

"I happen to like Candy, your better, and I mean BETTER half, and I think you should forget the whole thing and be nice to your girlfriend. Bring her roses and tell her the truth."

Michael sneered.

"That's the Russian answer for all things —"

Bring ROSES!", they chorused.

Allan was not finished, he looked pasty, not right.

"I wonder if she'll ever track me down, I mean I gave her the name of my restaurant and everything . . ."

They all agreed that the best treatment for guilt was a good game of poker to spread the guilt and regret around a little. As it was for the common good, and as Allan agreed to take paper, they played, not stopping till seven the next morning. ●

WELL AT LEAST YOU GOT OVER THAT BANANNA THING.

VI

Vietnam

World travelers are supposed to carry themselves with a certain level of detachment. We assume that along with cosmopolitanism comes a sense of being a "global citizen" in some way that rises above partisanship. Tony was not this. For Tony, Vietnam was everything. It is impossible to nail down exactly what it is about the place, and the people, and the food, that captured Tony so deeply, and for so long, but I think there's a key that we can see in the writing here in this section. In these pages, it almost feels like Tony has met his match with Vietnam, a boundless subject that is too vast for even him to render with its endless movement, life, color, ingenuity, pride.

I Was Hooked

An excerpt from the foreword Tony wrote for Graham Holliday's *Eating Viet Nam: Dispatches from a Blue Plastic Table*, originally published under the Bourdain Books imprint at Ecco in 2015.

Vietnam owns me. From my first visit, I was helpless to resist. Just a few months previous, I'd been resigned to the certainty that I would never see Vietnam; that my dreams of Graham Greene Land, that faraway place I only knew from childhood news reports, books, and films, would have to wait for another life. This life, I was sure, would finish in close proximity to a Manhattan deep fryer.

So, simply finding myself there, finally, outside the legendary Continental Hotel in Saigon, smelling Vietnam, hearing it, the high roar of thousands of motorbikes, I was overcome with gratitude and disbelief. Jet-lagged (back when I still got jet lag) and deranged by antimalarial meds, I staggered happily through the heat to the places I'd read about in the great nonfiction accounts of the French and American wartime years: the Majestic, the rooftop at the Rex, and of course, the very hotel where I was staying. I ate steaming, spicy bowls of pho on the street, and crispy fried quails, and was delightfully overwhelmed by the smells and flavors of Ben Thanh market. I ventured out into the Mekong Delta, where I got savagely drunk with an extended family of former Vietcong. I explored the islands and floating markets off Nha Trang, had many adventures, and made lasting friends.

And I changed.

My attitude changed, of course. Your eyes can't help but open when you travel and just to see the places I'd read so much about was surely life-changing. But something else changed on an almost cellular level, as if my very tissues had been penetrated by the smells and atmosphere of Vietnam, that heavy air, thick with odors of jack-fruit, durian, fresh flowers, raw chicken, diesel fuel, incense. Vietnam is a country of proud cooks and passionate eaters. And, after experiencing the spicy morning soups of Saigon, the notion of ever settling for a bland Western-style breakfast again was unthinkable.

I was hooked. I wanted more. I needed more. I left Vietnam that first time determined to do whatever was necessary to keep coming back—even if that involved something as undistinguished as making television.

Highway of Death

An excerpt from *A Cook's Tour: In Search of the Perfect Meal*, originally published by Bloomsbury in 2001.

I just had the closest near-death experience I've ever had.

And I'm about to have another one. Then another.

I'm hurtling full speed down Highway 1 on my way to Can Tho, sitting with Philippe in the back of a hired minivan, horn honking constantly, heading right up the center line into oncoming traffic. There's a water truck about a hundred yards ahead, coming fast in the opposite direction, showing no sign that he intends to pull back into traffic, also honking wildly. Linh and a driver are in the front seat, with two shooters behind us—and I'm convinced that any second we're all going to die.

During the war, Highway 1 was said to be dangerous: snipers, sappers, ambushes, command-detonated mines, the usual perils of guerilla insurgencies. I can't imagine it's any less dangerous now. Understand this about driving in the Mekong Delta: The thing to do is keep up a constant attack with the horn. A beep means "Keep doing what you're doing, change nothing, make no sudden moves, and everything will probably be fine." It does not mean "Slow down" or "Stop" or "Move to the right" or "Get out of the way." If you try to do any of those things on Highway 1 after hearing a car horn behind you—if you hesitate, look back over your shoulder, slow down, or even falter for a second—you will immediately find yourself in a burning heap of crumpled metal somewhere in a rice paddy. The horn means simply "I'm here!"

And there are a lot of people here today, just like us, tearing down the two-lane road at full speed and hammering their horns like crazy.

The water truck ahead is getting closer. And closer. I can make out the grille, the Russian manufacturer's logo on the hood. Our driver still has his foot on the gas, not slowing down in the slightest. We're right in the middle of the road, what would be a passing lane, if they had such a thing here. There's an uninterrupted line of fast-moving cars to our right, with no room at all between them in which to pull back in, a steady torrent of oncoming cars to our left, and the shoulders of both sides of the road are choked three- and four-deep with cyclists, motorbikes, water buffalo, and scooters—all of them loaded with crates of food, washing-machine motors, sacks of fertilizer, flapping roosters, firewood, and family members. So there is no room, none at all, should our driver suddenly decide at the very last minute to abort mission and pull out of the center. If he decides suddenly that the oncoming driver is definitely not going to yield in this maniacal high-speed game of chicken, that he's going to have to veer off the road to avoid collision, there is nowhere, nowhere, to go!

We're close enough now that I can make out the features of the truck's driver, the color of his shirt, the pack of 555 cigarettes on his dashboard. Just when our bumpers are about to meet, vaporizing all of us in an explosion of brake fluid, safety glass, blood, and bone, two cars to our right suddenly open up a space for us—and as if part of some hellish high-speed chorus line, we slip back into traffic. The water truck whips by with a terrific blast of wind, avoiding contact by less than a centimeter, and there's that peculiar vacuum pressure-drop effect you feel when on a train that is suddenly passed by another hurtling in the opposite direction. Philippe just looks at me, shaking his head, says, "Are we still alive? . . . I . . . I was sure that truck went right through us." He's not joking.

Every few moments, we do the same thing again, pulling out to pass—often pulling out to pass a vehicle that is already passing—taking up the whole highway, three-deep, screaming straight into cars and trucks doing the exact same thing in the other direction, horns blaring and honking, a sea of farmers and grandmas and children on rickety bicycles on both sides, the occasional added hazard of oxcart or water buffalo protruding dangerously into the road.

Again.

And again. This time, it looks like an army truck, olive drab, the back loaded with standing soldiers in fatigues. They're coming right at us, not slowing down at all. Our driver doesn't seem concerned. He's having a nice conversation with an equally oblivious Linh, hardly, it seems, paying attention to what must certainly this time be our imminent doom. He honks the horn. He keeps honking. He leans right on that thing like it's a magic wand that will somehow alter the laws of physics. His foot is still on the gas, the motor racing. I see Philippe's knuckles getting white, then whiter on the armrest of his seat, see Chris the shooter's eyes grow huge in the rearview mirror. There's a collective holding of breath among the Western contingent as we all brace for impact, think fleetingly of loved ones, prepare ourselves to be thrown through the windshield . . . Again, somehow, we're back in traffic, a momentary blast of air as the two vehicles nearly kiss paint. Then we're right back straddling that center line again, honking wildly at a slow-moving car in front of us, tailgating at 120 kliks per hour.

Whatever magic safety zone our driver thinks envelops our car, protecting us from harm, we're beginning to think he must be right. There's no other explanation for our continued survival. Again and again and again, we just miss colliding, so frequently and regularly that, after an hour on the road, we actually begin to believe it, even count on the idea that we are invincible—that some Vietnamese juju does indeed prevent us from slamming head-on into another vehicle. We run straight at the most unroadworthy twenty-year-old Soviet-made contraptions on four wheels, gas pedal flat on the floor each time, enduring that queer Doppler effect as they whip by, the horns going *WHOOoooANNnngggg* as the shock wave blows us sideways toward a family of four on a wobbly bicycle. On more than one occasion, we come so close to rolling right over a pedestrian or an overloaded bicycle that I'm sure we touched them. I think all of us, long ago, would have screamed at our driver to slow down, maybe even attempted to wrestle the wheel away from him (he's clearly a madman intent on destroying us all), but there isn't a single second when we're not paralyzed with fear, bracing for impact, or at least certain that if we were to speak, or distract him for even a split second, it would surely cause our instantaneous deaths.

Eventually, nerves shattered, blind faith takes over and we either try our best to ignore what's going on outside the thin layer of metal and glass around us or we simply pray, nearly hysterical with fear and nervous exhaustion.

The city of Can Tho is a low-rise river town with the colonial architecture of its French planners. We check into the Hotel Victoria Can Tho, one of the many luxurious foreign-run hotels one sees more and more of in Vietnam. It's stately, beautiful, with an airy whitewashed lobby, black-and-white marble floors, a pool and boathouse on the shores of the Mekong River, hardwood teak and mahogany rooms with comfortable beds, and satellite TV. There's a business center, a health and massage studio, a very decent restaurant and bar—and an antiaircraft battery down the street. As we drive by the gun emplacement, Linh reminds the shooters, "Not to photograph, please."

I order a mango daiquiri as soon as we check in. God, there's nothing like a fine hotel when you've survived multiple brushes with death. I splurge and send out my moldering clothes to be laundered, schedule an hour-and-a-half massage, and treat myself to a traditional Vietnamese lunch of chicken BLT club sandwich. Philippe, in a monogrammed hotel bathrobe, is already at the pool. Soon, I'm oiled up on a table, half-asleep, a tiny Vietnamese girl walking on my back, by now only vaguely aware how lucky I am to be alive.

I'm also beginning to think that there must be a lot of penile dysfunction in Asia. There's no other explanation for it. Just about every damn thing you can think of seems to have been thoroughly investigated for its potential wood-raising properties. If your waiter or a friend urges you to put something in your mouth that a few weeks ago you never would have thought of eating, chances are it is believed to "make you strong." Only desperation can account for what the Chinese, for instance, do in the name of "medicine." That's something you might remind your New Age friends who've gone gaga over "holistic medicine" and "alternative Chinese cures." They say there are sun bears in

China, hooked up to kidney drips like catsup dispensers, leaching bear bile into tiny bottles. Rhino horn. Bear claw. Bird's nest. Duck embryo. You've got to be pretty anxious about your penis to contemplate hurting a cute little sun bear.

And you've got to be really concerned about your penis to eat at the My Khanh Restaurant in Can Tho. Our waiter greets us and proudly takes us on the obligatory premeal tour of the grounds. It's a large, wooded park with a narrow cement pathway that winds and twists around zoolike cages of menu selections. Everything here is available for dinner. I lose my appetite as soon as I see the sun bear. There are snakes, bats, lizards, crocodiles, cranes, an eighty-kilo python, monkeys, and dogs. The dogs, our waiter assures us—not too convincingly—are not for sale. We pass ponds where one can catch one's own elephant fish or catfish. And in the middle of this torture garden, where the cages seem to radiate fear, are cute little bungalows where Chinese and Taiwanese businessmen come for dirty weekends, their mistresses in tow. They come to eat animals that most Americans have seen only on the Discovery Channel, to absorb, I'm guessing, the animal auras at close hand—before killing and eating them. The plan, then, I can only assume, is to settle the check quickly, rush back to the bungalow, and endeavor mightily to produce a hard-on. The management of My Khanh, our waiter proudly shows us, is putting in a swimming pool. It's a horrifying theme park of cruelty. And I'm sickened by it all. Bad enough to want to eat some of these creatures. But to want to stay here, close to your victims, to lie in bed with your mistress, listening to animals die—what kind of romantic weekend getaway is that?

Philippe and I settle for catching our own elephant fish in a murky, stagnant pond covered with green film, a small boy helpfully pointing out exactly where to drop our hooks. It takes about thirty seconds to catch our entrées.

For appetizers, we go for the relatively benign curried frog legs; a little ground snake with shrimp cracker, peanuts, garlic, and mint; and some braised bat (imagine braised inner tube, sauced with engine coolant). We eat no animals with cute bunny eyes. I just can't take that today. Philippe and I pick at our food unenthusiastically, a strong cloud of fermenting fish from the nearby *nuoc mam* factory doing nothing to improve our appetites.

No one should come here.

Our waiter is a friendly-enough young fellow, soft-spoken and attentive, but I can't get it out of my head that if I should suddenly decide to order some monkey, he'll happily slit the little fella's throat with the same friendly expression on his face.

I'm in much better spirits the next morning when we board a riverboat to go to the nearby floating market at Cai Rang. It's beautiful out, the sun creating pink-and-orange coronas around the edges of the clouds, the light on the water hypnotic. Bamboo frame houses with thatched roofs, tall palms, the crowded waterfront of Can Tho pass by. The river itself teems with activity. Net fishermen, their handwoven nets extended like the wings of giant moths over the water, dip and pull with ingeniously crafted levers of bamboo poles. Families in sampans pass by, sampans with lone women paddling from the stern and a baby sitting aft, boats overloaded with cinder blocks and building materials. There are floating gas stations: a thousand-gallon floating gas tank piloted by a chain-smoking old man sitting on top. The river traffic gets more intense as we near Cai Rang. Sampans are so overloaded here, so low in the water, I can't imagine how they stay afloat. Boats are piled high with sacks of rice, fertilizer, produce, potted palms, cages of live poultry.

And there are floating food vendors.

A chugging sampan pulls alongside our craft and inquires if we'd care for coffee. He's got a whole Starbucks rig set up at the helm. Attaching his boat to ours with a frayed rope, he sets immediately to work filling our order, one hand keeping his boat aligned as we speed along the river, the other steaming, filtering, and pouring some of that fabulous Vietnamese coffee into tall glasses. Another boat, this one selling baguettes, comes along the other side, and we buy a few of those, too. They're still warm, crunchy, and delicious, as good as any you'd find in Paris. A boat selling *pho* joins us and soon Philippe and I are digging greedily into bowls of outstandingly fresh spicy beef and noodles, a slice of liver, those brightly colored and crunchy garnishes making the flavors pop. I could eat here all day. Just float along and everybody comes to you. Pâté sandwiches, roll-your-own beef, spring rolls, sweets—all this in the middle of busy river traffic. At the market, there are floating fishmongers, livestock pens, fruit and vegetable wholesalers, bakers, plant sellers, all of them in waterlogged, porous-looking, questionably seaworthy vessels of indeterminate age. Slurping down the last of my morning *pho*, I'm thinking that this is living. Everyone smiles. Children shout "Hello!" and "Bye-bye!" and "Happy New Year!"—all wanting nothing more than to practice the few words of English they know. A dessert boat sells candied mango and banana, skewered melon, chunks of pineapple, whole jackfruit, durian, mangosteen, dragon fruit, and custard apple. Boats chug by with bundles of beautifully wrapped square and triangular *banh* dangling from the wheelhouse, an entire convenience store aboard, selling cigarettes, sodas, beer, and fruit juices in plastic bags. Women cook in woks of boiling oil on fast-moving boats, grill little packets of ground meat wrapped in mint leaves, fry little birds, boil noodles. Everything smells good. Everything looks good to eat.

Looking at the far shore, I can see doorless shacks built out over the water, nearly without furniture, except for an occasional hammock, the glow from a much-repaired television set. There are television aerials over medieval-style privies built out over the water. Watch the shore and you see every stage of domestic river life: mothers bathing their children, pounding laundry, scrubbing their woks in the brown water, laying out circles of rice paper to dry on rooftops, fastidiously sweeping their tiny primitive abodes, every inch clean and squared away.

It's something I'm seeing everywhere in Vietnam; what makes its food so good, its people so endearing and impressive: pride. It's everywhere. From top to bottom, everyone seems to be doing the absolute best they can with what they have, improvising, repairing, innovating. It's a spirit revealed in every noodle stall, every leaky sampan, every swept and combed dirt porch and green rice paddy. You see it in the mud-packed dikes and levees of their centuries-old irrigation system, every monkey bridge, restored shoe, tire turned sandal, litterless urban street, patched roof, and swaddled baby in brightly colored hand-knit cap. Think what you want about Vietnam and about communism and about whatever it was that really happened there all those years ago. Ignore, if you care to, the obvious—that the country is, and was always, primarily about family, village, province, and then country—that ideology is a luxury few can afford. You cannot help but be impressed and blown away by the hard work, the attention to detail, the care taken in every facet of daily life, no matter how mundane, no matter how difficult the circumstances. Spend some time in the Mekong Delta and you'll understand how a nation of farmers could beat the largest and most powerful military presence on the planet. Just watch the women in the rice paddies, bent at the waist for eight, ten hours a day, yanking bundles of rice from knee-deep water, then moving them, replanting them. Take a while to examine the intricate interlocked system of Stone Age irrigation, unchanged for hundreds and hundreds of years, the level of cooperation necessary among neighbors simply to scratch out a living, and you'll get the idea.

These people survived bombing, strafing, patrols. They outwitted the CIA, the NSA, satellites, AWACS, blacked-out C-130 cargo planes that had been tricked out with sensors and Gatling guns, staffed by whole teams of airborne intelligence analysts searching the ground below on winking monitors, B-52 strikes, hired killers, special units of "counterterror" teams, regime after regime of clannish leaders who cared nothing for them. They survived *The Beverly Hillbillies* and Bob Hope and the worst that America's lusts and America's culture had to offer. They beat the French. They beat the Chinese. They beat the Khmer Rouge. And they'll survive communism, too. A hundred years from now, the Commies will be gone—like us, another footnote in Vietnam's long and tragic history of struggle—and the rice paddies of the Mekong Delta, this market, and this river will look much as they look now, as they looked a hundred years ago.

I like it here. I like it a lot.

I'm Still Here

An excerpt from *A Cook's Tour: In Search of the Perfect Meal*, originally published by Bloomsbury in 2001.

It's *tim ran* time. This time, I'm going to eat something that will, I am assured, make me very, very strong. The strongest. Huong Rung (Flavors of the Forest) Restaurant is a bright beer-garden-like space, enclosed by trellis, its foyer crowded with fish tanks. I enter, sit down, and order a beer right away, steadying myself for what will probably be the most . . . unusual meal of my life so far.

A grinning waiter approaches, holding a wriggling burlap sack. He opens it, gingerly reaches inside, and extracts a vicious, hissing, furious-looking four-foot-long cobra. As I've ordered the specialty of the house, I assume the staff is inured to the sight, but when the cobra, laid on the floor and prodded with a hooked stick, raises its head and spreads its hood, the whole staff of waiters, busboys, and managers— everyone but my cobra handler—steps back a few feet, giggling nervously. My cobra handler, a nice young man in waiter's black slacks and a white button-down shirt, has a sizable bandage on the back of his right hand, a feature that does not fill me with confidence as he lifts the snake with the stick and holds him over the table, the snake training its beady little eyes on me and trying to strike. I knock back the rest of my beer and try to stay cool while the cobra is allowed to slide around the floor for a while, lunging every few moments at the stick. The cobra handler is joined by an assistant with a metal dish, a small white cup, a pitcher of rice wine, and a pair of gardening shears. The two men pick up the cobra, fully extending him; the cobra handler holds him behind the jaws, while the assistant keeps him stretched just ahead of the tail.

With his free hand, the handler takes the scissors, inserts a blade into the cobra's chest, and snips out the heart, a rush of dark red blood spilling into the metal dish as he does so. Everyone is pleased. The waiters and busboys relax. The blood is poured into a glass and mixed with a little rice wine. And the heart, a Chiclet-sized oyster-like organ, still beating, is placed gently into the small white cup and offered to me.

It's still pumping, a tiny pink-and-white object, moving up and down up and down at a regular pace in a small pool of blood at the bottom of the cup. I bring it to my lips, tilt my head back, and swallow. It's like a little Olympia oyster—a hyperactive one. I give it one light chew, but the heart still beats . . . and beats . . . and beats. All the way down. The taste? Not much of one. My pulse is racing too much to notice. I take a long swig of *ruou tiet ran*, the blood and wine mixture, enjoying it, not bad at all—like the juice from a rare roast beef—robust, but with just a slight hint of reptile. So far so good. I have eaten the live heart of a cobra. Linh is proud of me. Many, many sons. The floor staff grin, the girls giggle shyly. The handler and assistant are busily carving up the cobra. An enormous mass of snowy white snake tripes tumbles out of the cobra's body cavity onto a plate, followed by a dribble of dark green bile.

"This very good for you," says Linh as a waiter mixes the bile with some wine and presents me with a glass of *ruou mat ran*. It's a violent green color now, looking about as appetizing as the contents of a bedpan. "This will make you the strongest. Very special, very special."

I long ago came to dread those words. I take a long swig of the green liquid and swallow. It tastes bitter, sour, evil . . . just like you'd expect bile to taste.

Over the next hour or so, I eat every single part of the cobra. First, *ran bop goi*, a delicious shredded snake salad, heavily dressed with citrus and lemongrass and served in a hot pot. *Ham xa*, braised cobra with citronella, is also quite good, though slightly chewy. *Long ran xao*, however, the snake's tripe sautéed with onion, is absolutely inedible. I chew and chew and chew, grinding helplessly away with every molar. My chewing has not the slightest effect. It's like chewing on a rubber dog toy—only less tender. The tripe, while innocuous tasting, is impossible to break down. I finally give up, hold my breath, and swallow a mouthful whole and intact. *Xuong (ran) chien gion*, the deep-fried bones of the snake, is delightful—like spicy potato chips, only a lot sharper. You might enjoy these at a Yankees game, though very carefully. If one bone goes in at the wrong angle, it could easily pierce your esophagus, making the prospects of lasting through the ninth inning doubtful. *Ran cuon ca lop*, the cobra's meat, minced and rolled in mint leaves, is also delightful—a festive party snack for any occasion.

The manager comes over to present me with a plate containing a large tree grub, white with a black freckle-like mark on one end. It's alive, undulating, bigger than a thumb. Oh, Jesus, no . . . It squirms around, thrashing on the plate. *No*, I'm thinking. *No. Not that* . . . Fortunately, the tree grub is cooked before serving, sautéed in butter until crispy. When it arrives back at my table, perched on a little bed of greens, I warily take a nice-sized bite. It has the consistency of a deep-fried Twinkie: crunchy on the outside, creamy and gooey in the middle. It tastes fine. But I would have been much happier not having seen it alive.

Overall, though, not a bad meal. And I've eaten the still beating heart of a fucking cobra! (I'll be dining out on this story for a while.) For the very first time after eating food that will "make me strong," I actually feel something. I don't know if it's just nervous energy and adrenaline, but when I walk out into the street, I feel a buzz, a jangly, happy, vibrating sense of well-being. I think, *Yes, I believe I do feel . . . strong*.

"Monsieur Fowlair. Monsieur Fow-lair . . . ," someone is whispering.

It's the police inspector in Greene's *The Quiet American*, talking in my dreams. I wake up expecting to see Phuong, the heroine of the novel, preparing an opium pipe for me, and Pyle, the youthful CIA agent, petting his dog in a chair. I'm in my room at the Continental, carved fleurs-de-lis in the woodwork, ornate chairs, yards of intricately carved shelving. I can hear the clack-clacking of shoes on the wide marble floor outside the door, the sound echoing through the halls. Saigon. Still only in Saigon. The French doors leading onto the balcony are open and, though early, the streets are already filling up with cyclos, bicycles, motorbikes, and scooters. Women crouch in doorways, eating bowls of *pho*. A man fixes a motorbike on the sidewalk. Buses cough and stall and start again. At Givral's, across the street, they're lining up for coffee and the short, plump, fragrant-smelling baguettes. Soon, the "noodle knockers" will come, rapping their mallets to announce the imminent arrival of another yoke-borne kitchen, bowls and bowls of steaming fresh noodles. Linh has informed me of something called "fox" coffee, *ca-phe-chon*, a brew made from the tenderest beans, fed to a fox (though I have since seen it referred to as a weasel), and the beans later recovered from the animal's stool, washed (presumably), roasted, and ground. Sounds good to me.

I'm leaving Vietnam soon, and yet I'm yearning for it already. I grab a stack of damp dong off my nightstand, get dressed, and head for the market. There's a lot I haven't tried.

I'm still here, I tell myself.

I'm still here.

Hanoi

An excerpt from *Medium Raw: A Bloody Valentine to the World of Food and the People Who Cook*, published in the UK by Bloomsbury in 2010.

It's Christmastime in Hanoi again and the Metropole Hotel is lit up like an amusement park. In the courtyard, a monstrous white tree with bright red ornamental balls towers over the swimming pool. The decorative palms shine blindingly bright with a million tiny bulbs. I'm on my second gin and tonic and planning on having a third, settled back in a heavy rattan chair and feeling the kind of sorry for myself that most people would be very content with. There's incense in the air, buffeted about by the slowly moving overhead fans: a sickly-sweet odor that mirrors perfectly my mixed feelings of dull heartache and exquisite pleasure.

I often feel this way when alone in Southeast Asian hotel bars—an enhanced sense of bathos, an ironic dry-smile sorrow, a sharpened sense of distance and loss.

Today, this feeling will disappear the second I'm out the door. Once I'm away from the sight of the other lone Western travelers, each, I imagine, with their own weltschmerz-loaded backstory, their own unfulfilled longings, sitting there with their Gerald Seymours and their Ken Folletts next to unringing cell phones. After strolling ever so slightly tipsy yet confident through the lobby, the service staff in *ao dai*s and traditional Annamite headgear address me (as they do all the guests) in French: "*Bonsoir, monsieur . . . Ça va?*" I'm through the doors, and suddenly the air fills with the roar of a thousand motorbikes and those feelings are gone, replaced by a giddiness, a familiar rush of overwhelming glee at being back in the country I'm crazy in love with.

The only way to see Hanoi is from the back of a scooter. To ride in a car would be madness—limiting your mobility to a crawl, preventing you from even venturing down half the narrow streets and alleys where the good stuff is to be found. To be separated from what's around you by a pane of glass would be to miss—everything. Here, the joy of riding on the back of a scooter or motorbike is to be part of the throng, just one more tiny element in an organic thing, a constantly moving, ever-changing process rushing, mixing, swirling, and diverting through the city's veins, arteries, and capillaries. Admittedly, it's also slightly dangerous. Traffic lights, one-way signs, intersections, and the like—the rough outlines of organized society—are more suggestions than regulations observed by anyone in actual practice. One has, though, the advantage of the right of way. Here? The scooter and the motorbike are kings. The automobile may rule the thoroughfares of America, but in Hanoi it's cumbersome and unwieldy, the last one to the party, a woolly mammoth of the road—to be waited on, begrudgingly accommodated—even pitied—like the fat man at a sack race.

Linh is driving—and I've finally, after many hours and many times as his passenger, given up on the strictly Western practice of hanging on. Nobody else does. Not the three-year-old child whipping past me, standing in front of his father and mother. Not Grandma, riding side-saddle behind her son-in-law and daughter over there, or the hundreds of thousands of young men and women, chatting on cell phones or exchanging comments from the backs of other bikes. Somehow we all manage to stay aboard without gripping our drivers around the waist or shoulders—or even bracing ourselves from the back. Somehow it all works; we manage to move quickly—sometimes very quickly—through space, together and apart, without flying from our seats or colliding with each other. Thousands, millions of us, a moving conversation of words, glances, gestures, and the shrill honks of our horns with an ever-changing cast of characters snaking through Hanoi's Old Quarter, around its lakes, weaving through crosscurrents, breaking over and around the bigger, sadder four-wheel vehicles like stones in a river, barely noticing the souls trapped glumly and impatiently inside.

Is anyone in this city over thirty?

It seems not. Statistically, it is said that nearly 70 percent of the population are under that age, and, if the streets of Hanoi (or any city in Vietnam, for that matter) are any indicator, that number seems even higher. Nobody among them remembers the war. They weren't even alive for it. Much like our post–World War II baby boom, they must have gone straight home from the battlefield and done an awful lot of fuckin' around here. Everyone—*everyone*, it seems—is young and either on the way to eat, returning from eating, or eating at this very minute, absolutely choking the sidewalks on low plastic stools, filling the open-to-the-street shop houses, slurping noodles or nibbling on delicious-looking bits, drinking *bia hoi*, the fresh beer of Hanoi, with varying degrees of joy and seriousness of intent.

My old favorite, *bun cha*—juicy hunks of pork served in room-temperature, sweet-and-sour green papaya juice—are grilling over charcoal by the curb; bowls of *bun bo*, the bright, reddish, steaming mix of snails, noodles, and crab roe–infused broth are recognizable from the hunks of fresh tomato on top as I sweep by. Sizzling crepes; *banh mi* sandwiches—crunchy baguettes overloaded with headcheese, delightfully mysterious pâté, pickles, and, often, a fried egg; *bun bo Hue*—a sort of heartier, more highly testosteroned version of *pho* (noodles heaped with slices of beef and pork); slabs of blood cake—and nearly every delicious goddamn thing you can think of. Tiny electric-red slices of chili peppers, crunchy sprouts, Thai basil, roughly yanked cilantro, mint, green banana slices, wedges of lime everywhere.

Everywhere.

Parties of ten, twenty Vietnamese cluster around and hover over hot pots of beef parts and whole fish.

Or they just ride. If you're in a car, you're fucked for any of this. Most neighborhoods have no room for your spaceship to touch down. At best, you can glide slowly by, face pressed to the glass, or—if you care to torture yourself—open the window for a moment, let your nostrils fill with the complex admixture of a thousand and one delights, most of them unavailable to you. Sure, you can park a few blocks away, maybe—but then you may as well have walked. For the scooters and motorbikes, however, there's the convenience of *valet parking*. Oh, yes. Since nearly every available square foot of sidewalk is packed with tables, there is precious little space for bikes. But not to worry, because every little *com*, coffee shop, street stall, and eatery has a kid outside who will helpfully take your scooter and helmet, scrawl an identifying mark with chalk on the seat, and find some way to jam it in between the scores of others out front. It's the only way the system works. When you're done? He will helpfully extract it and have it ready for departure.

Some things never get old. Some things are just . . . classic. You never lose appreciation for them. Your enthusiasm may wax and wane ever so slightly, but you always come back. Whether it's the Rolling Stones' "Let It Bleed" or doing it doggie-style, good is simply . . . good. There may be other things in life, but you can pretty much spend eternity considering the matter of the former—or latter—and you'd be hard-pressed to improve on either of them.

I feel exactly like this with Hanoi-style *pho*. I may love the southern versions of this spicy noodle soup fiercely and appreciate—even need—from time to time the difference, the rougher, spicier, less subtle charms of Saigon's often cloudier, more assertive sisters. But I wouldn't marry any of them.

Using sexual metaphors to describe food is a practice blithely, even automatically employed by most food writers—yours truly being a frequent perpetrator. But it seems particularly appropriate when describing *pho* in Hanoi—even though it's usually a morning routine, as opposed to a late-night, post-bar, fall-into-sloppy-embrace kind of a thing. Visiting a popular *pho* shop, particularly later in the morning, after the first waves of hungry people on their way to work have been through, resembles nothing so much as the set of a porn shoot.

Here, as there, the landscape of desire is strewn with crumpled tissues, the spent expressions of human lust. Short pink plastic trash baskets overflow with little white paper balls, wet tumbleweeds are littered everywhere. Walk three feet up to the counter and they will cling embarrassingly to the soles of your feet, trail back to your table as if you are hurriedly exiting a peep-show booth. Unlike with sex, however, this walk of shame comes *before* touchdown. For one's efforts, after a long wait on line, the handover of a few dong (the unfortunate name for

Vietnam's unit of currency), a jostle, and a squeeze in between strangers at a low table on a sidewalk, one is rewarded with perfection.

Broth—usually (but not absolutely always) the savory-sweet extraction of many beef bones, heavy on the marrow. Not too dark—definitely not too light. Chances are, there are three or four enormous pots of the stuff going now behind the counter, steam rising to the ceiling, the proprietor ladling the stuff straight off the top. Locals will tell you it's all about the broth. If the broth isn't right, the best ingredients in the world aren't going to save it. Rice noodles. And they'd better be right, too. Too soft, too old, or too cooked? It's shit. Too chewy? Same. Handmade and cooked to order—or at least in constantly ongoing batches, please. Classically, in Hanoi, the meat component is beef—and beef tendon, but preferences vary as to the exact mix. The counter behind the glass of my favorite place in the Old Quarter is stacked with preboiled beef shoulders: the perfect balance of lean and fat; and many prefer this—and only this: sliced ever so thinly onto the surface of their broth, where it wilts and relaxes and nearly dissolves into sublime tenderness. Some purists, however, insist entirely on raw beef, sliced at exactly the right degree of thinness and at the very last minute, added to the broth on the way out, so that the customers can "cook" it lightly themselves in the hot broth of their bowl by simply tossing it gently with their noodles. I, like many locals, prefer a mix of raw and cooked. The unattractive-sounding tendon, cooked properly by a master *pho*-maker, should be the best thing in the world—even for the uninitiated. Rather than being rubbery or tough, as one would expect of tendon, it should have just enough bite, just enough resistance, dissolving into fatty, marrow-like substance after just a few chews—a counterpoint to the wispy, all-too-brief pleasures of the beef. There're usually very few of the slender, translucent little tubes in one's bowl, and if you're unhappy to discover one on your spoon, then they're doing it wrong.

You complete *pho* at the table—and unlike with many similar dishes, where everybody's got their own way of doing things, in Hanoi there seems to be an accepted orthodoxy. A dot or two of chili paste, a tiny drizzle of chili sauce, a generous squeeze of lime, toss lightly with chopsticks in the right hand—and spoon with the left. Ideally, one wants a perfect marriage of beef, broth, and noodle in each mouthful. Slurping is encouraged. As is leaning down into your bowl. As is lifting the bowl to near your mouth.

There will be a generous plate or basket of greens, herbs, and sprouts next to a bowl of *pho*—usually Thai basil, mint, and cilantro— and one adds as needed, periodically incorporating elements of freshness and crunch and a welcome bitterness to one's mix, and one can pick idly at the occasional leaf as well, as kind of a palate cleanser.

I am hardly an expert on this subject, by the way—merely an enthusiast. But this is what I have observed and been told, over time. What is not debatable is that a perfect bowl of Hanoi *pho* is a balanced meeting of savory, sweet, sour, spicy, salty, and even umami—a gentle commingling of textures as well: soft and giving, wet and slippery, slightly chewy, momentarily resistant but ultimately near-diaphanous, light and heavy, leafy and limp, crunchy and tender. There—and nearly not there at all. Were this already not enough to jerk a rusty steak knife across your grandma's throat, empty her bank account, and head off to Hanoi, consider the colors: Bright red chilies; the more subdued, richer-red toasted-chili paste; bright green vegetables; white sprouts. Pinkish-red raw meat, turning slowly gray as it cooks in your bowl, the deep brown colors of the cooked meat, white noodles, light amber broth. Nearly all God's colors in one bowl.

This is a sophisticated and deceptively subtle thing, Hanoi *pho*. I do not pretend to fully understand and appreciate its timeless beauty. Here, describing *pho* as more like love than sex would be more accurate—as there is simply not enough time on this planet, I think, to ever truly *know* it. It is an unconditional kind of love, in that it doesn't matter where you enjoy it—elevated only a few feet off a dirty street corner or at the sleekly designed counter of an overdecorated lounge. It contains, like the man said, "multitudes."

Sometimes I think I should feel a little guilty about writing stuff like the above.

It's porn. Albeit food and travel porn.

I had it, I lived it—and, chances are, most of the people reading this have not.

It seems ungracious to share some experiences. Though I'm sure it's difficult to accept, my parents brought me up to believe that showing off was a bad thing, a sign of generally bad manners. (I'm not saying those values took hold, just that I might have heard them mentioned.)

Some things I've seen, some experiences at tables and counters around the world, I feel a little bad telling people about. I may not hesitate to put them on TV at every opportunity—but that's . . . *different* somehow, in that it's somebody else, the evil camera people, the editors, doing the telling. This conveniently lets me off the hook.

But writing about sights and sounds and flavors that might otherwise be described as orgiastic—and doing it in a way that is calculated to inspire prurient interest, lust, and envy in others . . . that raises more questions in my mind as to . . . I don't know . . . the moral dimension.

Sitting here, choosing words, letter by letter, on the keyboard with the explicit intention of telling you about something I did or something I ate and making you as hungry and miserable as I can—surely that's *wrong.*

But fuck it.

Who doesn't like a good wank now and then?

VII

Restlessness

Many young men are restless. Not many turn restlessness into an art form. I think one of the most precious items in this collection is in this section: a few lined pages on notebook paper headlined "EVENTS AND PLACES VISITED" on which Tony, just barely eighteen years old, is on a trip by himself in Nice. He describes going days without eating and wandering around fantasizing about sleeping on benches. The words seem to depict a grim reality, but it's hard not to read the excitement and verve in the journal entries. Even when he repeatedly expresses a desire to go home, he doesn't end there. He keeps writing, and if anything his restlessness seems to only generate more restlessness. It is a dynamic that would keep him in almost constant motion for the rest of his life.

I'll Give It All Up Someday

An unpublished handwritten note, date unknown.

~~But~~ I'll give it all up some day. It will end, move to France and write my book, make my movies.

But I would ~~never~~ do it again if I could. I have seen moments of greatness in the long dance of craziness. Flashes of brilliance, drama, significance. I have learned, observed, loved, hated, ~~and bear~~ I have seen people in every state of elevation and depression, togertherness and totally off the wall, and always have ~~and always will tried to understand~~ why, I've tried to keep ~~looking~~ watching, try to understand and evaluate what I saw and apply it to what I will see in the future.

Untitled Play (Script?) About Television

Unpublished, date unknown.

A Holiday Inn motel room. Two beds with a night table in between stage center. Large picture window suggested to stage right, overlooking Boston skyline. A round table and two armchairs next to window. Mike and Jeff sit at table with feet up, looking out window.

MIKE: So this is it, Jeff. Has it come to this? A Holiday Inn room . . .

JEFF: —and a small cassette recorder . . .

MIKE: Just you and me, Jeff.

JEFF: Taking down our every thought.

MIKE: As time goes by . . . Gaze out the window; the Boston skyline. Someday, Jeff, we'll be riding around in a limo out there.

JEFF: Sometimes I think I'm just a soggy pair of bathing trunks. (*picks up trunks from table*)

MIKE: Life . . . is a cold meatball hero, Jeff . . . it starts out wet and warm and ends up cold and soggy. But someday we'll be famous, Jeff. Someday people will look at us as the Jack Kerouac, Allen Ginsberg, William Burroughs of our day. And they'll say, "I wish I was back there in 1969 in New Jersey." That's what they'll say. And they'll read my books and hear your records and see Sam's picture on the First National Bank. And they'll say, "Times must have been good." And times were good in those days, Jeff . . . But sometimes I think this is the end.

JEFF: I won't have Fulfillment until that little green message light goes on.

MIKE: The little green message light that spells "Mama."

JEFF: Beneath it it says RCA.

MIKE: Does it? RCA, THE VOICE OF CONFIDENCE. The voice of your asshole. Sometimes I think it's all over.

JEFF: It's all over for you, Mike, old boy.

MIKE: No! It's never going to be over for me! I'm no patsy! Don't count me out! . . . We're all good for another round.

JEFF: Just another Holiday Inn . . . It's all too real . . .

MIKE: It's all too real. . . . What does the future have in store for us? Will Destiny knock on that door, holding fresh towels and a new Kick?

JEFF: Just a soggy pair of bathing trunks.

MIKE: No, Jeff. It's going to be Big Cars and Fast Women. Kicks, Thrills, and new heights in Teenage Excitement! And Fulfillment . . . The Big "F" . . . along with fornication of course . . . memories, Jeff . . .

JEFF: Changing winds . . .

MIKE: Breaking wind . . .

JEFF: Crossing the tundras . . .

MIKE: Cruising the permafrost . . . ahhhhhhh . . . memories and mammaries . . .

JEFF: The long road to . . .

MIKE: What does the future have in store for us, Jeff?

JEFF: (*picking up Bible*) Maybe we can find the answer in Jesus.

MIKE: Let's rip this place up. Unconventional use of a conventional space. Very artistic. (*hurls oriental ninja star at wall*)

MIKE: O . . . O . . . O . . . she kissed me. The cocaine was some incentive I'm sure. I mean her lips were closed. But she did kiss me and hold on to me for a while. I'm in love. I'm in lust. Disgusting. I shouldn't allow myself to . . . But I want her. I want her real bad. For sure. I don't want to be in love with her. Love . . . Love and retardation go hand in hand. I want her to be in love with me. But I suppose that's always the case.

O, what a patsy. I'm walking into a setup. But I mean, should I accept that? That I'll never get what I really want and walk into it anyway? Shit. I always got what I wanted if I wanted it bad enough. I always got it. Not always in the way I wanted it . . . But I did get it. I got it, I got it . . .

I mean should I accept my physical, psychological . . . mental deficiencies or should I charge on. Crank it up all the way past redline . . . 100 milligrams of Ego. If I believe I'm NUMBER ONE maybe she'll believe it. SHIT . . .

What have I got? Lust? Need? At least I want something. I need something . . . I mean, is that an attribute or a disease? . . . I don't know. Nobody out there knows. A lot of them pretend . . . but I see you past that waving cigarette. I see what you got inside. You've got the Fear.

But I need something from you stupid wimps. I need something. I need a lot. I'm a junkie really. You all are. I need my music going all the time, entertainment. Action, cigarettes, reefer, sex, gratification, and only you can give it to me. More and more and more. I'm a television baby and nothing is enough. I need the music, the movies. You did this to me!! I guess that's our problem. Me and Jeff and Sam and Jean. Nothing is enough. We're all running on need. I look in the mirror sometimes tripping and I see a corpse trying to dress himself, belching smoke and guzzling drinks. We can't really be turning into our parents, I mean it would be too grotesque. (*laughs until laugh turns to cough*) I can't stop my ears my eyes my hands my eyes . . . something's got to come of it . . . I don't know. Maybe my mother was right.

Mother appears from nowhere in strange blue light.

MOTHER: It's always "I want, I want, I want." You never give. It's always "take, take, take." I just don't understand you.
MIKE: That's not true . . . I mean maybe it's true in some ways, all right . . . all right . . . but . . . but I'm doing something. It's all leading somewhere. It's not all inside me. There's something that somebody out there can relate to, learn from, laugh at or something. I mean . . . MY LIFE IS A WORK OF ART, GODDAMN IT!!

MOTHER: Bullshit.

MIKE: All right, all right. I don't know, maybe that was a bit cheeky . . .
I'm movin', Ma . . . This is your mess, you and that stupid tube over
there. I guess life isn't like the movies. You should have protected me
from that thing. It's dangerous. I think it did something to me. I don't
think I was given all my equipment when I signed up. Maybe I'm
missing a gland or something . . .

But at least I want. I want to do something. That's enough, isn't
it? It's better than being content. It's better than not wanting anything.
I mean my various neuroses and dependencies are just the price I
have to pay for wanting so much. I want to do, to go, to give. Really!
Really! Regardless of any reasons, superficial or otherwise . . . Ego
Fulfillment, whatever, I still want to create. To make something that
does something.

All right . . . maybe I've been too busy feeling to do anything.
Maybe I place too much significance in what I feel. Kerouac had the
same problem . . . I mean I'm sure, for Christ's sake, that I'd be a
lot happier of I didn't feel anything. It would be less messy for sure.
But the intensity of what I've seen and done and experienced. It's
important. Ignorance is bliss I'm sure, but if I had to do it all over
again, I wouldn't change a thing.

Cause and effect, Mom, I want to see what I can do to all those
people out there. Charles Whitman did it with a gun; I don't know
what I'm going to do it with yet, but I'm going to do it. It's going to be
BIG BIG BIG. I only feel good when I'm moving. And I'm moving.
Play it cool, Ma. I'm going to make it . . . I'll buy you a Mercedes.
Really.

MOTHER: Mike?

MIKE: Don't interrupt me, Mom. I'm going to do it! I'm going to blow
this country and live in Paris and drink wine and eat oysters! I'll write
great books. Hemingway on the Left Bank!

MOTHER: How are you going to . . . What a load of crap! With what
money??! Where are you going to live, how are you going to support
yourself??? Think!!

MIKE: Don't ask stupid questions, Mom. Goodbye, I thank you for everything . . . I can't stay here anymore. It's going rotten . . . everything is getting so confused and deformed. I'll write you from Paris, Ma . . .

Paris. A café table.

MIKE: Well, I made it . . . (*to waiter*) . . . *encore du Pernod, garçon.* The grass really is greener on the other side.
WAITER: *Il y a une femme qui voudrait vous voir, monsieur.*
MIKE: *Très bien*, Phillipe . . .
GIRL: Where were you last night, I waited . . .
MIKE: Sorry, sweetheart. Assignment on Venus came up and I had to split.
GIRL: Maybe we can make it tonight . . .
MIKE: That sounds—hold it a second. If you'll pardon me.

Bank robbers run from door holding money and guns. Mike stands and takes off jacket and nonchalantly shoots them all with large gun from his shoulder holster.

MIKE: I hope you'll excuse me for the interruption.
GIRL: Oh, that was all right. I rather enjoyed it, actually.
MIKE: Another glass of wine, maybe, and we'll go back to my hotel.
GIRL: Gee, what a guy!

It Tastes Like Victory

An excerpt from *Medium Raw: A Bloody Valentine to the World of Food and the People Who Cook*, published in the UK by Bloomsbury in 2010.

The kitchens of Les Halles, finally, and deservedly, are now being run by Carlos Llaguno Morales, who started cooking on the fry station many years ago. He is a fantastic cook—far better than I ever was—and, to my surprise, a much better organizer. The dark recesses of Les Halles' old cellars are now sparklingly clean and bright, compared to my time. The food-handling and control systems, a whole different story. And though the kitchen is the same size, with the same number of cooks, the dining room has expanded into the space that used to house the deli next door, nearly doubling the number of seats. Where, in the old days, we considered a night of three hundred and fifty dinners to be a Monster, they now do as many as six to seven hundred.

In 2007, I got the bright idea that I'd go *back* to Les Halles and work my old station. The Tuesday double shift, no less—where I used to come in at eight A.M., set up, cook the line for lunch, then slam straight into dinner, behind the stove the whole time. That the dining room had gotten so much bigger and busier, and that I'd gotten so much older, didn't really occur to me until the date was nearly upon me. I'd figured that it would make good television.

As the implications and likely outcome began to dawn on me, I struggled to find a solution, a distraction, some way to mitigate what could very well be a public butt-fucking of historic proportions.

So I invited Eric Ripert out for dinner and plied him with high-end tequila (which is something of a weakness of his), and when he was in suitably good spirits and nicely relaxed, the time was ripe. I suggested he join me for a rollicking good time cooking together at Les Halles. It'll be fun, you know . . .

The result is something I'm very proud of. I managed (just) to bully my way through the night (a not very busy one, by current Les Halles standards). It was hard. Very hard. Made harder by the fact that I could no longer read the dupes. When I'd try and slip on my reading glasses, by the time they reached my nose, they were invariably smeared with grease. My knees were creaky, to say the least. But my moves were still there. I could still—if just barely—do it. But at the end of the night, I knew that to do it again tomorrow—as any real cook would have had to do—was out of the question.

Eric, to my surprise, was smooth. I'd hoped that he, who'd never in his life worked in a turn-and-burn joint like mine, who'd never had to hustle out hundreds of plates—much less grill steaks in such quantities and at such speeds—I figured he'd be thrown for a loop. But no. He made it through elegantly, his uniform as snow-white at the end of the shift as when he'd begun. It was enraging. He does, to this day, however, complain bitterly about how "understaffed" the kitchen is at Les Halles. That it's "inhuman" to pump out so many meals with so few cooks. And "impossible." He won't let go of the subject, either.

I'm proud of the television show that came out of it—because it demonstrated in specific, realistic, and very visual terms not just how a busy kitchen works, but how fucking *hard* it is; how much it requires of a person, the kind of teamwork, the kind of endurance, the mindset, choreography, and organization—and what it takes away.

When people ask me if I ever miss it, my answer is always the same. No. I don't.

I know people want me to say yes. Yes, of course I miss it. But I had enough. I had twenty-eight years of it, I tell them, twenty-eight years. I was forty-four years old when *Kitchen Confidential* hit—and if there was ever a lucky break or better timing, I don't know about it. At forty-four, I was, as all cooks too long on the line must be, already in decline. You're not getting any faster—or smarter—as a cook after age thirty-seven. The knees and back go first, of course. That you'd expect. But the hand-eye coordination starts to break up a little as well. And the vision thing. But it's the brain that sends you the most worrying indications of decay. After all those years of intense focus, multitasking, high stress, late nights, and alcohol, the brain stops responding the way you like. You miss things. You aren't as quick reading the board, prioritizing the dupes, grasping at a glance what food goes where, adding up totals of steaks on hold and steaks on the fire—and cumulative donenesses. Your hangovers are more crippling and last longer. Your temper becomes shorter—and you become more easily frustrated with yourself for fucking up little things (though less so with others). Despair—always a sometime thing in the bipolar world of the kitchen—becomes more frequent and longer-lasting as one grows more philosophical with age and has more to despair about.

You're basically done—or on your way to being done. Your brain knows it. Your body knows it—and tells you every day. But pride persists.

What I do miss, I tell them, and will *always* miss, is that first pull on a cold beer after work. *That* is irreplaceable. Nothing approaches that. That's the kind of satisfaction no bestseller can ever beat—no television show, no crowd, no nothing. That single moment after a long and very busy night, sitting down at the bar with your colleagues, wiping the sweat off your neck, taking a deep breath, with unspoken congratulations all around—and then that first sip of cold, cold beer. It tastes like victory. Happy waiters, flush with tips, are ringing out, the cooks look pleased with you and with each other, and you remind yourself that nothing came back the whole night.

Maybe it's Curtis Mayfield, "Superfly," that comes on the sound system then—put on by a sympathetic bartender—or "Gin and Juice" (also for the old folks), or something the moment somehow, by collective will, requires: "Gimme Shelter" or the Stooges' "Dirt." Songs from some other time—not this one—songs that will always mean something to somebody present, but maybe you had to be there.

You look at each other with the intense camaraderie of people who've suffered together and think,

We did well tonight. We will go home proud.

There are nods and half-smiles. A sigh. Maybe even a groan of relief.

Once again. We survived. We did well.

We're still here.

At the Churchyard
Another Pointless Journalistic Play

An unpublished self-proclaimed "pointless journalistic play" about not believing in God, date unknown.

AT THE CHURCHAYARD
another pointless
journalistic play

ACT I
     The scene is a darkened churchyard. Trees out
front with a stone steeple. Small and quiet. It is
late at night. Two boys discuss things from the curb
in front of the church.
     Robert is tall with a pale white complexion, horn
rimmed glasses and long, bushy black hair. He is
nervous, playing with his fingers...
     Tony we are familiar with...

TONY-
     So, what's new, Robert?
ROBERT-
     Nothing much, just that I've found out something
really important.
TONY-
     Really? What's that?
ROBERT-
     That Jesus is the only way.
TONY-
     You're kidding.
ROBERT-
     No. I go and sit in the church now all the time.
TONY-
     C'mon, I know you've always had a good sense of-
ROBERT-
     I'm not kidding.
TONY-
     Promise?
ROBERT-
     I promise. I go there sometimes after I've seen a
all my friends and I don't feel right I go there an d
sit and think about my problems and myself and they
all come to the surface and I can solve them.

TONY-

Do you pray?

ROBERT-

No I can just go in there and I sit and think and I feel better. Like there's a force in there that makes me feel better.

TONY-

Ohh, Jesus, Robert....

ROBERT-

Like have you ever seen a drawing or a poster of a guy pointing and saying "There is only one Way" ?

TONY-

No......and I don't really see the significance.

ROBERT-

Well like, the wrong way is drugs and the right way is God.

TONY-

Until God ##### comes down and lights my cigarette I'm not impressed.

ROBERT-

So you think you don't believe in God?

TONY-

No I don't believe in God.

ROBERT-

There is a God. And you believe in him you just don't know that you believe in him.

TONY-

I believe in the electrical masses of energy theory. Stanley Kubrick discovered it... Like there are these huge masses of floating energy that exists. These masses of energy are what gives life to everything. Some people are aware of these masses and some people aren't. They give different names and meanings to them, but essentially the same. You can call it Fate, Luck, God, Satan or electrical masses... But I don't believe in some guy sitting up there waiting to answer your prayers.

ROBERT-
    He's there, alright. I can feel Him when I go
in the church sometimes late at night.
TONY-
    It's open all night?
ROBERT-
    Yeah.
TONY-
    Woah! 24 hour service..just like a Pathmark!
ROBERT-
    Sometimes it's closed, like there's no lock on
it, it just opens at certain times. Like when I've
done something bad and I come here, it won't open.
TONY-
    You're kidding.
ROBERT-
    No! I'm not kidding.
TONY-
    Sorry, Robert, I do not believe-
ROBERT-
    What do you believe in?
TONY-
    The only thing it is any use believing in is
yourself.
ROBERT-
    Do you believe in yourself?
TONY-
    I don't know why, but I guess I do. Like we
everything has gone wrong for the past month, just
about every aspect of everything... France, everything.
I was looking forward to getting out of here June
24th...dumpnig everything and getting out of here
forever. I was going to scrape off all the bullshit
and kind of start over....Now I find out I can't
go until August and I have to get a job.
ROBERT-
    I was going to commit suicide a few days ago,
but I came to the church and felt better again.
TONY-
    Jesus....

Diary Entries from France, 1973

Tony kept a record of his trip to France when he was eighteen years old. Unpublished.

EVENTS AND PLACES VISITED

Date July 19, 1973 12:51
Place Nice, France
Weather warm, dark

Amazing. The body so lost, so goddamn lost and the brain still functions. After isolation, disease, drink, overtiredness and boredom the old bean still works.

Here I sit, locked out of the train station at One AM, alone. My train missed it's correspondence and I am forced to wait an agonizing six and a half hours for an even more agonizing 13 hours on the train to Bordeaux. I want to go home. I haven't eaten in two days. I'm tired but have no where to sleep.

EVENTS AND PLACES VISITED

Date   I've considered the
Place   old newspapers on the
Weather   park bench idea but I don't want to wake up late or worse get arrested.

"On my Way Home" is what is running through my head, and how true it is. How much I want to be in the warmth and security of my La Teste home.

It's funny that I consider it home. But it's my only conceivable refuge. So. Nothing to do for six hours but write. WRITE all night. Keep that motherfuckin' brain and those shaky hands moving!

Date What I planned as a
Place lovely time in Florence
Weather living the life of
Hemingway has turned out
to be living on a train
living the life and observing
the diet of Ghandi.

An Italian is across the
street lying on a bench.
He takes occasional hits
on a bottle of cough
syrup he's got with him.
SO far from home.

People are getting into
taxis heading off to
expensive hotels with
big beds to fuck and
smoke cigarettes. Play
music and sleep in warmth.

Me, my pack is my pillow
the cement my bed — the

Date sky is my ceiling
Place and my kitchen is
Weather the ice cream machine
inside the station.

I have a cold. My
stomach and intestines
hurt. I have contributed
more shit and more vomit
to the Florence sewer
system than I do at
home in a year.

I played pool on a
broken table at the
café across the street.
I poured some tea into
myself [it being about the
only thing I can keep
down] and it was
in the midst of a doomed
game with myself that

Date The truth came
Place to me. The place
Weather I WANT TO BE.
I WANT TO BE IN
FAMILY BILLIARDS IN
BERGENFIELD NEW JERSEY,
STONED, LISTENING TO THE
QUADRAPHONIC MUZAK
AND GETTING BEATEN
BY "LUCKY" GOULD. A
HALF SMOKED LARK IN
THE ASHTRAY, SOME OF
PETES CARBABA IN HIS
PARKED CAR.
I WANT OUT —
But La Teste will do.

Date June 23, 1973
Place Paris - Hotel Colbert
Weather warm, breezy

Paris, with a cold. Jesus, why
did I have to kiss the little bitch?
My hair is gone. Cut. I feel
as if I'm on a pilgrimage of
sorts. My hair cropped, a new
place, no one to talk to.
But a nice hotel on the
left bank. Near a lot of
cafés, good restaurants and
Shakespeare and Co. bookstore.
I'll have to check it all out.

EVENTS AND PLACES VISITED

Date July 8

Place La Teste

Weather dark

Two weeks in this house. Paint dust and more paint. The mutt. Oh Christ. I've got to get a motorbike and get the fuck out of here. Bad Craziness.

No New Messages

No New Messages is a novel Tony began in 2008 but did not complete. Here are the never-before-seen chapters.

Chapter One

Really, the only question this time of night was Dutch-side shawarma or French-side. Both were served out of trucks. Both stayed open late. Only difference was the Dutch-side shawarma's sauce was a little better. And the Dutch-side joint was closer to the brothels—on the way home, in fact, which made it more convenient as Harry was at the brothels almost every night, usually drunk. In the interests of safe driving alone, the Dutch side made more sense.

Tonight, having decided early on Dutch side all the way, Harry stood in a light drizzle in the parking lot across from the bowling alley, leaning against the hood of his Jeep, carefully chewing his way through his shawarma. The pita bread had ruptured, leaking sauce and shredded lettuce onto the asphalt and his bare feet, but he didn't care. He'd just had sex with two women simultaneously, was pleasantly buzzed, and best of all, "Season of the Witch," the Donovan version, was playing on the unpredictably eccentric island radio station from his car—a development which had put Harry instantly into good spirits.

"Season of the Witch" was a good sign, he felt—as his moods had become, over the last few months, increasingly dependent on what song the tiny local station might play at any given moment. Speeding home on the island's narrow, twisting, badly maintained, and underlit roads, the right song—say . . . Bill Withers doing "Use Me"—could put him right in the zone. Harry would arrive home feeling perfect, drunk and satisfied. He'd crack another beer, light a joint, and flop into the pool for a float on the rubber raft. Staring at the moon and stars, the strangely comforting smell of whore's perfume gradually giving way to chlorine and cannabis and salt air, he'd feel comfortably the hero of some unwritten novel: debauched, heartbroken—but sympathetic.

The wrong song—a sad Roxy Music ballad, or something from his past life, like Bowie's "Changes," or one that got him just too amped up for drunken driving, like "Born to Be Wild"—and he felt sometimes like just stomping on the gas, straightening out the wheel at the next turn, and flying the Jeep out over the sea.

Donovan blaring, he peeled out of the parking lot, cigarette hanging from the corner of his mouth, bare foot on the gas pedal, feeling, momentarily, on top of the world. The streets were fairly empty at this hour and he managed them without weaving, making it over the mountain, through the unlovely tourist strip of bars and crap restaurants by the airport and past the neon-lit hell of Maho Beach without difficulty. There were still cruise passengers pouring from the casino—fanning out to their buses like disturbed roaches. They were wearing the usual tourist mufti for an evening of rhythm-machine-assisted calypso dancing, alcohol-assisted karaoke, and limbo challenge: rainbow wigs, brightly colored leis, and ugly shorts. They'd soon be tucked in snug in their beds back in their floating penal colonies—before it occurred to them they'd just spent a hundred bucks for a basket of fried fish and an artificially flavored piña colada. Question Mark and the Mysterians' "96 Tears" was on the radio now, the perfect revenge / I Hate You song for the scenery, and Harry briefly considered what it would sound like to crunch tourists under his tires if he pulled the wheel just a little to the left and plowed through the herd. He hated them because they were happy.

The song felt just fine for the moment, but rang hollow when Harry considered that he'd already been on top and was unlikely in the extreme to return there. Fact was, Harry thought, his mood growing a little more maudlin as he got closer to home, Tears for Fears' "Mad World" bringing him down (beautifully, but down just the same), fact was . . . he hadn't been happy when he was on top. The next song, a hair-metal classic for which Harry held a secret affection, bucked him up a little—enough for the last turn up the private road. The electronic gates to his villa swung open on command and he was home. Feeling the twelve or so beers, the Jäger shots, the two tequilas, and the half a Valium he'd taken on the way out the door at the brothel, he staggered blindly up the smooth terra-cotta steps, felt for the light switch inside the kitchen, and, finding it, grabbed a few leftover rib bones for the caretakers' dogs, who were sitting there like bookends, expectant looks on their faces.

Should he check his e-mail? Surely not.

That inevitable and forlorn-looking zero—in its nest of cruel parentheses next to the words "New Messages." He didn't want to see that now. Instead, he drank one more beer on the balcony— the rather spectacular vista of two oceans converging, the French capital in the distance, the swollen moon peeking through the silhouettes of palm fronds suddenly more rebuke than comfort. He padded off to bed and collapsed into clean white sheets that smelled slightly of bleach.

He slept on one side. Still unable to make the transition to center.

*Richard Stringer stood exactly 120 yards from his former place of busi-*ness and watched the workmen take down the sign with his name on it. He would have liked to have been closer, but the restraining order precluded him from advancing. There was a small crowd in front of the restaurant formerly known as Café Stringer: a photographer from the *New York Post*, the new general manager, a couple of waiters, and Richard's onetime partner, Chip. All of them hated him now.

Everybody hated him now, thought Richard. It was official policy to not like Richard Stringer. Richard Stringer was "over." Richard Stringer was "last week." An asshole. A joke. All the years, all the work . . . all the press . . . the time and effort he'd put in to make things work, to get the word out, to improve himself. What had he done that was so wrong? What had he done to deserve this?

The answer, he knew, was that he'd wanted it too badly. They'd seen that. And in New York, that was unforgivable.

He'd played the game. He'd cultivated the right people, he'd fed the right people—he'd been nice, really nice to the right people—even when he hadn't liked them. For the cause, for the show, he'd opened up his life, for fuck's sake—let them in, invited the whole world to share his most private and unguarded moments, something that had not come naturally (something he'd had to train for)—and yet they'd turned on him—all of them. At the first drop of blood in the water, all the people who'd flattered him, who'd schnorred free food off him, who only a few months ago had been vigorously kissing his ass, had quickly—with terrifying speed—devoured him. The quickness and ferocity of their attack had stunned him—as had their number. Every day they piled on: Journalists, clients, former friends—even his girlfriend had dumped him, dropping him like he was radioactive when the first negative cover story came out. They'd made Chip, with that greasy little rattail sticking out the back of his head—and his carefully cultivated two-day growth and his well-earned reputation as the most reptilian restaurateur in New York—Chip—the good guy, the injured party. How fair was that? And they weren't letting up, were they? After the lawsuit, it only got worse. From "hottest" and "sexiest" and "best" up-and-coming young chef in New York City—his three-star restaurant's bar three-deep with adoring girls in tiny black dresses every night—he'd become first punching bag, then pariah, and now, worst of all, an anecdote and a punch line. He was the best cook in New York and he had no kitchen. He was one of the country's "most eligible bachelors"—and he had no girlfriend. He was one of the most famous reality stars on television—and he had no job.

A pudgy girl in a sweatshirt passing by with two well-pimpled friends stopped in her tracks when she saw Richard, and right in front of him squealed, "LOOK! It's that chef from TV!" She whipped out a daisy-decorated cell phone and snapped his picture. As they headed off to wherever they were going, Richard heard them debating whether they'd just seen Bobby Flay or Emeril Lagasse.

Richard took a final look up and down East Thirty-second Street, picked up his luggage, and hailed a cab. Fuck them. Fuck them all. They'd miss him when he was gone.

Let that cocksucker Chip chase him for the money.

The cute flight attendant knew who he was. She kept looking at him and whispering to her coworkers in the galley, refilling his glass with un-characteristic speed. He was among fans—and he was happy. Some-where over North Carolina, when they'd served the in-flight meal, the cute one had leaned down and apologized for the food.

"I guess this isn't exactly as good as you're used to, Chef."

Richard had smiled politely and said, "No . . . no . . . this'll be fine." Then asked her name—as he always did when recognized, remember-ing to look directly into her eyes. When she answered that her name was Diane, he repeated it.

"Diane . . . It's nice to meet you, Diane. Thanks for looking after me so well."

She'd called him "Chef" and that felt good. Always did. Though he had, to be perfectly honest, abandoned that part of his life when he'd made the move into television, he still responded to the word. Someone yelled out "Chef" in the street, his head would always turn. He was done, he'd thought, with cooking. But that, he supposed, would never change.

The "Daube of Beef," designed, he surmised from the menu, by a chef who'd once worked for him, was execrable—an appalling brown smudge of near–pet food, baked into a plastic container. But Richard ate it obligingly. He was a good sport. No snob, he. Diane liked him. He didn't want to let her down. When they landed in Saint Martin, he'd wait for her by the baggage carousel. If she was on layover, he'd offer to take her out to dinner at La Samanna. Maybe a swim. He'd order for her, of course, a bottle or two of very expensive wine, a walk on the beach.

He needed a fan right now. And she'd do.

The sound of the caretaker sweeping the driveway woke him at six. Harry opened his eyes, fumbled for a cigarette on the nightstand, lit it, then lay on his back smoking, fighting the urge to check his e-mail. After a few moments, he lit another cigarette from the end of the first, heaved himself out of bed, and fired up his laptop.

The island dial-up service took forever. Three tries and he was finally on. He reluctantly typed in his screen name and code, positioning the cursor over the X, ready to close out when he got the inevitable bad news. Didn't want to dwell. Why ruin a perfectly good day?

Downstairs, the sweeping stopped. Monsieur Dufour would soon, if the usual pattern held, be starting up his little Renault. There'd be the sound of the gates opening as he headed into town for *Le Monde* and a fresh baguette. In about twenty minutes, the gates would open again as he returned. Followed quickly by his appearance outside Harry's window, skimming the pool in his usual yellow Speedo, a short, wrinkled old man—a veteran of the Algerian conflict, he'd told Harry once—now a gardener, pool cleaner, and caretaker, talking baby talk to his dogs and waiting for the usually quiet, sullen American tenant to leave, so he could make the bed, collect the dirty towels, and clean the house.

Harry didn't like to keep him waiting. He got into his usual island garb—cut-off jeans (no bathing suit), a faded T-shirt, and flip-flops—packed a towel, extra cigarettes, car keys, his cell phone, sunglasses, and wallet, rolled a joint for the beach, and got ready to go. Just before leaving he opened the safe and put the nickel-plated nine-millimeter SIG Sauer in his beach bag. He didn't know why he was taking it with him. Or even why he'd purchased the thing. He only knew it made him feel more comfortable these days.

On the way out the door, he picked up the fat hardbound edition of *Don Quixote* he'd been slogging through all summer, cracked a beer for the ride, and headed briskly for the Jeep. Didn't know why he persisted with the book. His attention span was for shit these days. Couldn't read four pages without getting restless, going for a beer, taking a dip, or nodding off. Maybe that's why he stuck with it. These days, Harry found himself sleeping with an intensity that bordered on the desperate. Life was something he endured between naps.

Messages: 98 New Messages (0)

Harry sighed. Not surprised but disappointed just the same, and after clicking on Write Mail, began to clack away at the keys.

To: laksa@fastmail.com
From: charliedontsurf@fastmail.com

Subject: Lucullus Dines with Lucullus

I'm presently a dark, walnut-brown color with red highlights. My hair, self-chopped with kitchen shears, is sun-bleached, salt-damaged, and sticks straight out from my head like burnt straw. Last night at the bar, someone said I looked like a "shorn Apache."

At the bars, the locals don't sit too close. I look like one of them, sure: the cut-off shorts, the faded T, flip-flops, a beer constantly in hand in its little foam coozy; but I've got, I think, too serious an expression. The dead eyes I used to turn on and off so well have become a permanent feature. I think I scare them a little. I drink my beers a little too fast. I scribble suspiciously in a little notebook. I stare out into space a lot—and I don't flirt with the bartenders or hit on the tourists when I get drunk. I appear, I think, always right on the verge of saying something, confessing to something way too serious for this island "paradise," something appalling and inappropriate to the laid-back Jimmy Buffett–esque context of life here.

Mornings I sit on my balcony and write. I fix myself coffee, do some push-ups if I'm not too hungover, try and smell free air and feel good about it. Then it's jump in the Jeep, put the top down, and head out for the local paper and (yesterday's) International Herald Tribune. I swing by the rental office to see if there's any forwarded mail. If I'm hungry, I'll stop by a little shack I go to for a beer, a salt-fish patty, and the latest island gossip. Then it's the boulangerie for a baguette, maybe the épicerie . . . to see what might have arrived from France. Often there's some great stinky cheeses, a few sausages, some charcuterie. God love the French. Wherever they go—they've got to have it just like home.

There's a very rough, wild, and beautiful beach—just across the border on the Dutch side. A long, narrow strip of sand and cliffs with rocky outcroppings, caves, and coral formations. The waves hit the rocks in the most majestic way and there are little stretches of beach completely isolated by cliff, so I can strip down, stretch out, swim naked, and smoke a joint as I please. Nobody recognizes me. The water is warm, fierce electric blue, and clear like high-end vodka.

When sunstroke threatens, I go back home, take a dip in the pool— and in that wonderful, half-drunk, stupid-from-the-sun state of truly enjoyable back-to-the-womb infantilism, take a dozy float in the late afternoon light, hibiscus flowers—taken by the wind—gathering around me. Then it's a nap on clean white sheets which smell ever-so-slightly of bleach, the French doors open to catch the trade winds, ceiling fan droning quietly overhead.

At night, there's really nothing to do but drink. I've taken to a joint at the end of the runway at the main airport—right on the water. You can watch the sun drop like a swollen ball of red lava into the sea. They've got amiable bartenders with beer guts and a liberal pouring policy, a good selection of old songs on the sound system (mostly cheeseball mideighties stuff like Tears for Fears, Depeche Mode, and so on—and the usual Marley-fest) and a typical expat crowd of rowdy South Africans, Aussies, French, Dutch creoles, and Yanks. All of whom can be counted on to misbehave worse than I do.

Nights I usually cook for myself and maybe a few friends. Watch the satellite, read on the balcony . . . pet the caretaker's dogs, then read Cervantes till I fall asleep. The quiet life of a gentleman of leisure in the tropics.

You'd like it here.

Miss you,
H

Harry regretted the "miss you" as soon as he'd hit the "send" button.

It was the only entirely true thing he'd said.

Ten thirty that night and Harry was drunk, but not driving too fast— moving at a good clip through the lowlands just beyond Maho, still managing to stay mostly on the road, and almost home now. It was dark here, no streetlights, the road twisting through the high grass near the cliff edges before turning inland and across the border. Harry liked driving this stretch. The road was well graded and recently paved—unusual for the island—and when the music on the radio was right and he was feeling good—like he felt now—it was as close to perfection as Saint Martin offered these days. The road turned and banked at graceful angles. There was no other traffic. He felt loose but in control, the view in front of his lights dramatic, the music washing over him. It had been a fine night at Defiance, one of the better Dutch-side brothels. The place had been packed with gang members—from the unfortunately named Bling-Bling Crew and the even-more-unthreatening-sounding Back Street Boyz—what at first blush would have seemed to be an unpromising development as one would have expected most of the girls to be busy. But to Harry's surprise, they were everywhere; dancing on the stage, lounging by the bar, chattering cheerfully with each other at tables, their brightly colored dresses fluorescing under the black lights. The hundred or so young gangsters—mostly awkward young men in cheap clothes—seemed to have spent what little money they had elsewhere. They stood docilely gaping at the girls onstage, none of them buying—unable to summon even much false bravado. According to the local paper, Harry knew that the leader of the Slings had been recently convicted for a typically inept jewelry store robbery in Philipsburg. The police had apprehended him at a nearby bus stop patiently waiting to make his escape. The Back Streeters' leader had just met with a yet more humiliating fate: His sister-in-law had shot him in the neck—then bitch-slapped him while he bled out in front of the neighborhood. He was now said to be in Curaçao, handcuffed to a hospital bed. Perhaps this explained why the crowd was so subdued—or maybe, thought Harry, a vacationing Crip or Blood had explained that *Sling Sling* and *Backstreet Boyz* were names not likely to strike fear into anyone over the age of eight. Harry would not have been concerned in any case. Shooting or stabbing white people was—in general—bad for business on an island whose only industry was tourism. Fucking up customers at a brothel was particularly unwise—as almost every such establishment was owned and operated by one of the old Saint Martin families—from whom also came the island's political class. For the minister of justice or prime minister to be—as well—a whoremonger, or at least to have a brothel in their portfolio of holdings, was a fact of life. Prostitution was legal on Dutch Saint Martin. The girls (the legally imported ones, anyway) were brought in on three-month "temporary worker" visas—for a one-time fee of a few thousand dollars. They operated as independents, paying a daily room rent to the house—and then working—or not working—as much or as little as they could. For Harry, it was a fairly guilt-free arrangement.

Unburdened by the lurking presence of a predatory pimp, the girls were free to practice their craft as they chose—with whom they chose—an exercise in free-market exchange which seemed to suit all parties. He often salved his conscience with this notion.

After a few beers at the bar, he had quickly scooped up two lovely, high-bottomed Colombian girls—a dark-haired one and a tousled bottle blonde—and, one on each arm, had let them lead him through the resentful-looking crowd to the back rooms. He'd paid two dollars for condoms at the desk, and the girls, giggling and disconcertingly playful, had taken him down the now familiar hallway to a little room at the end, where he'd quickly removed his shirt and kicked off his shorts. He'd put his half-finished beer down on the dresser by the ubiquitous and heartbreaking features of the Catholic whore's place of work: the postcard of the Virgin Mary, the burning votive candle, the box of Kleenex and tube of lubricant. He'd wondered which of the two girls' room this was. The dark-haired one—she'd said her name was Claudia—had begun licking his chest, while the other one—Lupe, he thought—had gently reached for his penis.

"*Que rico, papi,*" said Claudia, guiding Harry's cock into her friend's mouth.

"You have good time with us," said Lupe, in between sucks, "we are . . . professionals!" Both girls laughed. And Harry had laughed too, tears in his eyes.

Later, he'd had his usual shawarma and a couple more beers across from the bowling alley, watched the cornrowed Israeli-Arab owner break up a fight between two drunks . . . then, fortified by Curtis Mayfield, had burned rubber out of the parking lot and made for home.

He'd felt unusually good. The girls had been sweet and playful. Afterward, Claudia had told him of the house she was building back in Barranquilla, Harry easily picturing the one-story cinder block structure, rebar extending upward from the roof, the eternal indication of third-world optimism. Maybe next year and another season would bring another floor. Lupe had shown him a photo of her son in a baptismal gown and told him she would send him to America. Harry had tipped lavishly, kissed each on the cheek, told them they were beautiful in Spanish. Life, for the moment, was good.

When Steppenwolf's "Magic Carpet Ride" came on the radio, just as he hit the lowlands, Harry had seen it as a good sign.

He saw the tall grass by the edge of the road move just seconds before the man stepped in front of his lights. A dark figure—black and white like an elongated penguin—moving unsteadily, lurched two, three steps into the road and Harry had no chance at all to avoid him. His foot was still on the gas pedal when there was a tremendous THUD and the Jeep hit meat and bone. The man went spinning off the right front bumper, a terrible, slow-motion arc into the weeds. Harry stomped down hard on the brakes, suddenly stone-cold sober. The Jeep screeched to a full stop and he stuck his head out the window, looked back, and saw nothing, hoping the thing had never happened—that he'd imagined it. Everything looked the same. The Jeep, from where he was sitting— still behind the wheel—looked fine. The road was empty—as always at this hour. Harry listened, straining to hear something, anything, a cry, a groan, a call for help—movement somewhere out there in the dark. Nothing. Only the tree frogs and crickets, the buzzing of insects, the sound of waves chopping and sucking at the coral formations of the cliff bottom to his left. He put on his emergency flashers, opened the door, and ran toward where the man's body appeared to have flown.

It took him a few minutes.

The man wore a tuxedo. A white man in black and white formal wear—not something you saw much of on Saint Martin. He lay sideways in the grass, one arm tucked up behind his ear, one leg sticking out at an angle that was all wrong. Blood matted the man's hair and was already beginning to soak the ground around him. Harry got down on all fours, pressed a finger up against the man's neck like he'd seen them do on TV, put his ear by the man's lips, listening for breath. There was nothing. There was more blood coming, saturating the man's shirt, leaking from his nose and ears—and he'd pissed himself. Harry believed he knew what that meant. Years earlier, he'd found his cat, seemingly asleep on the floor—and it had been that sad puddle that tipped him off that kitty wasn't ever waking up . . . He stood up feeling sick and confused, not knowing what to do. Outside of his cat, it was the first dead body he'd ever seen . . .

He ran. After a few more moments with the body, determining beyond all doubt that the man would not and never would sit suddenly up, brushing himself off and exclaiming, "What the hell happened?," Harry got back in his Jeep, closed the door, turned off the emergency flashers, and drove away. He did not call the cops—who would have taken an hour to arrive in any case. He didn't drive all the way back to the Dutch capital to report the incident. He didn't think of a reason why he didn't do any of these things. He didn't give thought to any particular aspect of his life that this event could and would likely irreparably destroy: career (such as it was), reputation (ditto), personal happiness (what there was of it), financial security (a real consideration) . . . or his freedom (there was that). He knew only that he'd done a terrible thing. That he had killed another human being. That this, finally, was the worst day of an already totally fucked-up life—and that he had to get away. He drove straight home. He threw two buckets of water over the remarkably undamaged front end of his car and then sat up all night on his balcony, knowing that everything had changed.

The Hotel Rex was an eight-room affair near the very top of Pic Paradis, the island's highest mountain. The website BoutiqueHotelsofthe Caribbean.com referred to it as "charming, discreet and out of the way—with a commanding view of Orient Bay and Saint Bart's." It also said that the establishment, a red-tile-roofed structure consisting of white stucco main house and various bungalow-like outer residences, was a "family-run" operation. But Richard, only a few hours since check-in, wasn't so sure what kind of a "family" Mr. and Mrs. Denard comprised. They were an odd pair—to say the least. Mr. Denard was an older man—very tan and sinewy, though in his midsixties, and curiously scarred on his chest, back, and legs. Mrs. Denard—who insisted from the first on being addressed as Frances—was much younger— perhaps forty-two—also tan and fit—and also marked by injury: a small star-shaped scar over one eye—and evidence of a larger wound on her upper chest near the collarbone. They'd met Richard at the gate wearing sarongs. While swiping Richard's credit card at the front desk, Mrs. Denard had casually lit a joint.

"It's not going through," she'd sighed, after a few moments of waiting for the machine to spit out its little piece of paper. "You must be tired and hot. We can try again tomorrow."

A Vietnamese gentleman of indeterminate age—a gardener or houseboy?—silently picked up Richard's bags and carried them to the farthest-removed quarters, a gabled, one-bedroom bungalow built out onto the mountain's slope, supported at one end by concrete pylons driven into rock. An ancient tamarind tree provided shade for a spacious deck with hammock, small chair, table, and abalone-shell ashtray. An Indonesian wind chime hung from a nearby branch and small, yellow-breasted birds picked from a coconut-husk feeder.

"I hope you'll be happy here," said Frances, opening the French doors to his rooms: a well-lit bedroom furnished with a four-poster mahogany bed draped with mosquito netting, a matching Asian-style nightstand—a red chest of drawers—identifiably Chinese, decorated with coiled dragon inlay. The living area also featured predominantly Asian appointments: a cushioned rattan couch and chairs, an ornately carved cocktail table. The floorboards were wide, well-polished teak, adorned here and there with Middle Eastern throw rugs. There was a tiny but efficient kitchenette and a very large slate and glass bathroom with deep, Japanese-style *hinoki*-wood bathtub, a separate shower, and two sinks. A jade vase held a bouquet of African violets.

"There's no regular mealtimes . . . no bar per se . . . Nothing really," said Frances as the Vietnamese man dropped Richard's bags with a thud and padded away without a backward glance. "If you're hungry? Feel free to raid the fridge in the main house. We don't really eat breakfast, but there's always croissants and coffee around. From time to time, my husband will cook—and we'd be happy to have you join us if you give us a little advance warning. Let us know any time you're at loose ends . . . Pool's yours . . . any time you want it. Overnight guests, no problem—as long as they don't steal shit or pee in the pool. I'd appreciate you don't bring them by the main house till you get to know them."

With the contented look of someone who'd decorated the place herself, she did a half turn, a last-minute inspection, and left him, after an assessing smile.

Richard unpacked, slid into a pair of swim trunks, and sat out on the deck, smoking. There was a nice breeze up here—much cooler than the rest of the island, the wind chimes making a hollow, musical sound as they brushed together. He looked up and the Vietnamese man was standing there with a drink.

"Weh-kum drink," he said, putting a rum punch down on the small table. He stood there—for about two seconds longer than was comfortable—before leaving Richard to his thoughts. Richard sipped his drink, grateful for both the cold liquid and its alcohol content. After a while, he stood up, flopped into the hammock, and fell asleep to the sounds of Peter Tosh from the main house—and the smell of marijuana smoke. At one point, he woke to the sound of laughing.

Phil Cervieri pressed a tasseled loafer into the dead Bengali and pushed him down into the wet cement. It was—he had to admit—a bit of a cliché, to enshrine someone in a cornerstone; but sometimes, you just have to stick with the classics. They become, after all, classics for a reason. When the last of the body—chest and a bit of chin—disappeared below the surface of thick, gray slurry, Phil withdrew his foot, leaned over and wiped his shoe with a folded paper towel, then stood quietly for a few moments, among the heavy equipment and stacked palettes of construction material, waiting to see if his former employee would pop to the surface. A protrusion—a nose, a hand, a bit of tie or cuff—would be a bad thing. The construction crew—mostly hired from Curaçao—would be arriving in a few hours and he definitely didn't want them to see that. He lit a cigarette and smoked as the cement hardened and the likelihood of his onetime accountant breaking the surface diminished. Looking around the deserted site, he tried to picture it when it was finished: the placement of the slot machines, the hotel, shopping arcade, restaurant complex, multilevel parking facility, and infinity pool.

When the cigarette had burned down to the filter, he discarded it; picked his way carefully across the rutted property, avoiding the deep, water-filled tracks of the earth movers; and started up his car. "Piano Man" was on the radio, a song Phil loved, and he turned up the volume, cranked up the air-conditioning, and drove slowly away. He'd bill back the company for the clothes and the shoes. Fair was fair after all. This definitely came under the category of "expenses."

Hilma's Windsor Castle was just opening up when Phil arrived. He parked the car in a space by the RBTT bank a few yards over, heaved his large frame out of his seat, and loped over to the wooden stools by the trailer's flip-down counter and sat down.

"Good morning!" shouted Hilma from the back—where she was deep-frying Johnny cakes in a deep saucepot. "What can I do for you this morning?"

"What kind of patties you got today, Hilma?" he asked, giving her a kiss on both cheeks when she came over to greet him.

"Oh . . . let's see . . . We got chicken, beef . . . cheese and salt fish." She smiled.

"And soup? What's the soup today?"

"Oh . . . your favorite. We got a nice bullfoot soup. Just made it fresh. You want some?"

"Beautiful," said Phil. "Lemme get a soup . . . and two salt fish patties. And I better have a Dutch coffee with that." She'd already cracked one of the icy-cold Heinekens she kept in the freezer for the early morning regulars who worked construction and as security guards in the Simpson Bay area. She placed it, wrapped in a paper napkin, down in front of Phil—along with an ashtray—and went back to fill his order.

"You read in the paper today?" Hilma asked him, her back turned as she pulled two patties from the glass food warmer next to the refrigerator. "The hit-and-run by Cupacoy there? Poor man was killed."

"Probably a fuckin' tourist. Drunk . . . ," muttered Phil, not really interested.

"No," said Hilma. "Local man. I believe he's been by a few times.

Steve somethin'-or-other. Makin' some kinda movie down here. His name is in the article."

Suddenly, Phil was interested.

Chapter Two

NOTED FILMMAKER KILLED IN HIT-AND-RUN read the header of the local paper. Harry read on, trying not to look too interested, his usual coffee, orange juice, and croissant untouched. He'd woken up hoping it had all been a bad dream—but knew right away that it wasn't. For confirmation, he'd hurried down to the car and taken a peek at the front end. It wasn't bad. No blood at least—and the damage, unless you looked at it carefully, was minimal. The thick bumper must have taken most of the impact. Not eager to have the caretaker see him suddenly caring about the appearance of his car, Harry had resisted the temptation to give the thing a good scrubbing. So, frantic to know how the thing was being reported—and who, exactly, it was that he'd killed—Harry did his best to stick with his normal routine. He put on his usual garb, packed the usual things—and headed into Sandy Ground for his usual breakfast and newspaper at the tiny French café.

"Steven Lustgarden, the American producer/director/actor who had been living on Saint Martin for the last few years during the production of his latest film, was killed last night near Maho Beach—the apparent victim of a hit-and-run. Mr. Lustgarden had just attended the premiere of his eagerly anticipated major motion picture, *Inferno*, which was shot largely on location in Saint Martin using local actors. A crowd of cast, crew, and investors, many of them still assembled in the Diamond Casino's banquet hall when the body was discovered, were shocked by the news.

"'We can't believe it,' said Thierry Lasseur, who described himself as *Inferno*'s producer. 'Steve knocked himself out for three years to make this film. We—all of us who've been involved in the production— were looking forward to this night. And it finally came. The realization of Steven's dream. And now he is dead. We are terribly distraught. Saint Martin has lost a great friend. And a great artist.' Guests at the invitation-only event described the film as 'a triumph' and 'a really exciting thriller' and expressed the hope that Mr. Lustgarden's work will live on—even if he is gone."

There was—in typical style for the local rag—an unflinching color photo of the broken body sprawled out in the high grass, the legs of the cops and emergency response crew in the foreground. Harry stubbed out a half-finished cigarette, took a sip of cold café crème, and coughed, the cough quickly threatening to become a retch, then sat there for a few minutes, struggling to control his stomach, aware that he was attracting looks from the other customers.

What was this director doing, stumbling around in his tuxedo in the dark—a few hundred yards from the scene of his big night? And who was Steven Lustgarden anyway? Harry had never heard of him. Not in the States. Not on the island. He looked worriedly up from the paper at his Jeep, parked a discreet distance down the parking lot—dented part hopefully concealed from casual view. Nobody seemed to be paying undue attention. But that would change, wouldn't it? A promising filmmaker, an American no less, killed by an unknown hit-and-run driver? There'd be friends back in the States. Grieving relatives, partners, friends, lovers, wives, ex-wives . . . maybe even kids . . . What if he'd had kids? The thought he'd left some adorable tyke or tykes without a father pushed Harry down into his chair. People would be paying attention to this. Harry could no longer pin his hopes on the usual ineptness and disinterest of the Dutch-side police force. In a case like this, pressure would be applied. He'd be looking over his shoulder for the rest of his life. Not for the first time in the last few hours, Harry considered going home, sticking the business end of the SIG Sauer in his mouth, and pulling the trigger.

Instead, he went home, cracked a bottle of vodka, and spent the day drinking it. When he eventually crawled into bed, he didn't come out for two days.

Two days later, the headline read: CONFUSION OVER DEATH OF FILMMAKER.

"'Filmmaker' . . . that's being too kind, don't you think?" said Frances. She was sitting poolside at the hotel, Trung, their Vietnamese helper, spraying the flower beds. Two scraggly-looking dogs and a well-fed black cat slept in the morning sun. Another cat—a one-legged runt with a missing eye—hopped after a lizard among the empty deck chairs.

Her husband, Henry, put down his coffee and said, "Oh . . . I don't know. He did make films. Of a kind. Give the man his due. Unappreciated in his time, perhaps. Imagine what he might have become had he lived. Another John Landis. Maybe even a Harold Ramis."

"A late bloomer, you're saying," said the woman, putting down the paper, a hint of a smile on her face. "Appears that before he was hit by the car, he was shot five times. Causing some consternation among the local crime busters. They figured it for a hit-and-run until they dug five twenty-two slugs out of him."

"Imagine," said Henry, reaching over to tear a hunk of Frances's croissant off. He held it in the air, examining it for a second, before popping it in his mouth.

"You're getting slow. That never would have happened before," said Frances.

"I know," said Henry. "Complete clusterfuck. It's an amazement I still have bladder control. Pathetic. You'll be feeding me mush soon."

"No shit. You know you snore now. Sound like a fucking wood-chipper."

"That's a damnable lie," protested Henry.

"You want me to tape it? You scare the cats it's so loud."

"Maybe I should have my uvula removed."

"That would be a start," said Frances, sighing. "The police are looking for the car."

"What car?"

"The car that hit him, nitwit. The hit-and-run? They're looking for a white four-by-four with damage to the front end. Last person to see our auteur alive."

"Oh . . . that car . . . That should narrow it down. To just about everybody. This island? Who doesn't have extensive body damage to their car? It's a fucking demolition derby out there. People should drive more responsibly. Those roads are killers. Someone could have been hurt. Let that be a lesson to someone—whoever he is."

"You know, I'm beginning to think you have Alzheimer's. I'm paying close attention. Looking for symptoms. I'm watching you, Henry."

"So . . . ," said Henry, lighting a joint and reclining in his lounge chair. "What are we doing today?"

"Same as yesterday, I thought," said Frances. "Nothing."

"You see this?" said Phil, the day's paper in his hand.

"Yes," said Mr. Mansoor. "One could be forgiven for thinking it's a professional job." He looked unhappy beneath a smiling portrait of the shah of Iran. "The caliber and all . . . That's what they use, isn't it?"

"Well . . . sure," said Phil, lowering himself into one of two well-cushioned chairs on the other side of the desk. "But I'm thinking no. I'm thinking a broad done it. I mean . . . what professional shooter puts five pills into a person—all over the fuckin' place no less: legs, chest, shoulder—only gets two in the noodle? Then runs the fuckin' guy over? I'm thinking one pissed-off cunt. Steve-O? He had a few of those around."

"It's the timing that disturbs me," said Mansoor, grimly. "It's very . . . inconvenient. I mean . . . the movie comes out. Business is nearly concluded. The irregularities with the bank. Then this. It's worrying."

They sat there in silence for a moment, Phil watching as Mr. Mansoor stroked a well-tended mustache.

"You spoke with the accountant?"

"I spoke with him," said Phil.

"And what did he have to say?"

"He didn't have anything to say."

"Are you sure?"

"Oh, I'm sure," said Phil. "I'm 'He ain't ever sayin' nothing else' kinda sure."

"I see."

"Yeah."

"Well . . . One has to be sure."

"That was my thinking."

"So the problem has to be with the bank. Or with Mr. Lustgarden. Who unfortunately—and rather too conveniently—is no longer with us," said Mr. Mansoor, beginning to sound very irritated.

"We're looking into it," said Phil, trying to appear unconcerned. "I've got our boy—the cop—looking at it."

"I shouldn't rely too much on the commissioner's investigative skills—or powers of perception—if I were you," said Mr. Mansoor. "He's been good at doing what we needed him to do over the years. But actual police work? I don't think so."

"You have a point."

"This is a lot of money," said Mr. Mansoor. "And there's the principle of the thing."

"There is that."

"He had family, this Lustgarden? Someone we can . . . reach out to? A wife?"

"Afraid not," said Phil.

"So the usual . . . avenues of inquiry are . . . not available."

"I can get over to the bank and talk to them," said Phil. "I can ask around."

"The bank? Yes. Asking around? Here? No. That's not for you. Not for us. People will know who's asking and they'll want to know why."

For the first five days, Richard never left the hotel. Agoraphobic, not wanting to be recognized in his disgrace, he was grateful that Henry and Frances had appeared not to recognize him from television or care at all about his previous life. They, too, seemed never to leave the grounds. Though a mud-spattered Land Rover sat in the small lot, only once had Richard seen Frances use it—to run into Marigot on what was, apparently, the good day for French seafood. She'd returned with Bretagne oysters, turbot, and whelks, which—since he'd found himself eating with the strange couple most nights—Richard had volunteered to cook. From the day he'd arrived, he'd remained the only guest.

They ate by the pool, making light conversation—no one volunteering any information about themselves—talking about food, local lore, the occasional anecdote punctuated by long silences.

A few times, he was informed that he'd be dining alone. Something would be left for him in the kitchen—or he'd order in. His reluctance to go out went uncommented on, though Frances had taken to calling him "Grumpy"—for the constant, pained frown on his face. That was as far as it went. She didn't ask him what was wrong and he didn't tell her. It appeared quite natural at the Hotel Rex to do nothing and go nowhere.

He spent his time sleeping, either in his room or at the pool—at a respectful distance from the couple, who appeared to spend most of their hours there as well. He watched a lot of television. He read (slowly) from Liebling and M. F. K. Fisher and a biography of Carême. He explored his hosts' impressive personal library; hundreds of books in gorgeously fitted bookshelves, built, he was told, by a ship chandler friend. It was a collection of books you could discern nothing of with certainty. No central obsession or interest. Montaigne's essays—in French—sat next to a military history of the Congo. A trashy crime novel leaned against Pépin's *La Technique*. Books on forensic pathology and metallurgy neighbored up against biographies of Dean Martin and Graham Greene. Unlike most hotels and bed-and-breakfasts, there wasn't the sense that these were books left behind by departing guests. Almost everything was in hardcover and there were clearly some rare and expensive volumes. Though the library revealed little about its owners, there were some tantalizing points of interest: One late afternoon, idly perusing the shelves, he settled on an autobiography of Jonas Savimbi, the Angolan rebel leader. On the inside cover sheet was a handwritten inscription: "To my Great Friend," it read. "Thank You for all your Efforts, all your help and Dedication. I will never forget your Friendship."

It was signed by the author. Stranger yet, someone had drawn a very disrespectful mustache across the cover photo.

With little else to do, Richard found himself preoccupied with observing the oddest of couples and their daily routine at the hotel, looking for clues. He noticed, for instance, that Henry spoke French, Spanish, and Vietnamese. Vietnamese with Trung, the houseman; French on the phone and to deliverymen; English to Frances—and Spanish when he cursed. Frances, for her part, was the least squeamish woman Richard had ever seen. Third day at the hotel, he'd gashed himself while struggling with a French can opener. She'd stepped right in; pressed her thumb, hard, directly against the wound (a nasty rip); and applied pressure—a lot of pressure. This while tearing off a piece of kitchen towel with her teeth to improvise a dressing until she could round up the astonishingly comprehensive first aid kit. Amongst the bandages and Band-Aids was everything you'd need to treat anything, from bug bites to a sucking chest wound—forceps, tweezers, a scalpel, and what looked like morphine syrettes. More disturbingly, packets of a product called QuikClot bearing large-print instructions to "pour directly in wound in case of arterial injury." This last seemed to anticipate rather more severe mishaps than one would expect at a boutique hotel in the Caribbean.

Frances had cleaned him up quickly, dressed the wound with a butterfly closure, and wrapped that with gauze. Afterward, she'd inspected the dressing while puffing on a cigarette, offering to "stitch that thing up if the butterfly doesn't hold."

The scars on the couple continued to fascinate. What could possibly have befallen both parties to mark them like that? There was evidence of past slashes, punctures, and suturing all over Henry. And the two round patterns on Frances looked as if she'd once been shot. He began to dwell on the question—and when Frances caught him ogling her scars one afternoon at the pool, he decided it was time to get out more.

On a rented scooter, he began to explore the island, looking for places to eat. The food in the sit-down restaurants was appalling. Rubbery, invariably frozen snapper, extraneous garnishes—usually corn on the cob, zucchini, yellow squash, rice, boiled potatoes, christophene, pureed yam—arranged around the plate in a multicar pile-up of uselessness. Pesto was on everything—a state-of-the-art, all-purpose plate dressing, flavor note, and decoration. The French cooks were relentless in their application of every overused culinary trope in the repertoire of the eighties: squeeze-bottled sauces which had no relation to the dish, spices sprinkled on the rims of the plates—every other dish a lumbering French standard sunk deeper by overkill. Predictably bad "homages" to Creole flavors, dreary Asian fusion, soggy spring rolls, weak-ass "Thai" curries, bogus, never-fresh Vietnamese. No menu did not feature a limp, listless "tuna tartare" or goat cheese salad. Beef carpaccio was inevitable—as was the truffle oil it was usually drowned in. Lamb reeked of too much rosemary. Lobster was murdered with overrich, bisquelike sauce—made from base. Sushi—if one was foolish enough to try it—was always stone cold, the nori wet, the rice gluey. Steak was Argentine—it had made the trip from the pampas soaking in blood and water in plastic vacuum wrap. Once cooked, it appeared always with a huge knob of garlicky maître d'hôtel butter.

He sent a plate of food back once. An order of skate in brown butter and capers at a well-regarded bistro in Marigot. When the replacement had been just as old and awful as the first, stinking of ammonia, he'd mentioned it to the chef, sitting at the bar sipping pastis near closing time.

"This island . . ." The Frenchman shrugged, jerking his head at a black cook in his tiny, filthy kitchen. "And these people . . . what can I do?"

As if that explained—or excused—anything . . . *You're the one selling rotten fish, you lazy fuck*, thought Richard—though he said nothing. His chef days were behind him.

"Every leetle ting . . . gonna be all right . . . ," sang the cover band at the Sunset Bar, the inevitable (and in this case spectacularly inept) tribute to Bob Marley. *Ahhh . . .* , thought Harry, *the optimism of the stoned . . . and doomed*. Two more beers and oh, Jesus fuck, here it comes: a rousing version of "Margaritaville." The perfect song for the perfect fucking moment, he thought. Here he was tottering on the divide between another drink and suicide and could go either way—but no, no, it's Jimmy fucking Buffett and a song Harry hated deeply, the international anthem for every bald fuck with a ponytail and a Hawaiian shirt. He

hated that piña colada song too—which was probably coming next the way things were going, and then, of course, more Marley—and there really was something disturbing about a bunch of white South Africans singing along to "Get Up, Stand Up." By the time the band finally took a break, Harry was only dimly aware of it. He leered stupidly at a blond tourist across from him at the circular bar, her breasts hanging out—taking advantage, no doubt, of the Topless Girls Drink for Free policy at the Sunset. He turned away, embarrassed, when she suddenly looked straight at him. Funny, he thought, his life had once been described by the social whirlwind around it. He'd been the perennial life of the party, the center of attention, the raconteur . . . Now? Now he felt afraid of even the most impersonal interaction. When the girl had looked him in the eyes he'd felt tissue thin—as if even she could see directly into his guilty soul.

The knuckleheads were lining up behind a taxiing passenger jet at the beach end of the runway. When the plane took off, the wash from the turbines would kick up sand and bits of shell and rock and blow half of them back into the water—which was what they wanted. They were getting ready as the engines of the Air France 747 began to whine, whipping out their disposable cameras, hugging each other excitedly. One of these days, a piece of rock was going to shoot straight into one of these idiots' brain pans. And then who'd be sorry? Like Harry's Mom said, he recalled, smiling now, "It's only fun until somebody loses an eye!"

The revelations as to the actual cause of death of Steven Lustgarden had improved Harry's outlook somewhat—at least as regarded his future. But his future hadn't been looking too good anyway. There wasn't much to celebrate. He couldn't get the sound—and feel—of his car hitting the heavy weight of flesh and bone out of his head.

Harry punched the keys on his laptop with careful deliberation. He was drunk—but temporarily exhilarated. An offer of a job—followed by a moment of exhilaration—had led to this. He hoped it would be effective. Everybody likes dogs.

To: laksa@fastmail.com
From: charliedontsurf@fastmail.com

Subject: rat-tat-tat

Dogs like me.

There are a few of them at every bar—usually sad-looking strays upon whom some softhearted bartender has taken pity, providing regular food and water and a sort of home. At the Sunset there are two of them. And I think they recognized me immediately as a kindred spirit. They get excited when they see me approach. They sit by my bar stool, take pets behind the ears, sleep contentedly on the ground nearby while I drink my beer.

A tropical storm tonight. Rat-tat sounds on the corrugated metal roof, the big palm outside my window making that sound like a bellows flapping against a picket fence as it rakes the balustrade. The wind whips through the louvers in the living room and fills the eaves with a low, dolorous moan that lasts for minutes at a time, subsides, then begins again. The tree frogs stop their swinging-door cries. Dogs bark. The deck furniture scrapes around on the tile floor as it moves with the wind.

Funny. I was at the Sunset tonight, sitting there at the bar, scribbling (this actually) in my little notebook. The bartender, a Danish girl who usually feeds me free shots at regular intervals, saw me writing and joked, "What, are you writing a love letter?"

I laughed and said, "No . . . no . . . working on a book. You know me. Always working. I get paid for this shit."

But then, when she was gone, I thought about it a little. I thought the true answer to her question was:

"Yes . . . Yes I am."

H

Harry hit the "send" button too soon—and the message was on its way.

The dog business had been clever—though a little wide of the truth. In fact, the lone house dog at Sunset was a mangy, spavined, ill-tempered beast who growled at Harry's approach and who'd spent most of its time in his presence gnawing its own ass. The noise the rain made on his roof was a nice description—though not of this evening's weather, which was dead and humid. The only true thing was the bit about the love letter. And now, that was the one thing he wished he hadn't included.

Funny, he thought, as he peeled off his moist clothing and teetered toward the pool, it was always the truth that got him in trouble.

Dara Heyligger finished loading Heinekens and Red Stripes into the ice bins and looked at her watch. Two forty-five P.M. In exactly twenty-two minutes, Cynthia, the most regular of Dara's regulars, would arrive. She'd sit down, second stool from the left, remove her hat, clean her sunglasses with a cocktail napkin, appear to mull over her drink of choice for the afternoon, then order what she always ordered: a rum punch. She'd finish the first drink in about eight minutes, and order another one—which she'd linger over for a while, maybe twenty minutes. She would then pretend that she was giving serious consideration to cutting things short today—tomorrow was a workday after all—then she'd start in on the beers. By four o'clock, she'd be in her sad and wistful phase, slurring her speech and confiding in Dara (for the hundredth time) the unhappy details of her short-lived romance with a local charter captain. Her eyes would fill with tears but she wouldn't—if the pattern held— quite cry. By five o'clock, when the Cap'n Ricky's bar started to fill up, Cynthia would get her second wind, the influx of available—and soon-to-be-drunk—locals, and the anything-can-happen mix of tourists, giving her reason to hope that she wouldn't be going home alone tonight. She'd start getting loud—and lewd—by seven, and by eight o'clock, she'd be buying Jäger/Red Bull shots for some unfortunate desperado. Nine o'clock, she'd be glassy-eyed and done, sagging into her drink with her mouth half open, the other customers studiously ignoring her. Fortunately, she lived quite close—across the street in a little cracker-box condominium. She usually made it home without help.

You could set your watch to it. Dara chilled two highball glasses for the rum punches, made sure plenty of Cynthia's beer of choice was

close at hand, and moved the cocktail napkins a little closer to where—
any minute now—she'd be sitting.

There was a grim inevitability to the proceedings at Cap'n Ricky's.
And Dara—as five-days-a-week bartender, two P.M. until ten, Tuesday
through Saturday—gave the daily routine a lot of thought. It was her
regulars who really broke her heart. Enabling their relentlessly unvarying self-medication, their delusional behaviors, with alcohol took
its toll on her. Seeing Cynthia, for instance, or Bamboo John, or Billy
Koop—or any one of the score of tragic regulars who sat at her bar until
babbling and near comatose every night—she felt like a drug dealer.
She was selling them poison that they were only too happy to have. And
she was, she was pretty sure, watching them die in increments.

Cynthia would never find a nice guy to take care of her. Bamboo
John would never get his bar back (or his wife, or kids, or boat). And
Billy Koop would never again make sense at all. If Dara didn't get away
from this bar—and this job—she'd be feeding poor addled Billy his last
drink on earth. In this way, she wondered if she wasn't just like them.
Another dreamer going nowhere—another prisoner of Cap'n Ricky's,
only on the other side of the bar.

She handed Teddy the bar back a list of bottles that needed re-
stocking and asked for more ice. She cracked open a package of Bev
Naps, reloaded the Zip-Sticks, made sure there were plenty of paper
umbrellas for the blender drinks, then began cutting fruit with a small,
serrated blade. She was thirty-one years old.

Everybody wanted her.

This was small consolation to Dara, as she knew that after a few
beers, of *course* they'd all want a roll in the sack with a blonde—*any*
blond, well-proportioned, and reasonably good-looking bartender.
They saw the same creases at the corners of her eyes, the slight pooch
over her waistband that she did in the mirror each morning, the wages
of too much time in the sun, too many free Jäger shots—but through
beer goggles it didn't matter, did it? Blond—and not actively ugly—was
enough on this island. Everybody got around to hitting on you eventually . . . Eight o'clock, the boys would start getting suggestive. Nine
o'clock they'd start asking her number. By ten o'clock it was dirty jokes

and "Hey, love . . . What are you doin' after?" And this was from people who'd known her for years. These were her friends. Human behavior was getting her down. Cap'n Ricky's was getting her down.

People—the people who knew anyway—had been nice for a couple of days after Steven was killed. They hadn't leered or been stupid. They'd made consoling remarks—and then pretty much avoided her, unsure how to act around the recently bereaved. Which was as much consideration as one could reasonably expect on Saint Martin. Steven's death, though it had happened only a week ago, was still the past. And everybody at Cap'n Ricky's had a past.

Dara finished cutting the lemons and limes and skewering the pineapple chunks and filled the garnish trays with maraschino cherries and olives. She spread new kosher salt on a plate next to the sponge for margaritas, made sure she had fresh bar towels, arranged three blender heads in ready-to-grab fashion under the bar. Then she sat down on a stack of beer cases and had her first tequila of the day, wondering if anyone would ever see the movie she'd spent three years living with—and whether she had actually been any good in it.

She liked this time of day the best at Cap'n Ricky's. If there was a best time. No customers, her setup all done, first drink . . . She could sit and look out at the lagoon from her floating bar, the deck moving ever so slightly beneath her, watching the pelicans dive for food, thinking about things.

Everyone had seemed to love the film. They had cheered uproariously throughout—every time Dara had appeared on camera. They had clapped enthusiastically, and whistled and yelled throughout the titles. After it was over, they had all come up to Steven and clapped him on the back and hugged him and offered congratulations. And he'd looked so happy and proud in his tuxedo. On top of his game, triumphant. Sure, the writers from the New York papers had not, in fact, shown up. And the rumored studio types from LA had also been no-shows. Just a couple of sad sacks from the local papers. But Steven had done—finally—what he'd said he'd do. He'd made *Inferno*. He'd shown them that he really could do it, that he was what he said he was.

But was the thing any good?

Dara had lived with the film—and its producer/director/star—for so long that she couldn't tell. When the lights had gone down and the curtain gone up, she had found herself holding her breath waiting to appear on-screen. She'd barely noticed the rest. It had all gone by in a blur, inseparable in her mind from a dream. Whose dream, she didn't know. Down here, she realized, seeing Cynthia in her floppy straw sun hat and sunglasses, approaching the bar, dreams tended to become commingled with others. There were so many who'd bought into Steven Lustgarden's dream and made it their own. What happened now that Steven was dead?

Ten o'clock and her feet were killing her. She wasn't feeling the tequila or the Jäger or the beers she'd been drinking all night with her customers, but they'd catch up with her later—at Sunset—when she slowed down. Dara moved slowly away from the dwindling crowd at Cap'n Ricky's without saying goodbye. Her customers were too drunk to notice anyway. Ellen, the late-night bartender, would count out and close. She walked gingerly through the dark parking lot while feeling for the car keys in her bag. There was a hand on her shoulder.

"Dara . . . my love . . . where you goin'?"

It was a customer. Fourth stool from the left. Ronnie, a plumbing contractor from New Jersey, as she remembered, down for vacation. He'd said he was staying at the Pelican, she thought—before she'd started watering his drinks.

"Less have a drink," he suggested, spinning her around. "Less have a drink!"

"I'm afraid I have to go," said Dara, taking a step backward and falling out of her sandal. When she reached down to fix it, Ronnie stepped forward, pressing her against her car.

"C'mon," he breathed, "less have one drink. I like you. I wanna talk to you."

"You're bothering me," said Dara, a little afraid for the first time. Ronnie was all dead weight now, mashing her against the door of her battered Celica. "I don't want a drink."

"Sure you do," insisted Ronnie, reaching toward her face, trying to stroke her hair, but missing her head entirely. "C'mon . . . C'MON!" He had his face scrunched up in an ugly approximation of a sulking little boy—and Dara knew she'd have no problem with him. She'd handled amorous drunks before. Ronnie here was big—and drunk—but she knew she could handle him. A few sharp words, a quick move to the left or right, and things would be fine. Failing that, a knee to the balls would do the trick.

But she didn't get the chance. Suddenly, Ronnie stood straight up. His eyes opened and Dara thought she heard something crack as Ronnie's right hand disappeared behind his back, reappearing—disconcertingly—above the back of his head. He made a loud keening noise that sounded like "EEEEEEEEeeeeeEEE!!" and then spun on his heels and dropped straight to the ground like a stone going down a well. There was a tall, thin, much older man standing over him, a bare foot on Ronnie's neck. He was smiling sheepishly and smoking a cigarette.

"Appalling manners," said the man, sighing. "Really appalling. I sometimes think it's the end of Western civilization. I guess I should have waited for you to cry 'help' or something, but this kind of behavior. It really offends me." He looked genuinely unhappy and tired, his voice relaxed. It was a kind voice, the type of inflection you heard from a reassuring veterinarian talking about a sick puppy.

"I . . . don't think that was really . . . necessary," said Dara, taken aback. She'd seen this man before but wasn't sure where. "I could have handled it fine."

"I'm sure you could have," said the older man, foot still on Ronnie's neck. "Apologies. Personal thing really . . . I just hate to see that kind of thing." He looked down at Ronnie, who was moaning and barely conscious, his arm pushed up underneath his back in a very unnatural way. "Do you think, though, that I should break something else?" asked the man cheerfully. "I'm thinking it would be instructive."

"No. No. Please. I think that's enough," said Dara, not sure who was more frightening, the man on the ground or this soft-spoken old guy with the inappropriate smile.

"You sure? I could break his collarbone no problem."

"No . . . no. I don't think so."

"Maybe a rib or two?"

"No. I'm fine, really."

"You're fine, sure. But there's a certain social responsibility issue here . . . ," said the man, removing his foot from Ronnie's neck and pulling on his cigarette. "I mean, okay . . . *you* coulda taken care of shit-for-brains no problem. But what about the next time? You *know* this goof is gonna do this again . . . Maybe next time with someone not used to wrestling with drunks—someone less prepared."

Dara didn't know what to say to that. Just about all the women she knew were used to wrestling with drunks. But the man had a point. She hesitated.

"You might want to turn your back for a moment," said the man.

Dara, responding to something truly scary—maybe it was the flatness in the man's voice—did exactly that.

There was a THUD and then silence.

When she turned back, Ronnie's nose was sideways on his face and he wasn't moaning anymore. The man was gone.

"What are you? Fucking Batman?" said the woman in sunglasses, looking up from her newspaper. "I think sometimes I don't know you anymore, Henry . . . I mean . . . this is nuts. What are you doing? Lurking in fucking parking lots in a fucking cape? Doing good deeds? What's going on with you?"

"I wasn't lurking," said Henry. "I was checking the tires. Front right was a little low. I didn't want to go flat somewhere between here and Marigot. I just happened to be there. What do you want me to do? Ignore a young woman in distress?"

"I think you're menopausal or something. This is turning into some kind of hobby for you? It says here they're looking for the man who dislocated a tourist's shoulder, broke his arm, broke his nose, and generally fucked him up. A tourist, Henry. A tourist."

"Exactly, sweetheart," said Henry, rubbing sunblock into his face. "A tourist. What? Tourists are supposed to be immune? They get a free ride? Feel free to come down and waylay and molest our locals? The flower of our youth? This is our island, Frances. Ours. Cocksucker'll be back in Connecticut or wherever he came from in a few days—and nobody'll be looking for anybody. He'll be somebody else's problem."

"I think you should pursue safer activities in your golden years, darling. Really. Something less likely to invite . . . scrutiny. Something less—dare I say—dangerous? You're not a young man anymore. You'll hurt yourself you keep this shit up."

"So, what you're saying is—I should learn to crochet or something? Build ships in bottles? Take up stamp collecting. Is that where I am?" said Henry, looking hurt.

"I'm not waiting on you hand and foot when you break your fucking hip is what I'm saying. Jesus, Henry. You're old. Accept it. I roll on top of you, it sounds like I'm fucking a box of Triscuits. You're retired. Enjoy your life. Don't leave your wife with some fucked-up basket case. Don't go doing stupid shit that gets us busted after all this fucking time. That's what I'm saying."

"Everybody needs a hobby," said Henry.

"At the very least, Henry? Next time? Carry a fucking blackjack or a piece of pipe. All right? Man of your advanced years—your bones get brittle. You pop some guy in the fucking head you'll hurt your hand."

Looking disgusted, Frances took a sip of coffee, shook her head, and then dropped her sarong for a jump in the pool . . .

"Coffee's cold," she said. "And you're an asshole."

Chapter Three

A job.

The man on the phone had said a writing job. That they'd pay "better–than–New York" prices. And expenses. It was too good to be true, thought Harry, speeding toward the meeting in his best shirt and khaki pants. He was, after all, unemployable. Surely this man Cervieri knew that. Surely everyone in publishing or media had heard about the problem at *Esquire*; yet, this man had apparently not. Or maybe he just didn't care, thought Harry.

Maybe enough time had passed for him to be forgiven.

"It's for a European media group," said Mr. Cervieri, an outgoing fellow in expensive yet casual clothes. They faced each other at a table at the Sand Bar, the watering hole for the Yacht Club, a newly created mooring for gigantic "super-yachts" in the island's large inner lagoon. "You've probably never heard of us," he volunteered, answering Harry's unasked question. "We're a new outfit . . . part of a larger consortium of companies in the entertainment and financial services sector." Cervieri seemed to choose his words carefully, articulating with precision, pausing now and again to sip from an iced tea. Harry finished his Bloody Mary and signaled for another. "We're always looking for new material. In this case, one of our offices is very interested in a profile of a local personality. They thought you'd be perfect for it—what with your reputation and your being down here and all."

Reputation? Harry didn't know what to say. Hadn't this man read any of the hundreds of articles about his fall from grace? Google the words "Harry" and "plagiarism" and you'd get 1,114 mentions. Harry knew. He checked every day.

He sat speechless and confused, trying to not visibly enjoy his drink as much as he was—waiting to hear more. "Big fan," said Cervieri. "And our publisher is also a big fan. He's got *Look at Me* right now on his desk. Lovin' it."

Which was par for the course, thought Harry. That anyone—anywhere—would ever bring up another one of his nine books would be too much to hope for. They'd bury him with that fucking book, his first, youthful, exuberant, frat-boy-gone-wrong exercise in spoiled romanticism. All these years later—it continued to pay the bills. He did not, however, sitting here at the Sand Bar, feel like "Salinger on cocaine" or any of the other superlatives once attached to his name. He felt like a shaky, irrelevant alcoholic who wouldn't mind a few extra dollars and maybe a chance at professional redemption. This Cervieri character didn't impress him. He talked like he was playing a character. Harry didn't believe for a minute he'd read even *Look at Me* and he was, by the time he finished his second drink, pretty sure that this whole meeting was bullshit—that nothing would come of it. "Twenty-five thousand dollars," said Cervieri.

"What?" said Harry, attention suddenly returning to the matter at hand.

"The job pays twenty-five thousand dollars. Plus expenses," repeated Cervieri, seemingly concealing a satisfied smile. "It's the first issue of the magazine—we don't have a name for it yet—and the publisher wants to make an impression."

"He's made an impression on me," said Harry, actually sitting up in his chair. While he didn't yet need the money, it would certainly help. *Look at Me* couldn't sell forever . . . and twenty-five grand in the kitty went a ways toward improving his outlook. That someone would pay that kind of money for him felt flattering. He was in demand.

Somewhere.

"What's the subject—or I guess I should ask, who?"

"A filmmaker who died recently. Local guy. Or he lived here anyways. Maybe you read about him. Guy's name was Steven Lustgarden," said Cervieri, reaching for a menthol cigarette. "You know him? Or did you know him?"

"Uh . . . no," said Harry, "no I didn't," the room going sideways for a second. He felt himself flush violently red, his face burning, and he just managed to strangle a cough as he put down his drink—a little too hard.

"You okay?" asked Cervieri.

"Yeah . . . I . . . just . . . too much pepper in my drink. I caught a piece of horseradish or something," he stammered, eyes swimming. Looking into Cervieri's eyes now, wondering if he was a cop.

"He was a very talented guy—this Lustgarden fellow. A major talent. A lot of people said so. The French loved the guy. Don't ask me why—what do I know from movies—but they did . . ."

"So . . . ," said Harry, not knowing where this was going or what to do next.

"So. I have twelve thousand dollars cash right here," said Cervieri, sliding a thick envelope across the table. "And you get the rest when the article is done."

Harry sat stunned for a second, looking at the envelope. Twelve thousand dollars of tax-free, unreportable cash—and he wouldn't, he thought, even have to share with his agent. What magazine paid cash these days—or any days? On one hand, he was utterly confounded by what was happening, on the other, relieved that whatever this man Cervieri wanted, it seemed to be something other than a tearful confession.

"What . . . what do you want for this money?" he asked. "I mean, what kind of article? How many words? What . . . take on this guy? I mean . . . what are you looking for?"

"The piece works out, we're hoping for a continuing relationship. This could lead—we hope it'll lead to more work."

"Yeah, but what—"

"You better talk to my principal about that," said Cervieri, rising to leave. "He's over on Saint Bart's for the week and he'd like to meet you. You can spend a little time over there, talk about that with him. On us, of course. We're straight? You'll do the thing?"

"Yes," said Harry, not hearing the words coming from his own mouth, afraid to accept—more afraid to decline. "Sure. I'll do it."

Cervieri walked out the door, pausing by the bar to settle the check. The waitress came over and asked Harry if he cared for another drink.

"Your friend," she said. "He said you can have as many as you want."

He had two more—and then a third, before his stomach started growling and he became aware that he was hungry. Chewing distractedly on his celery top, Harry considered what was bothering him about the meeting—other than the fact of the too-eerie coincidence of Steven Lustgarden. There was something about the way Cervieri had talked—about his speech patterns—like someone not speaking their first language; the way those patterns had changed near the end of the meeting—as if he was reverting to a more familiar one. He'd seemed like a man who was not just used to but was, in fact, very comfortable passing envelopes of cash across tables. Maybe that was it.

*The Winair shuttle to Saint Bart's dropped out of the sky after a ten-*minute flight from Saint Martin, a steep, stomach-elevating descent between mountains. The wings shimmied and yawed before the small plane bounced down the tarmac, took a fast turn, and rolled up to the terminal. Harry was the only passenger aboard. He walked the short distance through arrivals, past the ticket counters and the baggage carousel, to the man holding a sign bearing his name. It was a forty-five-minute drive—through the town of Gustavia and then up and down steep, twisting mountain roads to a two-story hotel, the main building set back under heavy tree cover—cottages and rooms strung out along the beach behind. It was the high season on the island and a sweating and distracted-looking manager helped check him in, informed him that all charges were "being taken care of," and showed him to his room, a bungalow, slightly removed from the main hotel, up a hill with a sweeping view of the rocks and surf.

There was nothing to unpack, really. Harry had brought a couple of dress shirts, a bathing suit, extra shorts—and the khakis he was wearing now. After a shower, he changed, took a stroll down to the beach bar for a seventeen-euro mojito. The beach chairs were all taken—occupied for the most part by fat men and skinny women—so he took his drink back to his rooms, sat out on the porch, and waited to hear from his new employer.

To: laksa@fastmail.com
From: charliedontsurf@fastmail.com

Subject: Report from the Front

It's a slaughterhouse of bling, this island. Teeming with the newly rich, stacked in holding patterns to pay thirty dollars for a cab ride, twenty for a drink, hundreds for meals that would have been laughably dated and sub-mediocre in New York—or even Cincinnati—a decade ago. It's a tiny, beautiful island become a "moronic inferno" (credit here to Martin Amis). Never in the history of human conduct have you seen so many stretched faces, pumped lips, augmented boobs—and bad intentions. The younger women are pneumatically breasted semi-pros; the older ones— the onetime trophy wives, fighting the ravages of time with ever more drastic surgical extremes—sport jewelry in inverse proportion to their youth.

I've been to Cambodia during the Khmer Rouge days, and I've been to Uzbekistan, but God help me, I've never been anywhere so teeming with grotesques . . . a veritable Breughel painting of the seven deadly sins. Only sloth is missing from the picture as "vacationers" here indulge their dark urges and pursue old vendettas with a frenetic energy that borders on the desperate. Never have I seen such a vision of hell.

Lenin or Marx would have dropped dead at a mere glimpse of this unimaginable capitalist excess. Socialism would have died in its crib had its creators caught sight of this—they would have died, struck dumb on the spot, synapses and nerve endings overloaded with the sheer horror of it all.

Nearly FORTY dollars for a few spoonfuls of plain boiled lentils—served cold—with not so much as a carrot chunk as garnish. SIXTY smackers buys you a defiantly burned chicken leg or an indifferently grilled fish—this at a half-empty beach motel where our Real Masters, the people who rule this world, line compliantly up and cringe and beg and bribe for a table. That they do so to be peed on from a great height by a surly Frenchman who takes great delight in treating them with visible contempt gives me no satisfaction. Because ultimately, it is an aggressive act. Make it past the cordon to a plain white table, survive the capriciously sadistic selection process, and one may bask in the knowledge that while one eats one's cold lentils, one can see one's friends in the distance—doing without. More important, they can see you. In this way, decades-old scores are settled. An inappropriate remark twenty years ago in Saint Tropez. A bad joke about one's husband. Inadequate display of appreciation for a dress last year in Paris or Monaco or London. A bad haircut . . . Payback achieved.

Gaddhafis in Speedos, Mobutu mistresses, crackhead heiresses, Russian arms dealers, Italian race-car drivers turned gigolos, every variety of well-turned-out pimp and whore—every one of them scrabbling and scrounging over small stakes, fighting over bread crumbs more ferociously than the poorest resident of a São Paulo favela.

I swear to God, when I'm done here, I shall fly back to my beloved Saint Martin, take off my clothes, crawl under my bed, adopt the fetal

*position—and remain there for a week. My skull has been fucked, my
brain raped in devastating ways by what I've seen here. I fear I will
never be the same.*

Xx

H

The interior of the tender ferrying people out to the party was
plushly upholstered; early era Studio 54, or late back-of-the-limo
swank. Harry sat with Phil Cervieri and thirteen much-better-dressed
guests, engine throbbing beneath their feet as they plowed through the
chop into total darkness, the lights from Saint Bart's growing smaller
and more faint behind them and, finally, disappearing altogether. The
others seemed all to know each other and spoke—in a seamless mix of
Italian, French, and English—as though they hadn't seen one another
for a while. Harry found himself literally keeping his head down, chin
tucked to his chest, not speaking to the seemingly oblivious Cervieri,
who, though he clearly came from a different income bracket—and a
different world than the others—appeared perfectly at home among
these aged and temporarily drowsy predators.

Through the smoked-glass windows, Harry could now see absolutely nothing. He kept his gaze away from the other guests—particularly
the ancient vampire directly across from him, who, he believed, if he'd
gotten it right during the brief second he'd dared to look, was actually wearing an ascot. The man's wife was even more terrifying: heavy,
freckled and sunspotted cleavage, ears dripping with diamonds, her
mouth a rictus of gleaming white veneers, fear, and contempt. When
she laughed at something someone said, her violent, raspy bark rolled
through the deck like they'd struck an iceberg.

Suddenly—as if a flashbulb had gone off and stayed lit—the tender was flooded with bright, bright light. The doors at one end were
thrown open, the pilot cut the engine, and Harry saw that the entire
craft was sliding inside the enormous hull of a much larger ship, a giant, almost an ocean liner in size. The tender drifted gently up to an
interior dock, coming to rest next to a small, bright orange mini-sub.

Phil led him, blinking, out onto a gangplank, where uniformed crew assisted the guests onto the deck and showed them where to check their shoes. Waiters in nautical garb—little sailor suits with gold epaulets and sporty caps—offered flutes of champagne from silver trays.

Harry half expected someone to say, "Welcome, Mr. Bond."

"You're going to like Mr. M.," said Cervieri, leading Harry up the first of three flights of stairs.

"Is this his boat?" he asked.

"Yacht," corrected Cervieri. "It's a yacht. And no. It's a friend's. Second largest in the world, you want to know. Throws a party every year about this time."

They reached a heliport deck—with room and markings for two helicopters to land—and walked toward another flight of steps, music getting louder from above. The last flight of stairs and Harry could hear laughter and the clink of glasses, the low, ambient roar of conversation under the music. It was a feeling both familiar and enervating. He knew that smell, too. Expensive perfume, new leather, cigarette smoke, the faint chocolate aroma from the smoke machine. Once, he'd been the center of attention in rooms that smelled like this. Now he wanted to hide.

They emerged onto the party deck, where hundreds of guests clustered in groups around a laser-lit pool. A DJ spun vinyl under tented fabric. Tall women with long, graceful necks smiled at each other; serious-looking men with deep tans paused between remarks to examine—briefly—the platters heaped with sushi being offered before declining with a shake of the head. Two bars were each stacked three-deep with hopeful-looking, unattached women—the second string. The older, old-money crowd were sitting in groups. At the opposite end of the vast, open space, dead center, what looked like a professional recording studio—open on one end as if a wall had been removed to serve as a stage, a few musicians plugging in instruments. They looked familiar.

He knew some of these people, Harry realized with growing discomfort. He knew a lot of them. From magazines. From movies. From television and newspapers. And worst of all, from his past life. A young woman locked eyes with him for a second, then turned to her friend and said something, and Harry could well imagine what had been said.

He was grateful when Cervieri took a hard turn and led them down a hallway, past four Motherwells and a couple of Jasper Johnses, to a back staircase, where an expressionless security man with an earpiece let them pass without comment. Up a few steps to a smaller deck, overlooking the festivities, where a short, dark-skinned man with a neat mustache was talking quietly to a taller man with silver hair. When the shorter man saw Cervieri and Harry, he turned away from the other man—who left quickly and silently without saying goodbye—and gave Harry the briefest of smiles, as if such things pained him, extending a hand.

"Delighted to meet you. I very much enjoyed your book," said the man.

"Harry, meet Mr. Mansoor," said Cervieri.

"Enjoying the party?" asked Mansoor.

"Well . . . just got here," said Harry. "But very much impressed." Mansoor's accent was pure Oxford or Cambridge, the clothes, impeccable—Savile Row–tailored suit in tasteful pinstripes; bespoke shirt, open at the collar; nice shoes—probably Italian. Only the cufflinks were wrong: outsized, bright gold things—stamped with what looked like peacocks. He was . . . Pakistani? Or Iranian, thought Harry.

"It's all about Billy playing guitar," said Mansoor, indicating a dumpy, middle-aged man, now awkwardly slinging an old Stratocaster over his chest. "Our host is preparing to regale us. Van Morrison, most likely. Be prepared to look appreciative. He's been taking lessons."

And yes, indeed. There he was, Harry realized: Billy Conrad, second-richest man in the world, fiddling with the volume knob and the tremolo bar before strumming his first tuning-up chord of the evening. And now Harry knew why the musicians had looked familiar. That was Robbie Robertson taking his place on rhythm guitar. And was that Larry Graham on bass? Because for sure it was Aynsley Dunbar sitting down behind the drum kit.

"Now we pay for our sushi," quipped Mansoor. And sure enough, after a couple of false starts, the band went dutifully to work and to-gether launched into "Brown Eyed Girl." Mansoor and Cervieri stood smiling politely at the rail as Conrad and company ground through one more from the Van Morrison catalog. After a Creedence Clearwater and a lackluster stab at "Brown Sugar," sufficient homage had appar-ently been paid.

"Let's have a quiet word," suggested Mansoor, and the three of them walked down a hallway to a comfortable, unused conference room with a pitcher of ice water and three glasses set out at the center of the table, a large arrangement of flowers on a side credenza.

"Something stronger?" asked Mansoor. "Of course. You must. I'll have a whiskey myself."

"A beer'll be fine," said Harry.

"Beer then." Without bothering to look over at Cervieri, he added, "Phil?"

Cervieri stood up, picked up the receiver from a wall phone, and whispered a drink order. Three minutes later, there was a waiter with their drinks—and a tiny silver bowl of mixed nuts. Mansoor waited for him to leave before speaking.

"I'm not sure how much of this project my associate has discussed with you, but I believe he's given you the general outlines. The subject of our interest."

"Yes," said Harry.

"This is not, I should tell you, strictly a business matter. Yes, we are very . . . eager for a comprehensive article on the life and career of Mr. Steven Lustgarden. That's good journalism. And that's good business. It will be, I think you will come to find, a very interesting story. I don't know what you know of Mr. Lustgarden, but I can promise you that. He was a very . . . complex . . . character, to say the least. But you should know that there is a personal dimension. Steven was also a friend—and sometime business associate. I was—among other things—an investor in some of his film projects. While I can't say we were close, I was al-ways . . . amused and fascinated by his . . . exploits. A curious man. About whom I am personally very curious. This explains, to be frank, the rather generous fee we are willing to pay for your services."

"I understand," said Harry agreeably, though he surely did not. "And—I'm not so clear on this—what publication is this for?"

"Ahhhh," said Mansoor, leaning back in his chair and tenting his fingers—as if he'd been waiting for the question. "We're not sure, exactly of what we're going to call the thing. I run a media group out of Germany, mostly books, some film and television production, a newspaper here and there. This would be our first venture into glossy magazines." He smiled—as if at a private joke. "I was going to say that I am a man of 'many interests'—but that sounds so sinister, doesn't it? Like something the bad guy would say on one of your American television shows." He removed a peanut from the dish on the table, examined it, then replaced it.

"How about the . . . angle. The tone of the piece. I mean . . . what kind of magazine is this? You want some admiring, breezy sort of a thing . . . or uh . . . a harder look at the guy? I'm not sure what it is—"

Mansoor cut him off. "Investigative. I want a thorough, uncompromising examination of the life and times of Steven Lustgarden. Everything. From fucking to financials. To how he died."

"I'm not . . . I'm not a reporter, really. And I'm sure as hell not a detective," said Harry.

"We understand that," said Mansoor dismissively.

Cervieri leaned across the table and slid two business cards to Harry. One bore his own name—Philip Cervieri—identifying him as vice president of development for the Darius Media Group (the locations of presumed offices listed below in small type: "Berlin, Cyprus, Lichtenstein"). The other was a plain white card with the name and number of "Prosecutor Karl Roop," the address of the government office building in Philipsburg on the Dutch side of Saint Martin, and a telephone number.

"Karl is a good friend of ours from way back. He can get you up to speed on the investigation. I told him to expect your call."

"It's been very nice meeting you, Harry," said Mansoor, standing up abruptly, the meeting clearly over.

Harry, taken aback, struggled to remember all the unanswered questions he'd had for his new employer.

"Deadline!" he managed to blurt out, spilling a bit of beer as he rushed to stand, Mansoor and Cervieri already on their feet. "When do you want this thing?"

"Soon would be good," said Cervieri. "Really soon."

Mansoor was out the door and heading left. Cervieri waited outside the door for Harry, then guided him right, back toward the party. More people had arrived since they'd left, and the party was louder, more frantic. The live performance had ended; dance music was now thumping through the deck.

"There's boats headed back all night—and a car waiting for you on the other end. The meantime—enjoy the party," said Phil, taking his leave. Then adding—almost as an afterthought but not quite—"Help yourself to some pussy. It's free." He then patted Harry gently on the back and actually winked.

Which was Harry's cue to leave.

Chapter Four

Monday morning, when he drove his recently rented scooter to the cash machine, the screen kicked up "FUNDS NOT AVAILABLE FOR THIS ACCOUNT." He tried three other ATMs on the island—and in French, Dutch, and English got the same response. When he tried using his Visa at the market, the checkout clerk shook her head and said, *"Marche pas,"* before handing it back to him with a shrug. His AmEx got the same reaction—this time with a pitying smile. Richard Stringer had twenty-two dollars and thirty-seven euros in his pocket and was well and truly fucked.

Head reeling, he drove aimlessly for a while. Then he pulled the scooter to the side of the road, pulled out his cell phone, and called his mother.

"Richie!" she answered, her voice a mixture of desperation and relief. Richard could picture her, sitting at the kitchen table of her Wantagh home in a flowered housecoat, a Pall Mall in one hand, cold coffee in the other, her overweight cat, Minxie, somewhere close. "My God! I've been so worried!"

"I'm all right, Ma," said Richard. "I just had to get away."

"Some man was here. From the district attorney's office," she said. "With a subpoena."

"It's Chip, Ma. The whole thing with the restaurant. They froze my accounts."

"That miserable cocksucker. That rat fucking whore. I told you, I met that slimy little fuck, you shouldn't get in business with him. Didn't I tell you?" said his mother.

"You told me . . ."

"One look at him and I said. I said it'll end in tears. Didn't I say that?"

"You were right, Ma . . ."

"What is it he said you did? The man who came, he was inferring you was some kind of thief—"

"Implying," corrected Richard. "He implied. You inferred—"

"Don't talk to me like you're so smart. You're the one hiding out like some criminal! I'm not the one being called a fugitive!" She started to cry. "Oh my God . . . I was so worried! Where are you? You should see what the papers are sayin' . . . I'm so embarrassed. I can barely show my face!"

"I'm safe," said Richard. "I'm somewhere nice and I'm safe. I just couldn't take it anymore. I had . . . I had to get away."

"But you didn't do anything! Why should you have to run away? Why should that man—why should he be saying these things in the papers? Why are you letting him?" his mother pleaded.

"Because he fucked me, Mom. Because he got me so jammed up there was nothing I could do. He was looking for a way to take the business and he found one, okay? You were right. He was a fucking backstabbing snake in the grass. He was looking for a way from day one"—at this, Richard's voice began to choke up—"and I gave him one. I gave him one, Mom."

"You gave him one . . . ," repeated his mother, considering what this meant.

Richard went on to explain the vagaries of "business expenses" and pressing personal requirements—and the ensuing differences of opinion as to their interpretation.

"I was gonna pay it back. It's not like I was stealing. I mean—what the fuck? Chip gets a company town car—takes him everywhere he wants to go, twenty-four/seven. He puts his girlfriends on the payroll—they don't even work there. He's got half the Russian whores in Manhattan on the company insurance plan—and I'm a thief?"

"So why didn't you say something? You should fight. When people hear—they'd understand."

"It doesn't work that way, Ma . . . ," said Richard wearily. "Chip's got a sixty-million-dollar-a-year restaurant group. He's got half the press in town eating for free in his places. He's got lawyers who could tear anybody to pieces. Doesn't matter if you win. It'll cost you half a million bucks for him to lose! Even if you win, you lose." Which was a simplification—but true enough.

"What do you want me to do?" asked his mother.

"I need money, Ma," said Richard, sheepishly. "I need you to sell the car." He'd only last year triumphantly presented his mother with a brand-new Volvo. "I need you to sell the car and send me the money."

There was silence on the other end. Then his mother said, "I can't."

"What do you mean, you can't? Ma—I'm screwed here! I got like twenty-two bucks in my pocket!"

"They took the car. Some animal from the jungle came and put a yellow piece a paper on the car. From the marshal's service. Says I can't sell the car. They're coming tomorrow to take it away." At this, the poor woman burst into heaving sobs.

She'd loved that car.

Three days later, Richard found a job—working breakfast shift at the Galley, a small place built out on the lagoon side of Simpson Bay, next to the Rusty Scupper. It was something of a step down, but he was grateful for the job—which paid in cash. With a Yankees cap pulled down low over his forehead—and an incipient beard, which he was hoping would grow quickly—he was reasonably confident he wouldn't be recognized. And who would have believed it anyway? From pan-seared foie gras with tamarind-apricot chutney to eggs Benedict in the space of a month. Double-breasted chef's coat of finest Egyptian sailcloth, his name embroidered in royal blue, to a short-sleeved cotton/poly snap-front.

Six A.M. and Richard melted down the previous night's butter in a wide metal crock at low heat. The smell of home fries, roasting in bacon fat in the oven, brought him back twenty years, when he'd been just starting out. He stacked up five flats of eggs next to his workspace in the tiny kitchen, mixed batter for French toast, sliced orange twists and strawberry fans for garnish and sat them, in small plastic containers, in a bed of ice from the ice machine they shared with the Rusty Scupper. He made batter for the pancakes from a prepared mix, refilled the fryer with Mel-Fry, pre-seared frozen sausages, and removed four sheet trays of cooked bacon from the pizza oven, drained the fat into a crock for the next day's potatoes, and piled the cooked strips on paper towels. He sliced Canadian bacon on the deli slicer and pre-separated English muffins for Benedicts. He checked that his grated cheese, sliced mushrooms, onions, and peppers for omelette fillings were topped off, filled a small crock with hot water for his spoons and spatulas, made sure the two nonstick omelette pans were wiped clean and close at hand, made hollandaise out of the melted, clarified butter, nicked a stack of clean bar towels from the Scupper's storage space, and stood smoking by the pass to the dining deck, satisfied that his kitchen was squared away.

There was a curious satisfaction in the moment. The pleasurable feeling of minor achievement that comes with a complete mise-en-place, those few magic moments when his neatly sliced, diced, and stacked ingredients would remain unmolested, his stovetop and container rims still clean, the kitchen quiet and orderly—before the customers came and ruined everything.

An hour later and he was nearly—but not quite—in the weeds. A six-top of fat-necked vacationers sitting at the picnic table by the water had all ordered omelettes—two of them whites only; his poaching water for Bennies had gotten scummy and impenetrable with albumen, and he was having difficulty finding his prey in there. By forgoing some hideous product called Gold'n Griddle for the more appetizing butter as frying medium, he'd sacrificed ease: His French toast and pancakes were sticking to the griddle—taking more time and attention from the two omelette pans than he could spare. And if he got one more order for fruit and yogurt with muesli (which required a run across the kitchen to the glass-front refrigerator) he was going to leap through the window and strangle the lone slack-ass waiter who had been in the shit before the first order was in. The Galley's owner, an amiable but clueless Dutch/Curaçaoan with ruddy cheeks and a gin-blossomed nose, was already into his fifth Heineken and no help at all with coffees or check-dropping. Half the customers didn't seem to be paying anyway. The tented dining area was cheerfully uncaring chaos. Nobody gave a fuck. The tourists—used to the snail-paced service and indifferent attitude at the hotels—were just happy to get fed at all. The locals were apparently long inured to incompetence and bad food. By island standards, the new breakfast cook—and the snappy new garnishes of orange slice and strawberry fan—were a major improvement.

By eleven o'clock, it was all over. The heat of the day was coming on at full strength and the Galley's ten tables were empty. Richard sat at the edge of the deck with his feet over the edge, drinking from a cold bottle of beer. All in all a good day—considering. He was proud of himself for not falling completely in the shit, for managing to impose order on the incoming stacks of ineptly written dupes, for getting the food out in reasonable time. He was proud that he could still work alone behind a busy stove—regardless of how completely off the radar he'd fallen. A busy kitchen was still a busy kitchen. Breakfast could be a bitch. He'd done well. He took another long tug on his beer, peeled off his shirt to catch the sun, and lit a cigarette.

"Are you the guy who keeps stealing my bar towels?" said the voice behind him.

It was the bartender from the Rusty Scupper, the blond one with the serious attitude. He'd seen her before—she'd be coming in as he was leaving a few times, but they'd never spoken. Her expression discouraged that.

"What?" Richard said, blinking into her silhouette, the sun blinding him.

"My bar towels," she said. "They keep disappearing. Since you've started here, I don't have any. The ones I find, there's like egg crusted on them. Those towels are supposed to be for me."

"Oh. Sorry," he found himself saying. "I . . . I . . . thought—"

"They're for the bar," she stressed.

"Yeah. Sorry. Bad habit." He clambered to his feet and repositioned himself, eyes out of the sun. "I go through those things like toilet paper."

"Yeah. I know," she said, impatient with him, clearly ready to end this conversation. "Look. You can use five a day, okay? I can spare that many. End of shift throw them in the hamper behind the bar so I don't have to come looking for them, all right?"

"Yeah. Thanks," said Richard.

And that was that.

The film career of Steven Lustgarden, prior to the as-yet-unreleased Inferno, consisted of one film, *Dealers of Death,* an actioner whose story—according to the short summary on Amazon.com—concerned "international terrorism, espionage, and romance." Harry recognized none of the film's stars in the limited credits given—except one: Producer/director Steven Lustgarden had also, apparently, found time to play the lead role of Nick Chase, ex–Special Forces officer and freelance agent for the "National Intelligence Agency." There were no customer reviews in the comment section and the thing looked, on the whole, like a typical direct-to-video cheapie, something you'd expect to see on Cinemax late at night starring Steven Seagal or Lorenzo Lamas. Harry ordered a copy from the site, moved over to Google, and punched in "Steven Lustgarden." Other than credit listings for *Dealers of Death,* there was nothing.

Harry sat at his kitchen table, his laptop in front of him, two untouched reporter's notebooks and a yellow legal pad to his right. Two sharpened pencils and two ballpoint pens taunted him from an empty coffee cup.

Exactly how did one go about "reporting"? And was that what was really expected? Harry had the definite impression that his employers were not looking for a "brash, satirical romp" through Saint Martin—or a "sharply drawn first-person account of a descent into the ninth circle of contemporary hell," as some had described his best-known work. He doubted either had even read the thing. He flashed back to his first book tour—a twenty-city marathon—when such a thing had still felt glamorous and fun. He'd been standing in a mall in a Houston suburb, just outside the bookstore where he was to give a reading. He'd been smoking a last cigarette before the event began, unwittingly standing just in front of the life-sized poster of himself reading *Look at Me* in the window. A big man had approached him, pig-eyed and sour expression on his face, tilted his head as he'd looked at the poster, then at Harry. He'd peered at Harry with a look of pure suspicion and said, "So . . . I guess you wrote some kinda book." Harry had nodded and smiled, ready to say more. But the man quickly moved on. It had not been a question. It had been an accusation. Sitting at his table, years later, blank pages in front of him, he knew now why he'd been hired. He wrote some kind of book. Once. He'd been hired for that. And because he was there.

The thing was, they didn't even have crab bee hoon *on the menu.*

This after Harry had rather lavishly described the "ethereal" qualities of its noodles, the home-brewed "spicy hellbroth" from which its sauce was based, the "unearthly richness" of the giant Sri Lankan crab's flesh. He'd even speculated out loud that the crab's particularly unctuous texture was due to its former residence at the mouth of the Ganges River, a beneficiary, Harry had hinted, of a steady tide of human corpses on which the tasty carrion-feeding crabs had no doubt feasted. He'd attributed this dish to a tiny, no-name *kopi tiam* in Geylang, a grimy, never-busy coffee shop like hundreds of others in Singapore, a culinary "find" on a side street which he'd unwisely identified by number.

Food and restaurant coverage not being his usual beat, the response to the ensuing article had taken him by surprise. It had taken some obsessive traveling food blogger exactly two days from publication to track down the establishment and announce to his world of fellow food nerds that the article in the *Times* travel section was "bullshit"—that the "magnificent" and "authentic" *kopi tiam* did not serve crab *bee hoon* and never had served crab *bee hoon*. That no "wizened, third-generation" chef proprietor was in evidence—and that Harry had very likely made the whole thing up while sucking back vodka tonics by the Ritz-Carlton pool.

Which was pretty close to the truth.

The story's variance with the facts became a story itself, spreading first to other food websites and then to *Romenesko*—a journalism blog—before quickly metastasizing into gossip sites and then print media. Within a week the hounds were in full pursuit, fact-checking every article Harry had ever done, walking the cat backward, looking for more examples of laziness, exaggeration, cut and paste, plagiarism, deceit, and outright invention. And there was plenty to find.

Fact was, Harry had long since been ruined by Asia.

In his many private moments of self-justification for the acts which led to the wrecking of his career, Harry told himself that it was the condiments of Asia which had sent him over the edge—across whatever line had made it impossible for him to return to life as it had been before. It was the expectations raised, he'd say to his drinking buddies at the Brix bar beneath the Hyatt, or at the Highlander or any of the faux Irish pubs along Boat Quay where expats hung out and were likely to listen to him. "The condiments," he'd splutter. The bright colors of the sliced red chilies, floating in dark soy. The shrimp pastes and fish sauces. The side dishes of crunchy sprouts and greens. That. *That* was what did it. The thing that had begun the change—made his old life back in the States inadequate, insufficient, flat . . . and just *not . . . enough*. It was the graceful *ao dai*s of the women passing by in Saigon, the smell of burning joss and *huac nam*, the seductive, fertile background smell of durian in Cambodia and Jakarta—and Geylang for that matter. It was the sugar syrup they offered with your iced tea. It was the gongs and wind chimes of Bali . . . the call to prayer of Malaysia and Java, the rip of a million one-stroke engines in Hanoi and Beijing—the sense of being always someplace strange and wonderful, where every day it was a challenge just to do the simplest things.

Which was all bullshit, of course—as even Harry knew.

Fact was, he'd fallen disastrously, foolishly, and humiliatingly in love—and had chucked his whole life in its cause. Like a lovesick teenager—too infatuated to do his homework or to mow the lawn— he'd simply pushed the business of writing into the background—an annoying distraction from the main business of being heartsick and miserable. Work was something that needed to be dispensed with, gotten out of the way as quickly and easily as possible—so that he could go back to his close and constant scrutiny of the permutations of his romantic situation. He needed to examine, chart, deconstruct, and reexamine exactly how fucked he was—and to track, minute to minute, the never-changing situation for any evidence of change. He would dedicate his life to this new calling. Naturally, work like this required alcohol.

There was an old beater parked in the Rex's tiny drive when Henry woke up and did his morning recon of the grounds: a beige Hyundai—Dutch plates—with typically island features: smashed headlight, corrosion around the wheel wells, mismatched hood, the front bumper just hanging on with baling wire and duct tape. Not a vehicle anyone of sinister intentions would drive. Henry returned to the main house, put on coffee, did a few laps in the pool while it brewed, then poured himself a cup and plopped himself down in one of the chaise longues. He recognized Trung's nearly silent footfalls on the crushed-shell drive, heard him turn the faucet to the garden hose and begin his work watering the flowers and bushes. The neighbor's dogs woke up around ten minutes later and began barking at the cock crowing on the next property over. The construction crew at the bottom of the mountain started up their power saws and cement mixer. Children laughed. A baby cried in the distance. There was no wind.

About nine o'clock, a slightly sheepish-looking Richard emerged from his room with a young woman Henry recognized from the incident in the parking lot a few nights earlier.

"We meet again," said Henry, who generally hated coincidences, but in this case felt strangely pleased.

Dara's eyes opened wide. "Wow! You. This place is yours?"

"Your humble innkeeper. Welcome."

"You know each other?" said Richard, not that surprised as everybody, it seemed, knew everyone else on Saint Martin.

"Yeah," said Dara. "We met . . . the other night."

"We gotta head in to work," said Richard, not sure what else to say.

"There's coffee if you like," volunteered Henry.

"No. That's cool."

The two hurried—somewhat faster than they'd originally intended—to the car.

Henry waited until they were gone and went into the house. Frances was sitting cross-legged on the bed, cleaning a disassembled Desert Eagle.

"Our guest got lucky last night," said Henry.

"Really?" said Frances, putting down barrel and brush and cracking a big smile. "Cute?"

"The girl from the other night. The parking lot at the Scupper? I gather she tends bar there."

"Bruce Wayne unmasked! How awkward for you."

"Not really," said Henry. "I'm happy for the kid."

"Oh?"

"She seems like a nice girl. A little lost. Like him."

"He made himself lost," said Frances, picking up the gun barrel again and running the brush down its length. "Though I take your point."

"I think it's nice. Young love. All that," said Henry, pushing over some gun parts to lie on the bed.

"Jesus, Henry," said Frances, "he picked up the bartender from work. It ain't Abelard and Heloise."

"Just the same," said Henry. "It's nice."

For the second time, Frances stopped what she was doing.

She looked her husband in the face. "You know? You worry me lately."

Mitch Felcher, deputy secretary of national security to the vice president, sat across from Mr. Mansoor and puffed contentedly on a Romeo y Julieta cigar. He wore a crisp, white dress shirt and the color of light blue tie popular in Washington that year. His jacket was neatly folded over the chair next to him. His legs were crossed, one over the other, revealing a dark blue stretch sock too short for his trousers—strip of pale, hairless flesh visible on one leg.

"So," said Mr. Mansoor. "Is he—or isn't he?"

"CIA?" Felcher smiled. "No. In plain terms? Bottom line? No."

Mansoor, looking annoyed, leaned forward and fiddled with his own cigar, as yet unlit. "Excuse me, please. But what does that mean exactly?"

"It means that Mr. Denard is not now and never was an officer of the Central Intelligence Agency—nor is he acting on their behalf."

"My friend says he is CIA."

"I'm guessing your friend is Israeli?"

"My friend is in a position to know such things. He recognized him."

"Listen, Mansoor, I'll give you what I've got. It took some doing as they're not exactly big fans across the river these days. But . . . my office still has some friends." Felcher took another puff of cigar, tapped the ash into a gold ashtray in the shape of a peacock, and smiled, pleased with himself.

"His 201 file has been filleted. Completely. But I managed to get the bare bones from our end—and a rather fuller picture from other services. DEA had some paper on him—mostly speculative . . . but provocative reading just the same. Military records up to a point—then nothing. All very sixties, seventies. In brief? Your friend is not entirely wrong. Henry Denard served in Vietnam, where his specialized talents were noticed. War hero. He became—for a while—a contract employee of the Company. A very brief while. What he did exactly during that time I have no idea—and there's no way to find out—but I can guess.

I guess as well that while his "employment" was terminated in '75, he might have been used in an off-the-books capacity from time to time. Again, no paper trail. In '78, a burn notice went out to all stations advising no further contact. There's nothing else as far as Langley. From our friends abroad—and from the same people I gather you've been hearing things from—I hear he was picked up by the French for the occasional odd job. Times being tough after the House and Senate hearings for his line of work. The DEA stuff I saw suggests he did not confine himself to working for government agencies. There are explicit allegations—unproven—that he worked for . . . what do you call them these days? Mafia? There was an incident on this island a while back. Involving that bunch. And while I can't make heads or tails of any of it, it seems that a lot of people were killed. And that Mr. Denard—while friendless at Langley—still has chums abroad. And that's pretty much all she wrote."

"So. What the fuck are we supposed to do? This man is poking his nose around my business. He is causing problems. I don't know why— but he . . . I think he is after me. In whose pay could he be? On whose behalf does he come after me?"

"Is there anyone you might have pissed off lately, Mansoor?" asked Felcher.

"Other than the usual?"

"Other than the enemies of freedom? A few former business partners who tell lies about me? Terrorists? Islamist fanatics?"

"No one!"

"Listen . . . this guy is a burned-out case. From what I see now, he's an old man, retired quietly on an island and running a fucking bed-and-breakfast. He doesn't come and go—hell, he hasn't been off the island in over ten years. His phone logs tell us nothing. He's been— best we can tell—nowhere, seen no one, and interested in nothing more political than the local animal shelter and oceanfront overdevelopment. Back in the day . . . when he was somebody to worry about, he wasn't the sort to let on he was interested in you before . . . you know . . . doing what he did. Which was shoot people. Are you sure you're not being a little . . . paranoid? Just 'cause somebody recognized him? I mean . . .

this guy . . . is he gonna come after you 'cause one of your hotels is blocking his ocean view?"

"I think we can both agree that any interest—at this time—from a man such as this is not . . . a good thing? Potentially . . . possibly dangerous?"

Felcher sighed and closed his eyes, holding a hand up. "I think I know where you're going with this," he said, "and I don't think we should take this conversation any farther. This sounds to me like a private matter. Outside the purview of our shared efforts, and—if what you tell me is everything I need to know—in no way connected to or connectable to what we . . . have legitimately tasked you to do in the cause of . . . blah blah blah. Your business is your business. How you handle that business is of no concern to my office—as long as I don't have to hear about it, read about it, or even ever remember this conversation. Which I've forgotten already."

*Henry looked over the old man's shoulder at the nurse pushing the wheel-*chair, a quizzical look on his face.

"Don't worry about her," said the old man, putting the oxygen mask on his lap, "she's secure. They chucked her out when the new bunch came in. Works for us now."

The nurse gave no indication she'd heard, her face a mask of indifference as she pushed the old man's chair closer to the table and sat down next to him, with a quick glance at the regulator on his oxygen tank.

"I'll have a gin tonic," said the old man. "She'll have water. *Gazeuse.*"

The waiter who'd hurried over to their table headed for the bar, leaving the three of them alone at the far end of the pool deck. Henry, who'd arrived a half hour early for the meet, took a sip of beer, looked around for any new or unnaturally interested hotel guests, and leaned forward.

"So. Mansoor. Who is he when he's at home?"

It was between lunch and dinner at La Samanna, a luxury hotel on a gated compound by Baie Longue on the French Side. The poolside café was empty. Only a few seniors napped in the late afternoon sun under large beach umbrellas. A lone octogenarian swimmer wearing skullcap and goggles did slow laps in the pool.

"A douchebag," said the old man. "The new breed of douchebag. Not even new breed. New breed back in Iran-contra. Back in favor I gather. Everything old is new again."

"Iranian," said Henry. "What flavor Iranian are we talking about?"

"What flavor do you like?" said the old man bitterly. "Ex-SAVAK, of course. A general. But aren't they all. Left around the same time as the shah. No surprise there. Set up shop in Cyprus—then Belgium, then Panama. Frequent trips to Washington. On the books? He's an arms dealer. Shipping. A few hotels. Lately casinos. What does he really do? Intelligence peddler.

"Israeli agent. French agent. American agent. Leader of the resistance. Deep thinker. The man who has his finger on the Pulse of the Islamic Mind. Liar. Fantasist. Thief. And all-around scumbag. The Agency wouldn't touch him with a ten-foot pole."

"So. He's nobody," said Henry.

"Did I say that? Oh, no. Mansoor is in very good order in the circles that matter these days—particularly in these . . . *trying* times." He paused to take a deep hit of air from his mask. "No, no, no . . . Mansoor is everybody's favorite Iranian over at NSC, the White House. Won't hear a bad word about him. Hear him tell it, he's got ten thousand disgruntled Iranians just itching to march into Tehran. Just waiting for the word from Mansoor to chuck those nasty mullahs out. Make the Middle East safe for Exxon. A font . . . a gusher of intel on the folks next door as well—has been for some time. Which helps explain why things are going so well."

"Oh," said Henry.

The drinks arrived. The old man took a big slosh of gin and tonic, spilling some on his chin.

The nurse reached over to wipe up but he brushed her hand away, annoyed. Henry ordered another beer.

"So. Are you saying this guy's untouchable?" said Henry.

The old man put his glass down on the table a little too hard. There was anger in his voice when he spoke.

"What I'm saying, Henry, is that I've been out for nearly twenty fucking years. And I don't give a flying fuck what happens to this cocksucker. I've got a nice little business, tells bankers and businessmen how to not get their heads sawn off when they go abroad. How to drive better than the bad guys. If the secretary's selling the secrets of their new deodorant to the competition. We provide the occasional bodyguard. Occasionally, if somebody gets kidnapped? We might know somebody who can help. And I can tell you this. Since these retards came in? I can't get through the front door of my office without tripping over Agency people looking for work. Anybody with three functioning neurons at the Company . . . at NSA . . . even Defense . . . is looking to 'join the private sector,' and fast. That's how bad things are. That's what kinda bright lights are running the show."

"No offense," said Henry, "but I never thought much of you guys from the get-go."

"Yeah . . . yeah . . . ," said the old man, draining the rest of his drink in one gulp and signaling for the waiter. "HONEY! Another, please. *Encore de* gin tonic!"

"And you're not really answering my question," said Henry.

"What *is* your question, Henry?" said the old man. "If you're asking me if this guy goes missing is anybody going to come looking? *No* fucking idea. Maybe. Probably. Personally? You stick a cannon up his ass and pull the fucking trigger you'll be doing the world a favor. And the Agency—if that's what you're asking—even in their current deplorable state, would probably feel the same way. The White House, on the other hand? Who knows?"

Henry mulled this over while the old man's second drink arrived. A few more gulps seemed to improve his mood.

"What's the matter, Henry? I mean . . . look at you. You got out. After the kinda career almost nobody gets out of. You've got money. How much money, I have no idea. We tried to figure it out once, back in the day—but even the smart boys over in DOI couldn't track it down. The French clammed up and stayed that way—and clearly you've still got some good friends over in those parts, given your . . . continuing . . . situation here. Your former employers from that Italian fraternal organization seem to have . . . well . . . passed. You married the—pardon my crudeness—best piece of ass I ever saw . . . So what the fuck are you doing? Why are you asking questions about the shiftiest, most unreliable and frankly dangerous piece of well-connected international whale shit on the planet? Retirement boring you? Tired of living? What the fuck you want to mess with this guy for? Who do I think would come looking if he gets shot in the brain? Nobody. Everybody. I don't know. You ask me? He's still working for the Iranians. And *not* the good kind. I think—you ask me—and nobody asks me—I think he takes his orders from the mullahs in return for . . . I don't know . . . and I think he's been very successfully feeding this crop of credulous fuckwits in the White House exactly what Tehran wants him to feed them. Which seems to suit everybody fine 'cause that's what they want to hear. Get it?"

Henry pondered this silently over his rapidly warming beer while the old man finished his drink and signaled to the nurse that he was ready to go.

"I like you, Henry," he said, pityingly. "When I ran you? You did good work. And when I didn't run you—even when you made a big fucking mess, it wasn't my mess, and I appreciate it. You stayed quiet and away . . . and we never had to worry about you writing your memoirs, make a buncha old farts worry about losing their country club memberships—or causing problems for the kids at school. Nobody remembers you. Nobody cares about you anymore. Which is exactly the way things should be. Keep it that way. I don't like mysterious coded messages on my answering machine. I don't like flying. You know you have to check your wheelchair? They haul your ass onto the plane in a very undignified fashion. I haven't been manhandled like that since . . . Camp Runamuck; the scoutmaster got fresh. So, please. This is the last I want to hear of this. This time was for old times' sake. Next time? You do what I think you're thinking of doing—which is fucking with an

important source in a matter of highest national security? It'll be somebody else who comes down here. I don't know who—or who they'll be
working for. But I'm guessing they won't be sentimental like me. Now
fuck off home, take a couple a pills, and bone your wife. While you still
can."

VIII

Television

I don't know that we can confidently say Tony had a "love/
hate relationship" with television and his work in the
medium, but I think we can confidently say that it was mixed.
Working with him up close on his several shows, I know for a fact
just how much work and pride went into the production. Even when
he was frustrated, he delivered at the highest level of effort and
conscientiousness, and the awards and ratings that followed that
work were deeply satisfying for him and his colleagues. The excerpts
here, including a series he called "Reasons You Don't Want to Be on
Television," to me seem mostly to establish that while it was television
that raised his profile to true international celebrity status, he knew
he was a writer first. Perhaps his ambivalence about television was
deep-seated, as we see in "The Typewriter or the Television," in
which he describes being torn between writing and the "debilitating"
yet "potent" allure of the flickering screen, in a manner that sounds
alarmingly similar to his relationship with heroin.

Reasons You Don't Want to Be on Television

Number One in a Series

An excerpt from *A Cook's Tour: In Search of the Perfect Meal*,
originally published by Bloomsbury in 2001.

"While you're in the area, let's see where foie gras is made," said the creative masterminds of Televisionland. "We're making a food show, remember? All this trip down memory lane is nice and all—but where's the food? C'mon! You like foie gras! You said so!"

"Sure," I said. Why not? Sounds educational. Sounds interesting. I do like foie gras—love it, even. The swollen fresh livers of goose or duck, lightly cooked *en terrine* in Sauternes, or seared in a pan with a few caramelized apples or quince, maybe a little balsamic reduction, a nice fat slice off a torchon with some toasted brioche. It's one of the best things on earth.

We were right near Gascony, the epicenter of foie gras territory, so sure . . . let's do it! Let's make riveting, informative television, and scarf up some free foie while we're at it. How could we go wrong?

The previous night, I'd sat for the cameras and choked down an absolutely gruesome, clumsily prepared, three-day-old dino-sized portion of *tête de veau*—a terrifying prospect in the best of circumstances. Usually (the way I make it anyway), it's a slice of rolled-up boneless calf's face, peeled right off the skull, tied up—with a stuffing of sweetbreads—and served boiled in a little broth with a few nicely shaped root vegetables and a slice of tongue. It's an acquired taste, or, more accurately, an acquired texture: the translucent fat, the blue calf's skin, and the bits of cheek and thymus gland take some getting past before you can actually enjoy the flavor. The squiggly, glistening, rubbery-looking gleet is—or should be—pretty tender and flavorful. Accompanied by a dab of *sauce ravigote*, or *gribiche*, the dish can be a triumphant celebration of old-school French country food, a conquering of one's fears and prejudices. It's one of my favorite things to cook. The few (mostly French) customers who order it at Les Halles, when I run it as a special, adore it. "Ahhh! *Tête de veau!*" they'll exclaim. "I haven't had this in years!" I make it well. And I have always gotten a very good reaction from those I inflict it on. I eat my own, now and again, and I like it.

This stuff was different. First of all, I had ignored all my own advice. Sucked into some romantic dream state of willful ignorance, I'd overlooked the fact that for three days I'd been passing by that specials board with TÊTE DE VEAU proudly written in block letters in white chalk. Meaning that it was, without question—particularly considering this was off-season Arcachon—the same unsold *tête* on day three as they'd been offering on day one. Business was hardly so good, and they'd certainly not been so swamped with orders for this (even in France) esoteric specialty, that they'd have been making a fresh batch every day. How many veal heads were they getting in the whole town per week? Or per month? Even worse, I'd broken another personal rule, ordering a not-too-popular, potentially nasty meat-and-offal special in a restaurant that proudly specialized in seafood—a very slow restaurant specializing in seafood.

My brother, who is usually pretty daring in his tastes these days when it comes to food, had ordered the sole. I'd ignored his good example. During the meal, he'd looked at me as if I were gnawing the flesh off a dead man's fingers and washing it down with urine. By any parameters, it had been disgusting; undercooked, tough, seemingly devoid of cheek, tasting of some dark refrigerator, and, worst of all, absolutely slathered with a thick, vile-tasting *sauce gribiche*—a kind of mayonnaise / tartar sauce variation made from cooked egg yolks. I'd swallowed as much as I could for the benefit of the cameras, trying to look cheerful about it, and, far too late, simply said, "Fuck it!" then tried sneaking away half my food into a napkin concealed below the table (as I had not wanted to offend the chef).

So the next morning, at eight o'clock, feeling none too fine from what had easily been the worst head I'd ever had, I found myself standing in a cold barn, watching my genial host, foie gras farmer and producer Monsieur Cabenass, jam a pipe from a long, long funnel down the throat of a less-than-thrilled-looking duck and begin grinding what looked like a food mill until a fistful of cornmeal disappeared down the creature's gullet. All this before breakfast.

The funnel seemed to reach the very bottom of the duck's stomach. Monsieur Cabenass would give the ducks a stroke, nudge them not too forcefully between his legs, tilt their heads back, and then give them the business. Seeing such a thing with an undigested wad of veal head still roiling in your stomach tends to inspire the gag reflex. Global Alan, the shooter who'd been standing next to Monsieur Cabenass, certainly seemed to think so: He suddenly turned an awful hue of green and went running for the door, disappearing for the rest of the morning.

Though not feeling too good myself, I endured a learned discourse and demonstration of the entire process of raising and feeding ducks and geese for foie gras. It was not as cruel as I'd imagined. The animal's feet are not nailed to a board, as some have said. They are not permanently rigged up to a feeding tube, endlessly pumped with food like some cartoon cat while they struggle and choke in vain. They are, in fact, fed twice a day—and each time a considerably lesser amount comparative to body weight than, say, a Denny's Grand Slam breakfast. Monsieur Cabenass did not strike me as a cruel or unfeeling man, he appeared to have genuine affection for his flock, and, more often than not, the ducks would actually come to him when it was funnel time. He'd simply reach out an arm and they'd come, no more reluctantly than a child having his nose wiped by his mother.

He held up one particularly plump duck and let me run my hand over its swollen belly, its warm, protruding liver. He was not yet "harvesting," though he showed me some photos—a display akin to a highway safety film, and about as appetizing. Ordinarily, I like blood and guts, but rarely do I like them first thing in the morning. And never with the sound of a violently heaving and coughing cameraman in the distance. By the time we retired next door to the little shop where the Cabenass clan sell their products, I was not feeling well at all.

For my tasting pleasure, Madame Cabenass had assembled a spread of *conserve de foie gras, mousse de foie gras, rillettes de canard*, and confit, along with some sliced croutons of baguette and a bottle of Sauternes. The Cabenass product was top-drawer—it regularly takes the prize at competitions and tastings—but I like my foie gras fresh: not canned, not preserved, not in mousse, and not "*en sous vide*." In fairness, it had been a while since harvesting, and the fresh stuff was long sold. Any other culinary adventurer would no doubt have been thrilled. And while I do like Sauternes with my foie, not at nine o'clock in the morning. Foie gras should be enjoyed at one's leisure, not choked down in front of a camera in the cold, cruel morning after a nauseating *tête de veau* experience the night before.

There was a lot of food there. Once again, fearful of giving offense to my very kind hosts, I scarfed everything in front of me, smiling and nodding appreciatively, conversing (with the help of my not noticeably disturbed brother) in my tortured French. The drive back to the Norman Bates Passion Pit in Arcachon was the longest journey in memory. Global Alan, in the car ahead, had his head hanging out the window at a crazy angle, periodically drooling as we passed through quaint country villages, by Crusade-era churches and lovely old farmhouses. Alberto, the assistant producer, at the wheel of the lead car, was soon feeling bad, as well. My brother drove our car, feeling fine, taking the turns way too hard for my taste—my stomach beginning to flip and gurgle like some incipient Krakatoa. I held on for dear life, hoping to make it back to the privacy of my hotel bathroom before erupting. I just made it.

Five hours of rib-cracking agony later, I was lying, near delirious, in my ugly hotel room, trash bucket to my right, alternately sweating and shivering under a pink poly-blend blanket, the television remote control out of reach on the floor. I'd just been considering the possibility—however slight—that I might someday feel better, when suddenly, the TV show I'd not really been watching ended and the highlights of what was next flickered across my screen. The true horror of France revealed itself in all its terrible quirkiness. *This has to be a joke*, I thought. *It can't be! It's a punch line, for Chrissakes! No!* But it was happening. A ninety-minute biography—with clips—of the glorious career of that great French hero, the recipient of France's highest honors, Jerry Lewis. The great man's entire oeuvre coming *tout de suite* to my television screen, promising to bombard my already-toxin-riddled brain with a lifetime of mugging, simpering, whining shtick.

It was too much. I tried, in my desperately weakened condition, to reach the remote control, felt the blood drain from my head and the bile rise in my throat, and had to fall back into the pillows, inspiring a whole new bout of dry heaves. I couldn't turn the damn TV off, couldn't change the station. Already, scenes from *The Disorderly Orderly* were searing their way into my softened brain, causing me whole new dimensions of pain and discomfort. I picked up the phone and called Matthew, the one member of our crew who was as yet unafflicted, and begged for him to come over and change the station.

"Is it *The Day the Clown Cried*?" he asked. "That's a vastly underrated classic, I'm told. Never seen by American audiences. Jerry plays a prisoner in a concentration camp. That Italian guy won an Oscar for the same idea! What was it? *Life Is Beautiful*? Jerry was *way* ahead of his time."

"Please, you gotta help me," I gasped. "I'm dying here. I can't take it. You don't do something fast, I'm a dead man. They're gonna have to fly Bobby Flay in to shoot the Cambodia stuff. You wanna see Bobby Flay in a sarong?"

Matthew thought about that. "I'll be right over."

He showed up a few moments later—with his camera running. He stood over my bed, getting a "white balance" off my bloodless face. He filmed and filmed, while the room tilted and whirled around me, panning back and forth between me, moaning in my sodden sheets, and Jerry, in *Cinderfella*. He shot close-ups as I heaved and pleaded. Cutaways of the out-of-reach remote control, slow pullbacks to reveal the source of my torment, the distance between me and the remote as I groaned, promised, threatened. Just before he finally reached down and tossed me the remote, allowing me to put a merciful end to a scene from Jerry's masterpiece, *The Nutty Professor*, I heard Matt say, "This is gold, baby! Comedy gold!"

Don't make television. Ever.

Never Flinch

An excerpt from *A Cook's Tour: In Search of the Perfect Meal*,
originally published by Bloomsbury in 2001.

At the far end of the barn, a low door was opened into a small straw-filled pen. A monstrously large, aggressive-looking pig waggled and snorted as the crowd peered in. When he was joined in the confined space by the three hired hands, none of them bearing food, he seemed to get the idea that nothing good was going to be happening any time soon, and he began scrambling and squealing at tremendous volume.

I was already unhappy with what I was seeing. *I'm causing this to happen*, I kept thinking. *This pig has been hand-fed for six months, fattened up, these murderous goons hired—for me.* Perhaps, had I said when José first suggested this blood feast, "Uh no . . . I don't think so. I don't think I'll be able to make it this time around," maybe the outcome for Porky here would have been different. Or would it have been? Why was I being so squeamish? This pig's number was up the second he was born. You can't milk a pig! Nobody's gonna keep him as a pet! This is Portugal, for Chrissakes! This porker was boots and bacon from birth.

Still, he was my pig. I was responsible. For a guy who'd spent twenty-eight years serving dead animals and sneering at vegetarians, I was having an unseemly amount of trouble getting with the program. I had to suck it up. I could do this. There was already plenty in my life to feel guilty about. This would be just one more thing.

It took four strong men, experts at this sort of thing, to restrain the pig, then drag and wrestle him up onto his side and onto a heavy wooden horse cart. It was not easy. With the weight of two men pinning him down and another holding his hind legs, the main man with the knife, gripping him by the head, leaned over and plunged the knife all the way into the beast's thorax, just above the heart. The pig went wild. The screaming penetrated the fillings in my teeth, echoed through the valley. With an incredible shower of fresh blood flying in every direction, the shrieking, squealing, struggling animal heaved himself off the cart, forcefully kicking one of his tormentors in the groin repeatedly. Spraying great gouts of blood, the pig fought mightily, four men desperately attempting to gain purchase on his kicking legs, bucking abdomen, and blood-smeared rearing head.

They finally managed to wrestle the poor beast back up onto the cart again, the guy with the mustache working the blade back and forth like a toilet plunger. The pig's movements slowed, but the rasping and wheezing, the loud breathing and gurgling, continued . . . and continued . . . the animal's chest rising and falling noisily . . . continued and continued . . . for what seemed like a fucking eternity.

I'll always remember, as one does in moments of extremis, the tiny, innocuous details—the blank expressions on the children's faces, the total lack of affect. They were farm kids who'd seen this before many times. They were used to the ebb and flow of life, its at-times-bloody passing. The look on their little faces could barely be described as interest. A passing bus or an ice cream truck would probably have evoked more reaction. I'll always remember the single dot of blood on the chief assassin's forehead. It remained there for the rest of the day, above a kindly rosy-cheeked face—an eerily incongruous detail on an otherwise-grandfatherly visage. Imagine your aunt Minnie bringing you a plate of cookies as you sat in front of the TV, a string of human molars strung casually, like pearls, around her neck. I'll remember the atmosphere of business as usual that hung over the whole process as the pig's chest rose and fell, his blood draining noisily into a metal pail. A woman cook came running for the blood, hurrying to the kitchen with it after it stopped draining freely, the death and killing just another chore. More women walked briskly to and from the kitchen with other receptacles. Food was being prepared. And I'll never forget the look of pride on José's face, as if he were saying, "This, this is where it all starts. Now you know. This is where food comes from."

He was right, of course. I'm sure that had I just seen a Thoroughbred being inseminated, a cow being milked, a steer being castrated, or a calf breeched, I would have been equally ill at ease. I was a pathetic city boy, all too comfortable with my ignorance of the facts, seeing for the first time what was usually handled on the Discovery Channel (just after I changed the channel).

The horse cart, with the now-dead pig aboard, was wheeled around the corner of the barn to a more open area, where his every surface was singed with long bundles of burning straw. All the animal's hair was burned off, a time-consuming process that left black streaks and patches on his thick skin. He was then scrubbed and washed with cork, scrubbed again, and then—another brief but horrible Kodak moment.

I was smoking and trying to look cool, as if what I'd just seen hadn't bothered me at all. The pig was positioned head away, hind legs and butt pointed in my direction. Global Alan, one of the shooters for the TV crew, was standing next to me, shooting from a crouch as the men washed and rinsed the pig's upper body. Suddenly and without warning, one of the men stepped around and, with the beast's nether regions regrettably all too apparent, plunged his bare hand up to the elbow in the pig's rectum, then removed it, holding a fistful of steaming pig shit—which he flung, unceremoniously, to the ground with a loud *splat* before repeating the process.

Global Alan, professional that he is, veteran of countless emergency-room documentaries, never flinched. He kept shooting. You never know, I guess, what footage you might just be required to have during the editing process, but I had a hard time imagining the "pig-fisting" scene on the Food Network.

Reasons You Don't Want to Be on Television

Number Three in a Series

An excerpt from *A Cook's Tour: In Search of the Perfect Meal*, originally published by Bloomsbury in 2001.

Goofy with hash, I was worthless as a television host. I sat at the table with Abdelfettah and his wife, Naomi, eating a spectacular meal of wonderful thick *harira*, a lamb and lentil soup traditionally served to break the fast of Ramadan. There were salads, brochettes, and an absolutely ethereal couscous served with a Fez-style tagine of chicken with raisins and preserved lemon. While we ate, Matthew and Global Alan stood directly across from the table, both their cameras pointed from the hip straight at us, expectantly. Under the unblinking gaze of their lenses, I felt unable to say a single enlightening or interesting thing. Repartee with my kind hosts was beyond me. I shrank from the artificiality of the whole enterprise, the forced nature of turning to Naomi, for instance, and casually inquiring, "So, Naomi, maybe you'd like to tell me about the entire history and culture of Morocco, its cuisine, and, uh, while you're at it, could you explain Islam for us? Oh, pass the chicken, please. Thanks." I was enjoying the food, competently snatching fingerfuls of couscous and tagine between the excellent bread. But I couldn't talk.

Next to me, Naomi radiated unease. Abdelfettah looked, understandably, bored. Matthew cleared his throat impatiently, waiting for me to elicit a few recipes, some anecdotes. I liked my hosts, but Naomi, while quick, articulate, and informative off camera, froze when the cameras turned on. I couldn't do it to her. In my state of neurotic, hash-heightened sensitivity, I just couldn't put her on the spot, knowing the cameras would then move in for a closer shot. I certainly had nothing to add to the world's knowledge of Morocco. I was just finding a few—a precious few—things out myself. Who am I, Dan Rather? I'm supposed to face the camera and spit out some facile summary of twelve hundred years of blood, sweat, colonial occupation, faith, custom, and ethnology—as it relates to a chicken stew—all in a nice 120-second sound bite? I'm not even Burt Wolf, I was thinking. And I hate Burt Wolf. Watching him in his flawlessly white chef's coat, with his little notepad, pretending to take notes for the camera while he leans inquisitively over some toiling chef in a French country kitchen, the voice-over giving the viewing audience the short course on the French Belle Epoque. I used to watch those shows and want to leap through the TV screen, grab a fistful of Burt's chef's jacket, and scream, "Take that off, you useless fuck! Give the man some room, for God's sake! Let him work!" But I was Burt now. Worse than Burt—because I had no idea, no clue, what I was doing. In my madcap lurch around the world, I'd done no preparation. I knew nothing. About anything.

I could have pointed out, I guess, that the raisins and preserved lemon were distinctive of Fez-style tagine. I'm sure I could have described for the viewing audience the difference between couscous made from scratch and couscous made out of the box, talked about the way it's cooked—in the *couscoussier*—steaming over the simmering sauce from the tagine. I'm sure, if I'd stitched a smile on my face and gathered my thoughts, and had the heart to do it, I could have gotten Abdelfettah to discuss his hopes for his city, his planned music center, his art, knowing full well that that would have ended up on the cutting room floor. As Matthew squirmed and fumed, the clock ticked, each second dropping like molten lead into the vast pool of unusable footage. What was I going to say? Abdelfettah had found something here, but however beautiful, however righteous and unpolluted by the outside world it was, I knew I could never live this way. Maybe, I mused, if the cameras were gone, maybe then I could give myself over more wholeheartedly to the experience. Maybe I'd be more able to relax. But I knew better. Even with the added conveniences of a high-speed modem, hot tub, bowling alley, regular deliveries of deli food and pizza from New York, and Krispy Kreme doughnuts, I couldn't live like this. Ever. My hosts seemed so content and at home within the context of their city, their family, and their beliefs that I felt it completely inappropriate to nudge them into the automatic dumb-down that comes with addressing a lens.

My last meal at Abdelfettah's was *pastilla*, the delicate, flaky pigeon pie, wrapped and baked in *warqa* with toasted almonds and eggs, then garnished with cinnamon. Like everything I'd eaten, it was wonderful. But I felt pulled in twelve directions at once. I was not happy with being the globe-trotting television shill. I had been cold and away from home for far too long. I yearned for the comfort and security of my own walled city, my kitchen back at Les Halles, a belief system I understood and could endorse without reservation. Sitting next to these two nice people and their kids, I felt like some news anchor with a pompadour, one of the many glassy-eyed media people whom I'd flogged my book with around the United States. "So, Anthony, tell us why we should *never* order fish on Monday." My spirits were dropping into a deep dark hole.

I was being "difficult." I was being "uncooperative." I really was. An executive producer was flown out from New York to soothe my troubled conscience, to help me feel better about the enterprise. She showed me some rough cuts of earlier shows, pointed out that I wasn't doing that badly, if I remembered to look at the camera, if I'd only stop cursing and smoking and slagging other Food Network chefs all the time, maybe look at a map before visiting a country. Three minutes into this motivational meeting, the producer mentioned that her boyfriend had been kidnapped by aliens. She said this casually, as if mentioning that she'd seen the Yankees/Red Sox game last week. He'd built an alien landing strip in their apartment, she added, her tone frighteningly devoid of irony or skepticism. I waited for the part where she'd say, "Oh yeah, I know. He's nuts. Barking mad. But I love the big lug." That would have been enough for me. I waited, but nothing came. She continued gently pointing out my many deficiencies while urging me on. I think I even jokingly inquired if her boyfriend had mentioned any rectal probing being involved, a suspiciously regular feature of rural alien abductions. She didn't laugh.

I was alone.

I spoke with Naomi before leaving, apologized for myself, thanked her for enduring the crew and the cameras, expressed regret that I was leaving her beautiful home, and this amazing city, without really having gained any knowledge or real insight. She handed me a small piece of paper on which she'd copied a verse by Longfellow: "And the night shall be filled with music, / And the cares, that infest the day, / Shall fold their tents, like the Arabs / And as silently steal away."

I hoped so. I truly did. I had very high hopes for the desert. I needed it.

Panels

A comic panel written and illustrated by Tony from an unpublished zine he cofounded called *ZILTZ*, date unknown.

The Typewriter or the Television

An unpublished piece written in 1976 when Tony was twenty years old.

The typewriter or the television? Today, right now, I can either toil over the keys in pursuit of some saleable prose or I can wander over to the idiot box, flip on *Match Game*, and temporarily silence the noises my brain has been making. Just lie back on my bed, light up a joint, and stare at those over-the-hill mannequins in TV land going through the predictable motions. Never fails to cease the annoying thought process which can be so disturbing. Lost indefinitely in this distraction which is no longer what you would call a minor distraction; rather, a lifestyle. And it's so easy lying there forgetting the troubles of the real world, forgetting my lack of money, direction, and nicely calming down those frayed nerve ends. Slowing down the mental machine while I get a video tan. I could stay here forever. And I might. I don't even care what I watch anymore though I prefer something that's either really good or really bad. This makes me react and takes care of my reaction quota for the day. My palms sweat during the final heats of *The $20,000 Pyramid*, my pulse rises dramatically as I wait to see what today's Blockbuster Movie will be, and my sense of appreciation of art is teased slightly by the twisted postcard California neorealism of *The Brady Bunch*. By the time *Mary Hartman* rolls around I'm catatonic and blissful, ready to doze off to the late movie, and what a day. The grim specter of REALITY has not once reared its ugly head. When I think of all the money spent on drugs in my college years . . . When television is so much more debilitating, so much more potent, and it costs only pennies a day!! Maybe I'll kick the habit. Maybe tonight I'll sneak up on the vile tube and hurl it out the window, severing forever the umbilical cord that connects it to my stomach. But the consequences of such an action! By tomorrow I'll be pacing around the room like an animal in a cage. My brain will be racing feverishly, sweat pouring out from under my arms. I'll be running up and down to the refrigerator opening the door repeatedly hoping to find satisfaction. Scratching, biting my nails. Chain-smoking cigarettes and marijuana and wildly bemoaning my desperate condition, my unfortunate place in this hideous world, my most horrible dilemma, which is this:

My horrible condition is that I am a spoiled twenty-year-old college dropout with absolutely no idea of what I want to do. No longer supported by my parents, I wonder what and how. How to attain the wealth and material nirvana promised by my video-influenced youth. Somewhat burnt out by my years of consuming illegal drugs and jaded by an accelerated and accelerating lifestyle, I seek success as a writer. I labored under the misassumption for many years that my life was a work of art and that the world owed me a living. How, after two years out of college working as a cook, I turn to the publishing empire to give me a sign. From this twenty-minute product which I whipped out between *I Love Lucy* and *The Dick Van Dyke Show* I hope you can find some promise. If you are interested in any aspects of my off-key life, notably such ideas as: My Criminal Life at Vassar College, Provincetown Atrocities in the Kitchen, Tales of a Bicycle Messenger, or a myriad of other sordid tales dealing with the leftovers of the late sixties . . . drop me a line.

IX

The Restaurant

Where else could we end? Between food and world travel, the restaurant supplied Tony with the perfect middle ground for his writing talents: a stage-sized location where the outside world (in the form of diners and fads) combined with the inner world of the kitchen and its overworked cooks, joined together in a highly formalized dance, overseen by waiters, back waiters, and staff of all kinds. Did he love restaurants? Some, of course. But more than anything, I think it's where he felt most like he was in the center of a corner of humanity where he could look around and see that everything made some kind of sense. It's why he never merely wrote about the end result—the plates, the diners, the menus—but always about the kitchen as a system. A system that depended as much on the deep pockets of those diners as it did on the person who carried the urchins in through the back door, and then left again, to deliver more, and keep the system going.

This Was His Favorite Part of the Day

An excerpt from *Bone in the Throat*, originally published by Villard Books in 1995.

Tommy sipped his coffee in the empty kitchen. The night porters, Big Mohammed and Little Mohammed, had finished their work, he could hear them arguing in Arabic in the changing room. Otherwise, the kitchen was quiet.

This was his favorite part of the day. The cutting boards were rubbed clean and white; the stainless steel worktables and reach-in refrigerators gleamed. There were no other cooks due in until two thirty. A dishwasher would be in at noon to help him with the scut work and to catch up on the pots. Tommy would be undisturbed until then, free to cook at his own pace and in his own way. He went over the prep list taped to the reach-in door by the sauté station.

"TOMMY!" it said, in the chef's jagged block lettering. (The chef loved exclamation points.)

Veal stock not reduced enuf. FIX! Also: Roast Chix . . .
25# culls coming . . . Cook and shuck for pasta Tonite.
Need Sauce for Sword . . Any Ideas??
Also: Gaufrette Potatoes and Pommes Anna (sorry)

Tommy hated to make pommes Anna.

There was more:

Fill bottles with redpepper vin. and Cilantro Sauce.
Cut Fish—One Sword Puppy (make sure it's a puppy!) and one
    Salmon coming in. Sword cut 7 oz. Salmon usual.
SOUP!! 86 the old shit. Use squid from walk-in, any odds and
    ends in reach-ins. DO NOT USE SCALLOPS!
Mushie Sauce: Use portobellos, black trumpets, dried cepes.
    Step on it with regular mushies. Use demi after reduced.
    And PORT WINE!
Use any scraggly veg trimmings in veal stock . . .
Have DW pick over mussels when he comes in. Also shellfish.
One Pine Island Oyster and One Cherry coming in . . .
There's Veg cut already in walk-in. DO NOT MAKE!
When Ricky and Mel come in, have them clean out boxes,
    throw out Mystery Items.
I'll be in around 2:30.

Tommy looked at the last line. When the chef said he'd be in around two thirty, he meant maybe three thirty, or even four o'clock. "Mel" was the name given to any new inexperienced cook. It was taken from the Italian term *"malacarne,"* meaning "bad meat." The latest Mel was the new garde-manger, real name Ted, or something like that. Like all the other Mels, he was an extern from the Culinary Institute, spending a semester working in the real world for school credit. He was having what was sarcastically referred to as a Learning Experience, meaning he worked his ass off and the restaurant got some motivated labor dirt cheap. He'd shown up, like the others, freshly scrubbed, in his own new uniform, with the standard-issue black-vinyl knife roll-up under one arm and a copy of *The Professional Chef* under the other. But he worked like a Trojan, didn't bitch if somebody asked him to peel garlic or make hollandaise in bulk for brunch. Tommy considered asking Mel to shuck the lobsters but thought better of it.

The bell at the delivery entrance rang. Tommy walked down the narrow hallway and pushed open the heavy trapdoors to the street. It was the fish delivery. A short, unshaven driver wearing leather truss, work gloves, and rubber boots came in with a long cardboard box heaped with crushed ice. He dropped the box at Tommy's feet, a thin stream of water from the melting ice running out onto the floor. Tommy reached inside, first removing a wheel of swordfish, then an Atlantic salmon. He weighed both on the digital scale atop an ancient chest freezer, gave the salmon a perfunctory press with his fingers, checked the eyes and gills, and signed the invoice. He gave the driver the white copy and spiked the yellow on a nail on the wall next to a stack of shell-fish tags. Then he returned to the kitchen.

Tommy could hear Barry, the manager, in the upstairs waiter station steaming milk for cappuccino. He finished his coffee and shouted "SALAAM" to the two Mohammeds as they passed through the kitchen on their way out the door. He filled up the steam table with water and, his knees resting on the clean rubber floor mats behind the line, reached under and lit the burners. He switched on the range hoods and fired up the Frialator, the ovens, and one side of the grill. In a nonstick pan, he sautéed some chorizo and chopped scallions left over from the night before, then quickly beat in some eggs with a rub-ber spatula. He added a little fresh cracked pepper with a few turns of a steel peppermill, slid the eggs onto a salad plate, and, standing there at his workstation, ate quickly. When he was finished, he put the empty plate and the fork down on the prewash area of the dishwasher.

Moving on to his mise-en-place, he collected the pots he would need from the overhead racks and neatly arranged the house knives next to his cutting board. He filled a stainless-steel crock with hot water and dropped a handful of male and female spoons, a pair of tongs, and a spatula in it. He got a stack of clean kitchen towels from the changing room and laid them down on a shelf over his workstation.

He went in the walk-in and hauled out a tall plastic bucket filled with veal stock, then poured the stock into a double-weight Crusader Ware stockpot and started reducing it. He then went back to the walk-in and returned with a buspan of wriggling, one-clawed lobsters. He poured two quarts of white wine into a stockpot and added some bay leaves, some peppercorns, a bit of crushed red pepper, whole cloves, a sprig of raggedy fresh thyme. He found some vegetable trimmings in the sauté box, a drying half-onion, a few wrinkled carrots, some limp celery. He threw them in along with some leek tops and a head of garlic. He put a sheet pan over the pot and waited for the wine to cook down a bit and suck up the flavor from the spices and vegetables. He went back to the walk-in, wondering how much mileage he put in every day on his trips back and forth, then returned with a bucket of fish fumet and a bucket of peeled potatoes. The food-splattered radio cassette player was blaring an old Modern Lovers tune, "She Cracked," and Tommy bounced around in time to the music unembarrassed, as he was alone in the kitchen. "She cracked. I'm sad. But I won't." He sang along. He rubbed a few red peppers with olive oil and put them on the grill for red pepper vinaigrette.

Tommy turned back to the frantic lobsters. He emptied them out of the buspan and into the boiling white wine. "Sorry, guys," he said. "It'll all be over in a minute." He listened to them scraping their claws against the metal. After a few moments, the noise died down.

When the lobsters were cooked, he poured them into a colander in the pot sink and ran cold water over them.

He reduced some port wine for the mushroom sauce. Reaching into a cold bucket of shallots, he found there were dangerously few. His hand still wet, he started a night prep list on a piece of notepaper from the chef's clipboard, writing "Chop Shallots!!" He put some dried cepes in warm water to soak and, with a paring knife, trimmed away the gills and stems from a few handfuls of portobellos.

The old surf instrumental "Pipeline" by the Chantays came on the radio. Tommy smiled and decided it was an auspicious moment to begin the soup. He found his favorite pot in a corner under a worktable where he had hidden it the day before and put it on the range. He poured some olive oil into the pot, minced some garlic, and simmered it until transparent. He wanted to play air guitar along with the music, since no one was looking, but instead peeled the onions and chopped them into a fine dice. Remembering the red peppers on the grill, he spun around, grabbed them with the tongs, put them in a stainless-steel bowl, and covered them with plastic wrap to free the skin. He tossed the diced onions into the soup pot with the garlic and sprinkled in some thyme and some bay leaves. He seeded some red and green peppers, cut them into a medium dice, and added them to the pot. He poured a healthy hit of ground cumin in after. Soon the kitchen began to fill with the smell of garlic, onions, and cumin. He added the cut squid, chasing it around with a large steel paddle. He rooted around in the grill man's reach-in for a few minutes, coming up with some swordfish trimmings, a little lobster meat, and, wonder of wonders, a full crock of cherrystone clams, already shucked. He strained the clam juice in with the fish fumet that was already heating on a back burner and added the clams to the squid, along with the lobster and swordfish. When the fumet was hot, he poured it into the soup pot, added two cans of crushed tomato, a couple spoons of paste, and a gallon of red wine. He cut ten of the peeled potatoes into large dice and threw them in the pot, too. He finished the whole dark, wonderful mess with some crushed red pepper and a little Tabasco sauce and left the pot to simmer.

He lit a cigarette and felt around under the station for the chef's ashtray from the night before. He couldn't find it at first. He looked through the tilted speed rack, pushing aside the greasy bottles of Tabasco, olive oil, white wine, brandy, Worcestershire, rice wine vinegar, and lemon juice. He finally found the ashtray on an overhead shelf, tucked behind the chef's $450 custom-made Japanese knife in its rosewood scabbard. There was a small glassine envelope peeking out of the scabbard, and Tommy slipped it carefully out from next to the knife. The envelope had a colorful, rubber-stamped image of a toilet on it. He quickly rolled up a bill from his wallet, peeled back the tape on the envelope, and after a quick look in both directions, took a short, measured sniff of the bitter contents.

"Oooohhhh, baby," he said out loud.

As always, the chef showed up late: around three thirty. He went straight for his knife, disappearing back into the changing room for a good five minutes before he reappeared in his whites, looking noticeably refreshed. Tommy didn't say anything. The chef tuned the radio to a classic-rock station, lit a cigarette, and drifted upstairs to the bar, returning a few moments later with a shaker glass of Coca-Cola and ice.

"What's the soup?" he asked Tommy.

"Check it out," said Tommy, proudly, "Portugee Seafood Chowder."

The chef lifted the lid off the still-simmering chowder. "That smells fuckin' great. If I think I can hold anything down, I might have a bowl for breakfast. You get the lobster squared away?"

Tommy nodded. "Yeah. And I hated every minute of it. We should get the dishwasher to do that shit."

"The dishwasher'll throw half the fuckin' lobster meat in the trash. They don't get the knuckles. And he gets upset. He's not too crazy about getting involved with shellfish. I think it's a religious thing."

"I got a fish sauce together," said Tommy. "Mustard tarragon vinaigrette with crispy leek garnish. That okay?"

"Yeah, that's fine," said the chef. "An oldie but goodie."

"I haven't cut the leeks yet," said Tommy. "I wondered if you'd let me use your knife. The house knives just mash them to shit."

"Looks like you were at my knife already. Half the fuckin' bag is gone," said the chef.

"It was half empty when I found it. I just did a tiny poke," said Tommy.

"That was my wake-up, man," whispered the chef. "You don't need the shit. I need it."

"Sorry I tapped it," said Tommy. "Spur of the moment. Mea culpa. Sorry."

"Now I gotta go east," said the chef, jerking his head to the east. "They got nothing uptown, it's too hot in the forties. I was gonna go over later, but now I gotta go sooner. I don't want to turn into a fuckin' pumpkin halfway through dinner."

"Really, I didn't do a lot," said Tommy.

"Now I gotta go over there," said the chef.

"Why don't you just send a busboy later. Hector's coming in in an hour," suggested Tommy.

"I thought about that," said the chef. "I don't like doing that anymore. It's not too cool. What if he gets popped? They'll probably deport the guy. On top a that, you know Hector. I sent him over there a few times, now he thinks he can shake me down for a steak dinner for his shift meal. Can't you see Hector, the fuckin' busboy, sittin' up there, munchin' on a twenty-ounce sirloin and all the waitrons and the manager are trying to choke down their shepherd's pie? Doesn't look too good. On top of that, the son of a bitch eats his steak well-done. I got principles."

"So you're going over now?" asked Tommy.

"Yeah, can you set up my station?"

"Yeah, sure." He hesitated. "Well, since you're going, can you pick me up a couple?"

"You have any money?" asked the chef.

"Enough for two bags."

"You got twenty extra till next week? I'm short."

"All right," said Tommy, reaching for his wallet. "But I gotta have it back."

"No problem," said the chef. Though Tommy knew it would be a problem.

"So, you're gonna get four?" Tommy asked.

"Two for me, two for you," said the chef. He turned and headed for the door.

Don't Eat Before Reading This

Originally published in *The New Yorker* in 1999.

ood food, good eating, is all about blood and organs, cruelty and decay. It's about sodium-loaded pork fat, stinky triple-cream cheeses, the tender thymus glands and distended livers of young animals. It's about danger—risking the dark, bacterial forces of beef, chicken, cheese, and shellfish. Your first two hundred and seven Wellfleet oysters may transport you to a state of rapture, but your two hundred and eighth may send you to bed with the sweats, chills, and vomits.

Gastronomy is the science of pain. Professional cooks belong to a secret society whose ancient rituals derive from the principles of stoicism in the face of humiliation, injury, fatigue, and the threat of illness. The members of a tight, well-greased kitchen staff are a lot like a submarine crew. Confined for most of their waking hours in hot, airless spaces, and ruled by despotic leaders, they often acquire the characteristics of the poor saps who were press-ganged into the royal navies of Napoleonic times—superstition, a contempt for outsiders, and a loyalty to no flag but their own.

A good deal has changed since Orwell's memoir of the months he spent as a dishwasher in *Down and Out in Paris and London*. Gas ranges and exhaust fans have gone a long way toward increasing the lifespan of the working culinarian. Nowadays, most aspiring cooks come into the business because they want to: they have chosen this life, studied for it. Today's top chefs are like star athletes. They bounce from kitchen to kitchen—free agents in search of more money, more acclaim.

I've been a chef in New York for more than ten years, and, for the decade before that, a dishwasher, a prep drone, a line cook, and a sous-chef. I came into the business when cooks still smoked on the line and wore headbands. A few years ago, I wasn't surprised to hear rumors of a study of the nation's prison population which reportedly found that the leading civilian occupation among inmates before they were put behind bars was "cook." As most of us in the restaurant business know, there is a powerful strain of criminality in the industry, ranging from the dope-dealing busboy with beeper and cell phone to the restaurant owner who has two sets of accounting books. In fact, it was the unsavory side of professional cooking that attracted me to it in the first place. In the early seventies, I dropped out of college and transferred to the Culinary Institute of America. I wanted it all: the cuts and burns on hands and wrists, the ghoulish kitchen humor, the free food, the pilfered booze, the camaraderie that flourished within rigid order and nerve-shattering chaos. I would climb the chain of command from *malacarne* (meaning "bad meat," or "new guy") to chefdom—doing whatever it took until I ran my own kitchen and had my own crew of cutthroats, the culinary equivalent of the Wild Bunch.

A year ago, my latest, doomed mission—a high-profile restaurant in the Times Square area—went out of business. The meat, fish, and produce purveyors got the news that they were going to take it in the neck for yet another ill-conceived enterprise. When customers called for reservations, they were informed by a prerecorded announcement that our doors had closed. Fresh from that experience, I began thinking about becoming a traitor to my profession.

Say it's a quiet Monday night, and you've just checked your coat in that swanky Art Deco update in the Flatiron District, and you're looking to tuck into a thick slab of pepper-crusted yellowfin tuna or a twenty-ounce cut of certified Black Angus beef, well-done—what are you in for?

The fish specialty is reasonably priced, and the place got two stars in the *Times*. Why not go for it? If you like four-day-old fish, be my guest. Here's how things usually work. The chef orders his seafood for the weekend on Thursday night. It arrives on Friday morning. He's hoping to sell the bulk of it on Friday and Saturday nights, when he knows that the restaurant will be busy, and he'd like to run out of the last few orders by Sunday evening. Many fish purveyors don't deliver on Saturday, so the chances are that the Monday-night tuna you want has been kicking around in the kitchen since Friday morning, under God knows what conditions. When a kitchen is in full swing, proper refrigeration is almost nonexistent, what with the many openings of the refrigerator door as the cooks rummage frantically during the rush, mingling your tuna with the chicken, the lamb, or the beef. Even if the chef has ordered just the right amount of tuna for the weekend, and has had to reorder it for a Monday delivery, the only safeguard against the seafood supplier's off-loading junk is the presence of a vigilant chef who can make sure that the delivery is fresh from *Sunday* night's market.

Generally speaking, the good stuff comes in on Tuesday: The seafood is fresh, the supply of prepared food is new, and the chef, presumably, is relaxed after his day off. (Most chefs don't work on Monday.) Chefs prefer to cook for weekday customers rather than for weekenders, and they like to start the new week with their most creative dishes. In New York, locals dine during the week. Weekends are considered amateur nights—for tourists, rubes, and the well-done-ordering pre-theater hordes. The fish may be just as fresh on Friday, but it's on Tuesday that you've got the goodwill of the kitchen on your side.

People who order their meat well-done perform a valuable service for those of us in the business who are cost-conscious: They pay for the privilege of eating our garbage. In many kitchens, there's a time-honored practice called "save for well-done." When one of the cooks finds a particularly unlovely piece of steak—tough, riddled with nerve and connective tissue, off the hip end of the loin, and maybe a little stinky from age—he'll dangle it in the air and say, "Hey, Chef, whaddya want me to do with *this*?" Now, the chef has three options. He can tell the cook to throw the offending item into the trash, but that means a total loss, and in the restaurant business every item of cut, fabricated, or prepared food should earn at least three times the amount it originally cost if the chef is to make his correct food-cost percentage. Or he can decide to serve that steak to "the family"—that is, the floor staff—though that, economically, is the same as throwing it out. But no. What he's going to do is repeat the mantra of cost-conscious chefs everywhere: "Save for well-done." The way he figures it, the philistine who orders his food well-done is not likely to notice the difference between food and flotsam.

Then there are the People Who Brunch. The "B" word is dreaded by all dedicated cooks. We hate the smell and spatter of omelettes. We despise hollandaise, home fries, those pathetic fruit garnishes, and all the other cliché accompaniments designed to induce a credulous public into paying $12.95 for two eggs. Nothing demoralizes an aspiring Escoffier faster than requiring him to cook egg-white omelettes or eggs over easy with bacon. You can dress brunch up with all the focaccia, smoked salmon, and caviar in the world, but it's still breakfast.

Even more despised than the Brunch People are the vegetarians. Serious cooks regard these members of the dining public—and their Hezbollah-like splinter faction, the vegans—as enemies of everything that's good and decent in the human spirit. To live life without veal or chicken stock, fish cheeks, sausages, cheese, or organ meats is treasonous.

Like most other chefs I know, I'm amused when I hear people object to pork on nonreligious grounds. "Swine are filthy animals," they say. These people have obviously never visited a poultry farm. Chicken—America's favorite food—goes bad quickly; handled carelessly, it infects other foods with salmonella; and it bores the hell out of chefs. It occupies its ubiquitous place on menus as an option for customers who can't decide what they want to eat. Most chefs believe that supermarket chickens in this country are slimy and tasteless compared with European varieties. Pork, on the other hand, is cool. Farmers stopped feeding garbage to pigs decades ago, and even if you eat pork rare, you're more likely to win the lotto than to contract trichinosis. Pork tastes different, depending on what you do with it, but chicken always tastes like chicken.

Another much maligned food these days is butter. In the world of chefs, however, butter is in *everything*. Even non-French restaurants—the Northern Italian; the new American; the ones where the chef brags about how he's "getting away from butter and cream"—throw butter around like crazy. In almost every restaurant worth patronizing, sauces are enriched with mellowing, emulsifying butter. Pastas are tightened with it. Meat and fish are seared with a mixture of butter and oil. Shallots and chicken are caramelized with butter. It's the first and last thing in almost every pan: The final hit is called *"monter au beurre."* In a good restaurant, what this all adds up to is that you could be putting away almost a stick of butter with every meal.

If you are one of those people who cringe at the thought of strangers fondling your food, you shouldn't go out to eat. As the author and former chef Nicolas Freeling notes in his definitive book *The Kitchen*, the better the restaurant, the more your food has been prodded, poked, handled, and tasted. By the time a three-star crew has finished carving and arranging your saddle of monkfish with dried cherries and wild-herb-infused *nage* into a Parthenon or a Space Needle, it's had dozens of sweaty fingers all over it. Gloves? You'll find a box of surgical gloves—in my kitchen we call them "anal-research gloves"—over every station on the line, for the benefit of the health inspectors, but does anyone actually use them? Yes, a cook will slip a pair on every now and then, especially when he's handling something with a lingering odor, like salmon. But during the hours-of-service, gloves are clumsy and dangerous. When you're using your hands constantly, latex will make you drop things, which is the last thing you want to do.

Finding a hair in your food will make anyone gag. But just about the only place you'll see anyone in the kitchen wearing a hat or a hair-net is Blimpie. For most chefs, wearing anything on their head, especially one of those picturesque paper toques—they're often referred to as "coffee filters"—is a nuisance: They dissolve when you sweat, bump into range hoods, burst into flame.

The fact is that most good kitchens are far less septic than your kitchen at home. I run a scrupulously clean, orderly restaurant kitchen, where food is rotated and handled and stored very conscientiously. But if the city's Department of Health or the EPA decided to enforce every aspect of its codes, most of us would be out on the street. Recently, there was a news report about the practice of recycling bread. By means of a hidden camera in a restaurant, the reporter was horrified to see returned bread being sent right back out to the floor. This, to me, wasn't news: The reuse of bread has been an open secret—and a fairly standard practice—in the industry for years. It makes more sense to worry about what happens to the leftover table butter—many restaurants recycle it for hollandaise.

What do I like to eat after hours? Strange things. Oysters are my favorite, especially at three in the morning, in the company of my crew. Focaccia pizza with *robiola* cheese and white truffle oil is good, especially at Le Madri on a summer afternoon in the outdoor patio. Frozen vodka at Siberia Bar is also good, particularly if a cook from one of the big hotels shows up with beluga. At Indigo, on Tenth Street, I love the mushroom strudel and the daube of beef. At my own place, I love a spicy *boudin noir* that squirts blood in your mouth; the braised fennel the way my sous-chef makes it; scraps from duck confit; and fresh cockles steamed with greasy Portuguese sausage.

I love the sheer weirdness of the kitchen life: the dreamers, the crackpots, the refugees, and the sociopaths with whom I continue to work; the ever-present smells of roasting bones, searing fish, and simmering liquids; the noise and clatter, the hiss and spray, the flames, the smoke, and the steam. Admittedly, it's a life that grinds you down. Most of us who live and operate in the culinary underworld are in some fundamental way dysfunctional. We've all chosen to turn our backs on the nine-to-five, on ever having a Friday or Saturday night off, on ever having a normal relationship with a non-cook.

Being a chef is a lot like being an air-traffic controller: You are constantly dealing with the threat of disaster. You've got to be Mom and Dad, drill sergeant, detective, psychiatrist, and priest to a crew of opportunistic, mercenary hooligans, whom you must protect from the nefarious and often foolish strategies of owners. Year after year, cooks contend with bouncing paychecks, irate purveyors, desperate owners looking for the masterstroke that will cure their restaurant's ills: Live Cabaret! Free Shrimp! New Orleans Brunch!

In America, the professional kitchen is the last refuge of the misfit. It's a place for people with bad pasts to find a new family. It's a haven for foreigners—Ecuadorians, Mexicans, Chinese, Senegalese, Egyptians, Poles. In New York, the main linguistic spice is Spanish. "*Hey, maricón! Chupa mis huevos*" means, roughly, "How are you, valued comrade? I hope all is well." And you hear "*Hey, baboso!* Put some more brown jizz on the fire and check your meez before the sous comes back there and fucks you in the *culo*!" which means "Please reduce some additional demi-glace, brother, and reexamine your mise-en-place, because the sous-chef is concerned about your state of readiness."

Since we work in close quarters, and so many blunt and sharp objects are at hand, you'd think that cooks would kill one another with regularity. I've seen guys duking it out in the waiter station over who gets a table for six. I've seen a chef clamp his teeth on a waiter's nose. And I've seen plates thrown—I've even thrown a few myself—but I've never heard of one cook jamming a boning knife into another cook's rib cage or braining him with a meat mallet. Line cooking, done well, is a dance—a high-speed, Balanchine collaboration.

I used to be a terror toward my floor staff, particularly in the final months of my last restaurant. But not anymore. Recently, my career has taken an eerily appropriate turn: These days, I'm the chef de cuisine of a much loved, old-school French brasserie/bistro where the customers eat their meat rare, vegetarians are scarce, and every part of the animal—hooves, snout, cheeks, skin, and organs—is avidly and appreciatively prepared and consumed. Cassoulet, pigs' feet, tripe, and charcuterie sell like crazy. We thicken many sauces with foie gras and pork blood, and proudly hurl around spoonfuls of duck fat and butter, and thick hunks of country bacon. I made a traditional French pot-au-feu a few weeks ago, and some of my French colleagues—hardened veterans of the business all—came into my kitchen to watch the first order go out. As they gazed upon the intimidating heap of short ribs, oxtail, beef shoulder, cabbage, turnips, carrots, and potatoes, the expressions on their faces were those of religious supplicants. I have come home.

Food Is Sex

An excerpt from *Kitchen Confidential*, originally published by
Bloomsbury in 2000.

I n 1973, unhappily in love, I graduated high school a year early
so I could chase the object of my desire to Vassar College—
the less said about that part of my life, the better, believe me.
Let it suffice to say that by age eighteen I was a thoroughly undisci-
plined young man, blithely flunking or fading out of college (I couldn't
be bothered to attend classes). I was angry at myself and at everyone
else. Essentially, I treated the world as my ashtray. I spent most of my
waking hours drinking, smoking pot, scheming, and doing my best to
amuse, outrage, impress, and penetrate anyone silly enough to find me
entertaining. I was—to be frank—a spoiled, miserable, narcissistic,
self-destructive, and thoughtless young lout, badly in need of a good
ass-kicking. Rudderless and unhappy, I went in with some friends on
a summer share in Provincetown, Cape Cod. It was what my friends
were doing and that was enough for me.

Provincetown was (and is) essentially a small Portuguese fishing village all the way out on the fishhooked tip of the Cape. During
the summer months, however, it became Times Square / Christopher
Street-by-the-Sea. This was the seventies, remember, so factor that
in when you conjure up the image of a once quaint New England port
town, clogged with tourists, day-trippers, hippies, drifters, lobster
poachers, slutty chicks, dopers, refugees from Key West, and thousands upon thousands of energetically cruising gay men. For a rootless
young man with sensualist inclinations, it was the perfect getaway.

Unfortunately, I needed money. My on-again-off-again girlfriend spun pizza for a living. My roommates, who had summered in P-town before, had jobs waiting for them. They cooked, washed dishes, waited tables—usually at night, so we all went to the beaches and ponds each morning, smoked pot, sniffed a little coke, dropped acid, and sunbathed nude, as well as indulging in other healthy teenage activities.

Tired of my drain on the household finances, one annoyed and practical roommate hooked me up with a dishwashing gig at the restaurant where she waited tables. Dishwashers (sudsbusters, a.k.a. pearl divers) were the most transient breed in the seasonal restaurant business, so when one goofball failed to show up for work for two days, I was in. It was my introduction to the life—and at first, I did not go happily.

Scrubbing pots and pans, scraping plates, and peeling mountains of potatoes, tearing the little beards off mussels, picking scallops, and cleaning shrimp did not sound or look attractive to me. But it was from these humble beginnings that I began my strange climb to chefdom. Taking that one job, as dishwasher at the Dreadnaught, essentially pushed me down the path I still walk to this day.

The Dreadnaught was—well, you've eaten there, or someplace like it: a big, old, ramshackle driftwood pile, built out over the water on ancient wooden pylons. In bad weather, the waves would roll under the dining room floor and thud loudly against the seawall. Gray wood shingles, bay windows, and inside, the classic Olde New England / Rusty Scupper / Aye Matey / Cap'n What's décor: hanging fishnets, hurricane lamps, buoys, nautical bric-a-brac, the bars fashioned from halved lifeboats. Call it Early Driftwood.

We served fried clams, fried shrimp, fried flounder, fried scallops, french fries, steamed lobsters, a few grilled and broiled steaks, chops, and fish fillets to the mobs of tourists who'd pour into town each week between the Fourth of July and Labor Day.

I was surprisingly happy in my work. The Dreadnaught managers were an aged, retiring, and boozy lot who stayed out of the kitchen most of the time. The waitresses were attractive and cheerful, free with drinks for the kitchen and with their favors as well.

And the cooks?

The cooks *ruled*.

There was Bobby, the chef, a well-toasted, late-thirtyish ex-hippie who, like a lot of people in P-town, had come for vacation years back and stayed. He lived there year-round, cheffing in the summer, doing roofing and carpentry and house-sitting during the off-season. There was Lydia, a half-mad, matronly Portuguese divorcée with a teenage daughter. Lydia made the clam chowder for which we were somewhat famous, and during service dished out the vegetables and side dishes. She drank a lot. There was Tommy, the fry cook, a perpetually moving surfer dude with electric blue eyes, who even when there was nothing to do rocked back and forth like an elephant to "keep up the momentum." There was Mike, an ex-con and part-time methedrine dealer, who worked the salad station.

In the kitchen, they were like gods. They dressed like pirates: chef's coats with the arms slashed off, blue jeans, ragged and faded headbands, gore-covered aprons, gold hoop earrings, wrist cuffs, turquoise necklaces and chokers, rings of scrimshaw and ivory, tattoos— all the decorative detritus of the long-past Summer of Love.

They had style and swagger, and they seemed afraid of nothing. They drank everything in sight, stole whatever wasn't nailed down, and screwed their way through floor staff, bar customers, and casual visitors like nothing I'd ever seen or imagined. They carried big, badass knives, which they kept honed and sharpened to a razor's edge. They hurled dirty sauté pans and pots across the kitchen and into my pot sink with casual accuracy. They spoke their own peculiar dialect, an unbelievably profane patois of countercultural jargon and local Portugee slang, delivered with ironic inflection, calling each other, for instance, "paaahd" for "partner" or "daahlin" for "darling." They looted the place for everything it was worth, stocking up well in advance for the lean months of the off-season. A couple of nights a week, the chef would back his Volkswagen van up to the kitchen door and load whole sirloin strips, boxes of frozen shrimp, cases of beer, sides of bacon into the cargo area. The speed racks over each station—containing bottles of cooking wine, oil, etc., for easy access during service—were always loaded with at least two highball glasses per cook; Lydia liked to call them "summertime coolers," usually strong Cape Codders, Sea

Breezes, or Greyhounds. Joints were smoked in the downstairs walk-in, and cocaine—always available, though in those days very expensive and still considered a rich man's drug—was everywhere. On payday everyone in the kitchen handed money back and forth in a Byzantine roundelay of transactions as the cooks settled up the previous week's drug debts, loans, and wagers.

I saw a lot of bad behavior that first year in P-town. I was impressed. These guys were master criminals, sexual athletes, compared to my pitiful college hijinks. Highwaymen rogues, buccaneers, cutthroats, they were like young princes to me, still only a lowly dishwasher. The life of the cook was a life of *adventure*, looting, pillaging, and rock-and-rolling through life with a carefree disregard for all conventional morality. It looked pretty damn good to me on the other side of the line.

But if there was one moment when I saw clearly what I wanted, it was at the end of that summer.

I'd moved up a bit by now. Mike had gone missing on a meth jag, and I had been promoted to the salad station, plating shrimp cocktails, cracking oysters and cherrystone clams, mixing canned lobster meat with mayonnaise, and filling champagne glasses with strawberries and whipped cream.

The Dreadnaught line was a long, narrow affair: a cold station by the exit door to the parking lot, a double-decker lobster steamer where we'd kill off the one-and-a-half- and two-pounders by the dozen, stacking them up like cordwood before slamming shut the heavy metal doors and turning the wheel, giving them the steam. Then came a row of deep fryers, a range, a big Garland pull-out broiler, a few more burners, and finally a brick hearth for charcoal grilling, all of this bordered by the usual pass-through on the other side—wooden cutting board /counter with sunken steam table, and below that, the low-boy reach-in refrigerators for reserve supplies. By the far-end open hearth, where Bobby, the chef, worked, was a Dutch door, the top half kept open so incoming tourists could get a peek at some lobsters or steaks grilling as they entered and get in the mood.

One weekday, a large wedding party arrived, fresh from the ceremony: bride, groom, ushers, family, and friends. Married up-Cape, the happy couple and party had come down to P-town for the celebratory dinner following, presumably, a reception. They were high when they arrived. From the salad station at the other end of the line, I saw a brief, slurry exchange between Bobby and some of the guests. I noticed particularly the bride, who at one point leaned into the kitchen and inquired if any of us "had any hash." When the party moved on into the dining room, I pretty much forgot about them.

We banged out meals for a while, Lydia amusing us with her usual patter, Tommy dunking clams and shrimp into hot grease, the usual ebb and flow of a busy kitchen. Then the bride reappeared at the open Dutch door. She was blond and good-looking in her virginal wedding white, and she spoke closely with the chef for a few seconds; Bobby suddenly grinned from ear to ear, the sunburned crow's feet at the corners of his eyes growing more pronounced. A few moments later she was gone again, but Bobby, visibly trembling, suddenly said, "Tony! Watch my station," and promptly scooted out the back door.

Ordinarily, this alone would have been a momentous event. To be allowed to work the busy broiler station, to take the helm—even for a few minutes—was a dream come true. But curiosity got the better of all of us remaining in the kitchen. We had to look.

There was a fenced-off garbage stockade right outside the window by the dishwasher, which concealed the stacked trash and cans of edible waste the restaurant sold to a pig farm up-Cape from the cars in the parking lot. Soon, all of us—Tommy, Lydia, the new dishwasher, and I—were peering through the window, where in full view of his assembled crew, Bobby was noisily rear-ending the bride. She was bent obligingly over a fifty-five-gallon drum, her gown hiked up over her hips. Bobby's apron was up, resting over her back as he pumped away furiously, the young woman's eyes rolled up into her head, mouth whispering, "Yess, yess . . . good . . . good . . ."

While her new groom and family chawed happily on their flounder fillets and deep-fried scallops just a few yards away in the Dreadnaught dining room, here was the blushing bride, getting an impromptu send-off from a total stranger.

And I knew then, dear reader, for the first time: I wanted to be a chef.

Kitchen

An unpublished handwritten poem about three A.M. in the kitchen, date unknown.

KITCHEN

3:AM
ALONE IN THE KITCHEN
AFTER A MIDNIGHT REEFER
A PILE OF NEWSPAPERS
WITH BITS OF HEADLINE
STACKED TO READ:
"A NOTABLE NIGHTINGALE
FOR VIOLENT YOUTHS"
FLUORESCENT OVERHEAD
MAKES THE FAMILIAR KITCHEN
MY KITCHEN.
THE FAMILY KITCHEN,
UNCANNILY LIKE A FAST FOOD JOINT

WHAT WITH GLEAMING FORMICA
SHINING STEEL
SPOTLESS LINOLEUM

I WAS AFRAID TO SPEAK LOUDLY
TO YOU ON THE PHONE

FOR FEAR OF SOMETHING.
- DISTURBING THE OWNERS PERHAPS
STRANGE
TO BE FRIGHTENED OF ONE'S OWN KITCHEN.

A. BOURDAIN

An Exquisite Corpse

The last piece Tony wrote before his death, unpublished, undated.

INT: An Irish bar, somewhere in New York City. A MAN sits at the far end corner, drinking beer from a pint glass. He is in his forties, with what might once have been rough, simian good looks, but his hair is suspiciously dark for his age—a last attempt at vanity. He is tall with wide shoulders but he's out of shape, what could have been an intimidating presence, but he now hides behind words.

He slouches back in his bar stool as if observing. At the other end of the bar, VINNIE, the bartender, reads the New York Post while an overhead TV plays silently above the Irish bric-a-brac. VINNIE is young and chiseled with a model's good looks.

It's early in the day and there is no one else at the bar.

A WOMAN enters the bar and sits down on a stool near the MAN— but not too near. She is diagonally across from him, separated by two seats. She, too, is in her forties, a handsome woman, though clearly not as beautiful as she once was. She is dressed down, for comfort, with a large, expensive, but old bag which she carelessly deposits on the seat next to her.

MAN: That smell. It's what? Disinfectant? Floor cleaner? Slight background of puke. It's the smell of every morning bar in the history of the world.

VINNIE (*TO THE WOMAN*): What can I get you?

WOMAN (*WITHOUT YET ACKNOWLEDGING THE MAN, THINKS FOR A MOMENT*): Just a club soda.

VINNIE: Club soda. You want a lime with that?

WOMAN: No lime.

MAN: The smell I'm used to. It doesn't bother me. But you know what bothers me? The fruit flies. You see the fruit flies? They hover over the bottles. Some bars, they wrap the bottles in plastic wrap, end of the night. But Vinnie doesn't do that. Little fuckers hatch in the lemons and limes or some shit. So, good thing you didn't do the lime.

WOMAN: It's Vinnie?

VINNIE: Yeah. Vincent. Vinnie. Whatever you like.

WOMAN: What do you do, Vinnie? When you're not bartending? You don't look like somebody who just bartends.

VINNIE: I'm an actor.

WOMAN: Oh? What have I seen you in?

VINNIE: I've done a few *Law and Order*s. Some other stuff in the pipeline. You know how it is.

WOMAN: I love that show. I'm sure I've seen you in it. I must have seen all of them a couple of times.

MAN: And the big screen over the bar. On silent. Always on silent. Set permanently to the sports channel. Soccer in this case. The preferred clientele being Irish and all.

Am I bothering you? Should I just shut up and drink my beer?

WOMAN: Talk all you like. That doesn't mean I have to listen to you.

MAN: True enough.

There's a long, awkward silence. VINNIE washes some glasses.

MAN (TO VINNIE): What can I say to that? I mean . . . what can a person say? Lady doesn't want to talk. You gotta respect that.

WOMAN: I'll have a vodka. And tonic.

MAN: Uh-oh. Change of plans?

WOMAN: No change of plans. I want a drink. This is a bar. They serve drinks. I will have a drink.

MAN: I'd offer to buy you one but funds. Funds are limited.

WOMAN: Really? I would have thought otherwise. Looking at you. The watch. Expensive. The shirt's not cheap either.

MAN: Relics from another time I'm afraid.

WOMAN: Easy come easy go.

MAN: Not so easy as you'd think . . .

WOMAN (*DRINK ARRIVES; SHE DRINKS HALF OF IT QUICKLY*): Really? (*snorts with derision*) I kind of doubt that. It's a problem—the kind of problem I'd like to have. Shall I buy you a beer? Would that be helpful? Not to be nice. I just—it's distracting. Me sitting here, enjoying my cocktail—and you, nursing those last few ounces of warm beer.

MAN: That would be much appreciated. Thank you.

WOMAN (*TO VINNIE*): Another beer for him. And me—again.

VINNIE: Vodka tonic?

WOMAN: Yes. A little bigger pour on the vodka this time, you don't mind.

VINNIE: Sure.

MAN: What's money for anyway? I had money. Why even bother? Better things go, more you make, more you make, the more people you need. The more people you need, the less time you have . . .

Then what? You making money for who? Women who don't love you, houses you don't live in, a car you don't drive. You know how much it is to keep a car in New York City? A garage?

WOMAN: No, actually I don't. I wouldn't.

MAN: Seven hundred and fifty dollars a month. A month! And that's before you tip the garage attendant on Christmas.

WOMAN: What kind of car?

MAN: What?

WOMAN: What kind of car did you have? When you had a car. Assuming it's no longer with us. I'm curious to know what kind of car.

MAN (*UNCOMFORTABLE*): A Dodge. Challenger.

VINNIE: Sweet!

WOMAN (*TO VINNIE*): Is that a good car? A fast car? Big engine?

VINNIE: Yeah. Fast as fuck. Thing's a beast . . .

MAN: Yes. It was very fast.

WOMAN: A sports car. Two seats . . .

MAN: Well, there's seats in the back but . . .

WOMAN: Sure. Fake seats. The kind of seats you'd cram into as a teenager—a short ride to the mall. This car, I'm gonna guess, is all about the driver.

MAN: It's always about the driver.

WOMAN: And this car, you drove in New York City. In traffic. Where you never get that thing above what—thirty miles an hour? And every time you park your car—because you have to park—you gotta put it in another lot. Which is like—what? Fifty dollars a pop? Not exactly wind in your hair, wild and free like the commercial. And, the car is too young for you to start with.

MAN: I don't know. Sometimes, late at night, bombing up Amsterdam or Park Avenue, you can hit the lights just right. You're moving along with the yellow cabs, like in a school of fish, just going and going . . . you think it's never gonna stop—that you can keep going forever.

WOMAN: And I gather that you thought at the time that this car would make you more attractive to women? Was that a factor in your choice of automobile?

MAN: No.

Actually. To tell you the God's honest truth, I was aware . . . I was fully cognizant of the ramifications, of the message this car sent. I knew it wouldn't make me younger. I knew there would be an implied subtext . . . an indicator, a hint of douche when I pulled up at a restaurant, a hotel valet. That I'd have to live the car down.

It was a car for a selfish person to be honest.

And I want to be honest with you.

VINNIE: Detroit's finest, man. I would totally drive that car.

WOMAN: I'm trying to picture you in this car. Alone. Driving the streets. Radio on, looking out at the world. Or were you looking? Did you notice things as you drove by them?

MAN: Sure, I noticed. But you have a point. I'd listen to the radio and think. Mostly about myself I grant you. I was, I thought, in those days, a pretty interesting subject.

WOMAN: And now?

You seem to still think you're fairly interesting. You talk a fuck of a lot. You must think you have interesting things to say—worth sharing with the world.

MAN: Now?

I bore myself.

I bore myself stupid.

WOMAN: That must be awful. Rejected by your first and best audience.

MAN: Yes. It is awful. And a condition unmitigated by alcohol. In fact, aggravated. It's the writer's worst nightmare, isn't it? To be a boring old fuck at a bar.

WOMAN: Probably inevitable. Writing isn't normal. Takes an aberrant personality to think you have a story to tell.

MAN (*LAUGHS*): Okay . . . Yeah. You're probably right. You ARE right. How about you, though? You feel good about yourself? How's your life going that's so great?

WOMAN: I work. I work a lot.

MAN: I have a faint recollection of that feeling. The technical satisfactions—a collection of small things—coming together to make one, larger thing. Yes. It comes back to me. That must be nice.

WOMAN: Nice? I tell waiters what to do. I tell cooks. I call somebody when the dishwasher doesn't work. I call the man who picks up the grease from the deep fryers. I smile and stand there in heels and tell rich fucks who I'd otherwise not brake for if they popped up in front of my headlights on the Taconic that I'm happy to see them. I ask them if they have any allergies. And I pretend to believe them when they tell me they do. Yeah. It's a wonderland.

MAN: But the money's good?

WOMAN: I get by. I can afford this drink. If I choose to have another, I will be able to afford that too. Nobody's calling me on the phone threatening to shut off the lights or put a lien on my paycheck. When I go to the supermarket, I buy the name brand, not the generic. If I want to go someplace nice with some girlfriends from work, I can go. Not Tahiti. But a beach. Somewhere.

MAN: The beach. That's a thought. I used to live on the beach. I had a place.

WOMAN: Of course, I don't go.

MAN: Where?

WOMAN: The beach. I say I'm gonna go. I mean—I've been. I tried . . .

But two days? After two days of sitting in the sand, staring into space? I just can't.

MAN: Really? The idea of laying in a hammock, big pile of To Be Read books next to you . . . frothy, frosty drink in hand. Doesn't appeal?

WOMAN: No. I had to put such things—I hadda put that shit aside. I'm not the kind of person who can do nothing.

MAN: See, that's where we're different. That's a fundamental difference. I am quite good at doing nothing. I excel at it. For a time, I made a profession of it. I was paid to do nothing.

WOMAN: That is a pure stream of shit.

MAN: No. I mean it. I got paid to tell stories, to write stories that would never, ever see the light of day. Year after year. After a while, I'd know going in. A fucking hamster wheel. Just running round and round.

WOMAN: This sounds like an enviable position, my point of view. It's like you're paid to be a whore—but you don't actually have to fuck.

MAN: It was not so wonderful. It was not wonderful at all. It grinds you down. All that free time. The bad part of your brain starts talking to you.

WOMAN: Really? I can't say I'm sympathetic. No. Not at all.

I work. Like real work. I don't have the luxury of existential crises.

MAN: But . . . Making a living.

WOMAN: Yes.

MAN: And the money is good.

WOMAN: Yes. You keep asking about money. It's annoying. Like it's any concern of yours. It's none of your business.

MAN: No. I'm sorry. I just wanted to know. I was curious. If you—you know—get by. Such things . . . I don't know. I'm interested.

WOMAN: It's good enough for my situation.

MAN: Situation?

WOMAN: Yeah. I'd call it a situation. Wouldn't you? Deadbeat husband of twenty years leaves me high and dry—drops off the fucking grid—not even worth going after in court because he's got nothing left worth taking in any case. Not for nothing, but I'd call that a situation.

You cockSUCKER! You miserable piece of fucking SHIT!!

MAN (*MAN LEANS FORWARD, HIS FACE CONTORTED WITH RAGE*): You fucking WHORE! You ruined my fucking LIFE!!

The man begins to cry.

VINNIE: Whoa! Get things under control, people. I can't have this at the bar.

WOMAN (*LOWERS HER VOICE TO AN INSISTENT HISS*): Whore? WHO's the whore? You fucked your assistant. You fucked your actresses, you fucked your porn star—and worst? Worst of all? You sold your own ass, you sold yourself, your own life, everything you were—down the shitter.

MAN (*REGAINS COMPOSURE*): You're right of course. But, Jesus fuck. My best FRIEND. You fucked my best friend. That was in bad taste.

WOMAN: Your best friend? That asshole was hitting on me from day one. Some friend. Fuck him. And fuck you. Fuck you in the ass. Fuck you in the lungs . . . Just . . . fuck . . . you.

She pauses, anger purged somewhat.

I will admit to a revenge motive.

MAN: Revenge for what? I hadn't done anything. Yet.

WOMAN: Sure you did. You betrayed me. Just 'cause you didn't—just 'cause you say you didn't stick your dick in somebody doesn't mean you didn't betray me.

MAN: You knew it all along. Minute they called, said "come out to the coast—we have meetings" . . . you knew.

WOMAN: Yes. I knew. I knew it would all go bad.

MAN: I thought you were jealous.

WOMAN: Jealous? Of course you'd think that. I was jealous of your great success. No. What I really felt? Fear. Because I knew you wouldn't survive. That you'd get stroked a bit, somebody would roll you over onto your back, stroke your belly, you'd get paid some money, and that you'd fuck it up—you'd fuck everything up.

You're soft.

I knew that place would destroy you.

MAN: Soft? Jesus!

WOMAN (*LONG PAUSE*): Soft is not a bad thing. You were kind once.

Do you remember that?

MAN: No.

WOMAN: You were kind. And gentle.

And you needed help.

You let me help.

MAN: Yes. Maybe. Yes.

WOMAN: So, what's this all about? Why am I here? Why—after all these years, of what?—nothing—you reach out, call me? How does this help anything?

MAN: I guess I felt the need to express . . . regrets.

WOMAN: Regrets? About what? What's the point? You really want to look back? Start adding it up? I became a drunk. I am a drunk. They took our CHILD away. You want to express regrets?

MAN: Yes. Regrets. Big regrets. What if I told you I had a gun in my pocket. That I was going to shoot myself. Would that impress you?

WOMAN: Don't make me laugh.

VINNIE: Hey!! No guns in here!!

MAN: Did I say "gun"? I kid. I kid. I was just kidding. It's a hypothetical.

WOMAN: You were always overdramatic. A fucking child. The grand gesture. Poor me. Look what you made me do—

Suddenly, the MAN produces a pistol, tucks the barrel under his chin, and closes his eyes. The WOMAN lunges forward and pulls the gun down and away but it fires. A single shot that strikes VINNIE in the cheekbone. He slumps back into the bottles, bounces forward, the back of his head a mess, slumps to the ground, obviously dead.

MAN: Shit shit shit shit shit!! Is he all right?

WOMAN (*STANDS UP AND LOOKS BEHIND THE BAR TO THE FLOOR*): He is most definitely not all right.

MAN: Oh fuck . . . what am I gonna do?

WOMAN: Give me your glass.

MAN: What?

The WOMAN picks up his glass, pours out the remains of his beer behind the bar, puts it in her bag. She does the same with her glass.

WOMAN: Now the gun. Give it to me.

The MAN, stunned, lets her take it. She puts the gun in her bag.

WOMAN: Now, go to the bathroom and wash your hands. Wipe off the faucets when you're done.

THE MAN sleepwalks into the bathroom obligingly. She produces a packet of wet wipes from her bag and begins wiping down the bar and the stools. The MAN returns.

You touch anything else?
MAN: No. I don't think so.
WOMAN: You ready to go?
MAN: My life is over.
WOMAN: Our lives were over a long time ago, my love. We don't exist. We weren't even here.

Acknowledgments

Thank you to Jessica Mileo and William Callahan at InkWell Management for their dedication to helping me curate Tony's work. I couldn't have done it without your steadfast support, superb organization, and eagle eyes. Thanks also to Laurie Woolever for taking the time to give the book an early read. I am lucky in so many ways to share this journey with each of you.

I am very fortunate to work with two brilliant publishing teams who greeted this project with excitement. I cannot express enough gratitude to them for championing this book, in particular Gabriella Doob, Helen Atsma, Sonya Cheuse, Miriam Parker, Alicia Gencarelli, Renata De Oliveira, and Allison Saltzman at Ecco, and Paul Baggaley, Ian Hudson, and Nigel Newton at Bloomsbury.

Thank you to Patrick Radden Keefe for generously providing a foreword with so much heart. Tony would have loved it.

Finally, I am thankful for the trust and clarity of Ottavia and Ariane Busia-Bourdain. You make this work a pleasure.